The Complete Sermons of Martin Luther

Volume 5

Edited by
Eugene F. A. Klug

Translated by
Eugene F. A. Klug, Erwin W. Koehlinger,
James Lanning, Everette W. Meier,
Dorothy Schoknecht, and
Allen Schuldheiss

BakerBooks
A Division of Baker Book House Co
Grand Rapids, Michigan 49516

Published by Baker Books
a division of Baker Book House Company
P.O. Box 6287, Grand Rapids, MI 49516-6287

The Complete Sermons of Martin Luther (seven-volume set)
ISBN 0-8010-1199-X

Volumes 1–4 published 1983 as *Sermons of Martin Luther* (eight volumes). Reprinted 1995 as *Sermons of Martin Luther: The Church Postils* (eight volumes in four volumes).

Volumes 5–7 published 1996 as *Sermons of Martin Luther: The House Postils* (three volumes).

Printed in the United States of America

For information about academic books, resources for Christian leaders, and all new releases available from Baker Book House, visit our web site:
http://www.bakerbooks.com

Volume 5

Sermons on Gospel Texts for Advent, Christmas, New Year's Day, Epiphany, Lent, Holy Week, and Other Occasions

Dedicated to
Concordia Theological Seminary
Fort Wayne, Indiana
in recognition of its sesquicentennial
1996
and 150 years of faithful service
in preparing over four thousand pastors for
the holy ministry in
The Lutheran Church-Missouri Synod

Contents

ACKNOWLEDGMENTS

A number of valued co-workers participated with me in this project of translating Luther's HAUSPOSTILLE, or "House Sermons." In each case they gave their service freely, without the thought of reward, for the joy of reading Luther in the original German and putting his thoughts into contemporary, idiomatic English. The number of sermons translated varied with each individual. Almost all of the translation team were retirees who expressed appreciation for being enlisted for the task of putting their expertise into meaningful application in this way, so that others might have the joy and opportunity of reading Luther's sermons. He, after all, still remains a lively subject almost five hundred years later, not only for the sake of theology, but also for the existential insights his contributions afford in many other directions; for what he has to say opens windows on life at the time of the Reformation. This stirred the interest of the translators and we are confident it will also do so for readers in our day as well.

The members of the translation team are listed here in alphabetical order:

Erwin W. Koehlinger, Ft. Wayne, Indiana, retired business executive, with theological background early in life.

James Lanning, Ft. Wayne, Indiana, library assistant at Concordia Theological Seminary, Ft. Wayne.

Everette W. Meier, Alliance, Nebraska (now deceased), retired from the pastoral ministry and college teaching.

Dorothy Schoknecht, Kalispell, Montana, retired from teaching chemistry and biology, also German.

Allen Schuldheiss, Kalispell, Montana, retired from the pastoral ministry.

There were three keyboardists assisting me with the considerable task of setting the translations into camera-ready typesetting and formatting: Margaret Gruber, Helen Crowley, and Patricia Crawford, all on the staff of Concordia Theological Seminary, Ft. Wayne, Indiana. I wish also to pay tribute to my wife, Dorothy, for the arduous task of proofreading the hard copies of the manuscript before the completed disks were sent to the editors of Baker Book House. Prompted by a proposal from Paul T. McCain that Luther's HAUSPOSTILLE be published in English translation—the new American edition of Luther's Works does not include them—Baker Book House responded favorably to this suggestion and, learning that we already had a translation underway, expressed interest in our work. Needless to say, the support and encouragement of this publishing house to see the project through to completion was deeply appreciated.

Eugene F. A. Klug,
Editor and Translator

PREFACE

Historians like Preserved Smith and James Froude, among many others, have cited Martin Luther's career as the beginning point of modern times because of the profound, pervasive influence his life and work exerted in various directions—theological and ecclesial reform, schools and educational restructuring, government and politics, social and economic improvements, and the like.

It is impossible to proceed very far without at some point feeling the impact of Luther's person upon human history since 1521. His stand at the Diet of Worms in April of that year has, with good reason, been judged to be the continental divide of modern world history. His is a giant presence, like a skyscraper, inspiring awe the closer one stands or tries to embrace its totality, but most profitably appreciated when viewed from a distance as it provides the bearing point for all else on the horizon.

Luther's productivity—even without the aid of modern word processing devices—is widely recognized to have been truly incredible, really legendary. The Weimar edition of his works, launched in 1883, exceeds one hundred volumes presently and is still incomplete. Many excellent biographies of his life have appeared through the years; but the definitive statement of his theological impact and production has yet to be written, and probably never will, whether by friend or foe. The field is simply too vast, even though Luther was and remained very clear and uncomplicated in every utterance and situation. Scholars today generally agree that from the time of the posting of the 95 Theses in 1517, and especially the Leipzig Debate in 1519, the hallmark of Luther's theology was his great consistency, his unwavering and unchanging stance in theological expression, an excellence that is undoubtedly owed to his total commitment to and vast knowledge of the Biblical text.

Luther studies through the years have drawn various foci at the hands of researchers. They have riveted their attention upon his Bible translations, his lectures and commentaries, his pioneer catechetical achievements, the polemical treatises, his voluminous correspondence, the famous table talk, sermons, and so forth. Usually such probings include also the claim of new insights into the man and his theology. That is probably true, but it merely highlights the insurmountable task confronting scholars. Undoubtedly, it is also possible to compose and produce a study of Luther's theology based primarily on his sermons. But the task is awesome. The estimate is that there are somewhere between two thousand to three thousand sermons or fragments that can be traced to Luther. These comprise some thirty plus volumes in the Weimar edition!

In comparison, our efforts here are modest in scope. We have narrowed our focus on the so-called HAUSPOSTILLE of Luther, the sermons which he delivered in the famous Lutherhalle, or Luther house, in Wittenberg, the old monastery of the Augustinians. Luther had been a member of this monastic order since 1506 when he completed a one-year probationary novitiate, and in a sense he really felt he had not left it until June 13, 1525 when he married Katharina von Bora, who had been a nun. Luther had lived in the old monastery ever since joining the faculty at Wittenberg in 1511. Here he had his living quarters, often preached for the Augustinian chapter, and eventually also delivered his lectures as professor of Biblical theology at the university. Elector Frederick the Wise had designated the old monastery to be the family home for Luther and Katie, as Martin affectionately called his bride. She was up to the challenge, and with him established a model parsonage family and home. Together they rejoiced over a circle of six children that gladdened their hearts, but then also saddened them when Elizabeth died as an infant and Magdalene as a vivacious teenager.

The HAUSPOSTILLE, or house postils or sermons, need to be distinguished from Luther's KIRCHENPOSTILLE, or church postils. The term "postil" itself derives out of the Latin phrase *post illa verba textus*, "after those words of the text," and refers to the commentary or homily which followed upon the reading of the standard pericope, the Gospel or Epistle, by the preacher at the service of worship. The church postils of Luther originated in the earlier period of his life, roughly from the time of his temporary exile for safekeeping at Wartburg Castle (1521–22) until 1525. Prompted in part by the elector, Luther resolved to put devotional and sermonic material into the hands of the people, first of all the fathers and heads of households, for the sake of their children and servants, and then also to assist the clergy, who at that time were ill-prepared to deliver sound homiletical messages and sermons to their people in the parish churches. Strictly speaking, many of these were simply sermon studies or helps, rather than sermons preached in person, and were designed by Luther to help the reader extract the gospel truths out of the chosen Scriptural text.

The house postils or sermons, on the other hand, which constitute the volumes of our translation, were delivered by Luther in the intimate circle of his family members and a few others. The Luther household was often quite extensive—a real test for Katie's ingenuity at balancing the family budget!—because of relatives, students, and associates who were domiciled there or regularly present at Luther's elbow for one reason or another. Among these were two individuals who were key figures in the preservation of the so-called house postils preached in the Lutherhalle: Veit Dietrich, who served Luther as amanuensis, a kind of graduate assistant, and Georg Roerer, who was a called assistant at the parish church, St. Mary's, under Dr. John Bugenhagen. Georg Roerer was also part of the translation team that worked with Luther on the translation of the Old Testament from the Hebrew. It is significant that Luther himself often referred to his own divine call into the parish ministry at this congregation from 1514 onward, serving alongside Bugenhagen until his death in 1546.

Both Veit Dietrich and Georg Roerer were present at the time Luther delivered the house postils. The period of years for these sermons was between 1531 to 1535. It followed upon a lengthy span of time before that, virtually a year and a half, when Dr. Bugenhagen had been absent from his parish introducing the Reformation and evangelical church order in Luebeck and Braunschweig, thus leaving Luther with the pastoral burdens at Wittenberg, along with his university lectures. Accordingly, the only explanation cited in the historical accounts for the reason why Luther initiated these house sermons in the old Augustinian monastery, his home, is that he experienced persisting illness, fatigue, and weakness during these years, and thus only seldom felt well enough Sunday mornings to occupy the pulpit in the town parish church as long as Bugenhagen was back to fill the pulpit. In no way do the accounts imply that these house sermons were to rival the ministry at the main church, as competing conventicles of a sort. For one thing, they were generally preached later in the day when Luther felt stronger. Apparently, as a true and faithful preacher, he never felt fulfilled until he had shared pertinent and timely thoughts for the day on the basis of the standard Gospel lesson for the church year with the members of his household and devoted circle of friends. In one of his recorded comments at the table, he states that he considered it his duty to do so, both by virtue of his office and as a responsible father in his house.

Veit Dietrich and Georg Roerer both made stenographic notes of these house postils, transcribing them later into finished form. Luther, at this time in his life, regularly spoke from an outline that had been carefully thought through ahead of time, in order to get hold of the Konzept, or chief point(s) he wanted to make, as he himself explained concerning his preaching. Thus, homiletically his style might be described as combining expository with topical, the chief point or conceptual thread coming really from God himself through the text of Scripture. Apparently, he was a deliberate speaker who spoke slowly and distinctly, a characteristic which would have allowed time for an expert note-taker to do his recording. Thus through these two faithful scribes, two versions of Luther's house postils have come down to us. In general, they may be said to complement each other, rather than being duplicates in carbon copy sort of manner; but efforts to collate them or to try to extract the "authentic version" out of them have usually foundered. The result is that they stand side by side, in tandem, as parallel versions, as in the source which we have utilized for our translation, volumes 13a and 13b of LUTHER'S SAEMMTLICHE SCHRIFTEN, also known as the St. Louis edition, launched in 1883 and completed in 1910. This edition, in turn, drew on the Walch and Erlangen editions that preceded its publication, as well as multiple other and earlier editions of Luther's works. The definitive, full-scale study of Luther's sermonic materials still beckons to be written. Scholars face a Mt. Everest sort of task in such pursuit. We will content ourselves with the translation of the sermons in St. Louis edition volume 13b, the house postils as recorded by Georg Roerer.

There is a rationale which justifies our choosing this version. In recent years the consensus of scholars has more and more moved in the direction of Roerer's transcription of Luther's house postils as the source most complete, exact, and trustworthy. This, in spite of the fact that Dietrich's version appeared in print early, in the 1545 Wittenberg edition of Luther's writings, a production that enjoyed Luther's approval and blessing. Matthias Loy, with others, completed an English translation of Dietrich's version of the house postils, with a few omissions, in 1871. But today the verdict is that Roerer, who spent twenty-four years as Luther's faithful colleague, and conscientiously recorded Luther's sermonic efforts—not only the house postils but all of the master's messages at public preaching appearances where he was present—was by all measurements the most objectively reliable scribe, a truly skilled factotum. He had mastered a shorthand that combined Latin and German abbreviations and he was intent on recording only that which Luther had actually said without adducing augmentations or thoughts of his own, or inserting one of his own sermons where he could not find one of Luther's for a given day of the church year in his notes. The latter charge is sometimes suggested against Dietrich's version, though, of course, it is debatable, since the contents of the Dietrich version are otherwise fully in harmony with Luther's theology.

The fact is, Roerer's version of the house sermons also came to light early, in 1539, published under the auspices of Andreas Poach of Jena, but lacking Luther's approval—a rather common happening as regards the Reformer's multiple writings. Roerer himself remained in closest trust of his mentor, and after Luther's death, until his own death in 1557, he was engaged in compiling the really first comprehensive edition of Luther's works. The result was the Jena edition of 1559, which then also included Roerer's version of the house sermons Luther had preached in the period 1531 to 1535. Included in this version are a few sermons Luther preached during those years, either at St. Mary's, the Stadtkirche, or occasionally at the castle church when the elector of Saxony or members of the ruling house were in attendance. But always the purpose on Roerer's part was to complete the church year with pertinent sermons Luther had actually personally delivered, with his thoughts assiduously transcribed and retained. We have indicated which these sermons are with a notation; all others belong to the house sermons of Luther, delivered by him in the Lutherhalle. The calendar year is noted for each sermon.

A final word needs to be said concerning our venture to translate Luther's house postils. As on many other subjects, Luther has a word concerning the challenge and difficulties of translating the thoughts and words of an author into one's own language—in his case from the Hebrew and Greek of the Bible into idiomatic German. "The plowing goes well," Luther observes, "when the field is cleared," but the task can be difficult and frustrating, and "we had to sweat and toil before we got those boulders and clods out of the way, so that one could go along nicely."

We can resonate to these sentiments. It has been our endeavor first of all to be accurate in reproducing Luther's thought faithfully and then secondly, especially in the final editing, to strive for an idiomatic translation that moves smoothly and remains as true as possible to the underlying fact that these were sermons, and as such they were to have the character of rhetorical pieces, delivered by Luther in a real, existential sort of situation, the Sitz-im-Leben of the chapel audience in the Lutherhalle, during a somewhat trying period of Luther's life.

We are only too ready to admit, as Luther puts it with himself in mind, "Ah, translating is not every man's skill as the mad saints imagine. It requires a right, devout, honest, sincere, God-fearing, Christian, trained, informed, and experienced heart" (cf. Luther's On Translation, LW 35, 188–194). If we have failed the reader on the first count in any way, we hope at least to be seen as having striven for the second tier of faithfulness as Luther portrayed it.

THE EDITOR

FIRST SUNDAY IN ADVENT

First Sermon—1532

Matthew 21:1–9

And when they drew nigh unto Jerusalem, and were come to Bethphage, unto the mount of Olives, then sent Jesus two disciples, saying unto them, Go into the village over against you, and straightway ye shall find an ass tied, and a colt with her: loose them, and bring them unto me. And if any man say ought unto you, ye shall say, The Lord hath need of them; and straightway he will send them.

All this was done, that it might be fulfilled which was spoken by the prophet, saying, Tell ye the daughter of Sion, Behold, thy King cometh unto thee, meek, and sitting upon an ass, and a colt the foal of an ass. And the disciples went, and did as Jesus commanded them, and brought the ass, and the colt, and put on them their clothes, and they set him thereon. And a very great multitude spread their garments in the way; others cut down branches from the trees, and strewed them in the way. And the multitudes that went before, and that followed, cried, saying, Hosanna to the son of David: Blessed is he that cometh in the name of the Lord; Hosanna in the highest.

1. This Gospel has two parts. The first treats of Christ the Lord's entry into Jerusalem riding on a donkey. The second part, as recorded by St. Luke (19:41–44), tells how when the Lord drew near and viewed the city of Jerusalem he wept over it. Let us begin by speaking of the first part.

2. You have often heard that a person is a Christian not by birth through his father and mother, also not because his name is John, Peter, or Paul, but because Christ has written his name in heaven, yes, in his heart. For by baptism we die and through it are told: You, oh man, who before were a child of Adam and were called Hans, Peter, Paul, shall no longer be only that, but you shall be called Christian. A human being is constituted by flesh and blood; but to

be a Christian one must be baptized and be washed clean from sins by the blood of Christ. Whoever has been baptized bears Christ's name and is called Christian. Hence, if he who bears Christ's name is asked, Are you called Hans, Peter, Paul, he indeed may answer and say, Yes, my father called me Hans, Peter, Paul, or the like, but now I am a Christian and also bear that name because I was baptized and washed clean with Christ's blood. Because of the man, Christ, I am called Christian. He is called Christ; I am called Christian, not because of my holy life, but because I have put on Christ by my baptism and have inscribed his name on my forehead, yes, imprinted it on my heart.

3. This is the point of this Gospel, that we should receive and hold to this King whose name we bear, after whom we are called Christians. True, death also comes to John, Peter, Paul, but a Christian does not die. John, Peter, Paul are also buried, but a Christian neither dies, nor is buried, but lives. It does not matter that I, Peter, or Paul die. Because I am a Christian, like Peter and Paul, I will come out of the grave resurrected. For Christ, from whom I have my name, promised this to all Christians, in order that we may learn to believe what this King gives us: deliverance from sin, death, and hell. The prophet Zechariah, whom the Evangelist here quotes, wrote of this: "Behold your King, who is meek, gentle, and helpful," and wants to rescue and save you. He is the epitome of righteousness and wishes to lavish his righteousness upon you. He is Life personified, and comes to give you life. That is what Christ signifies for us, and for his sake we are called Christians.

4. This is a sublime message which we ought gladly to hear with thankful hearts to God, so that when death comes we can be comforted and say, I, Hans, Paul, Peter lie here sick, but because I am a Christian I am ready to die in Christ whose name I bear and to whom I steadfastly cling. In that way neither Hans, Paul, Peter comes into hell, nor remains in death, but comes into Christ's bosom and lives.

5. That is a different sermon from the one that is preached with good works as the basis. True, Hans, Paul, Peter should and must do good works. But this sermon reaches higher. Granted, Hans, Nick, Paul, Peter, you are pious and do good works; but you still need something more, namely, to be a Christian who can say from the

heart, I believe on Jesus Christ, who truly is the King that comes to me with gentleness and grace, rescuing me from sin, death, devil, and hell; into him I have been baptized, in him I believe, with him I remain, and unto him I die. In this way a person overcomes death and leaves this life for eternal life.

6. So much for the first part and the prophetic proclamation spoken by Zechariah and the Evangelist here, "Say to the daughter of Zion, see, your King comes to you," merciful, righteous, and a helper! He wishes to make you holy and righteous. That means this King does not come in order to condemn the people and throw them into hell. Moses comes to judge and accuse (John 5:45). The devil comes, too, in order to accuse, judge, and kill. Judges, kings, and emperors are there to rule and to inflict death, for that is the office enjoined upon secular powers by God. But this King does not come to condemn but to help, to redeem from sin, to pardon and forgive. That is the way we should perceive him, and it is to such a King that we are called. God grant that we embrace and hold tightly to him. Amen.

7. The second part, as St. Luke tells the story, treats of Christ's weeping over Jerusalem. The people who went before and followed him cried out, "Hosanna, to the Son of David," God be praised, the King is at hand, all is well. But the Lord looked up and as he viewed the city began to weep, saying, "If you, even you, had only known on this day what would bring you peace!" He cries over those who pay no heed to such preaching. He had every right to be angry, to strike down with thunder and lightning, if he had wanted to judge them by what they deserved. But he weeps because they are so obdurate and unwilling to recognize the time of their visitation: Jerusalem, you will be stormed, young and old massacred, and the city leveled!

8. With sorrowful heart Jesus announces what will happen to Jerusalem, citing the reason why: "because you did not know the time of your visitation." As much as to say: My coming to you was in mercy, bringing help and comfort, deliverance from sin and death, and above all eternal life. All of this was out of sheer goodness and mercy, without any rights or deserts on your part. Will you let the devil so dominate you that you not only reject my proffered goodness and grace, but even scoff at me for it? Your rejection smells to high heaven and clings to you forever.

9. The gospel is presently being preached, too, in copious measure for all to hear what sort of King Christ is and how he is to be perceived. But townspeople, peasants and nobility trample their pastors and preachers under foot; the high and mighty of this world persecute the gospel. What will come out of this? Christ seeks to be gracious to them, brings the market to their door, and they strike him dead. What can be more irrational than to bring a man silver and gold, right to his house, and say to him that this is all his, if he will only put out his hand and receive it, but he rebuffs and strikes dead the one who seeks to deliver it right into his lap? Anyone witnessing this would say that the man is crazy, and he would be right. Well, now, here it is not a bag of gold but another kind of treasure announcing that when it comes time for you to die you have Christ's help and assurance that you will have eternal life, and then, irrationally, in spite of his offering you such a treasure, you push him away and scorn him! That is the reason why he here weeps.

10. We need to consider this well. This King's entry and coming overflow with mercy and with very great comfort. But when he is despised, in fact persecuted and rejected in unbelief, he then sheds tears. I have often said that a plague must come upon Germany. Our rulers and leaders are guilty before God of so great a folly that a terrible bloodbath is bound to come, so that nobody will know where to run. And then the King will say to you, I came to your house, offered you everlasting life, but you turned away, swilled yourself full, did as you pleased, and, to top it all off, persecuted my gospel. This calamity will be added to your judgment.

11. That's the way things went at Jerusalem. When Christ came there saying, My dear daughter, open the door, your King has come, what did she do? The bride proceeded to bring him to the gallows. He then dealt with her so severely that nobody today knows the site of Jerusalem. Now 1500 years have elapsed and the Jews no longer inhabit Jerusalem but are dispersed, some here, some there, scattered throughout the world. They sit on their bag of possessions and have nothing but oppression to endure from rulers and lords under whom they prospered for a time with their fraudulent dealings but now are robbed of their goods and driven out of the country. In the end their misery will be compounded by

fear for their very lives. They would no doubt gladly go back to their land and rebuild their city, but there's no hope in that. Like a wayward daughter who refused to listen then, she will find her King turning a deaf ear to her now.

12. Therefore, my dear children, young and old, big and small, don't ever let yourselves come to such a pass that you think and say, The gospel is something I can have any day, something I eventually will want to learn. Seize the opportunity now, while the Lord is near, as the prophet says (Isa. 55:6), "Seek ye the LORD while he may be found, call ye upon him while he is near." If we fail to see that he closes the door, there is no way to get in; for he will let us cry and knock in vain, as he did the foolish virgins who came after the door was closed, crying, "Lord, Lord, open to us." Thereupon he answered, "Verily, I say unto you, I know you not" (Matt. 25:11–12). So with us, too, if we fail to watch. Then not even a single preacher will manage to keep one iota of the gospel straight, as I experienced under the papacy when I was a monk. I did not hear a single monk who could have told me who Christ was, or the Ten Commandments, the Lord's Prayer, the Creed, what it means to be a Christian, the meaning of the Sacrament, of baptism, the pastoral office, marriage, and other articles. Nobody could explain how to derive comfort from these doctrines. But now that this is all clearly and thoroughly preached, people don't know how to scorn it enough! In times past, cloisters and churches were built at excessive cost; now not even a hole in the roof of the parish pastor's house gets repaired to keep him dry. I'll skip the shabby, scornful treatment, though it merits tears and lament to see such contempt.

13. For this reason I urge you young folks to be on guard; perchance you will see and experience the impending doom upon Germany. A storm will overtake Germany and not skip by. God could not unleash it upon Jerusalem as long as so many pious people, David and the prophets, lived there and lay buried there, yes, even God himself lived there. Jerusalem was his own dear fortress and dwelling place of which he himself said, "Here do I dwell, my heaven is here." Nevertheless, because of her sin, because she did not know the time of her visitation, God punished Jerusalem terribly and laid her waste. That is why I am not as much disturbed by people's greed, harlotry,

fornication, so prevalent now everywhere, as I am by the despising of the gospel. Avarice, harlotry, and unchastity are indeed great and terrible sins, sins which the Lord God punishes severely with plague and famine, though land and people still survive. But this sin is not adultery or harlotry; it is not even of human origin but of the devil, causing God's fatherly visitation of grace to be so terribly despised, laughed to scorn, and mocked. Such sin, you may be sure, prompts God's severest judgment to WIPE IT CLEAN!

14. The first phase of God's punishment, after the time of Christ's ascension, stripped the Jews of everything; later in the postapostolic days it came upon the Gentiles, too, just like the Jews, when after they had come into the fellowship of the gospel and Christ's kingdom they shamefully despised the time of God's gracious visitation. God stripped them of all spiritual goods, all churchly offices, so that not a single doctor of theology remained who could rightly expound and teach the meaning of a simple part of the Decalogue. The second part of God's judgment came at the hands of the Turks who devastated the cities and slaughtered men, women, and children, leaving neither young nor old to survive. Such is God's punishment upon the devilish sin of refusing to recognize his time of visitation. Greed, undoubtedly, is a great sin no matter where it appears, with prince or peasant, but far worse is this sin of despising God's Word. It will break men's necks. So let's be on guard! If God tolerates our sinful foibles, may he at the same time keep us from falling into this eternally damning sin of Satan! For it was over this sin that our Lord God shed tears here. All their sins would not have undone the Jewish people, if only this awful sin of despising God's visitation had not been added thereto, for Christ, their King, had come to help them. But when a person refuses to hear God's Word and despises it, he is beyond all counseling and help. For that reason be circumspect, be pleased to hear, read, and speak God's Word gladly, for then you do God the highest service and yourself the greatest good. Though the world despise it, do not be sidetracked by that; in due time it will find out and understand what it has done.

15. Remember what happened in Lot's case at Sodom. The Sodomites not only did not want to listen to pious Lot, but sought to drive him out of the city. Our Lord was ready to pardon their sins and

wanted it proclaimed that he wished to be gracious to them and have them return to him, but they refused to hear, despising and mocking him instead. As a result God rained hellish fire upon them and utterly destroyed their city. Their sin was not merely the base wickedness but their unwillingness to tolerate his Word. For a hundred years the first world mocked at Noah who at God's behest set about to build the ark at the time of the flood. They harassed the preacher of righteousness. When the ark had been completed God did not send pestilence, famine, or sword, but the flood waters to engulf and destroy them all, just as Sodom and Gomorrah were totally wiped off the map without a trace, leaving not even a dog. The destruction of Jerusalem was similarly total, and the same will happen to us, if we fall into this sin. Our Lord God can prepare an angel to rescue Lot and Abraham, set Noah at building the ark for his rescue, command the apostles to flee Jerusalem; he can uphold and save us in similar manner; but Germany will not escape suffering. If the Turk does not do it, the Last Day will. For the shameful despising of the gospel by the German people will not go unpunished.

16. Thus this Gospel treats of two things: first, that Christ is a Saviour unto eternal life; and second, that one must not despise God's Word. Christ sorrows over the city of Jerusalem, as though to say: Jerusalem will be leveled and the Jews scattered around the world, and yet I see that nothing dissuades them. They disdain the time of visitation, they refuse to ponder it, no matter how sweetly it is preached to them. All right then, he who won't accept advice cannot be helped. The person who not only is weak but on top of it all tramples with his feet the one who tries to help and guide him, how can he be helped by anyone? It is too much! We are sinners, and on top of it choke the one who tries to save and carry us. That is no trifling human sin, but of the devil. Such people are possessed by threescore devils. No one would strike dead the one who comes to the rescue except the pernicious devil himself or those whom he possesses. If my son were to throttle and slay me because I was trying to help him, I would have to say that he was totally crazy.

17. Accordingly, our Lord God wants his Word to be honored and will tolerate no less; and if it is not, he will not allow that to go unpunished. We have plenty of examples: the flood, the cities of Sodom

and Gomorrah, Jerusalem. Before the Last Day, new heresies will also appear, so that, as Christ says, if it were possible, the very elect themselves would be misled. God preserve us and give us his grace, so that we remain the faithful remnant that receives Christ and sings, Hosanna, God be praised, we have this King and are called Christians, knowing why and for what reason we bear that name because of our King into whose name we have been baptized and through his blood washed clean. Therefore, let us sing Hosanna and pray God to keep us faithful always. Amen.

FIRST SUNDAY IN ADVENT

Second Sermon—1533

Matthew 21:1–9

1. The Jews had many beautiful and precious prophecies concerning the coming Messiah, or Christ, their King, how with his coming he would establish his everlasting kingdom and eternally help and save his people from all evil. The message was evident in all the preaching of the prophets as they so splendidly spoke to the masses about the future kingdom of Christ. The Jews had these wonderful promises.

2. But there were also false preachers and carnally minded teachers who led the people to understand that Christ would come riding on horseback in worldly splendor like an earthly monarch for whom everything depends on pompous ostentation. From such false preachers the people conceived their fleshly minded notions that led them to expect they would all become lords. Even today the thought still prevails that when the Messiah comes they will all become lords and have the heathen as their servants. People still gawk after that sort of Messiah or Christ, in no way longing for a Messiah, or Lord Christ, who would rescue them from sin and eternal death.

3. In order that the Jews might be forewarned and not be deceived by such carnally minded teachers, God many years earlier proclaimed that Christ would not come as a worldly king with great pomp and worldly might, but as a poor beggar to Jerusalem, the chief city of Judah, where the temple stood with its divine service. He would be riding upon a donkey, as today's Gospel lesson also testifies. So that the Jews might not excuse themselves and say, If only we had known that our Messiah was to be a poor king, we would have accepted him, had the prophet but indicated this clearly long ago. So the whole story unfolds openly in broad daylight: Christ comes riding along like a beggar on a borrowed donkey without saddle or other

trappings, necessitating that the disciples place their cloaks and garments on the donkey in a makeshift arrangement for the poor king. Accordingly in no way could the Jews now excuse themselves. The prophecy had been perfectly clear: when Christ would ride into Jerusalem, he would not do so as some earthly monarch with armor, spear, sword, and weaponry, all of which betoken bloodshed, severity, and force; but as the Evangelist says, meekly, or in the words of the prophet, poor and lowly. It is as though the prophet wanted to forewarn everyone to take good note of the donkey and realize that the one riding is the Messiah indeed. So, be aware and don't be gawking for a golden throne, velvet garments and pieces of gold, or impressive mounted retinue. For Christ will come in lowliness, meek and sorrowful of heart, for all to see, riding on a donkey. That would be the extent of the pomp and splendor he would display with his entry into Jerusalem.

4. Christ manifests this openly by the manner in which he rides into Jerusalem, not furtively, but publicly, in bright daylight, accompanied by a vast throng, even though he comes like a beggar; and, as the Evangelist reports, the crowd that went before and that followed shouted loudly to the true Son of David, wishing him well and godspeed for his kingdom. They wondered over his preaching, understanding well enough that the donkey would not save them; but they hearkened to his preaching as regards the right way to be saved. All of this had been told the Jews long before by the prophet, in what manner Christ would come, namely, not with worldly pomp but poor and riding on a donkey, in keeping with the prophecy that the Lord would ride into Jerusalem on an ass. All of this, I say, was given as a warning to the Jews, in order that they might not be offended by the lowly situation of their King and fall into the delusion that their King, the Messiah, would come in worldly splendor. They were rather to understand that their Messiah and King would come poor and lowly, appearing as the lowest of the low.

5. On the other hand, however, as the prophet Zechariah states, this poor Beggar-King possesses might different from that which any ruler or king ever possessed, or ever exercised upon earth, no matter how great and mighty these rulers were or ever could be. His might is equivalent to his name, *JUSTUS ET SALVATOR*, not a rich, splen-

did, magnificent king before the world, but Righteous and Saviour, that is, the one who would bring righteousness and salvation with him, and assail sin and death. He would be known as sin's foe and death's destroyer, the champion over sin and death for all who believe in him and receive him as their King, not offended by the poor, borrowed donkey. These believers will have their sins forgiven, and death will not harm them, for they will have eternal life and not die. And even though physically they would die and be buried, yet it should really not be called death but a sleep. This is what the prophet wants to teach us about this King whom he titles with two names, Righteous and Saviour. It's as though he were saying, This King is and shall be called sin's devourer and death's strangler, who extirpates sin and knocks death's teeth out; he disembowels the devil and rescues those who believe on him from sin and death, conducting them to be among the angels where eternal life and blessedness are.

6. He lets the other kings have their finery, castles, dwellings, money and goods, their delicacies of food and drink, clothing and dwellings more costly than the average person has; but they do not have the art which this poor Beggar-King possesses. For neither emperor, king, or pope, with all their might, is able to help with the smallest sin, nor with all their money and goods heal the least of illness—I won't even speak about their capacity to rescue from eternal death, everlasting punishment, and hell. But Christ the King, who is righteous and a Saviour, even though poor and lowly and comes riding a donkey, prevails not only over *one* sin, but over *all* my sins, and not only over mine but *all the world's sins.* He comes not only to heal my illness but to take away death, and not only my death but also the world's death.

7. Tell this, the prophet says, to the daughter of Zion, open your mouth and shout, so that the daughter of Zion and Jerusalem be not offended by his lowly coming but open eyes and ears to hear what is proclaimed, "Rejoice greatly, O daughter of Zion; shout, O daughter of Jerusalem; behold, thy King cometh unto thee." Don't gawk with your eyes but let your ears give insight to your eyes. Your King has no great stallion, no spurs, no saddle; he is poor and rides a donkey. And yet there's no king like him; he removes your sin, rescues you from death and hell, and gives you everlasting holiness and righ-

teousness, eternal life and blessedness. So don't pay any heed to the wretched way in which he comes and then later also shamefully dies on the cross. For he does this all for your sake as Savior to help you, to sanctify you and rescue you from death.

8. If we don't want to understand this with our ears, but accept only that which our eyes see and our hands touch, we will miss our King and be lost. There's a big difference between this King and other kings. With the latter everything is outward pomp, great and gallant appearance, magnificent air. But not so with Christ. His mission and work it is to help against sin and death, to justify and bring life. He has placed his help in baptism and the Sacrament, and incorporated it in the Word and preaching. To our eyes Baptism appears to be nothing more than ordinary water, and the Sacrament of Christ's body and blood simple bread and wine, like other bread and wine, and the sermon, hot air from a man's mouth. But we must not trust what our eyes see, but listen to what this King is teaching us in his Word and Sacrament, namely, I poured out my blood to save you from your sins, to rescue you from death and bring you into heaven; to that end I have given you baptism as a gift for the forgiveness of sins, and preach to you unceasingly by word of mouth concerning this treasure, sealing it with the Sacrament of my body and blood, so that you need never doubt. True, it seems little and insignificant, that by the washing of water, the Word, and the Sacrament this should all be effected. But don't let your eyes deceive you. At that time, it seemed like a small and insignificant thing for him to come riding on a borrowed donkey and later be crucified, in order to take away sin, death, and hell. No one could tell this by his appearance, but the prophet foretold it, and his work later fulfilled it. Therefore we must simply grasp it with our ears and believe it with our hearts, for our eyes are blind.

9. That is why the Evangelist repeats the announcement, "Tell the daughter of Zion," and the prophet says, Rejoice and be happy, Zion, dance and spring, for your King comes to you. What sort of king? A holy, righteous King, a Saviour and Helper, who wants to make you holy and be your Redeemer. He brings you his holiness and righteousness as a gift, that you might be free from sin, righteous and blessed before God. He comes, too, as Saviour and Helper, to give

you life and by his death to deliver you from eternal death. Therefore do not be offended at his lowly appearance, but thank him for it and be comforted, for it was all for your good, to rescue you from sin and death, to make you righteous and blessed.

10. That is our King, our dear Lord Jesus Christ, and this is his kingdom and office. Dollars, crowns, castles, and vast kingdoms don't constitute his mission. For if we depended on that and died, our life would be nothing. But it is his office and work that we know that through his suffering and death we are redeemed. On this we rest and can say: through the righteousness of my King, the Lord Jesus Christ, I am justified. For that purpose he became poor and wretched, let himself be nailed to the cross, to make me holy and to drown sin and death in me. Whoever believes what the gospel declares has what it says. For that purpose Christ instituted holy baptism, thereby to clothe you with his righteousness. It is tantamount to his saying, My righteousness shall be your righteousness; my innocence, your innocence. Your sins indeed are great, but by baptism I bestow on you my righteousness; I strip death from you and clothe you with my life. That's Christ's true regimen; his office and mission are summed up in this, that he daily strips away our sin and death and clothes us with his righteousness and life.

11. We must certainly receive this message eagerly and gratefully, by it becoming more pious and godly. Unfortunately there's the opposite side, that by this teaching the world becomes more and more hostile, wicked, and malicious; yet not through fault of the teaching but of the people, thanks to the pernicious devil and death. Today people are possessed by seven devils, whereas before it was only one. The devil now bulldozes the people so that even under the bright light of the gospel they become greedier, slyer, more covetous, crueler, lewder, more insolent and ill-tempered than before under the papacy. Why so? Not through fault of the teaching but because the message is not met with thankful acceptance; people cast it to the wind and pay more attention to money and goods than to the blessed treasure which our Lord Christ brings to us. Hence our Lord God scolds again, saying, Have you no appreciation for this—that through the suffering and death of my only begotten Son I have removed your sin and death? Well, then, if that's the way you want it, I will

multiply sin and death sevenfold for you. And whereas before only one devil possessed and troubled you, now seven worse devils will afflict you. No station in life—peasant, burgher, aristocrat—is spared, from highest to lowest, as they give their lives shamelessly, carelessly, to greed, gluttony, drunkenness, immorality, and all manner of shameful depravity.

12. Therefore I exhort that you listen eagerly and lovingly to this Word, receive it with deep gratitude, and beseech the Lord God from the bottom of your heart for a firm faith to cling to this teaching. You may be certain that this will bear fruit day by day, as you become more humble, obedient, loving, chaste, and godly, for it is in the nature and art of this teaching to create godly, decent, obedient, and pious people. But if people refuse to receive it with loving and ready hearts, they will become seven times more wicked than before they came to know this teaching, as experience shows. Be forewarned therefore; the hour is coming—it cannot be avoided—that the ingrates will be afflicted and punished. They will then receive what now they have earned. God will certainly find them out.

13. Therefore learn this Gospel well; it is certainly meant for us. Because this King came in poverty to the Jews, they were offended by him and refused to accept him. The prophet Zechariah had long before informed and forewarned them not to be gaping for an earthly king who would establish a worldly kingdom. They were to learn that their Messiah and King would be the Saviour who would redeem them from sins and death. But it did not help; they refused to listen. See to it, therefore, that you don't become just like the Jews and end up with the same judgment. Be thankful to God, gladly and willingly receiving this King; otherwise the miserable devil will be your lot with howling, weeping, and gnashing of teeth. Against this may God graciously defend us. Amen.

FIRST SUNDAY IN ADVENT

Third Sermon—1534

Matthew 21:1–9

1. The Gospel for the first Sunday in Advent is also read on Palm Sunday, and later again in the summer on the tenth Sunday after Trinity, in connection with the Lord Christ's weeping over the city of Jerusalem. Thus three times each year the Gospel concerning the Lord Jesus' entry into Jerusalem is treated. There is much to learn from it, but the prophecy which the Evangelist quotes from the prophet Zechariah is the chief thing, "Rejoice greatly, O daughter of Sion, shout, O daughter of Jerusalem: behold, thy King cometh unto thee; he is just, and having salvation," and so on.

2. This was spoken by the prophet Zechariah many years earlier. The Jews were to discern from this what kind of Lord their Messiah and King would be, so that they might not miss him when he came. For the Jews opined that he was to be a secular lord who would govern the whole world, and that when he came his entry would be like the king of Babylon, or Alexander the Great, or Julius Caesar of Rome. To ward off such erroneous notions the prophet had forewarned them carefully, describing accurately what kind of king he would be, so that they would not miss him or allow him to pass them by because of failing to understand correctly the promises spoken by all the prophets.

3. Two parts, therefore, are embraced within the prophet's statement. First, he exhorts us to receive this King when he comes to us, showing what it is the King brings us. Second, he warns and arms us against being offended by Christ's poor and wretched appearance, foretelling that he would come poor and riding on a donkey.

4. First, then, in the words of the prophet, "Rejoice greatly, O daughter of Zion; shout, O daughter of Jerusalem," dance and spring, for I bring you a good, joyful message, "behold, thy King cometh unto you," to help you, to be your righteous King and Saviour. The

Jews understood these words differently, as though their Messiah's and King's advent would restore their old rights to them, since the Gentiles had robbed them of their possessions and taken away their kingdom. When our King comes, therefore, he will deliver us from bondage and yoke under the Gentiles and make us great and free lords—that is how the Jews understood these words then and to this very day.

5. In order to rid the Jews' hearts and minds of these carnal and worldly minded ideas of their Messiah's kingdom, the prophet states very clearly and emphatically that he comes "lowly and riding upon an ass." As much as to say, by outward appearance this King is a beggar, no hat for his head, no shoes for his feet, and, moreover, the donkey on which he rides is not his own. The Jews might well have asked, How can this be? The poorest beggar in the world, owning nothing, how can he be the world's King? That's why the prophet declares that this King will bring righteousness and salvation. He indeed rides on a donkey like a poor, wretched man, sans spurs and saddle; and yet he is rich in that he comes with righteousness and as Saviour.

6. Had the Jews correctly understood this word of the prophet Zechariah, they would not have erred so utterly. To be a worldly king with cities, territory, goods, gold, and wealth, as the Jews dreamt of their Messiah and still dream today, is not to be poor. The text is very clear on this point: "Behold, your King cometh to you poor (lowly)," that is, not with mounted escorts, possessing territory, people, or wealth. Hence this King cannot be a worldly king or lord. Had the Jews paid attention and been rightly stirred by these words, it would have been impossible for them to have been mistaken about the Messiah.

7. But like all factious spirits, so with the Jews. They latch on to a saying of Scripture and interpret it according to their own preconceived ideas and opinions, thus missing Scripture's true sense. So the Jews also! They read the prophet's words, "Behold, your King comes to help you," and immediately they concluded that, if he is a king, then certainly he must come with great pomp mounted on a horse as is customary for worldly kings. It certainly is not Christ's fault that the Jews did not receive him, since he had long before made it known by the prophets that he would come in lowly estate.

But the Jews held fast to their carnally minded opinions and let Christ pass by, just as today they mock at us for receiving the poor King who does not even own a donkey, let alone a pair of shoes. The Jews, therefore, cannot be excused, because the text plainly teaches, Behold, your King comes to rescue you, though he himself is poor, riding on a donkey.

8. We must learn to take hold of Christ, therefore, in line with the prophet's portrayal, as Saviour and Redeemer who has come for our sakes to help us. He was promised to Adam and all the patriarchs, and even so comes for our comfort and salvation. Accordingly he bears a twofold title, Righteous Judge and Saviour, who declares us righteous and free from sin, desiring to save us from death and give us eternal life. This title belongs alone to this King, Christ. If God were to deal with us strictly, according to our sins, we would die and be condemned. But Christ, the King, stands as the Righteous One for us, takes away our sin, and gives us everlasting righteousness. Those are our Lord Christ's true colors, as portrayed by the prophet, to be righteous and to free us from sins, as the prophet Jeremiah states (23:6): "This is his name whereby he shall be called, THE LORD OUR RIGHTEOUSNESS," that is, our Lord who will make us righteous.

9. Someone is bound to ask, How does this King make righteous? After all, the Ten Commandments came through Moses, and better commandments couldn't have been given. By keeping these commandments a person would be righteous. What is lacking that this King could supply to make men righteous? True, the Ten Commandments given through Moses are indeed as excellent as could be, but they were not able to make a man righteous and holy. He shows us wherein righteousness consists, but is unable to give it to us, because we cannot keep and fulfill the Ten Commandments. And just as Moses leads us to the Ten Commandments, so our reason directs us to the natural law which teaches us not to harm or hurt anyone, and so on. But thereby we are not righteous before God. To be really righteous is something we obtain only through Christ the Lord's death and shedding of blood; it is the Holy Spirit's gift to us, to believe and hold fast to the word, "whosoever believeth and is baptized will be saved." That is the way we become righteous.

10. This King's second title is that he comes as Saviour and Redeemer, which is to say, as Christ redeems us from our sins to make us righteous and holy, he will also deliver us from death and give us everlasting life. Moses did not have it in his power to do that. He says indeed, if you keep God's commandments, you will live; if you do not keep them, you will die and be lost. But that only amounts to showing the way to life, not giving it. For that reason the prophet says, Rejoice, you daughter of Zion, your King comes to you, a Saviour; take care that you receive him with great joy. He does not merely point to righteousness with his finger, like Moses, but grants you righteousness, that through him you might be righteous. Nor does he merely point at life from a distance, as Moses did, but rescues you from death, gives you eternal life, and also the Holy Spirit to believe it. Thus only through Christ do we become righteous, holy, and forever blessed.

11. No worldly king could give such gifts. Christ is the only kind of king able to redeem from sin and deliver from death. His rule is with righteousness and salvation. And he offers us such redemption from sin and deliverance from death through his gospel, declaring, Whoever believes on me is righteous and has eternal life. That is why the prophet here warns the Jews: when your Messiah and King comes riding in lowliness, don't turn your backs on him, but receive him with rejoicing; be concerned not to let him pass by, even though he comes in lowliness; for if you let him slip past you, the fault will be yours, not his, because he foretold it long ago, that he would come in such lowly form and you should not take offense because of his poverty.

12. The second part of our lesson deals with taking offense. The King will come with righteousness, and as Saviour, performing wonderful miracles also, but the miserable devil gets people to be offended in him. Oh, say the Jews, what sort of guy is he? He wants to help us when he cannot even help himself? Will he, dependent on bread handouts, possessing nothing and needing help himself, help others and be their king? The prophet foretold this all, so that people would not turn their backs: he will come in such wretchedness that all men will be offended by him, as recorded in Isaiah 53; yes, he will also be crucified. Now therefore believe these words and do not be offended in him.

13. But it was to no avail. The Jews renounced this prophecy and to this day they fancy that their Messiah will come with great pomp, gold, and wealth, and destroy the Gentiles. Because of these notions they reject this King and refuse to inquire into the prophet's meaning. They ought certainly abandon such carnally minded notions of a worldly kingdom, because the treasures which this King brings are spiritual and heavenly. But nothing comes of it—the Jews persist in their carnally minded thinking.

14. But the rejection of Christ does not happen only with the Jews, but also among us, for the high and mighty scorn us because of our gospel and sacraments. What folly, they say, that I should let myself be baptized with water poured on my head, supposedly to be saved thereby; or that some poor parish preacher, barely able to put a coat on his back, should pronounce forgiveness and absolve me from my sins; or that by receiving bread and wine in the Sacrament I should be saved. On that basis they despise a Christ-preacher. For it goes with the territory to be despised by reason of Christ's poverty. As a result, when a man becomes a preacher he is more despised than some lowly knave of no reputation. There is no station in life quite as scorned and humble as that of a preacher. That happens not because of us or the preacher, but because Christ is despised on all sides in the world. No wonder that the aristocrats and plutocrats say, Why should we believe some tramp-like, beggarly cleric? Why doesn't our Lord God send us a fine pulpit-prince to preach to us? Him we would believe. However, just as Christ's preachers are despised, so people also despise his baptism and the Sacrament of the Altar. Virtually no peasant retains respect for them, let alone burghers or nobles. Under the papacy people mocked at indulgences and pilgrimages, and yet they were highly regarded. Now, however, the prevailing word is, Huh, if all you can do is preach about Christ and faith, I'm fed up with that already, I've heard it all many times before.

15. Thus the world is offended at Christ, his gospel and sacraments, as St. Paul declared concerning him; his gospel, too, is a despicable and accursed thing in the eyes of the world, and is called the devil's teaching by the worldly wise and smart alecks. And so, just as miserable as Christ's entry into Jerusalem, so his teaching and works

are regarded too. He opts to be a beggar, and so the rich and learned trample over him with their feet, and the hale and hearty reject him. But no one ought to despise Christ in that way, for he is our Saviour and seeks to give us everlasting life. It ought not faze us that he comes in poverty. He requires neither armor nor mounted cavalry for his message; but simply proclaims, "Whoever believes in me shall have everlasting life."

16. These then are the two parts of this Gospel. First, we need to receive this King, for he is sent for us, to help us. Every troubled conscience therefore should pay heed to this King's word. Second, we need to guard against being offended and should say: It matters not a whit that this King is despised; I will nonetheless treasure him like a precious jewel, for the Scripture states, "Blessed are they whosoever shall not be offended in me," and "whoever endures to the end shall be saved." If we reject him now, we are left with as little excuse as the Jews. So, let us not say, If our prince accepts the gospel, then we will too. We have already heard that, as this King Christ was despised when he rode into Jerusalem, so will his teaching be to the end of time. However, when he returns in glory, he will hold his despisers in contempt. Then will the fools who now are rich and smart alecky be poor and in dire need. May our dear Lord and King Jesus Christ give us grace and the Spirit to receive him gladly, believe his gospel, and through him be saved. Amen.

SECOND SUNDAY IN ADVENT

First Sermon—1532

To render the service due our Lord God, to hear and learn his precious Word, just as he entrusted and gave it to us, to discern what he wants with us and what we may expect from him, so that we are not like swine, unable to do anything: this is why we should hearken to today's Gospel. For he is not letting his Word be preached to stones. Nor is our preaching about how to live our life here—because that is taught elsewhere—but how we are to achieve salvation. So, today's Gospel is about the Lord's second advent, about what will happen when the world comes to an end. It reads as follows:

Luke 21:25–36

And there shall be signs in the sun, and in the moon, and in the stars; and upon the earth distress of nations, with perplexity; the sea and the waves roaring; men's hearts failing them for fear, and for looking after those things which are coming on the earth: for the powers of heaven shall be shaken. And then shall they see the Son of man coming in a cloud with power and great glory. And when these things begin to come to pass, then look up, and lift up your heads; for your redemption draweth nigh. And he spake to them a parable; Behold, the fig tree, and all the trees; when they shoot forth, ye see and know of your own selves that summer is now nigh at hand. So likewise ye, when ye see these things come to pass, know ye that the kingdom of God is nigh at hand. Verily I say unto you, This generation shall not pass away till all be fulfilled. Heaven and earth shall pass away: but my word shall not pass away.

1. In this Gospel the Lord announces his return on Judgment Day, which is to occur with grandeur and majesty. Last Sunday you heard about his riding into Jerusalem on a donkey, minus all pretentious show. He had no place to call his own, not even a foot of space; and besides, he later was even crucified. He is facing a poor, miserable future, not as a master but as a servant, whose desire was to

serve, and to serve in such a way as to die for us. Just as he himself says (Matt. 20:28), "Even as the Son of man came not to be ministered unto, but to minister, and to give his life a ransom for many." To sum up, during his first advent he rendered the greatest service, a service which no angel, no creature was able to render, and prepared the kingdom for his believers and elect. But when the number of the elect is complete, he will return not as a servant but as a master, in order to free us from earth, maggoty mire, death, and decay.

2. This is what the Lord proclaims in this Gospel: he cautions his Christians against becoming secure, so that the day of his coming might not come upon them unawares; he comforts them also so that they will not be terrified at the signs which will precede Judgment Day but rather rejoice that their redemption is drawing near.

3. To begin, the Lord warns us Christians against setting a date for our life here on earth. But we are to know that our Lord and Redeemer will come from heaven, and should, therefore, expect his return at any moment. Consequently, we have but a left-handed half-hold on this life, but with our right hand and open hearts we await the day that our Lord will come in glorious majesty and splendor so great that human tongues will be unable to put it into words.

4. Today's Gospel warns and exhorts us to bear this in mind seriously—for here in this life there is nothing enduring—so that we do not do as the ungodly who say, Oh, who knows when Judgment Day will come? We must not become like those secure and ungodly people who crowd their hearts with surfeiting and concerns about earning a livelihood. For what will happen before Judgment Day is this: everybody will build, marry, surfeit, become secure, and in so doing burden their hearts, as if there were nothing else to do but that. Judgment Day will suddenly overtake these people who live this way, and Christ will come unexpectedly. When they are at their securest, when things rock with drumbeat, merriment, and dancing, they will suddenly be laid low and burn with a fire that will never be extinguished.

5. The Lord tells of this before it happens and wants us to be guided accordingly. Those who ignore what he has said will suddenly find themselves in the thick of things. While they devote themselves to building, to courting and being courted, to living high and carefree,

fire and brimstone will fall upon them from above and below. Just as happened to Sodom! The people ate greedily, drank to excess, danced, made merry, without offering Lot a single farthing, just like the burghers, peasants, and aristocrats also do today. At that time Lot announced to them, God will destroy you with fire; but they laughed at him and said, What are you talking about, you dear man? And what happened? At sunrise the next morning, the heavens grew black, a fierce storm arose that went crash! bang! From that moment on they were in hell. The same thing is happening today. When our people of high and low station hear talk about Judgment Day, they say: Oh, if only in the meantime I would have something to eat and drink, and money to count until Judgment Day comes! But if the best they can do is count dollars and live recklessly, while someone announces to them, Beware, Judgment Day is coming, they dismiss it with a laugh. Ah! You are such a fool! Do you really think that Judgment Day is coming? and so on! Judgment Day will propel its way in and crack suddenly like lightning does in the morning and during the night. To whom then will the crowns of silver and gold, houses, jewelry, and finery belong?

6. For this reason Jesus says, My dear disciples and Christians, do not follow the ungodly, careless crowd; but be on your guard. Right before your eyes you will see them burdening their hearts and ridiculing in the bargain. Be vigilant, for Judgment Day will come quickly, like lightning, so that no one will be able to escape it. Just as a mouse is caught in a trice, so suddenly will misfortune strike them.

7. This warning of Christ we should take to heart and mark well, for we cannot avert it. We have to hear and see how wanton everybody is. But let's listen to what Christ says, await his return, and pay no attention to what the ungodly and secure of the world are doing. For the Lord sincerely cautions us to look for his glorious return, because it is a sure thing. The ungodly will be plunged into the abyss of hell, while we, on the other hand, will be liberated from the earth and from all of earth's misery.

8. That is the one thing we ought to learn today, to prepare ourselves for the Lord's return, just as we confess in our Creed that our Lord Jesus Christ will come to judge the living and the dead. For what our Creed states briefly, this Gospel states profusely and assur-

edly, declaring in addition what the situation will be like in the world before the Lord returns, namely, Christ will be despised, and the preachers of the gospel will be regarded as fools. The wicked masses, on the other hand, will live riotously and in boisterous gaiety, as though nothing else mattered. This is not to say that it is wicked and wrong to take nourishment, but as they go at it, they overload their hearts. Were they merely to put a burden on their hands, there would be no problem; for work is a necessity. But when they overload their hearts, that is what is evil and forbidden, namely, to put all their hope in becoming rich and famous. They have no interest in Christ and scorn God's Word and Judgment Day. To overload the heart means to be so occupied with the worldly that the heart cannot focus on Christ's Word, just as our merchants, burghers, and peasants today who think only about how they can become rich, not giving a tinker's damn about the Word of God.

9. That's the way things will be, says Christ, when Judgment Day nears. The whole world will act secure. Don't let this disturb you, Christ admonishes, do not follow them; do not do what they are doing; cling to me. Nor be afraid; keep your head high, and see to it that, when I come down from heaven, I shall be able to find you! Then you will experience no distress, for I shall come to deliver you. But those who overload their hearts and show no concern for Judgment Day will find that death has suddenly overtaken them. The fellow who frolics and dances merrily with his wench, will then suddenly find himself flat on his face, and, while his next-door neighbor counts his shekels of silver and gold, he will suddenly be knocked flat with his money bags and all. That's what the situation will be like at that time; that's the bottom line.

10. All indications today, therefore, are that Judgment Day is not far off. For the world has certainly made a very good start in that direction, beckoning it more and more. The mad chase after material things is beyond calculating. Among the common masses the smug self-security is so strong that they laugh contemptuously at preachers. And this overconfident level will grow even worse. People will become so secure that they will refuse to tolerate any preaching at all but will chuck it completely and say with contempt, You are a fool, why do you care a straw for still more preaching? Already this think-

ing is widespread among our burghers and peasants. Whoever lives to see that day will understand these words well.

11. For this reason Christ says to his disciples and Christians, Be on your guard so that I do not find you in this rowdy crowd. When they say, Nothing to worry about, at that very moment they will be lying flat on their faces. That's what happened when Lot warned his sons-in-law; they laughed at him contemptuously. Their thinking, you see, went like this: Oh, this city has stood for such a long time; it will stay standing for a while yet. However, the next day before they ever got up, they were dead and engulfed in fire. That's the way the world wants it. Christ, of course, is vindicated. He faithfully warned the world and still today has the message preached. But to no avail. Really, people ought to be terrified and realize, this man who has preached these things to us will not lie to us. But they continue feeling secure and say, For the time being I'll go on drinking my beer. All right! It will serve you right. You did not want to listen; I have warned you; therefore, I shall suddenly smite you. Whereupon they will have to say that they got what they had coming. Now they don't trouble themselves at all about it. But the Lord says, The day will come, like lightning, let us be forewarned!

12. Such are the conditions prior to Judgment Day. We need to learn from this and not fret because we see these things happening, but say: Christ predicted beforehand that the world would become so savage, coarse, greedy, and so on. Well then! That's the way it is, and it is even going to get worse. That's the way it was with Sodom in Lot's day and worldwide at Noah's time. All these things are told us for our comfort, warning, and learning, that we understand what it all means. The ill-bred masses do not know what it is all about; but we are to know and be on guard so that we do not fall in with them! Eat and drink we must, but in such a way that we do not encumber the heart, for all is contingent on the Lord's coming and knowing that the resurrection of the dead and life everlasting lie in the future. If I am aware of that, then I can peacefully fall asleep, awaken, study, eat, or drink; and let Judgment Day come when it will, it cannot come too soon for me.

13. Yes, because of sin we wish that it would come; for in this life the name of God is not hallowed, but instead it is maligned, his king-

dom impeded, his will not done on earth, daily bread withheld from us, our guilt constantly increasing, and temptation continuing without end. Therefore, we pray: Heavenly Father, let thy kingdom come; deliver us from evil. Help, God, help, let your might be felt in all directions, and make an end of things. If thus we accept warning, watch, and pray, we can then rest assured that Judgment Day will not terrify us. The rest of the world, however, must be afraid, but it is their own fault, for they do not want to prepare themselves for the coming. It is for that reason also that Judgment Day must come upon the world suddenly, not for Christ's sake, who has given them sufficient warning, but on account of their guilt—because they refused to take heed.

14. Second, moreover, the Lord comforts and counsels us to rejoice when we see eclipses of the sun and moon, comets, and all of creation being transformed by change and increasing entropy. He says, When your eyes behold the sun and moon turning topsy-turvy, it is then time for creatures to die. It is just like a man whose eyes are distorted and unfocused, for whom things are half-dark, and whose eyes see things topsy-turvy; his end and death are near. Consequently, when the eyes of the world are skewed and distorted, then know that the end of the world is near. Lift up your heads and don't be afraid, for your redemption is drawing near.

15. We ought to write these words upon our hearts with gold letters, for they are immeasurably comforting to all who believe in everlasting life. When, says Christ, you see that the world is vile and coming apart at the seams, don't become frightened, you are my disciples and Christians. But let them fear who are directly affected by it all, the secure, vulgar burghers and peasants who do not care a rap about what is going on. Even if a given day were to have three periods of darkness, they would still be lying in the beerhouses and drinking themselves full. For this reason Christ says, When you see heaven and earth cracking apart, people more and more evil, and everything going out of joint, then be happy, be elated. About whom? About yourself? No, about me, for I am coming; it will be a bit terrifying, for if I am to destroy the world, it will exhibit horror and turn our eyes. But I am there, be not afraid, you will be delivered. This we must keep in mind: we believe that our Lord Jesus Christ will assur-

edly come, and we shall have eternal life; however, just when this day and hour will come, we actually do not know; but we are pretty close to knowing, for the Lord says, "When these things begin to come to pass, then know that it is not far off." For this reason we must be ready, every day, every hour.

16. Jesus tells a parable about the fig tree and other trees, not a terrifying, frightful parable about fire, but a beautiful, comforting, lovely parable about trees. "When the trees now shoot forth," he says, "ye see and know of your own selves that summer is now nigh at hand." So also, when the sun grows dark, you should say, the trees are budding; and when the sea and the waves roar, the trees are blossoming beautifully. Why? Because we are to be set free forever. The signs which will occur in sun, moon, sea, and earth, the world will regard as threatening pikes and halberds. But you, my disciples and Christians, are to think of them as beautiful blossoms. You ought to rejoice; for the kingdom of God is coming to you because you believe and are baptized, because you suffer and because you petition and pray.

17. These two things we must learn: be strong in faith and be forewarned and comforted. When we see the world's sundry troubles, we should pay no heed to them, but be on guard against all who follow blindly along like stupid blockheads. God's wrath will suddenly come upon them. We, however, are to rejoice and wait for the Lord, who will come in the clouds with his angels and deliver us from all misery. This is the message Christ leaves with us today. That is why we observe this day. May God grant us his grace so that we may lay hold on and remember it. Amen.

SECOND SUNDAY IN ADVENT

Second Sermon—1533

Luke 21:25–36

1. This Gospel has two parts. The first is about the signs which occur before Judgment Day. The second is an exhortation encouraging us not to be terrified at what is going to happen.

2. First then the modus operandi of our Lord God from the beginning of the world has been that when he purposed something new, it was preceded with wonderful signs. For example, when he wanted to punish the Egyptians and rescue his people, to make of them a special people, all manner of marvelous signs, some bad, others good, preceded. Bad, for example, when he punished the Egyptians with frogs, locusts, hail, murrain, and the like, until finally in a given night he killed all the firstborn, and the rest of the pursuers drowned in the Red Sea. Good, like the wondrous miracles on behalf of the Jews, leading them on dry land through the Red Sea, while drowning their enemies, providing manna, and the like. It was an indication that God purposed something new for this people, to establish a new government and order. The same was true when he toppled the unbelieving and obdurate Jews, in order to establish the new kingdom of Christ. As Christ hung on the cross, graves were opened, the dead came forth alive and went into the city of Jerusalem. Also, a very abnormal darkness fell over the whole land, and the curtain in the temple was torn in two pieces from top to bottom. All this was the beginning of a new order and the end of the old, marking the fall of Judaism and the beginning of Christ's new kingdom.

3. By experience the Jews were well aware of God's pattern of doing things. That is why the apostles come to Christ and ask him what kind of signs will precede the destruction of Jerusalem and the end of the world, even before the dawning of Christ's kingdom.

4. Concerning the destruction of Jerusalem the Lord replies, When you see an army encamped around Jerusalem, then know that the end of the Jewish priesthood and kingdom is not far off. There-

fore he advises them: Hurry from the country and flee to the mountains; for Judaism will be smashed, the time for mercy is over.

5. Similarly he also teaches them about Judgment Day: When you see signs affecting the sun, moon, stars, sea, water, mankind, and the heavens; when these come to pass—and don't wait around until you are sure of everything coming to an end, nor say that people have seen signs like this before—then, says he, take heart; however, don't think these signs a joke, for they are a positive indication that Judgment Day is now fast approaching.

6. The question is, which signs will they be? Also, will they all occur before Judgment Day? However, we ought not raise questions like this. For the Lord describes the place where these signs will be seen, namely, in the heavens, the water, earth, and mankind, and states that when these things begin to happen, then look up. For this reason I believe that some, though perhaps not most, of the signs, will occur later, even though Judgment Day were to dawn right now. Therefore we should be content with the Lord telling us where we are to look for the signs; and when we see any of them, we should prepare ourselves for what lies ahead, and not wait until they all have happened, so that we are not caught unawares.

7. Two kinds of signs occur in the sun and moon. First, they lose their brilliance. Whether this is a rarity or not, maybe even natural (for we can calculate some of this scientifically and predict it before it happens), doesn't matter, for it is a sign, as clearly stated in Matthew. But, besides this, such signs can occur in the sun without man knowing about them beforehand, suddenly, contrary to all calculations, like the darkness when Christ hung on the cross. For the experts explain that darkness like this occurs in the sun with the new moon. However, should it occur in the full moon or in the first quarter of the moon, it does not happen naturally. The darkness at the time of Christ's suffering on the cross occurred during the full moon. Accordingly this darkness was an especially extraordinary wonder. Even though we have never seen such a thing, it may occur quite suddenly.

8. Now during these past twenty years we have seen many other singular things, all of which have been unusual and peculiar, for example: a rainbow encircling the sun; the sun fragmented, with mul-

tiple suns appearing; also recently, within the space of two years, three comets appeared; and in other places earthquakes occurred.* So it is not beyond belief that something which has previously never happened may nonetheless take place. Certainly we have warning enough just in the sun that we should not be complacent but expect the blessed return of our Lord Christ.

9. The other signs, about which Christ informs us here, are the great roaring and surging of the sea, that it boils turbulently as to swallow up everything. It is just like a man, when he's about to die of natural causes; first he becomes sick, contracts a fever, contagion, or other illness, all of which are signs that he is about to die. In a similar way the world may become sick, heaven groan, sea, earth, and people show signs of illness, writhing with terrible distortions before everything is totally destroyed.

10. As regards signs among people I am totally convinced that we have experienced it. On that score the miserable pope has contributed a great deal with his doctrines, ordinances, and laws, causing pious hearts to be greatly terrified by proclaiming that it is necessary to pray, fast, hear masses, make pilgrimages, and that it is a mortal sin if they fail to do this. Terrorized like this, nobody could know when enough is enough, because true comfort, forgiveness of sins through Christ, had disappeared completely. As a result people ran to St. James and tormented themselves with pilgrimages, fastings, and other works, to the point in my estimation that there could not have been a greater misery on earth. I myself have seen many who were unable to bear such deep anguish, on account of which they fell into despair through intense fear and terror, and were seized with horror before God's dreadful judgment.

11. For by his preaching the pope had nearly succeeded in scaring us to death of Christ; we considered him to be a stern judge. I, too, had been one of those who expected Christ to be nothing more than a severe master, and as a result I called on the Virgin Mary to stand by me and be my advocate before this judge. Others did the same thing because that was all they knew. We all said, The judge is coming, the judge is coming; I have been a bad boy, help, dear Virgin

*The editor cites the years 1531, 1532, 1533.

Mary, otherwise there is neither comfort nor help nor counsel for my poor soul. That's how we babbled, and people did not know what else to do. For they had lost Christ, the true and only Saviour. So I regarded this sign, for the most part, to be nothing, just as I also thought that most of the other signs in the heavens had also occurred. But whether there are still more signs to come is something you can be very sure of; and in order that we leave nothing undone as we prepare ourselves for this day, is something the Lord teaches us hereinafter.

12. At the end of this part the Lord mentions another sign when he says: "Men's hearts failing them for fear, and for looking after those things which are coming on the earth." Here he talks about another fear, a very great fear, which springs from the fact that men will be terrified at the signs before Judgment Day. They are not wicked, unbelieving people, but pious and God-fearing hearts who heed the warning of the signs. The ungodly and unbelieving live on in their security, scorn all warning and signs, continuing to think that many of those signs have already occurred, while Judgment Day failed to make its appearance. The upright, however, profit from such signs and on that account are apprehensive and afraid. These are but few and will always be so, the secure masses. We must, therefore, not think of Judgment Day as coming in the distant future, but anticipate it every day.

13. Now, in the second part the Lord comforts his Christians who are horrified by the things coming upon the earth, so that they are not afraid but rather rejoice. This also is a very necessary admonition. For that's the way it is: Those who ought to be afraid are not afraid; and, on the other hand, those who ought to rejoice do not, but rather are terrified. Now under the papacy we understood nothing about this. Though it has been read about and preached year after year, men still have not understood what Christ so graciously preaches to us.

14. "And then," says Christ, "shall they see the Son of man coming in a cloud with power and great glory." The resplendence will be of a different kind than when emperors and kings come parading by. For then the whole sky will be full of angels and saints; they will shine forth more brightly than the sun, with Christ in the midst of them, soaring with Christ in the sky. Each saint, that is, each Christian will

pass judgment upon the damned who stand below on earth, trembling and shaking. In the clouds you will see nothing but the faces of the saints and elect; on the earth you will see nothing but the faces of the damned. For the damned will stand on earth; the saints, however, will be seated on the clouds. It is my hope that we, too, shall be sitting there, we who believe in the holy man who is called Jesus Christ.

15. "And when," says Christ, "these things begin to come to pass, then look up, and lift up your heads," that is, you are not to be terrified at the sign, but joyfully lift up your heads and say: "Blessed is he that cometh in the name of the Lord." For those who have believed in me and suffered for my sake and died in faith have nothing to fear. Let those be terrified who did not believe in me. But you, do not be afraid, for this is the way it must be. If the world is to be destroyed, then before this happens it must be fractured with violent upheaval, else this great structure cannot collapse. Just like when death reaches out for a sick person, he turns and wrenches, turns his eyes away, twists his mouth, grows pale, and becomes completely disfigured, thus will it also be for the world.

16. For this reason I say to you: Do not be terrified at this, but lift up your heads as they who view it with great pleasure. Then observe, "your redemption draweth nigh." "Your," he says, you who believe; the others, who do not believe, will be damned. To you believers salvation is coming. The day brings both with it: To those who believe and have been made righteous he brings heaven; to the rest, however, he brings hell and eternal damnation.

17. That is what the Lord says to the righteous. They will be terrified when sun and moon thus divert the eyes, the heaven will be filled with fire. For the saints are not that strong; even Peter and Paul would have to be terrified at this if they were alive. But be of good cheer. True, the sight will be awesome, terrifying to behold, but it is not aimed at you but at the devil and the unbelievers. Salvation and joyful redemption portend for you who have longed and prayed for so long that my kingdom should come to you and you be totally cleansed of all sins and delivered from all evil. That for which you have prayed with all your heart for so long will now come to you.

18. For this reason you may well call Judgment Day a day of damnation and salvation, a day of sorrow and joy, a day of hell and the king-

dom of heaven. As the Lord says in Matthew 24:30, "And then shall all the tribes of the earth mourn." God willing, we do not want to share in that. But we leave that for the pope and his cardinals and bishops, the factious spirits, burghers, and peasants who now pursue their wantonness, malign the gospel, and cause all kinds of misery and misfortune; they will have to pay for what they did. But we who have to cringe before them now, we who mourn and are troubled, will at that time rejoice; we will then see them going down into the abyss of hell.

19. Therefore, no matter that creation trembles, and sun and moon become black and dark in terrifying aspect, do not for this reason be alarmed, do not crawl into a corner but courageously look up, fight off despair, remembering that you are in need of my redemption and have often desired and wished for me. If I am now to come to you and deliver you, then I must first overcome those who hold you captive, else you will not be set free. When someone lies captive in a dungeon, he cannot be rescued unless the dungeon be broken open. Consequently, you will not be set free until the world comes to an end.

20. Therefore, when this commences, do not turn in that direction. The rod has been made, but it is not intended for you but for those who have caused you to cry out. So, accept this coming as the advent of your redemption. The purpose of my coming is not to cast you into hell but to deliver you from the vile, sick, infirm, and wicked life of this world, to separate you from the devil and his servants, and to place you among the angels where you will not suffer but live in everlasting glory.

21. To provide comfort is also the purpose of the beautiful parable of the trees which he spoke. In the spring, he says, when winter is finally ended, and the whole earth revived, when cold gives way to warmth and barren trees bud and green, tell me, how does all this begin? Is it not true that first the trees bud, and thereafter burst into leaf? Then everybody says that winter is gone, and summer is on the way.

22. Let this parable be your doctor and the trees your textbook from which to learn how you are to wait for Judgment Day. For just as summer comes soon after the trees run with sap and leaf out, so, when the earth quakes, heaven trembles, sun and moon look woebegone, do not be frightened, but say, Behold, the sap and leaves, soon will come eternal heavenly summer and the winter of this world will

fade away. Life on earth is dreadful and barren when everything deteriorates as it does in winter; but it will end and fresh, fruitful summer and eternal life will come.

23. The Lord speaks very clearly: "So when ye see these things come to pass, know ye that the kingdom of God is nigh at hand." He does not say: When this begins, then interpret this to mean that the hellish kingdom of the devil has come, but that the kingdom of God is near. He says this to indicate that the kingdom of the devil is to be destroyed. For we live here among ungodly, wicked, deceitful, avaricious people, who revile the gospel and deliberately cause all kinds of misery. Now we have to see and hear this and daily reckon with the evil. From this, says Christ, I want to free you by my coming, so that you no longer have to endure such wantonness. For this is exactly what happened to Lot; he lived at Sodom with innocent eyes and ears in the midst of vile people who did him much hurt by their lewd conduct and tortured his righteous soul; as St. Peter says (2 Pet. 2:7), he had to see their sins and hear their filthy conversation, things not fit to be repeated. But when the sins became ripe like a boil and God could no longer hold back, two angels came to lead pious Lot out of the city. Then a terrifying spectacle occurred, as the heavens grew dark along with thunder and lightning; the clouds broke open, fiery brimstone rained down, and the earth opened and swallowed up everything. Without doubt Lot became terrified and thought his experience to be as painful to him as to the city. But his consolation was that he knew that this horrible spectacle did not affect him as it did the Sodomites, the wicked, wretched scoundrels who did not believe and did not want to reform. Because of this rain of fire they not only experienced paroxysms of horror but also were destroyed and plunged into the abyss of hell. To Lot, however, that fire was like a beautiful tree which buds and now begins to green. For in this he experienced God's help and merciful deliverance from the ungodly.

24. If we live that long, the same will be our experience on Judgment Day. It will be awesome to see heaven and earth set ablaze, and ourselves suddenly carried away and changed. That is terrifying. But Christ says that we are not to keep our eyes fixed on what is happening but to listen to what he is here explaining, namely, that it is a beautiful bloom, a fine, succulent branch. For this reason we are to

keep ears carefully attuned to how he explains it and not to what it appears to be. True, no human being will escape being terrified by what will happen. But one must rivet his heart on the Word and, bracing himself against his reason, say, We must not be terrified. The signs are but beautiful blooms announcing that my Redeemer and redemption are near. So, welcome, O God, my beloved Lord and Redeemer, and come, as I have often prayed that your kingdom should come to me. Whoever can welcome the Lord Christ in this way will in a trice be transported into a glory like that of the sun where he, too, will shine as brilliantly as the sun.

25. In this way our dear Lord Christ teaches us how to discern Judgment Day correctly, to know what he means for us and why we hope for and await his return. The pope preaches that Christ is a stern judge with whom we must become reconciled through good works, such as calling upon the saints and having the benefit of their intercession if we are not to be damned. There's nothing in that about Christ being our Redeemer. But the papacy always paints him coming to judgment and smiting with the sword and rod of his mouth, both of which signify wrath and punishment of the world. John and Mary are also pictured as standing at Christ's side, to indicate that we are to seek their intercession and that of other saints and set our hope on this. And good father Bernhard* also writes that if Mother Mary shows her breasts to her Son, he cannot refuse her anything. These are sure indications not of trust in Christ but of belief that Christ comes as a judge. However, in this Gospel he teaches us differently, namely, that he will come not to judge and damn us but to redeem and save us, and to fulfill all for which we have petitioned him, and to bring us his kingdom. To the ungodly and the unbelieving he will come as judge and punish them as his enemies and the Christians' foes, who have afflicted Christians with all kinds of misery. But to the believers and Christians he will come as a redeemer. This we should believe firmly, rejoicing in his coming and taking care that when he comes, as St. Peter says, we shall be found in faith and godliness, walking before him in peace and without blame. To this end may God grant us his grace. Amen, Amen.

*Bernard of Clairvaux.

SECOND SUNDAY IN ADVENT

Third Sermon—1534

Luke 21:35–36

1. In this Gospel the Lord is preaching about the coming Final Judgment; he warns and teaches his own how they are to conduct themselves. This teaching is meant not for the ungodly and non-Christians, but solely for his own disciples and Christians. The sermon itself consists of two parts. The first part is a prophecy in which he foretells how things will be when the Last Day is near at hand. The second part is an admonition that men should pray and always be watchful, so that they will be found worthy to escape everything that's going to happen and to stand before the Son of Man.

2. The ungodly are not at all concerned about the Last Day—even though it were already hard on their heels. There is such obstinate blindness and filthy leprosy in the world that death holds no terror for a man even though he knows full well he must die. Actually, as St. Augustine says, death is every individual's Last Day. That's why it is such an awful thing for a man to feel so secure that he fears neither death nor the Last Day, as St. Augustine also remarked. Read all the books and you will find no image on earth more frightening and dreadful than death, the certainty of which looms up before everyone—and yet they keep right on living the kind of lifestyle in which they surely don't want death to catch up with them! In contrast with such a death even an accidental death is not so terrible. It surely is bad enough when a man breaks his neck, drowns in water, or in some other way dies accidentally and suddenly. But it is much more terrible when one knows that he is going to be eternally lost but nevertheless pays no heed. Hence, death is not terrifying for him who has no fear of death, as is the case with believers, or with young children who have had no experience with death. But that death is awful when one is not only aware of it but is actually at the point of confronting it, as is the case with the ungodly and unbelieving when death stares them in the face and they must enter its portals.

3. But now, even though death and the Last Judgment which follows are terrifying—and for the ungodly especially so—nevertheless, just as the ungodly pay no heed to the death which is imminent every hour, so also in their false security they disdain the Last Judgment. This very security is all the more culpable and serious because it involves their eternal death. Without any real concern or fear, they continue to live for the moment, refusing to break with their carousing, gluttony, avarice, and other sins and vices—until the Last Day overtakes them and in body and soul they ride into hell and are eternally lost. That's why it is such a terrible thing in our present world that carousing, gluttony, scraping, scratching, and other vices are taking over to such an extent that there's no stopping them anymore. It makes one shudder to have to live among such people. A few sometimes think of doing better but they are slow getting started; others never even think about mending their ways.

4. For this reason also Christ is here primarily preaching only to his Christians and believers, comforting them so that they should not be terrified, no matter what kind of death they will die. After all, they have a gracious God who gave his dear Son on their behalf; why then should they still be fearful? If you truly believe in Christ, then even if you fall and break your neck in two, or drown in water, or perish in some other way, or the Last Day takes you away, nothing is going to harm you. With a gracious God and a faithful Saviour, what reason have you to be fearful? God is your friend and Christ died for you! It is to such people, who have come to terms with their dying, that this gospel is preached; not to the ungodly. Even if the meaning of the signs were perfectly clear to these people, they would still not be impressed. So let them go and be hanged! May we, however, be found among those precious few who believe in God and fear him not as a judge but as a father. It's enough that the ungodly must fear him as Judge.

5. This is how events will transpire before the Last Day, Christ now tells us. The world will shrivel up and become horrible and frightful-looking. The eye of the world is the sun. So also a man becomes wrinkled and deteriorates when dying time arrives; his eyes start growing dim, and his lips turn pale. So will it also be when the world begins to break up and nears its end; the sun will darken, there will be earthquakes, and men will be filled with dread. To sum up,

heaven and earth will look as if they are about to die. You, however, do not fear when the sea roars and the waves pile high as if to crash together over your heads.

6. But these signs of which the Lord speaks here will not continue forever. For the sun will shine and the earth will produce grass and grain until the Last Day, as written in Genesis 8:22: "While the earth remaineth, seedtime and harvest, and cold and heat, and summer and winter, and day and night shall not cease." I say this because some have had dreams and asserted that one year before the Last Day comes, the earth will produce neither grains for fruits, and that seven years before, wives will not bear children. These and similar bablings are human notions and dreams without, yes, contrary to, Holy Scripture. For Holy Scripture, as Christ already says in this Gospel, teaches that when people are the merriest and most secure and in highest spirits, that's when our Lord God will hurl his Last Day at them and in an instant overwhelm them all. One he will find building, another one courting, a third gorging and carousing—yes, the whole world living it up in pleasures and all kinds of lusts. However, before the Lord's Day actually arrives, the sun will be darkened one or two days—even as now the sun has several times become dark—and the sea will rage one week, perhaps two or three, as has often happened and will happen again, and yet this raging will not continue forever. Men will be filled with dread as we have already seen.

7. When you shall see these things take place (so Christ says to his Christians—the ungodly understanding none of it), then do not become terrified, but instead look up with joy, and lift up your heads, for this means your redemption is drawing near. Soon thereafter the Day of the Lord will come. The Lord will appear in the clouds with many thousands of angels, and at the same time you will be caught up with them to meet the Lord in the air. The ungodly on earth will grovel in fear, screaming to high heaven for help and cursing themselves for not having recognized God but instead having despised his Word. Yes, then the tables will be turned! Those who here on earth in this life were rich, powerful, merry, and superior will then be wretched and accursed. On the other hand, the pious and God-fearing who were oppressed and miserable on earth will then be rulers. And so let those then be miserable who are now scraping and

scratching to pile up wealth, putting no faith in the gospel, wanting to hear nothing about death, asserting they would rather enjoy the good life here a hundred years and let the Lord God have his heavenly kingdom! You, however, be truly happy and in highest spirits because the day of your redemption is at hand.

8. Our Lord Christ wanted very much to impress these sweet and lovely words upon the hearts of the disciples and his Christians so that they would not be terrified by the signs but instead remember that these are meant for the "wicked rascals" and not for the Christians. And speaking now for ourselves personally, we have seen many signs in the past twenty years. One time—four days in succession—I witnessed such roaring and raging that the Elbe could not flow because of it. Also, earthquakes have often taken place; seven years ago there were places in the Netherlands where land was submerged and people drowned. The sun has been repeatedly darkened. Under the papacy I observed many who were so alarmed that they shuddered and despaired, so much so that nowhere could they find peace. We Christians carefully record such signs and pay attention to them; the ungodly, however, disdain them.

9. The parable of the trees is truly lovely; Christ gave it to his disciples and Christians to convey even more effectively the comfort he had already brought them. Our Lord God has written the Last Day not only into books, but even in the trees so that whenever we see the trees leafing out in spring we should always recall this parable and the Day of the Lord. The leaves on trees do not point to winter—when it freezes, snows, and gets cold—but rather they point to the joyous time, that is, to spring and summer. So also you, Christ says, when you see these signs you can be sure that the time of your redemption is near when you will be delivered from all misfortune and from this vale of tears itself. So what Christ is teaching us here is that we should learn to regard these signs for what they truly are. When they actually appear, our Lord God will then take us out of this world and this vale of tears and transplant us into that other life where there will be no more misery or sorrow. The ungodly of course do not regard the signs in that manner, but Christians follow the teaching of Christ, their Lord, and therefore regard the signs as sure indicators of their deliverance.

10. Now follow the warning and admonition, that Christians should be vigilant and prayerful. Christ says that before the Last Day, the world will be gorging and carousing, occupied with earning a livelihood and obsessed with horrible anxiety as they scratch and scrape—something we behold all around us today. There is a common proverbial saying about such people: the longer they live, the worse they get, or also, the older, the more tight-fisted. The old amass money but don't dare touch it because they can't be sure about surviving today—let alone tomorrow. So, says Christ, it will be when the world itself grows old; it also will be scraping and scratching and, as he says elsewhere, the world will build, plant, marry, and be given in marriage just as they did in the time of Noah before the flood. God warned the world through Noah, announcing the flood a hundred and twenty years beforehand. But how did our lovely, charming world respond? Preaching to it was like preaching to a wall; people kept right on eating, drinking, marrying, and giving in marriage up to the very day that Noah entered the ark. That's how it happened: when they were the very least concerned, the flood overwhelmed them and swept them all away. The very same spirit exists in our own time: business as usual, worldly cares, gorging, carousing beyond all measure. There is no fidelity, no real faith left among earth's inhabitants.

11. For that reason Christ warns and admonishes his disciples and Christians: "Take heed to yourselves, dear children, lest your hearts be weighed down with dissipation and drunkenness and cares of this life." When the world makes the biggest show with its scraping and scratching, that's a sure sign that the day of my final coming cannot be far away—that day which will suddenly and instantly overtake them. One he will catch counting coins, a second carousing and revelling, a third dancing and leaping. But just as a snare drops suddenly over little birds, to catch and throttle them before they are aware of it, so also that day will suddenly and unexpectedly overtake all the inhabitants of earth. Therefore beware of gorging and carousing and the anxieties of making a living.

12. If someone says, does that mean we should not eat or drink? Or that a man should not provide for his needs? And should a man not work and be concerned? Answer: Yes of course! Eating and

drinking are a "must." Working for a living is not forbidden—but avarice surely is! Christ permits all of his disciples and Christians to provide for themselves, to till the ground and work. Obviously he knows well enough that his Christians, as long as they are in this world, will very much need to have food, drink, clothing, and provisions. What he forbids is sinful worry and covetousness. In our present world we note that everybody wants to enjoy the high life—a sure sign that the Last Day is not far off.

13. And, therefore, says Christ, when you see such signs and, in addition, the world's abominable false security, plus its carousing, gluttony, scraping, and scratching, then remember your redemption is close at hand. Do not be sorrowful; this wrath will be poured out over the world, which on that day will perish instantaneously with all of its children. You, however, my disciples and Christians, Christ says, are not of the world but, on the contrary, only guests and strangers; the world is only your stopover for the night. And so be watchful always and don't forget the Lord's Prayer; pray that God's kingdom may come to you—as I also taught you.

14. Christ is, of course, not talking here about natural sleeping and waking, as if the body must always be awake and never sleep, day or night—something impossible. On the contrary, he is speaking about spiritual wakefulness, namely, that our soul and spirit always be alert, and that we pray diligently and keep remembering the Last Day. If we are thus engaged, that day will not catch us unawares, as it will overtake the ungodly. St. Paul, in 1 Thessalonians 5, also makes a distinction between the children of darkness and the children of light, saying in verses 2–5,

> *For yourselves know perfectly that the day of the Lord so cometh as a thief in the night. For when they shall say, Peace and safety; then sudden destruction cometh upon them, as travail upon a woman with child; and they shall not escape. But ye, brethren, are not in darkness, that that day should overtake you as a thief. Ye are all the children of light, and the children of the day; we are not of the night, nor of darkness.*

15. And so Christ's will is that we be watchful, keeping ourselves in fear of God and good conscience, praying that we may escape all temptation and distress and be found worthy to stand before the Son

of man. St. Peter also teaches this (2 Pet. 3:11–12), admonishing us: "Seeing then that all these things shall be dissolved, what manner of persons ought ye to be in all holy conversation and godliness, looking for and hastening unto the coming of the day of God. . . ." May our Lord and Saviour Jesus Christ grant that to us all. Amen.

THIRD SUNDAY IN ADVENT

First Sermon—1532

Rightly to worship our Lord God on this Sunday and holy day in keeping with his express will of how we are to serve him, we need to sanctify this holy day by hearing Christ's Word, the Word that sanctifies everything. For it alone is holy, and for that reason we speak it, preach it, and give heed to it. Today's Gospel lesson is as follows:

Matthew 11:2–10

Now when John had heard in the prison the works of Christ, he sent two of his disciples, and said unto him, Art thou he that should come, or do we look for another? Jesus answered and said unto them, Go and shew John again those things which ye do hear and see: The blind receive their sight, and the lame walk, the lepers are cleansed and the deaf hear, the dead are raised up, and the poor have the gospel preached to them. And blessed is he, whosoever shall not be offended in me. And as they departed, Jesus began to say unto the multitudes concerning John, What went ye out into the wilderness to see? A reed shaken with the wind? But what went ye out for to see? A man clothed in soft raiment? Behold, they that wear soft clothing are in kings' houses. But what went ye out for to see? A prophet? Yea, I say unto you, and more than a prophet. For this is he, of whom it is written, Behold, I send my messenger before thy face, which shall prepare thy way before thee.

1. In this Gospel our dear Lord Jesus teaches two thoughts. First, we should consider his Word precious, worthy, and holy because much is dependent on this as we shall learn later. Second, he shows the atrocious crime of unthankfulness of those who hear the Word and see the miracles but still despise the same and fail to believe.

2. First, then, people should listen diligently to the Word of Christ which is preached to them. This is indicated by what John did. Even though in prison, as soon as he heard that Christ had begun to do

miracles, John sent his disciples with orders to ask whether he was the man who should come, that is, whether he was the Christ of whom Moses and the prophets of the Old Testament had prophesied and preached, and, later in the New Testament, so much would be preached. To summarize, they were to ask whether he was the promised Christ of whom it was written that the Jewish kingdom and Moses' teaching and the covenant would discontinue. The Jews were to listen to Christ, what he was preaching, that he would inaugurate a new teaching, a new covenant not only among the Jews, but also among the heathen of the entire world.

3. The Jews knew this well because it had been prophesied loud and clear. Therefore, because it was soon after John's imprisonment that Christ began preaching of eternal life and the kingdom of God and doing miracles, John wanted to direct his disciples to Christ. So he sent his disciples to Christ that they would not only hear the prophet's testimony, but with their own ears hear the preaching and with their own eyes see the miracles about which for so long a time the prophets foretold. Then from his preaching and his miracles they would recognize that he was the man and true teacher for whom until now the whole world had been waiting.

4. This sending of his disciples amounts to John saying, Go and learn who is the true doctor and preacher. I know it well that he is the true Christ, but the people do not believe this. Therefore, you go to him and hear for yourselves from him personally, so that you will divorce yourselves from me and the entire Jewish school of thought, in order to cling to this man on whom your and the entire world's salvation depends. This, then, is the final meaning of John's message to Christ, namely, that his disciples should personally hear and see Christ, come into fellowship with him, believe on him, and be eternally saved.

5. How did Christ reply to this question? He said neither "yes" nor "no" when they asked whether he was the one. Rather, he answered with his works and said, You see, hear, and comprehend that I am he. Even as Isaiah and the other prophets had prophesied that Christ would heal the lame, cause the blind to see, and the like, this you see before your very eyes; you are in need of no further instruction or answer, if you are willing to accept the evidence.

6. This is an unusually wonderful sermon which includes everything that one should preach about Christ—what constitutes his kingdom and how precious his Word is. His kingdom is a kingdom in which the blind, the lame, the lepers, the deaf, the dead, but especially poor sinners and all who are wretched and worthless have a hearing and find comfort and help. We should diligently proclaim this teaching of Christ and tell of his kingdom in which he is a King where the wretched, the poor in body and soul, find the help which the world with all of its resources is unable to give. There has never been such an excellent doctor as he, to give sight to the blind, cleansing to the lepers, and so on. Nor has there ever been a preacher who could preach the gospel to the poor, that is, draw to himself and comfort the sorrowing, the distressed, the conscience-stricken, and bring cheer to shrinking hearts and those drowning in distress and grief.

7. Moses is the greatest of preachers, but he lacks the skill to comfort the poor sinner. A replay of all of his sermons finds this theme: you must keep the Law or be damned. This causes great distress. Those who feel their sin and yearn to be relieved of the burden try to live according to the Law, but never find peace, nor can they gain a happy heart and conscience. How the saints of the Old Testament complained as they grew weary of Moses' regimentation and expressed a longing for the kingdom of grace as promised in Christ! For example, Psalm 14:7: "Oh that the salvation of Israel were come out of Zion! when the LORD bringeth back the captivity of his people." Also Psalm 102:14: "For thy servants take pleasure in her stones, and favour the dust thereof." The hypocrites think that if they outwardly keep the Law, fast, do not commit adultery, they are in no need of the gospel or of Christ. They feel there is no urgency. God will take them into heaven because of their praying, fasting, and almsgiving. These are the satisfied, self-righteous individuals who are not in need of God's grace.

8. Now it is true, one must have Moses' preaching in order to encourage people in discipline and behavior, just as government needs hangmen and jailers to punish renegades who do not conform, but rather fornicate, steal, are avaricious, and are usurious. But when the hour comes that you must die, tell me, of what good is the teaching of Moses even though you have followed it to the letter? Is it not

true, you will need to confess and say, Dear God, even though I am not an adulterer, a thief, a murderer, I require, nevertheless, that you will be gracious and merciful, else, in spite of all my good works I must despair.

9. One may read an example of the latter in *Vitis Patrum* (Lives of the Fathers). One of the fathers stood for three days in one spot, constantly lifted his eyes to heaven sighing and mourning. When his disciples inquired as to what his problem might be, he answered, I fear death. Then his disciples began to comfort him, saying, Why should you fear death since you have led an exemplary life and have been diligent in keeping God's commandments? But the teacher replied, I tell you I am much afraid; as you say, I have been diligent in keeping God's commandments, but nevertheless I know that God's judgment is different from human judgment; consequently, I cannot rid myself of fear. He had come to the realization that, when a procession of his deeds was marshaled before God's judgment, God's judgment is so acute, serious, and severe that our righteousness and good works cannot hold up, or survive.

10. Even if we preached the Law and did good works, yet when it came time to die as the aforementioned father, we would have to say, Oh, God, where is help now? Such a person would be among the wretched, not knowing what to grab or hold on to. For he would lack that of which our Lord said, "The poor have the gospel preached to them." He would see and have no more than the Law, which leaves him a bad conscience, fear, and distress and in no way can bring him comfort.

11. In contrast, the gospel is a message from Christ which says to the sinner, My son, be comforted and happy. Do not be frightened. You should know that Christ has commanded that his righteousness, which is divine and eternal, has been imputed to the poor, the miserable, the distressed hearts. His righteousness in your stead will wash away your sins, bring forgiveness, and satisfy a just God. This grace is offered through his Word. Do not doubt. As you hear, so believe, and then you will experience the same.

12. The gospel is a gracious, blessed teaching, a happy tale, and a comforting message. It is as if a rich man said to a poor beggar, Tomorrow you shall have one hundred thousand gold pieces. That

would be a gospel, a joyful message which he is happy to hear and which gladdens his heart. But what are money and goods in contrast to this comforting teaching, which states that Christ accepts the wretched and is a King who wishes to help the sinner caught in the Law trying to obtain righteousness and eternal life.

13. Christ states, My kingdom is far different from a worldly kingdom. In the earthly kingdom the strong get the help. As the saying goes, whoever outwits the opponent, succeeds in tying him up. Being in charge here is with the sword which strikes and hits in every direction. It tolerates no disobedience or crime. It has hangmen, whips, swords, water, and fire, in order to punish and keep order.

14. But in Christ's kingdom things are different. He does not operate with strong, holy people but with weak, poor sinners of whom Christ said: "The blind receive their sight, the dead are raised up." Now to raise the dead is a great miracle; but a far greater, wonderful miracle, one which does not receive the recognition, is that God has ordained a king to preach the gospel to sinners. Of such a King and such a gospel the Law and Moses do not preach. Here the rule is that whoever is a sinner belongs in the devil's and death's kingdom. This sounds as though God were a King of the holy and pious, who have a far greater degree of piety than an earthly kingdom demands. This is true. For Moses' kingdom is God's kingdom and the sermon he preaches is God's Word. The earthly kingdom is also God's kingdom. He demands that it remain and we be obedient. But it is the kingdom of the left hand. Here he delegates authority to father, mother, caesar, ruler, hangman.

15. Over his own rightful kingdom he himself rules and he does not delegate to father, mother, government, jailer, but himself preaches the gospel to the poor. We must learn that when the time comes that our pious works don't help and we find ourselves saying, I have done what I could; I have served my father and my master faithfully, I have defamed no one, and have not grumbled; I have faithfully instructed members of my household, my children, and employees; as far as possible I have ruled well; I have caused my neighbor no injury, nor have I stolen nor have I committed adultery. But to what avail? That will not help now. With all this the human heart will not be satisfied; it is frightened when it finds nothing which

can stand before God Almighty and his judgment. A deep need causes you to say, I have heard that the King, my dear Lord Jesus Christ, has performed various miracles which no one could imitate. Among these is that the gospel would be preached to the poor, for which he was ordained by God that he should bring comfort to frightened hearts. Therefore I will not lose heart or despair, but rather accept this teaching because it belongs to me, who am poor and miserable. There is no other help to be found, neither within me nor in the entire world.

16. The prophet Isaiah in speaking of Christ (50:4), says, "The Lord God has given me the tongue of the learned, that I should know how to speak a word in season to him that is weary." The word referred to has been taught by God. God has placed his word on my tongue that I may know the right moment to speak to the weary, to comfort the timid conscience. The Evangelist explains this when he says that Christ preaches the gospel to the poor. For this reason he, Christ, was made King that he should evangelize, that is, comfort and strengthen the poor, timid, sorrowing hearts. Therefore, his kingdom is known as a kingdom of comfort and help, in which the timid are no longer frightened and overcome with fear, but rather are comforted and made to feel happy. This does not happen through the preaching of the Law, but alone through the gospel. It is the Good News that Christ has atoned for our sins, that through his suffering we have been saved from eternal damnation. It is his realm and office to proclaim the gospel to the poor. That is what he wishes, because he will not come to the self-righteous who do not deem themselves sinners and do not feel the need of the gospel. They consider it abusive heresy which forbids good works. To them it is best to preach Moses and the Law.

17. The other part of this Gospel is that the Lord says, "Blessed is he, whosoever shall not be offended in me." Yes, truly blessed. The entire world is offended with this King and his teaching in which everyone ought to rejoice. As we see from the Gospels, the Pharisees, the scribes, the high priests, the priests, the Levites, and all who held themselves in high esteem considered Christ a betrayer and his teaching heresy. No matter what he preached they would misinterpret it to make it wrong. Indeed they say the heretic has been inspired by the

devil because he preaches that the Lord will plunge the pious and righteous into hell and lift sinners into heaven. This is the same as the papists are preaching today. Does this mean that good works count for nothing, they ask, and heaven will be opened to evil knaves? Our dear Lord Jesus had to endure similar slander from the Jews.

18. But the text says, "Blessed is he whosoever shall not be offended in me." Now if you understand Christ correctly, accept his Word, and come into his kingdom, you would come to understand that the gospel does not forbid good works, but rather teaches and encourages that good works be done. We should seriously endeavor to do nothing contrary to God's Word or conscience—support secular government, the emperor, the king, permit the use of sword, the rod, and whatever is necessary to maintain discipline. Government, sovereigns, and rulers should punish evil, stealing, and so on. Why, then, do people take offense at the holy gospel and slander it as though it taught that one should not do good works? The gospel does not reject or forbid good works. What it does forbid is that, when this life is over and we embark on another life for which there is no counsel or help, we rely and trust in our earthly life and good works, rather than looking to Christ with unshakable confidence, relying on his work and merit, that through him we will find grace and eternal salvation in the life beyond.

19. Accordingly God has given us a body with many members, in order that here on earth we should not be idle, go with our feet, pitch in with our hands, speak with our mouth, and the like. To guide us he has given us his word, the Ten Commandments, by which we should judge all our works. Our works should never diminish God's honor or our neighbor's good. The gospel doesn't merely say that we should do this, but states we should diligently pursue this (good works). When man leaves this world naked and alone and comes before God's judgment then the gospel gives a different kind of comfort, one on which his heart and hope may rely.

20. You have likely led an exemplary life—that is very good—thank God for it. But in death do not rely on that as though God should give you heaven for it. Rather, hold fast to this King, our Lord Jesus Christ, who as the Evangelist indicated was to fulfill his office to make the blind see, the lame walk, and so on, to preach the gospel

to the poor and bring comfort to miserable, frightened hearts. For he has not been placed in authority by his Father in order to hang and mangle us for our sins but rather to console the troubled conscience, uplift, comfort, and help unto life eternal.

21. Those who do not recognize him for that, those who do not accept his grace but rather take offense at his teaching and despise him as did the Jews and hypocrites still do today, he will deal with in his own good time. The stumbling block is the same, namely, that the world is offended at the teaching of Christ, that it does not want to rely on God's grace, but wishes to rely on its own work and merit. Consequently, it criticizes the gospel as a deceptive teaching which forbids good works and makes people profligate and wild.

22. Further, the world is offended that Christ is so miserable and poor. Case in point: just as he carried his own cross and permitted himself to be crucified, he urges Christians to take up their cross and follow him in spite of temptation and sorrow. Such thinking is foreign to the world, which shies away. As we see, even if the gospel is acknowledged and the individual sustains risk or pain, because of the gospel, he may fall away like worm-ridden fruit in summer.

23. Third, it is also an offense if our feelings cause us to pay greater attention to our own heart and conscience than to the gospel of Christ. I must make the personal confession that my own coming and going affects me and concerns me much more than the grace of our Lord Jesus Christ, as proclaimed in the gospel, comforts me. This offense is not as common as the first two because only true Christians are afflicted with the same, as I myself grapple with it. This causes grief for many, and if it were not for the support and help of the Holy Spirit no one could survive this offense.

24. In summary, then, Christ says: "And blessed is he, whosoever shall not be offended in me." With these words he is prophesying that people will take offense at this teaching of the gospel and that because of the gospel they will be despised and persecuted. A bit further in the Gospel Christ states it more definitely and clearly when he scolds the cities: "Woe to you Chorazin, woe to you Bethsaida, woe to you, Capernanum," and so on. And he complained about the Jews and said: But whereunto shall I liken this generation? It is like unto children sitting in the marketplace and calling unto their fellows, and saying, We

have piped unto you and ye have not danced; we have mourned and ye have not lamented. I want to say, John is an exemplary, self-effacing preacher, who ate nothing but wild honey and locusts, drank nothing but water and led a self-effacing life, but what did it help? You Jews blamed him, saying, He has a demon and despises us. I eat and drink and am friendly with all people; therefore I must be a glutton and a drunkard and a friend of tax collectors and sinners. No matter what one does, one cannot please these poisonous serpents, hypocrites, the work-righteous. If one leads a normal life, it isn't right; if another leads a self-effacing life, that isn't right either. How then shall one please this shameless world? That might happen perhaps, if one praised everything it did, even though it does nothing right.

25. Such offense, contempt, and persecution one must endure. Thus it was when Christ himself preached and with his miracles literally and loudly demonstrated that the blind see, the deaf hear, the lame are healed, the lepers cleansed, the dead raised—nothing helped. His Word was despised and he, the dear Lord Jesus, was nailed to the cross; and the apostles were banished and found security nowhere because of the preaching of the gospel. What do we have to complain about? What surprise is it that the world today despises the gospel and tramples righteous preachers? It was no different for Christ and the apostles, who not only preached the Word but performed great miracles the like of which we cannot do—we only preach the simple, vexatious Word.

26. We simply need to let it happen as it will. It will never be different with the gospel. It is and remains a teaching which causes offense but not to the unimportant people. Experience has shown that it remains a teaching which causes offense, not to ordinary people, but to the self-righteous, the wise, the mighty of this earth. It is well with those who know that it is God's Word which restores, comforts, strengthens, and makes secure against such offense. Those who do not receive it inflate themselves with their good works, become proud, fall away from God's Word, and rely on their own self-righteousness. They consider the gospel an annoying, rebellious teaching, against which one stumbles and which causes one annoyance. There are many of this type in the world and the populace considers them the greatest saints and the smartest people. Therefore Christ

said: "We have piped unto you, but you have mocked," and so on, and it is the same today. If one preaches the gospel, it does no good; if one preaches the Law, it does no good either. If one whistles, no one wants to dance; if one sorrows, no one wants to weep. One simply cannot make the wicked world happy or sad. It is a people that understands neither the gospel nor the Law, nor wishes to understand. One cannot make them into sinners nor can one comfort them because of their sins. One cannot make them blind or seeing, as we have an example before our eyes, in our adversaries, the papists.

27. This is finally another matter, that the gospel is a message which is terribly despised and that we should pay no attention that the pope, bishops, monks, priests, townspeople, and peasants do not ask about the gospel. It happened to our dear Lord Jesus himself and his own people to whom he was promised and to whom he was sent as Saviour. They were offended by him. Even though he did his wonderful miracles before their very eyes they could not be persuaded to accept his teaching; indeed they crucified him. Therefore, we may say, Dear Lord Jesus, if this happened to you when you came with your marvelous miracles, then I may well be silent if I am despised, ridiculed, and persecuted because of the gospel.

28. To summarize, in today's Gospel we have two excellent, lofty teachings. First, Christ is a King of grace, full of comfort, and through his gospel he encourages the distressed conscience, comforts those who have sinned, and wants to help them obtain eternal life. Even though the powerful governments of this world are also God's kingdom, nevertheless, they are his kingdom of the left and will eventually cease. This eternal kingdom, however, is his true kingdom which comes to us through his Word. To the extent that we lock ourselves into this Word, we can say with complete confidence when we die, I believe in Jesus Christ who through his death can and will save me, who gives sight to the blind, cleansing to the lepers, and life to the dead. On him I rely and am saved. Second, though all the world is offended, angered, and finally falls because of him and his gospel, we pay no attention to their offense and falling, but rather accept this King without offense, cling to his Word, and through him gain eternal life. As he says, "Blessed is he whosoever shall not be offended in me." Grant us that, dear Lord Jesus Christ. Amen.

THIRD SUNDAY IN ADVENT

Second Sermon—1533

Matthew 11:2–10

1. In this Gospel our dear Lord Jesus Christ admonishes us to esteem his holy gospel and avoid offense. You have heard other aspects of this Gospel previously, but today we will discuss how Christ commended and praised the godly man, John the Baptist, as he said to the Jews: "What went ye out into the wilderness to see? A reed shaken with the wind? But what went ye out for to see? A man clothed in soft raiment? Behold, they that wear soft clothing are in kings' houses. But what went ye out for to see? A prophet? Yea, I say unto you, and more than a prophet." It was as though the Lord were saying, You Jews appraised John the Baptist like a cow looks at a new door. He came to you, but you didn't bother to ask who he might really be. You perceived him to be like a swaying reed or a dandy clothed in soft garments or a prophet. But I say to you he is neither a reed, nor a man in soft clothing, nor a prophet. He is rather the messenger of whom it is written that he should precede the Lord to prepare the way for him.

2. Christ, the Lord, did not preach this sermon for the sake of John the Baptist, for John the Baptist would not have benefited from it. Nor did he preach this sermon for his own sake. He has no need of such a sermon. Rather he preached this sermon for the sake of the Jews that they might recognize John the Baptist and understand his mission. The Lord presented three images of how the Jews perceived John the Baptist—none of which characterized him.

3. First, the Jews perceived John the Baptist as a reed swayed back and forth by the wind. They considered him a preacher who spoke and extolled man's wisdom, someone who preached about material, temporal possessions, ever changing, transitory, and fleeting. But Jesus said, John the Baptist is not a reed. Remember, you Jews, John the Baptist is not to be perceived as a waffling preacher who wavers to and fro, contradicting his own word in his preaching. You

very much prefer one who preaches about temporal, transitory possessions, geared as you are to this world and things, hoping for an earthly kingdom. What John preached about was not an earthly kingdom, but a heavenly kingdom, which neither death nor the devil can demolish. John's sermon about the kingdom of heaven stands like a bulwark and will not waffle as you do. You Jews are the sort of preachers who take handouts of barley and mouthfuls of bread (as the prophet Ezekiel prophesied about you and your kind [13:19]) and preach lies to your people and they love it that way. For a hundred gulden you preach what the people like to hear. These are the reed-like preachers who will hazard neither life, reputation, nor advantage, but accommodate themselves to what people want to hear. But that doesn't amount to anything, to preach when things prosper, but be silent when the situation is adverse. John the Baptist is a different sort of preacher. He persists, speaks out, and does not keep silent to win people's favor. He dares to speak up and tell it as it is.

4. Second, the Jews perceived John the Baptist as an individual going about in fine clothing. But Jesus said, John the Baptist is not a man clothed in fine garments; he is not clothed in effeminate, soft clothing; rather his clothing is rough and coarse. He wears a camel's hair pelt, goes barefoot and bareheaded—that is the way he is garbed and goes about.

5. This was said for the sake of the people who gladly accepted John's preaching and gospel as long as it coincided with their thinking and feeling—like our peasants who demand on the basis of Christian liberty to have a right to temporal benefits. But if they are to give even as much as one penny to the pastor, or do the least little bit for the sake of the gospel, the devil won't let them do it. The whole world is so inclined: if a gospel is preached that fits their needs and advantage it is a fine gospel. But if one tears away the old skin to crucify and kill the old Adam, and for the sake of the gospel put one's life and limb at risk, then it is a repulsive sermon which no one has any stomach for. Therefore Christ says, John the Baptist is a rugged man clothed in harsh garb and skins; similarly, John's preaching and gospel are not soft and tender sermonizing catering to all sorts of self-gratification and all types of wantonness in the custom of the world; rather it is an earnest, piercing sermon that may cause one

pain rather than self-gratification. We may enjoy food and drink as long as God gives and grants them; but to blame the gospel when we lack these things, that ought not be.

6. In the third place, the Jews perceived John the Baptist to be a prophet. But Christ said, John the Baptist is greater and worthy of more esteem than a prophet, for a prophet is of much less importance than John the Baptist. Those duly called prophets were imbued with the Holy Spirit primarily to proclaim Christ's imminent coming; in short, they predicted what lay in the future. John the Baptist is not numbered among those who foretold coming events; rather it was his calling and duty to identify the Messiah personally, face to face. You Jews, therefore, must no longer be waiting for the Christ to appear, because Christ has already come and is at hand; and, by the same token, you should not consider John the Baptist a prophet, but recognize him rather as the messenger preceding the Lord, to prepare his way. So in order properly to recognize this unconventional man in the camel's hair pelt, John the Baptist, know that he is called the Lord's messenger whose duty and calling it is to precede the Lord and prepare the way for him. When you see this messenger you know that the Lord himself is at hand.

7. This was a very necessary sermon for the Jews, for therein lay their destiny. Here was the bottom line: they would either be lost if they failed to heed this herald's message, or eternally saved if they welcomed him. It was foreordained that the old regime, instituted and ordained by God through Moses, with its rules, priesthood, and ceremonies, should cease and be abrogated, replaced by a future kingdom whereof the prophets foretold long before. The Sovereign of this kingdom was now at hand, ready to inaugurate this kingdom. That is why it was necessary for the Jews to recognize this King and learn that the old regime must now cease and the new begin. John the Baptist was sent to implement this, to teach and instruct the Jewish people as he himself said (John 1:31), "that he [the Messiah] should be made manifest to Israel; therefore am I come baptizing with water."

8. So now the Lord Christ says: Note well, you Jews, and pay close attention that you perceive John the Baptist properly, for John will teach you correctly. His preaching focuses directly on the King, the promised Messiah. You know that the Messiah is to come; you daily

await him. I warn you and sincerely beseech you, go to John. Listen to the man who is preparing the way for the Messiah. Let John tell you who the Messiah and Christ is, then you will not go astray or err.

9. The devout Jews accepted this warning and listened to John the Baptist and his sermon (namely, "Behold the Lamb of God which takes away the sins of the world"; the Messiah is at hand and stands among you). It astounded them and gladdened their hearts to know that God's promise to their forefathers, foretold by the prophets, was now fulfilled. The others however, threw everything to the wind, both Christ's warning and John's witness. Christ faithfully warned the people, and John steadfastly witnessed to Christ, saying, You have the Lord and Messiah now present; he is at hand; he is the one of whom I told you (John 1:30): "After me cometh a man which is preferred before me: for he was before me." The Messiah is here now; he existed before me and will soon succeed me; before I cease to preach and before I die, he will come forward and preach. So John witnessed. But the unbelievers and stiffnecked despised him, saying, Did the devil bring that fool here? He tries to convince us of something we cannot believe.

10. For this reason the Lord Christ wished to admonish the Jewish people to be very attentive to the words of John. For when they asked, Has the Messiah come? John answered, Yes, he has come. He is at hand. You will soon see him step forward and preach. Truly he is already here. Because the Jews heard this, they should have said, Very good, we wish to see who he is. Had they done that, they surely would have met the Messiah and could not have missed him. For Christ came forward and began to preach the gospel of the kingdom of God and performed many miracles. Thus John had given prior witness to Christ. But because the Jews were unwilling to believe, the fault is theirs alone for having missed the Messiah. They were certainly warned sufficiently.

11. John testified and said, "He walked among you." He comes and moves about among you like any other person. He stands up and preaches, as I have done and preached before him. I have discharged my office, pointing you to him who comes after me, who arises openly to preach after me. I am the predecessor who prepares the way—he is the Lord.

12. The Jews should have believed this witness of John, prepared the way for Christ, opened the door, and welcomed him. As at royal court before one sees the prince, a young lad precedes, and when the prince appears, everyone bows submissively, just so it should have been here. When the Jews encountered John the Baptist, they should have recognized the importance of his calling, followed him, and said: Lord here are the temple, the priesthood, and the kingdom; whatever your pleasure, we are ready to follow you. But they let John witness, let the Lord himself step forth, preach, and do miracles, but despised it all, yes, even murdered the Lord. Those who clung to him were saved; the others who despised him and persecuted him were damned. Not only were they damned, but also scattered and dispersed, and the heathen have taken the place of the Jews.

13. Since we Gentiles have now taken the Jews' place, John the Baptist witnesses and preaches among us as he formerly witnessed and preached among the Jews. For we have John the Baptist's word and spirit, and we pastors and preachers are for our time what John the Baptist was at his time. We let John the Baptist's finger point and his voice ring out. "Behold, the Lamb of God, which taketh away the sin of the world." We are spokesmen for John the Baptist's sermon, pointing to Christ and saying that he is the only true Saviour to worship and cling to. Such preaching must go on until the day of judgment, perhaps not always the same in all places and at all times, but, nevertheless, it must go on. For it is the same sermon, the same finger with which John the Baptist pointed to Christ as the Lamb of God.

14. Now it boils down to this: if we are as pious as the Jews, accept John's preaching, and follow where his finger directs, we will not miss the Lord. For John's preaching and his finger point to none other but the Lord. If we do not accept this preaching and ignore his pointing finger, we will miss Christ, the Lord, like the Jews. For radical spirits will come and the pure Word will again be lost. Then people will seek for Christ, the Lord, and not find him. There is no other way. No other finger points so directly to Christ. There is no other preaching about eternal life to be expected than John's preaching and finger pointing. If we neglect that finger and that preaching, all is lost. That's what happened to the Jews and Turks, and it will also happen to us if we don't take heed. Deceitful, evil preachers and

teachers will likely ensue when we are inattentive. The Jews and the Turks now seek Christ the Lord, but they do not find him. For all is dependent on this messenger, John the Baptist, on his preaching and finger pointing. Whoever believes his preaching and heeds where his finger points will meet the Lord and be saved, if only he holds to and abides in this faith.

15. We now also have this sermon and finger. Christ the Lord is with us and among us; let us be careful to cling firmly to him. If we cling to him, he takes us into his kingdom and we remain with him eternally. But what should I say? See how things are! Peasants, burghers, and nobility persecute this preaching and teaching, and our own people are lazy. With one finger they could cling to the gospel but they don't. But when John's preaching and finger are gone, and if war comes, no one will tolerate such preaching, for war brings lasciviousness and the gospel is silenced. If the gospel isn't taken away in this manner through war and bloodshed, it will be taken away through lies and false teaching. At the present time we are at peace and have the opportunity to hear and implement the gospel. Whoever is wise will cling with faith and confidence to that man to whom John points. However, if we permit John's preaching and finger pointing to pass us by, Christ the Lord will also pass us by and judgment will follow—murder will reign in the body and untruth will engulf the soul.

16. This is what Christ is saying to the Jews: You perceive John the Baptist to be a reed, a man in soft clothing, or at best, a prophet. But he is no reed, nor a fop in soft garment, nor a prophet. I want to describe him to you very graphically: he is the angel of the Lord who precedes the Lord. Just as a herald precedes the prince and says, "Give way, make room," just so, John the Baptist is the herald or forerunner of the prophesied King and Messiah. Look up, he says. Note the one I am pointing out with my finger. Let him be your King; if you receive him, you have God, life, heaven, in fact everything. If you do not, you are lost. Receive this witness and preaching of John the Baptist, for the one whom John the Baptist points to with his finger is the true Messiah and Saviour.

17. Thus Christ warned and admonished the Jewish people. But what good did it do? They likely considered John the Baptist an ex-

traordinarily great man. Yet, even though John testified of Christ, they paid no heed to his witness and thus let the true Messiah pass them by. They paid dearly for this and to this day are paying dearly. May God guard and keep us, so that we do not lose John's sermon and his finger pointing through gross ingratitude for and scorning of the gospel. Should it be that we forfeit John's preaching and finger pointing we may then conclude that we had it coming. May God protect us!

18. To summarize, we must pay close attention to John's finger pointing, his word and preaching, while they are available, as the prophet Isaiah states (55:6): "Seek ye the LORD while he may be found"; (49:8): "In an acceptable time have I heard thee, and in a day of salvation have I helped thee." Now is the time of grace, the day of salvation, of help and salvation (2 Cor. 6:2). Now the Lord is near and to be found; if we neglect the opportunity, if we wait too long, it will be like under the papacy. Take me as an example. In the monastery I castigated myself along with the rest; I could not find the door into heaven; if I had died, I would have gone to hell. We were earnestly seeking the Lord, but something was missing. What was it? Namely this, as the prophet said: "Seek ye the LORD while he may be found; call upon him while he is near." When the Lord has passed by and is gone, then no calling or crying will avail. To have Christ in our midst with John's preaching and his pointing to Christ is a great treasure. For this reason we must be forewarned, careful to hold onto this treasure. This is no light matter; if the treasure is once lost, it is lost forever.

19. This is the bottom line, then, when Jesus speaks of John the Baptist as the one of whom it is written, "Behold, I send my messenger before thy face which shall prepare the way before thee." When Christ the Lord comes all governments will cease, and they will say: "Blessed is he who comes in the name of the Lord." We gladly want to serve this King with all that we have, with all our strength. That is the mission and message of John the Baptist, to prepare the groundwork for our accepting Christ, the Lord, as our King. When my time comes to yield up my spirit and enter into eternity, this messenger, John the Baptist, must lead the way, pointing me to Christ with his preaching and finger-pointing, that I may not lose him. Our dear God and Father sustain us with this messenger's witness and finger, granting us grace to follow where he points, so that we come to Christ and through him are saved. Amen.

FOURTH SUNDAY IN ADVENT

First Sermon—1532

You know that on holy or festival days we are to pay homage to God, that is, hear his Holy Word, which is the greatest and most exalted service we can render God in this world. This is precisely what we want to do today on this Sunday, as we listen to what our dear Lord Jesus Christ proclaims to us, as recorded by St. John in the first chapter (John 1:19–28):

And this is the record of John, when the Jews sent priests and Levites from Jerusalem to ask him, Who art thou? And he confessed, and denied not; but confessed, I am not the Christ. And they asked him, What then? Art thou Elias? And he saith, I am not. Art thou that prophet? And he answered, No. Then said they unto him, Who art thou? that we may give an answer to them that sent us. What sayest thou of thyself? He said, I am the voice of one crying in the wilderness, Make straight the way of the Lord, as said the prophet Esaias. And they which were sent were of the Pharisees. And they asked him, and said unto him, Why baptizest thou then, if thou be not that Christ, nor Elias, neither that prophet? John answered them saying, I baptize with water: but there standeth one among you whom ye know not. He it is, who coming after me is preferred before me, whose shoe's latchet I am not worthy to unloose. These things were done in Bethabara beyond Jordan, where John was baptizing.

1. This is one of the truly great Gospels about the most precious article of our faith, wherein nothing is said about the Ten Commandments or about good works, as occurs in other Gospel lessons. But taught here is Christ, who he is and what he has done. The foremost and vital thing in this Gospel is that the Evangelist says: John the Baptist was a "Zeugnisz," a witness, who gave testimony concerning Christ. The word "testimony" is very significant. To us Germans "Zeugnisz" is not a clear word. "Zeugnisz" indicates a sermon or dis-

course about Christ. So the Evangelist now wants to show that the matter at hand is of great consequence, that we are to give ear to the preaching of John the Baptist, that his testimony is a matter of record and his preaching about Christ is to continue in the church. He, therefore, praises John the Baptist very highly for having stood so firm, and he has no desire to alter his testimony but to let it stand as a matter of record for that person who is called Christ.

2. The Jews sent members of the high council, priests and Levites from Jerusalem, to John the Baptist and had them ask the question: Are you Christ, Elias, or a prophet? But John remained unruffled and said he was none of them. Then they asked him: "Who art thou? What sayest thou of thyself?" He said: "I am the voice of one crying in the wilderness." I am a voice which is crying aloud, "Prepare the way of the Lord." That's what I am. Now you know who I am. I am one who is bearing testimony and preaching about the man who is called Christ. I am not the man himself. I have no desire to be Christ or Elias or a prophet. I am satisfied with having the honor of being a voice and preaching about the man. The man you are seeking is close by. He is Christ and the Prophet proclaimed in Deuteronomy 18:18; he is the one you want. However, if you wish to know who he is, hear me out: I am going before him and am preparing the way for him. He is coming after me. If you do not listen to what I am preaching, you will not find him.

3. Thereupon, since John brushes them off like this, the messengers become indignant and irate, and ask: "Why baptizest thou, then, if thou be not that Christ, nor Elias, nor that prophet?" Who has ordered you to practice a new way? By this new activity of yours you are causing the people to open their mouths in wonder and surprise, and are doing something we are not. John, however, has no fear of their indignation and anger, but continues with his testimony, saying:

I baptize with water: but there standeth one among you, whom ye know not. He it is, who coming after me is preferred before me, whose shoe's latchet I am not worthy to unloose.

He taunts them with his cheerful reply. He wants them to understand, My baptism is only a testimony. I am preaching and baptizing because I want to lead you to him. He is in your country and is now thirty years old. He will soon come after me; and before I was born, he already was. And this man is so great that I am not worthy to untie the thongs of his sandals. Say no more about my supposedly being that man. I am satisfied and happy that I am worthy to function as his voice and preacher, that I am to tell the people about him.

4. Here you have a fine, glowing, splendid example of John thrusting and shoving aside all those who want to control the Christian church, just as they did in those days and as the pope, monks, and others who desire to be Christ himself are still doing today. John the Baptist is greater and holier than all the popes; nevertheless, he says to the Jews: I do not know how to help or advise you, and I include myself here as well; but I know of one who is able to help you and me. I am not worthy of rendering him even the most menial service. Let's all go to this man. I am baptizing and preaching about him; he is the man; he is among you; embrace him; I, too, am going to embrace him. Thus John the Baptist points the entire world away from himself to the man who is and is called Christ, saying, It is written in the prophet Isaiah that there is one coming who will cry aloud in the wilderness, "Make straight the way of the Lord." I am that one. I am that preeminent preacher. I am not supposed to be the Lord, but the voice preceding the Lord. I am the one who is preaching, Make way, the Lord is coming. Make straight the path of the Lord. Remove from the way sticks, stones, and all other obstacles. Clear the way; here comes the Lord. That's the kind of preacher I am. I am not the Lord himself. But I teach that the Lord is coming.

5. We ought to mark well this testimony of John the Baptist in order to learn to distinguish between these two sermons (the sermon on faith and the sermon on good works) and to know when each is appropriate. When one is preaching and speaking about eternal life, good works are then not at all in place. But they must be accomplished by the man of whom John testifies that he is not worthy to untie the thongs of his sandals. In this life we have to speak about good works and obedience, for man must eat and drink, lead a chaste life, and perform good works. But in yonder life, good works come to an end. Thus one ought to heed this sermon which says that the Lord, the one to whom John has pointed, has come. Doctrine must

remain pure. We are to preach and teach that whoever believes in him of whom John testifies will be saved.

6. Thus we, too, cry out aloud in our wilderness. Nor must we ever stop doing so, but continually point people to Christ. For the devil does not intend to allow this testimony about Christ. He devotes all his energy to opposing it and will not desist until he has struck it down and suppressed it. In this respect, we humans are weak and stubbornly perverse and are more likely to become attached to saints than to Christ. Within the papacy they have preached about the service rendered by these beloved saints, that one ought to rely on their merit. And I, too, believed and preached thus. St. Ann was my idol, and St. Thomas my apostle. I patterned myself substantially after them. Others ran to St. James and strongly believed and firmly trusted that, if they conformed, they would receive all they wished and hoped for. Prayers were said to St. Barbara and St. Christopher in order to avert an early and sudden death, and there was no uncertainty here. So completely is man by nature bent on renouncing this testimony of John the Baptist.

7. For this reason it is necessary constantly to persevere and adhere to John's testimony concerning Christ. For it requires toil and effort to continue with word and testimony, for a person at death to be able to say, I must die, but I have a Saviour concerning whom John the Baptist testifies; on him and on no other creature, either in heaven or on earth, do I rely. However, that a person can die as cheerfully by believing in St. Barbara, in an indulgence, or in a pilgrimage to Rome, as in the man to whom alone John the Baptist points, is out of the question. Also, that a person can build as strongly on monkery or monastery life as on holy baptism is a forlorn hope. What I am telling you is that it is easier for us humans to believe and trust in everything else than in the man Christ, who alone is all in all, and more difficult for us to rely on him in whom and through whom we possess all things. Wealth and possessions are perishable things. Yet you can depend on it that for the sake of wealth and possessions people will kill, steal and rob, and risk life and limb. The average person is happy when he has wealth and possessions and unhappy when he does not have them. But when it comes to John the Baptist's testimony and preaching he cannot do or risk a thing. Isn't this an evil, perverse disposition?

8. The priests and Levites listen to John. He testifies and preaches to them about Christ, saying that the Lord is at hand. They listen all right. But they stand and look at John just like a cow looks at a new gate and ask, Are you Christ, Elias, or a prophet? Just as though they had not heard a single word he was saying. Thus they stand there, and with hearing ears they do not hear. Why is that? They are having other thoughts. They are thinking about a Christ who is to come riding on a great steed, arrayed in gold, and who establishes a temporal kingdom on earth. For this reason their hearts are hard. Were such a Christ, Elias, or prophet to come along who coincided with their thoughts of him, they would receive him. Submerged in such thoughts, they are not hearing John's testimony. But as soon as they hear about Christ, they at once look to see whether he is coming through the gate riding on a beautiful stallion and in golden array, with a mighty army.

9. The same situation prevails today, when we teach that to attain the life to come, people have to know the teachings of Christ and confess the article, I believe in Jesus Christ, and so on. That is something neither pope nor monk understands, even though they have already heard the message. A Carthusian simply replies, My religious order will see to it that I am saved. Similarly a friar thinks, Because of my gray cowl God will grant me heaven. They are looking through painted glass. The thinking of the world is as follows: you can build your life on things, you can make merry with eating, drinking, fornication, even with a drink of malmsey (wine); but with St. John's witness and preaching you cannot be happy. Isn't this a tragedy? A monk and his conscience are happy when he is able to say, I have kept my orders, poverty, chastity, obedience, just as I have vowed. A priest soothes his conscience when he celebrates Mass or prays at the seven canonical hours. But when they hear the testimony of John the Baptist, that Jesus Christ baptizes with the Holy Spirit or has shed his blood on the cross for the forgiveness of sins, they all fall asleep and begin to snore. Ought it not hurt to the quick that we humans are setting our hearts on created things, but are unwilling to do so on John's testimony and preaching alone?

10. For this reason the Evangelist John laments in his Gospel that John the Baptist's testimony preaches and teaches about Christ, but

the world is not accepting it. Yes, even those who hear it and should, therefore, be getting joy, hope, and comfort from it, are gaping at something else and are permitting this testimony to slip on by. This is the way of the world. If a peasant has a hat full of coins, he becomes so cocky that he does not know whether to walk on his head or on his feet. But let someone tell him about Christ, he will say, What is this? Ah, the way death, thunder, and lightning strike upon the world, that's the way loud protests should be voiced against this testimony of John the Baptist! Peasants, burghers, nobles, masters, servants, one and all, become bored at what they hear and learn, saying, What testimony! What gospel! What Christ! Would that we had Joachim's silver dollars and pretty women!

11. We see this everywhere among the smart professionals. They gape at John the Baptist to see whether he be Christ, Elias, or a prophet. They would be happy to have a Christ, Elias, or some prophets according to their liking. Yes, but what the Lord God has in mind is this: Man, you ought to accept Christ just as God sends him, not as you want him to be. I, too, wanted to make myself a Christ in accord with my conception of him, to fast three days or do other things, and after that say: This is well pleasing to God; by this means I hope to be saved. But that's not what Christ wants. That's the way the Jews are waiting for Christ. He is to come as a worldly king with many horses, chariots, and riders. And they are waiting for Elias; he is supposed to come with chariots with flaming torches; and the prophets with many and great miracles. No, it is not thus. God sends John with testimony and with the teaching that says, If you will receive John with his testimony, then you will have Christ at your door; therefore, receive John and his witness. But the Jews did not want to do this. As a matter of fact, they mocked John with his baptism, and as a result they also ridiculed Christ himself.

12. The same thing is still happening with John's testimony today. His word and preaching are despised. We proclaim, The Lord is here; receive him. But nothing comes of it. Yes, Christ and his gospel are rejected. On this account our Lord God sends to the despisers of his gospel so many fanatical spirits that they lose Christ. What will happen in the world is this: when our peasants, burghers, nobles raise enough money, numerous preachers will appear who will help

them deny Christ. John the Baptist shakes off the Jews like lice and says, "I am not Christ; I am not Elias, nor a prophet." But these despisers, who do not want to accept John's testimony nor believe what we are preaching, will fall into the hands of other preachers who will say, "I am he." So with Zwingli and others! That's the way it goes, and it can go no other way when the Word has been lost. We are now preaching, but you are not listening. Hereafter, once it's gone, it's gone for good.

13. It is, therefore, important that we learn from the example of John the Baptist to preserve this testimony concerning Christ. For from the moment this testimony and doctrine are gone, people begin to preach about human works, monkery, and false godliness, sanctimoniously thumb the nose at people, whereupon all true comfort comes to an end and they miss the true way to salvation. For when John with his testimony is silenced, heaven is closed, and people will come into hell. The same thing applies to monks with all their good works, with their vowed poverty, chastity, obedience, masses, fastings, and prayers; they must ultimately despair, since they have understood nothing of this testimony. For there is no other way to heaven than through this testimony of John concerning Christ.

14. Therefore, this Gospel deals with the great article about Christ, that we should receive him, kiss and embrace him, cling to him, never allow ourselves to be torn from him nor him from us. This is the chief article of Christian doctrine, and on it rests our salvation. When one possesses this central truth, good works will then follow immediately; a person will lead a godly life, obey parents, be subject to government, and each in his station serve his neighbor. When a person clearly discerns these things, with each teaching rightly in place, all is well. The Ten Commandments teach what is good in this life; but to speak of yonder life, for that only the testimony of John avails. There the word is: "I am not worthy to unloose his shoe latchet." Also: "He it is who baptizes with the Holy Spirit and with fire." This means that Christ, who has come into your midst, will enlighten and enkindle your hearts with the Holy Spirit, die for you, and give you eternal life. The Ten Commandments belong to this life; however, the gospel and this testimony of John concerning Christ belong to eternal life.

15. This is what made John stand so firm and confess and not deny. May God grant that we likewise stand firm, never altering his testimony, neither in preaching nor in hearing. It is, you see, very necessary. For by nature we have the tendency to fall easy prey to other things. Everything in the world is a temptation and an obstacle to offset this testimony of John. Money, goods, wife, child, feigned godliness are obstacles to deter us or lead us away from this testimony. For this reason I exhort you all to take heed and not allow this doctrine to be taken from you. Eat and drink what you will; just don't let anyone take this doctrine from you. May God graciously preserve us in it. Amen.

FOURTH SUNDAY IN ADVENT

Second Sermon—1533

John 1:19–28

1. This Gospel agrees almost to a tee with last week's except that other words and persons are found here. Otherwise it teaches the very same thing, namely, that all power reposes in this person called Christ, and that we should not ignore but welcome him, neither let him pass on by nor look for another.

2. For God resolved that this man should be all in all; whoever comes to him will find redemption from sin, death, and hell. This man is all things; he is the way, the truth, and the life; through him alone all patriarchs, prophets, and apostles from the beginning of the world have been saved. This John the Baptist well knows. For this reason he steers people away from himself to this man, so that they will not ignore so great a treasure.

3. And it was for this reason that the Lord God sent John the Baptist. For well he perceives that we humans are trying to save ourselves in all sorts of ways: one enters a monastery and becomes a monk; another fasts; a third sleeps on the ground. In short, everybody is seeking a special way and his own way to heaven. Therefore God says: I don't want it like this; I am giving you the word about my Son, Jesus Christ. He will show you the right way to heaven; whoever ignores my Son is overlooking the way to heaven, though he fast himself to death and pray like a fool. On the other hand, whoever comes to this my Son finds forgiveness of sins and eternal salvation, and neither devil nor death can hinder him.

4. All the patriarchs and prophets followed this way, and they were saved through Christ. And if anyone should have been able to get to heaven through righteous living and good works, it presumably should have been the patriarchs, the prophets, John the Baptist, and the apostles who did and suffered so much. But they all discount their own holiness and rely firmly on the woman's seed, who was to crush the serpent's head.

5. At the time of Christ, however, the Jews did not want to follow this way, thinking: Who is this carpenter's apprentice anyway? We have to fast, look grim-faced, give alms; that will be the best and shortest way to heaven. What can this poor wretch and beggar do to help us?

6. Now then! They did experience the help this beggar can give. For this reason God arranges for the beloved John, like the trumpeter before the prince, to walk ahead of the Lord Christ and blow the trumpet. When one hears the trumpet, opens his eyes, and sees who is following the trumpeter, he knows this has to be the right man.

7. When, for this reason, the Jews dispatch their messengers to him and have them ask, Are you Christ, Elijah, or a prophet? He replies: I am not. And when they persist, Who then are you? What do you have to say about yourself? He says, This is what I want to tell you: "I am the voice of one crying in the wilderness, Make strait the way of the Lord," that is, I am the trumpeter walking ahead of the prince. When I preach, listen very carefully; for he will come immediately after me, that is, the one who existed before I was ever born. He will baptize you with the Holy Spirit, while I, a servant, baptize with water.

8. This is my office. I was sent to blow my trumpet. By this you are to know the right man is here. I am a voice crying aloud, a preacher to whom you are to listen. Now the next person, the one who is coming after me, he is the one. Thus did the prophet Isaiah prophesy: "I am the voice of one crying in the wilderness, Make strait the way of the Lord." I am that preacher. It is my office to announce, Look, your Lord is coming. He is already in your midst, but you don't know him. But this is the reason I am preaching. I am preaching so that you learn to know and accept him. The next preacher, the one who is coming after me, is unquestionably the one. I am preaching and discharging my office, but he is not preaching as yet. He is at hand but has not yet begun to preach. However, he will come shortly after me, and then you can listen to him. So be alert, so that you don't miss him, but pay attention to what he has to say.

9. As John had preached, so it also came to pass. For immediately after his baptism Christ appeared in Galilee with his miracles, chose twelve apostles and seventy-two other disciples, and sent them out to

preach. Shortly after his baptism by John he has the message preached, "Repent: for the kingdom of heaven is at hand," that is, Christ is at hand and is the very one of whom John is testifying. It happened as John said it would. The voice in the wilderness is heard, and shortly thereafter the Lord comes. That is what John made known, stating, After me is coming the one who is going to assume the preaching office after me; he is the one, cling to him. But then he also adds: "He was before me." To the Jews this would have been blasphemy had they at that time understood what he was saying. For John was six months older than Christ; yet John says that Christ is before him. However, with these words he wanted to talk about the divine majesty of the person. For before Christ became man, he had been in heaven. Accordingly, later on he also talks about the glory of the person: "I am not worthy to unloose his shoe's latchet." But at that time the Jews did not comprehend.

10. Here it should have been quite natural for the Jews to have thought and said, Ah, what kind of a man or person must he be before whom John humbles himself so deeply and says, I am not worthy to perform the most menial task for him? Dear John, who are you that you should not be worthy? I am, says he, exactly who I'm supposed to be; however, compared with this man I am nothing. Thus he sheds all his own glory and states that he would be content if he could just wipe off his shoes.

11. So that the Jews might not think that he is humbling himself far too much, inasmuch as he had instituted baptism and was a remarkable preacher, he gives them precise information about his baptism and states: I carry a sign just like the rest of the prophets; Jeremiah wore a yoke around his neck (Jer. 27:2); Isaiah walked barefoot and naked when he prophesied to the Egyptians and Ethiopians that they would be plundered and stripped naked by their enemies (Isa. 20:2). And God has always given each new preacher (prophet) a sign. So, says John, I, too, am preaching something new and have a new sign. I am preaching that you should prepare the way for the Lord, that you should wash and cleanse yourselves. But I could not preach this if the way were not prepared beforehand. Since you are to wash yourselves also—it is a sign that you are unclean and dirty—I am beginning this washing and bathing; but the one who is

coming after me will provide a different and better cleansing for you and baptize you with the Holy Spirit.

12. So now everything is being aimed especially at this, that they should not allow this man to pass on by but bear in mind John's preaching and say: Look, John has told us about one who will come after him; he certainly must be the one who now is so conspicuous by his preaching and signs.

13. But what happened? Of course they heard John well, but did not believe his testimony. Christ, mighty in words and deeds, they saw but did not accept. And on top of all this, they beheaded John and crucified Christ. They were the kind of people who not only despised God's Word but also killed the beloved prophets and thereafter crucified the Prophet above all prophets.

14. Things are going the same way today. For Christ must still be crucified, not only in his person but also in his members. Just like John, we are happy to show everybody the right way to salvation and tell them that apart from Christ there is no forgiveness of sins and no everlasting life. But what is happening? The more faithfully we steer people to Christ, away from their own works, as from a false to the true cause of their salvation, the more vehemently our opponents scream heresy and condemn us. Before long it's into the water, fire, or whatever, for whomever they pounce on because of this. The pope wouldn't dawdle long if he caught hold of us. I, Dr. Martin, am already—God be praised!—excommunicated and condemned to death.

15. Why are they so antagonistic toward us? Why can't they tolerate us? For no other reason than that with John we preach that the pope and his priests and monks should humble themselves just like John did, likewise unworthy to clean his shoes. For truly John was holier than they are and yet said, I shall regard my holiness as nothing if I could just achieve the grace to take off or clean his shoes, then I would be satisfied. This is the kind of humility we would like to foster with everyone through the gospel, and for this reason we admonish everybody in keeping with our calling: Be as upright and holy as you want, you can never be as holy as John; fast and pray as long and as much as you want, we do not forbid you this. However, do this too: cast all your holiness at the feet of Christ, confessing that with it you will not gain heaven; and say, with all my holiness I would gladly be the least; all my

good works and honorable living are as wornout shoes compared to the sublime, pure, perfect, and great righteousness which our dear Lord Christ has merited for us by his suffering and death.

16. This is our message, that they should let the Lord Christ alone be holy. However, pope, bishops, monks, and priests do not want to do this, but forever scream like crazy people, that faith alone does not do it; good works also contribute toward it. Accordingly, they do not want Christ's holiness to be their treasure as did John. He tosses aside all his holiness and equates it with an old rag that is casually used to wipe dirty shoes clean. He freely acknowledges that his holiness is not worth as much as a wornout shoe. Much less will he deem it fitting to wipe his nose, comb his hair, clothe him, give him food, and so forth. So John, but not the pope and his doers of good works who in no way can tolerate having their holiness called old rags! In fact, they wonder whether the Lord Christ is worthy to receive gifts or offerings of their righteousness and holiness as alms.

17. The Jews heard about this humility of John, that he attributed everything to Christ; however, they not only scorned it but persecuted John on account of it. The same thing happens today. As with John, so for all who bear witness like he did. However, such persecution and scorn as befell the Jews will also, if God so wills, befall our despisers, persecutors, and blasphemers.

18. For this reason we should take careful note of John's exemplary humility. The holy man John, as Christ himself testifies, is without equal among all who have ever been born of women, far, far superior to all the priests and monks who have ever lived; nevertheless, he humbles himself very deeply and states that he, in spite of his holiness, is but a tramp, unworthy to wipe off Christ's shoes. Truly, an example for us to emulate.

19. We are to do good works and work hard at doing them, for God has so enjoined and commanded in the Ten Commandments. But when it comes to this man who is called Christ, you should humble yourself like John, and throw all the good works you have ever done at his feet and frankly admit that you are not fit to wipe off Christ's shoes.

20. Before men it is indeed a fine, clean, beautiful adornment, if you can show that you are no adulterer, no thief, no murderer, that

you give alms, that you are diligent in your calling. Such things one can boast about in the world and before men, like with velvet, silk, and gold apparel. But when we stand before our Lord God and his tribunal, then we must confess: in your presence, Lord, my best velvet, my gold apparel is worse than an old rag. Do not judge me according to my works; I am but a beggar in old rags and tatters, and pray God to accept me as I am; I will be satisfied with that.

21. Paul puts it the same way in Philippians 3:5–8 where he says: "I am an Israelite, as touching the law, a Pharisee and, as touching the righteousness in the law, no man can censure me." It is remarkable when someone can boast in the presence of people in this way. Nevertheless, he says, I count all this holiness, for Christ's sake, to be sheer loss and dung, and it is my greatest joy and highest comfort to be found not in my own righteousness, which is from the Law, but in the righteousness which comes through faith in Christ and is imputed by God to faith. So that I might be able to enjoy such righteousness of my Lord, I deem all my righteousness to be dung. Here Paul paints it much worse than John does. John deliberately diminishes what he does, calls his good works a dirty rag, but Paul calls them filth and dung. But that is plenty and enough said about our holy living.

22. We should regard such examples as highly commendable and be diligently engaged in living before the world in all modesty and respectability, so that people have nothing to accuse us for. That, however, is the way things are here on earth and how it also ends. As one can see, an upright man is buried as a scoundrel and a pious woman as an adulteress. But to deal with that and eternal life, then let your response be: I cling to the man Christ and to his holiness which he promises and grants me in baptism, in Word and sacrament; I myself am but a poor worm. For in this way we must differentiate between our earthly life and holiness, and eternal life and holiness that avails before God.

23. Gentiles have also been amenable to decency and respectability and for the sake of the fatherland have done and endured much; and about this they do reasonably boast. But here, when death comes, the roads part. Then all we have done and endured falls astern. For by this means we do not receive forgiveness of sins and righteousness before God. From where, then, do we obtain righ-

teousness and holiness that avails before God and for eternal life? That's when it is necessary humbly to say with John: Lord, here comes a poor rag, an old, torn, filthy rag, or, as Paul says, stinking dung. In the eyes of the world it may well be fur, velvet, and gold apparel, but before you, Lord, let me be an old rag with which I can wipe off your Son's shoes, and for his sake grant me his righteousness. Accordingly, it is through the righteousness of this man that I get to heaven, since by my own righteousness I must needs go to hell.

24. From this it follows that we must roundly conclude that monks and priests, monasteries and whatever else they may be called, all belong to the devil in hell. For by their good works they are not seeking to please God with due obedience, by leading an honorable life here on earth and not offending anyone, but are thinking that thereby they will be saved. For this reason also they sell their good works to others. This indeed is to deny and ridicule Christ. We should be aware of this abomination and learn here and now to counter such seducers and say to them: You poor soul, are you trying to save me with your works and holiness? John the Baptist, Paul, Peter, were unable to do this, though much holier than you, else they would not have thought and preached so modestly about their holiness.

25. If the papists were to have used monasteries as nurseries of instruction in rearing children and permitted young people to study Scripture, it would have been a fine thing. However, this they did not do, but with their monastic life they instructed people on how to get to heaven; yes, they were even wildly enthusiastic about it. That is why they left no stone unturned when they adopted monastic life, so that by outward life and good works here on earth they might gain not only good reputation but also heaven.

26. In summary, then, let us learn from today's Gospel that we ought to live chastely and honorably among people, be diligent and active in good works. For such obedience God enjoins upon us in his Law and wants from us. And where we do not render it, he will respond with the rod, with the executioner, with the sword, and finally also with the fire of hell. Over against our fellowmen, I say, we are obligated by God's command. But before God we say: Before you, Lord, I am lost on account of my holiness and works; because of them I long to be merely an old rag at the feet of Christ, my Lord;

for because of my life I am worthy of nothing else but to be cast by him into hell; but, since he has come to redeem me from sin and death and to sanctify me, I desire his eternal holiness. This is how we come to heaven.

27. This neither pope nor bishops want to hear, for they are well aware that convents and monasteries, Masses and all their false worship would not survive for long. For this reason they are so adamant about this; the majority for the sake of the belly, the minority in the hope that they will be saved thereby. But not so with John, nor with Paul, neither of whom want to retain their righteousness and holiness. What all Christians should do and say with Paul is this: My holiness is plain filth and dung; and with John: My holiness is a rag when I compare it with Christ's holiness and deeds. However, with their Masses, vows, fastings, and prayers the papists wish to be neither dung nor rags; they beat us to death because of this, since we do not agree with them but point people to another and better way. Now then! it is a viper's brood which can never produce anything good. They will find what they are looking for. Let us look to the mouth and finger of John with which he bears witness and points, so that we do not close our eyes to or lose our Lord and Saviour, Jesus Christ; for to the present day John still very diligently, faithfully, and richly points and directs us here, in order that we might be saved. May our dear Lord God and Father grant this to us through his Son Jesus Christ. Amen.

FOURTH SUNDAY IN ADVENT

Third Sermon—No date given

John 1:19–28

1. Today's lesson treats of John the Baptist's answer to the questions of the priests and Levites who had been sent to him from Jerusalem by the Jews. Dispute had arisen concerning this man who bore the name Christ. The prophets had prophesied and proclaimed that Christ would come and be a King over the whole world. About that there was no doubt, since this was taught throughout Holy Scripture by all the prophets. However, in this lay a problem. Because Christ would not come with great show and outward pomp, it was a question whether the Jews because they failed to recognize him might miss him. For they had dreamt and thought that Christ would come like a secular king, arrayed in gold, with conventional armament and thousands of horsemen. Instead, he came riding on an ass, without any worldly pomp and trappings, without money and shoes; and the donkey upon which he rode was not his own but borrowed. In short, even though he was a King, he did not even have a penny in his pocket.

2. There was real concern, therefore that the Jews might miss their Messiah and King. For this reason John the Baptist needed to sound the alarm, preach in the wilderness, baptize, and say: Look up, your Christ is at hand; be alert and careful, so that you do not miss him; don't be gawking for his advent with many thousands of horses. By such preaching he opens wide the eyes of the Jews, causing them to ask, Ah, who is this person preaching and baptizing in the wilderness, and we, the people of Jerusalem, know nothing about it? By his preaching and baptizing, therefore, John creates a great stir, causing everybody to think that he is a prophet. Even Herod and the scribes regarded him as a great personage.

3. That was the reason for sending the emissaries to John. The Jews had him questioned so that they might not go wrong or miss the boat. However, they do not inquire about his preaching and teaching, but merely about his person, power, authority, and appearance.

They were much too conceited to inquire about his doctrine or to address him themselves. However, so as not to lose their reputation among the people, they say: Oh! we are sending our intermediaries to him; we are sending priests and Levites to ask him whether he is the Christ or Elijah or some prophet.

4. To this John responds: You Jews should not hang onto my skirts; I exhort you to follow Christ, who is now among you; do not scorn or pass him by. When I now preach and baptize in the wilderness, raising a hue and cry, my purpose is to get people to come by, observe, and inquire about what I am preaching and teaching, and why I am baptizing, so that through my preaching and baptizing they might be brought to Christ, believe in him, and not despise him. This is my office. And the reason I am preaching and baptizing and creating such a stir in Judea is that I might bring everyone to faith in him. It is for your benefit that I am preaching about Christ, so that you are forewarned and recognize that the one I am proclaiming is the true Messiah who has come to redeem you.

5. John now acknowledges, I am not Christ, I am not Elijah, I am not a prophet. His job is to steer the Jews away from himself to Christ. And yet it was vital for John to raise a great hue and cry in the Jewish homeland, otherwise the Jews would have overlooked the Messiah and let him pass on by. Also, the Lord had John the Baptist adopt such an outwardly austere life so that the Jews would regard him as a holy man, come to him, and inquire into the purpose of his preaching and baptizing. And he answered them: I am baptizing with water so that you will know that the Messiah has come. You Jews, therefore, need not wait for him any longer; he is already at hand and been born; and now, thirty years old, he is presently preaching and performing miracles. I have preceded him in order to inform you that he has come. The one to whom I am now pointing is the true Messiah and Lamb of God who bears the sin of the world.

6. It was for the sake of the Jews that John the Baptist came, so that they would not let Christ pass on by and lose him. Now had the Jews been devout, they would have availed themselves of the opportunity and thought within themselves: Here is a truly great and holy man; there must be something to all the fuss he is creating in the wilderness with his preaching and baptizing. He says that the Messiah

is already here in person who would now in turn after him carry out his office, preach, and perform miracles. Verily, we must bear in mind what sort of a man it is about whom such a remarkable, holy man, John the Baptist, testifies and to whom he is pointing. Certainly, John would not exhort us to cling to him without good reason. This is what the Jews should have said. For John the Baptist exhorted them earnestly, saying that the one to whom the people will cling, who will come after me and preach, that person will be the Christ. I am preceding him, but you should know that, since I am still teaching and baptizing and still in office, he is coming. And my reason for being here is to let you know about him. Indeed, in his person everything converges: time, testimony, place, and everything that Scripture prophesies about Christ. The time is now, for according to the word of the prophet Isaiah, I am to let my voice be heard in the wilderness and proclaim that the Messiah is now here. When I stop preaching, he will begin. I, John the Baptist, am the witness, for I am testifying concerning the Messiah, he is already here. The place where he will begin is when I say, he has come into your midst; his shoes I am not good enough to untie; he will baptize you with the Holy Spirit and with fire. He is right here in this country and will do things better than I; take heed to him and do not let him pass on by. This is my earnest admonition.

7. The Jews have the question put to John the Baptist: Are you Christ? Are you Elijah? Are you a prophet? Since you are none of these, why are you creating such hubbub in our country by your preaching and baptizing? John replies: Listen to me, and follow me, I want to lead you to the right man; thereafter you dare no longer say, we did not know this. For so it pleased God that I should go before with considerable clamor and excitement to point him out to you, so that you are without excuse.

8. Thus John faithfully appealed to the Jews, but the Jews disdained John's admonition and allowed Christ to pass on by. John portrayed Christ accurately so that the Jews could not have failed to recognize him, stating that he who is standing in your midst is Christ who comes after me and also preaches. But the Jews inquired neither about witnesses, person, time nor place, and they allowed Christ to pass on by. They did indeed see Christ personally make his ap-

pearance after John; they heard him preach, saw him perform miracles, but with seeing eyes they did not see and with hearing ears they did not hear; they did not take his words and preaching to heart, and, worst of all, despite all the kindnesses he showered upon them they slew their own Messiah on the cross. This is another reason why later on they were utterly devastated and destroyed by the Romans.

9. The Lord God permitted punishment to befall the Jews as an example for us, so that we would not do what they had done. They missed their Messiah and have been hoping and waiting for him for 1500 years, but their hoping and waiting are in vain. And into the bargain the Jews are despised by all peoples on earth; they have neither kingdom nor country in which to live. They would gladly have him come now; even if it was in the form of a beggar, they would be happy. It has often happened also that some no-good upstarts have arrogantly panned themselves off as the Messiah and deceived the Jews. And since the Jews allowed themselves to be persuaded and believe it to be true, following after them and causing turmoil, many were put to death. Even today they open all their windows when it thunders, because they think that he will come with the thunder. But at the time he came they scorned him, and that is why even now they suffer harm. Now they would welcome him with open arms, but he will not come, for his return will be in glory on Judgment Day in order to judge the living and the dead.

10. All that the Jews experienced serves as a prototype and an example for us, so that we, too, might not pass Christ by and miss him, as the Jews did. He, of course, does not come to us in his physical presence, and yet he personally does come to us and is with us spiritually and efficaciously. To the Jews he came in the flesh; to us he comes in the Word. However, just as the Jews refused to follow Christ at that time, so today people fail to receive him. Now the whole world despises his Word and gospel. The pundits and power wielders of the world say: Indeed, how much credence should we give to these beggars who are preaching today? If great bishops and princes were to preach, we would be happy to believe what they say. However, because these are poor, lowly, despised people who do the preaching, how can we believe them and accept their message? The Jews took the same tack against John the Baptist, the Lord's forerun-

ner. Oh, they said, John comes like a bushman out of a cave and preaches the baptism of repentance for the forgiveness of sins. Who is he that we should believe his preaching? If the high priests at Jerusalem were to stand up and preach these things, we would believe. Similarly Christ in his day was scorned personally by the Jews, along with all his preachers, John the Baptist, Simeon, Anna, and others. So also now he and his teaching are despised, with all faithful teachers and preachers, by the whole world. In his day they did not receive him because he went about in such lowliness and wretchedness; today his gospel is scorned because it is the word of the cross.

11. It is said of the Poles that they speak and believe whatever their king believes and think that they have spoken very wisely. Such people will also enter heaven when their king enters in. Now assuredly Christ is the true Lord of heaven and he says that, "Where I am, there will also my servants be." But into that heaven, where Christ and his servants are, you may be sure that his despisers cannot comfort themselves with the thought that they will enter with him too.

12. For this reason no one should mistakenly allow himself to be swayed by what his prince, king, or even the pope believes. None of these can vouch in your behalf at the judgment; but you by yourself must give account of your faith. If you believe as your prince, king, or even the pope believes, you must also hear what Christ will say to you: Since you have believed as your prince, king, or pope believed and have served them, so go now and let your prince, king, or pope reward you. Had you believed in me and served me, I would have rewarded you as well. So, because you believe in Christ, have been baptized into him, and serve God in your station and calling to the best of your ability, Christ in turn will bless you. He will say to you, Because you have believed in me and served me, because you did not allow yourselves to be led astray or turned away from me even though you heard that my gospel is condemned by the whole world and called heresy and devil's doctrine so I want to honor you both here and there, and blessed you will be. You will be holy; my angels will lift you up on their hands, and you will have everlasting life.

13. For this reason we should not be concerned with how the world regards us or that it persecutes us as heretics; rather we should look forward to what we shall receive in heaven for enduring shame

and persecution, just as Christ teaches (Matt. 5:11–12), "Blessed are ye, when men shall revile you, and persecute you, and shall say all manner of evil against you falsely, for my sake. Rejoice, and be exceedingly glad: for great is your reward in heaven: for so persecuted they the prophets which were before you."

14. The dear Lord Christ comes to Jerusalem riding on an ass, his larder is not stocked, even though he already was a King. He had on occasion been hungry, and had to leave the Royal City still hungry; Martha and Mary of Bethany fed him. Such care he did not experience in the Royal City of Jerusalem or from his own people. He got nothing to eat. He hoped they would invite him, perhaps as a guest. However, since no one would invite him, he traveled, as Mark reports, to Bethany, to Martha and Mary, who gave him something to eat.

15. Now, just as Christ was despised by his own people, we find the same thing happening today still. Hold on, they say, is that supposed to be the gospel which this poor beggar is preaching? If emperors, kings, princes, pope, or bishops had preached it, it would have had the appearance of being a gospel. But our Lord God will not concede that then it is the gospel when and to the extent it suits them, but when and to what extent he wants it to be. Christ does not want to wait until Herod and Caiaphas come and with great pomp lead him into Jerusalem, but says, I shall be King and Lord and ride in when and how I choose; my gospel is to go forth when and how I want, and it is nobody else's concern. He who believes will be saved; he who refuses to believe will lose it and will be damned.

16. That's the way things are also going at the present time. Since everybody is taking exception to the word of the cross and its preachers, Christ is scorned everywhere in the world. But that does not offend or deter us at all, for we must now do what the pious and God-fearing people did at Christ's time. They did not take offense at Christ's person, but joyfully received him and loudly sang: "Blessed is he that cometh in the name of the Lord! Peace and blessedness in highest heaven!" Nor did they pay any attention to the fact that the Pharisees became violently angry and forbade them to sing and to praise God. Also the little children gladly received him, believed in him, and praised God, neither inquiring first for Herod's or Caiaphas's counsel.

17. We do the same thing now, and so indeed we should. If Duke George and the bishop of Mainz do not now wish to accept the gospel, let them desist; what concern is it of ours? We are free. Christ is the true King and Lord. He was poor here on earth just like he wanted to be; however, in heaven he has retained for himself a well-set table. If for his sake we here endure hunger, thirst, disdain, and persecution, he will say to us: Because you have acknowledged me as your King and Lord, even though I was so poor that I had nowhere to lay my head, you shall now see my, yes, your everlasting, unspeakable treasure and riches. You will have a table where nothing will be lacking for all eternity, and you will never hunger or thirst; if for my sake you have fasted, you shall now eat and never hunger. Therefore, hold on and don't let this vexation that my Word is called heresy in the world, and that for the sake of my Word you must endure persecution, tear you away from me. I have prepared a table for you where you will bountifully enjoy an end to what you have endured.

18. Thus John the Baptist pictures Christ in this Gospel as dependent on no one for their counsel. From this we should learn to believe in Christ and not first gawk at how and what the emperor, kings, princes, pope, bishops, or prelates believe. For each will have to answer for himself. For this reason may everyone heed what Christ has preached and taught in his gospel, not what emperor, kings, princes, pope, or bishops believe and command to be believed. May our dear Lord Jesus Christ grant that we acknowledge this and retain it. Amen.

HOLY CHRISTMAS DAY

*First Sermon**

Luke 2:1–14

And it came to pass in those days, that there went out a decree from Caesar Augustus that all the world should be taxed. (And this taxing was first made when Cyrenius was governor of Syria.) And all went to be taxed, every one into his own city. And Joseph also went up from Galilee, out of the city of Nazareth, into Judaea, unto the city of David, which is called Bethlehem; (because he was of the house and lineage of David:) To be taxed with Mary his espoused wife, being great with child. And so it was, that, while they were there, the days were accomplished that she should be delivered. And she brought forth her firstborn son, and wrapped him in swaddling clothes, and laid him in a manger; because there was no room for them in the inn. And there were in the same country shepherds abiding in the field, keeping watch over their flock by night. And, lo, the angel of the Lord came upon them, and the glory of the Lord shone round about them: and they were sore afraid. And the angel said unto them, Fear not: for, behold, I bring you good tidings of great joy, which shall be to all people. For unto you is born this day in the city of David a Saviour, which is Christ the Lord. And this shall be a sign unto you; Ye shall find the babe wrapped in swaddling clothes, lying in a manger. And suddenly there was with the angel a multitude of the heavenly host praising God, and saying, Glory to God in the highest, and on earth peace, good will toward men.

THE ACCOUNT OF CHRIST'S BIRTH AT BETHLEHEM

1. This is the narrative for the festival marking the birth of our dear Lord Jesus Christ, about which we want to preach. It is a good arrangement in the church year to commemorate the story in this way, especially since there is such power in it. It is the ground on which our Christian faith rests. This history is something our young folks need to become acquainted with and the average person learn very well, in order that they might know where to ground their Chris-

* Preached at the *stadtkirche* (St. Mary's), the parish church in Wittenburg, Christmas Day afternoon, 1532.

tian faith. Our Lord God's power and might sustain this text over against Satan's fury, so that under the terrible darkness of this world and the popedom, our young people and people in general may know the meaning of Christ's birth, suffering, death, and resurrection.

2. This Gospel has two parts. The first has to do with the account itself and its meaning for today, that Jesus Christ was born at Bethlehem. The second part is the message of the angels telling of its fruit and power, and how we are to profit from it. The narrative should be impressed upon the minds of the young people and people in general in order that they may know the article they confess in the Creed, "I believe in Jesus Christ, born of the Virgin Mary." The meaning especially needs to be assiduously pointed out, besides the history, so that we relish its true goodness.

3. As St. Luke tells the story, he points out precisely at what time, what year, what place, and the manner of Christ's birth. It was at Bethlehem, in Judaea, at the time when the Roman Empire was at its zenith under its most notable caesar and when the first general census was taken. The decree was given by Caesar Augustus that all the world should be enrolled and taxed. In obedience to this decree Joseph and Mary went to be enrolled, and for this reason they journeyed from Galilee to Bethlehem in Judaea. The time for Mary's delivery came and she gave birth to her son, the Saviour of the world, in a strange land and place, away from home, and because the town was so crowded there was not even room in the inn.

4. That is the account briefly told. From it one may see and learn that the Lord, immediately with his birth into the world, distinguishes sharply between his kingdom and the world's. As regards the world it is as though he is not cognizant of it and its jurisdiction; and contrariwise the world's acknowledgment of him is virtually nil both as to his person and his kingdom. Yet Christ does not strip Caesar Augustus of his power and rule. He lets him issue the decree for the worldwide taxation, and what is more, lets him tax the parents, Joseph and Mary, too. Caesar rules things in his kingdom with absolute authority basing his decisions on the canons of sound reason and wisdom, strict law and order. All this Christ allows to take place, except only that he wants his kingdom to be distinguished from caesar's. For that reason he conducts himself as though caesar's realm and the

world's did not concern him; and in turn the world and caesar act as though this King and his kingdom were of no account to them.

5. Christ indeed was born in Bethlehem, the very town in the land of his fathers from which Micah, the prophet, foretold that the Messiah should come:

> *But thou, Bethlehem Ephratah, though thou be little among the thousands of Judah, yet out of thee shall he come forth unto me that is to be ruler in Israel. (Micah 5:2)*

Yet he is a stranger in his fatherland. Another, namely, Caesar Augustus, is supreme king and ruler. For Christ there is barely room in a stall and manger. He is born in a strange locality where he has no home, in cold winter and at night, in a place and at a time when he is totally forsaken by everyone and without the usual necessities for such a moment. Miserable were the circumstances, with a world more hostile and loveless towards this King than to lions and bears. It does not so much as open a little room for him or give him a warm place, but shunts him off to the barn with the cattle. There, in great lowliness, this noble Son and great King was born, wrapped in swaddling clothes and laid in a manger. These are signs and testimonies enough to show that the world cares not a hoot about him, but disdains him. By the same token through the configuration of things connected with his birth, this King demonstrates that he does not stand in awe of the world but would begin a new way and kingdom, even though he chose meanwhile to be in the world.

6. To distinguish well between these two kingdoms is a great art which very few people rightly master. What usually happens is that the rulers of this world want to rule over the church and contrariwise the spiritual leaders want to take over the town hall. Under the papacy it was considered to be good government when the two were mixed together. The fact was that it was very bad. As long as the bishops were still pious, the distinction was respected; they served the church and honored caesar's rule. But their successors mixed the two realms, grabbed the sword and became worldly lords. The present state of affairs is that the squires and nobles want to govern consciences and give orders in the church. Similarly, when the spiritual

lords now assert themselves, they take the sword from the secular lords, as happened under the papacy.

7. At all events Christ was born at Bethlehem, of a natural mother, in a manger and diapers, in a world where Caesar Augustus ruled and governed, no less also in Bethlehem. Similarly, there is no Christian on earth who has no need for the world. Now then Christ's and caesar's realms are to be distinguished as follows: Christ's kingdom, briefly stated, is a spiritual realm and yet exists the meanwhile in the kingdom of this world. Christ and Christians live in and use this world, as St. Paul teaches (1 Tim. 6:7). Caesar's realm is a worldly kingdom which directs and sets things in order, governs with law, conducts war, rules with the sword, and so on. With such worldly things Christ has nothing to do, but his kingdom and office have to do with saving souls from sin and death, and to succor where the world cannot help.

8. For this reason he conducts himself over against the world as though he did not know it, and the world vice versa deals with him as though it does not know him. Really what should have happened is that the citizens of Jerusalem ought to have crept out to Bethlehem on their knees and welcomed their King, or at least that the mayor of Bethlehem should have gone into the stable to offer him service and waited upon him. But no one came, neither from Jerusalem nor Bethlehem, none paid him heed. He is stuck away in a stable and for his part does not present himself as a King or Lord, but as a poor beggar who has come to earth to declare that he is no worldly king, nor does he have a physical realm, but that his kingdom belongs in another world and life.

9. Whoever would be a preacher or teacher, or simply just a Christian, must direct all he does to the end that it serve that life and recognize that the *causa finalis,* that is, the end purpose of the spiritual realm and heavenly rule in which Christ is King and Lord is how man ought live in this world. People's lives in this world belong under the governance of caesar who had authority to direct things, put evildoers to death, make marriage laws, regulate the rearing of children, build, plant, divide the land, and the like. Christ, on the other hand, has and gives everlasting peace, eternal life, and salvation.

10. True it is that Christians live their lives here upon earth, eat and drink in this world, just as Christ, their King, also ate and drank

and shared in life here. But Christians do this as pilgrims and strangers, as guests in a lodging place, as Christ also did. In an inn the master of the house sees to it that there is food, drink, bread, meat, wine, beer; the guest is not in charge of that. He does not instruct the landlord how to run the house. He does not tell the manager how to go about buying food stuffs; rather, he asks the innkeeper whether there is bread and meat for him that he might eat, since he is weary from travel. So also, Christ has not come to earth in order to seize power from Caesar Augustus and teach him how to rule. But he uses the worldly realm and the manger, until he has fulfilled the mission for which he had been sent. This is what St. Paul teaches in 1 Corinthians 7:29–31:

> *But this I say, brethren, the time is short: it remaineth, that both they that have wives be as though they had none. And they that weep, as though they wept not; and they that rejoice, as though they rejoiced not; and they that buy, as though they possessed not; and they that use this world, as not abusing it; for the fashion of this world passeth away.*

In other words, a Christian's end purpose is not his life on earth, to marry and be given in marriage, eat, drink, be clothed, rejoice, buy and sell—though like a guest for an hour or two these things satisfy life's need—but he pursues another goal which endures once this all ceases.

11. This distinction must be carefully noted: *finis politiae est pax mundi; finis ecclesiae est pax aeterna,* that is, the end purpose of the government is temporal peace, while the ultimate end of the church is not peace and comfort on earth, nice homes, wealth, power and honor, but everlasting peace. Caesar does not care whether I die a blessed death and come to everlasting life, nor can he be of help against death, but must himself die just like me. Death comes to him as to the lowliest beggar. Caesar's jurisdiction pertains to this temporal, transitory life; but where this temporal life ceases, there the rule of the Christian church intervenes. Let this be the goal and purpose for which the Christian realm strives and aims: to proclaim the treasure for troubled and anguished consciences which Christ has earned for and committed to his church, namely, the forgiveness of sins and everlasting peace.

12. The pope has dispatched this distinction and made a worldly government out of Christ's kingdom with his decretals. Now Christ did not come in order to cancel out the old, secular government, but to establish a new spiritual realm. He has not stripped secular government in any way but given it its due. He uses this world but he does not govern this world in worldly manner like a secular king. He takes from the world a little bread but does not instruct how bread should be produced, leaving that to caesar. So much for the first part of the Gospel.

13. The second part of this Gospel treats of the angels' message which is the chief part of this Gospel and clearly shows that Christ's kingdom is a much different realm than that of the world. For if our dear Lord Christ had wanted to be a worldly monarch, then the high priests of Jerusalem, Annas and Caiaphas, or other prominent people of Bethlehem, would have come and celebrated his birth by preaching and singing, "Glory to God in the highest." But now it is the heavenly spirits, the holy angels of God, the princes who belong to that kingdom who come. These heavenly princes do not turn their eyes upon the world but upon this King born in the stable and laid in a manger. Thereby they indicate that the kind of kingdom this King possesses is one over which neither Caesar Augustus nor Herod could rule, but only God himself could be King and Lord, in which only angels and sanctified people are.

14. Accordingly, the account of the Lord Christ's birth is opened up straightway and brought into the light with the angels' coming. Christ's kingdom is set apart and distinguished from worldly government. The indication is that it is a heavenly, eternal realm, even though its rule is begun here on earth. When you, therefore, ask what sort of king Christ is, the answer here is that he is heaven's and the angels' King, and yet the King of heaven lies here in the manger without jurisdiction over the manger but as a guest on the earth, having another, a higher, realm to govern, of which the angels preach as we will hear.

15. Also it is made plain who those are who belong to this King's realm, namely, those with troubled hearts and broken spirits. Those who strive after worldly rule, power, and eminence do not belong to this kingdom. True it is that a Christian may and could be a worldly

ruler, governing over land and people, but he does so in obedience to God and out of Christian love, ruling in line with his calling and in service to the world, considering himself to be a servant in the house and a guest in the inn, as David, already a king, said (Ps. 39:12): "I am a stranger with thee, and a sojourner, as all my fathers were." Those, however, who seek after and contend for worldly power and lordship do not belong in this King's realm. Here belong the poor, needful people, for whom Christ came to earth. For that reason his kingdom is to be perceived as a kingdom for the terrified, sorrowful, wretched people.

16. The purpose for which the angels come in their dazzling and glorious brilliance, to the great fright of the shepherds, is to declare the truth that such wretched, sorrowful people, who do not seek after great wealth, power, and eminence, are the only ones who come into this King's realm. They do indeed live in this world's realm, exercise its power and rule when it is their lot, just as their King, Christ, uses the swaddling clothes, milk, and crib. But they do not contend for or seek after it, but keep their eyes on the eternal realm in which there is everlasting peace and eternal life. This is what the text signifies when it says that "the shepherds were sore afraid." For the angels appeared to them in shining brilliance and light, lighting up the darkness of the night, as though heaven were on fire; and for the shepherds it seemed as though it was nothing other than lightning. In this way it was demonstrated that this King was born for those who live in fear and trembling, and that they alone belong in his kingdom. They were the ones to whom it should be preached, as the angel announced to the terrified shepherds, "Behold, I bring you good tidings of great joy."

17. What is this joy? Listen to what the angel says. "Behold, I bring you good tidings of great joy, which shall be to all people." That signified that this joy would be proclaimed to all people, but only those would be receptive whose consciences were stricken and hearts troubled; these are the ones that belong to me and to my message, and to whom I proclaim something good. Is not this a wonder that this joy would be dearest to those in whom the conscience was most disquieted? There, where fear and terror reigned, this glorious, precious, sweet joy was to come, there where the human heart could

grasp and receive it only with difficulty. The shepherds were witnesses to this brilliant light which overpowered the world's darkness, and yet they were terrified by it and feared greatly. Ought one really be terrified by joy and be fearful before such beautiful light? Indeed, as the text says, the shepherds were frightened by the dazzling light of the Lord that shone around them. And that is the way it must be, and no other way.

18. Note this well, however, and never lose hold of it: the angel said that Christ, born at Bethlehem, is not a terror-filled cause for sorrow, but great, comforting joy, for which a terrified heart wishes and yearns. The world rejoices when things are good and it has money and possessions, power and glory. But a troubled, sorrowful heart craves nothing more than peace and comfort, to know that it has a gracious God. And this joy, whereby the sorrowful heart has rest and peace, is so great that all the world's joy reeks in comparison. For that reason poor consciences need to be preached to as the angel here preaches: Hear me, one and all, who are miserable and sorrowful in heart, for I bring you a joyful tiding. You must not imagine that Christ is angry with you. For he did not come to earth and become man for that reason, that he might shove you into hell. Much less was he crucified and died for that purpose; instead he came that you might have great joy in him. In short, there are no sour grapes with him.

19. That is the right explanation and understanding. If you wish to define Christ correctly and portray him truly, who and what he is, then note carefully how the angel distinguishes and portrays him, namely, that he is and is called, "Great Joy." I personally learned this the hard way under the papacy, for no one ever taught me anything else than that Christ was a stern Judge who would pass judgment on me according to my deserts and works. I was used to thinking at all times, therefore, how I might produce good works that I might reconcile Christ my Judge. In no way could this be termed "Great Joy," and "Unto you is born this day a Saviour," but rather the preaching of hellfire. What was missing for me was that I could not name Christ rightly with the name the angel gave, "Great Joy," as he most surely also is: great, sweet, precious joy.

20. This sermon, as stated, pertains only to the poor, terrified consciences; they are the ones who should learn this definition and pic-

ture Christ as nothing other than joy personified. It is in the nature of things that those who are ready to grant that Christ is sheer joy allow it to become nothing but terror for themselves. And, on the other hand, those for whom this definition is not intended, turn it for themselves towards fleshly security. Those to whom it does not pertain learn it quickly, while those who ought to take hold of it have difficulty. But they ought nonetheless grasp it, since it applies to them alone. Therefore, all who gladly believe in their hearts that Christ is nothing other than pure joy, these have learned well. When these folks come to hear that the first world was destroyed by the flood, that Sodom and Gomorrah were wiped off the map by fire and brimstone, and similar terrible visitations like these of God's wrath and judgment, they immediately respond: Be that as it may; I perceive who Christ is and I believe that he is rightly named "Great Joy."

21. The devil, however, does not readily let us have this belief, but always wants good works added in, and highlights for poor, troubled consciences the most terrifying stories and examples of God's wrath and judgments, tormenting and torturing them in order to melt them down with terrors.

22. For that reason a person must learn to keep Christ and all other works carefully separate, no longer dwelling on them fearfully and with terrors of conscience, nor plaguing and torturing oneself with thoughts of God's wrath and fearful judgments upon the ungodly. He must instead affirm: I know for a fact that God destroyed the world with the flood, reduced Sodom and Gomorrah to ashes with fire and brimstone, cut down the Assyrian king with his army before Jerusalem in one night. But all of this I enjoin upon the ungodly world, the papists, Turks, counterfeit Christians, and stiff-necked sinners. For myself, however, there's something else. I am fearful and anxious, and for that reason I must remember that Christ is known by no other name than the one the angel gives, namely, "Great Joy." Here I see another picture before me, that a virgin sits in a darkened stable in Bethlehem with a dear, gracious child in her lap, whose name is "Great Joy."

23. This is what the angel would want us to learn through this sermon, so that all sorrowful hearts and anxious consciences might recognize and grasp Christ according to his true picture. Where Christ puts

on a sour face, there he drowns the world with the flood and cuts down kings and tyrants; but here he has no sour face, but friendly and loving, and is called "Great Joy." For whose good? For all troubled hearts. This, then, is a golden text, which we ought to learn well, so that we might know how to comfort ourselves in time of sorrow and trial.

24. How is this great joy portrayed? The angel shows this as he announces further: "For unto you is born this day in the city of David a Saviour, which is Christ, the Lord." The words, "Christ, the Lord," sound terrifying to us. In the pope's theology, and our own weak nature, it makes us think of the hangman with his gallows, rope, and sword. But it is actually a comforting word, especially because with it stands "Saviour," that is, a helper who brings bliss and salvation. Whoever has no fear and cross does not need this Saviour. But those poor sinners who are in fear and angst are in need of Him, for none can help them except this Saviour, Christ the Lord, born this day in Bethlehem.

25. Therefore, we should take the angel at his word and not make a liar out of him. He gives Christ his right name, the one that alone fits. He is and is called the only Saviour. For on the last day, when he will come to judge the living and the dead, he comes first of all as true helper, directing us towards genuine help, rescuing us from devil, death, pope, wicked evildoers, and from this wicked world. If he were not to come on the last day, he would not be a rightful Saviour. But he will come on that day, in order to show himself as Saviour indeed, not in order to judge those who rejoice in him, but so that he might judge and punish pope, cardinals, bishops, and the ungodly world, all of whom blasphemed and persecuted him. He will come in order to settle accounts with those who tore up their inheritance, that is, first of all, the devil, and then the tyrants and wicked of this world who plague mankind, peasants, burghers, nobility alike.

26. Accordingly, wherever Christ is, in the manger or at God's right hand, whether called Lord or Judge, as we confess in faith concerning him, he is at all times our Saviour. Everything that he has done and will yet do has this significance and this purpose, that we might be saved. God grant us his grace that we may receive and ever hold fast to these things. Amen.

HOLY CHRISTMAS DAY

*Second Sermon**

WHAT THE ANGELS PREACHED AND ANNOUNCED TO THE SHEPHERDS

1. Beloved, you have heard the story of this day, how Christ Jesus, God's Son, was born into this world, and what we are to learn from this. Now while this occurred in Bethlehem, according to the Evangelist, the angel of the Lord, accompanied by many thousands of angels, appeared with extremely brilliant light to sing and proclaim this birth to the two or three shepherds in the fields tending their flocks nearby. This was the angel's sermon:

Luke 2:10–12

Fear not; for, behold, I bring you good tidings of great joy, which shall be to all people. For unto you is born this day in the city of David a Saviour, which is Christ the Lord. And this shall be a sign unto you; Ye shall find the babe wrapped in swaddling clothes, lying in a manger.

2. This is the first sermon preached concerning this newborn child, our Lord Jesus. It was delivered for us on earth by the angels from heaven, and even though we deal with this sermon year after year, we still keep on treating it as though new. For even if it were preached and heard every year, yea every day, we could never exhaust its meaning till the end of time.

3. The angel's sermon was indeed most necessary. Christ might have been born a hundred times over, but it would all have been in vain if it had not been preached and revealed to us. What profit would it be to a man to have a treasure and yet not know that he has it? It's like the man who has an inkling about a treasure of gold buried in the cellar of his house but doesn't know for sure how to get at it; what pleasure or joy does he have from it? That is true for every-

*Preached in the afternoon on Christmas Day at the parish church, 1534.

thing in this world: A buried treasure is a useless treasure, as the proverb has it, *ignoti nulla cupido,* "what a person is unaware of doesn't excite him"; there is neither delight nor disgust for what is not real nor likely to come to pass. This is especially true in spiritual matters. If the angels had not proclaimed this holy, wonderfully joyous birth and revealed this treasure to people, no one would have yearned for this treasure, let alone relished it; none would have rejoiced. The bottom line is, as stated, what a man does not know cannot be dear to him.

4. That is why the truly preeminent point in today's Gospel is that the angel's proclamation made this birth known, to show us this treasure, so that we are not left unawares of having a treasure in hand, unable either to rejoice over it or be comforted by it. Hence the pronouncement: "Fear not: for, behold, I bring you good tidings of great joy."

5. These are truly key words, for the one speaking them is the angel of the Lord. The shepherds are terribly frightened by the great and dazzling light accompanying the angel's appearance and encompassing them with the Lord's brightness in a most unusual happening. In just a split second the dark night was lit up like fire and everything, heaven and earth, fused together as one mass. The shepherds were hardly accustomed to such a light and message, and consequently, they were terribly frightened. The angel observes this and, therefore, speaks gently to them, "Fear not," as though to say, you have no reason to fear; but the fact that you do plainly shows that you are not yet aware of the very precious treasure God has given to you, otherwise you would not be afraid but would be of good spirit and happy at heart. That's the reason for which I have come, to make this treasure known unto you. So, listen to me: I bring you joyful tidings, truly joyful, against all your sorrow, fear, and terror.

6. He does not merely say, I make known to you a great work and wonder, but, "I bring you tidings of great joy." Now no one can rejoice over something he does not know about. The man who after being told and informed still refuses to rejoice over it is a fool. The world is full of such fools who have had God's heavenly and eternal gifts proclaimed to them and yet do not rejoice over them, though they know about them. Accordingly the angel does not merely term the birth of our Lord Jesus Christ a wonder, but a joyous thing, for it

is his sincere intention to bring a message that would be overpowering, not useless, but avail to make us rejoice over Christ's birth, and not just a little bit but with exceeding joy. The wondrous work of God which I am making known to you, he states, is a birth that will cause you wondrous joy.

7. Here was the reason why: The devil had subjected all mankind under sin and caused terrible, incalculable grief beyond human comprehension. In the first place he precipitated us into original sin, including death with it, and not only death but also all manner of evil. Daily in this world we live with murder, lying, betrayal, stealing, robbing, and all manner of shameful evil, depravity, and vexation, so that literally no one's life or property are safe for a moment, but everything is in terrible turmoil! But beyond such evil there is even a greater one, as God's Word tells, in that the devil takes hold of people so totally that they become mad and foolish. As a result of this wickedness and sin, the human race has become little more than a stinking, shameful, disguised tool of the devil. So despicable has he made mankind through sin that we could not possibly become more base. Eternal death and God's wrath take us by the throat; we are never at peace but constantly plagued in body and soul here on earth, making it an enormous, woeful, fear-ridden kingdom of the devil.

8. If we rightly think about it and weigh one against the other, however, such pitiful, and heartrending calamity in no way compares with the glory of this precious treasure and joy of a Saviour, who is Christ the Lord, born for us. And with his message the angel wants earnestly to divert our eyes and hearts from our devil-induced grief and sorry condition to this child, purposing thereby like a golden-tongued preacher to show us that the grief and sorrow brought upon us by the devil cannot in any way compare with the salvation and joy that is ours in this newborn child. It is a fact, when this joyous image reigns in a person's heart, then the evil launched by the devil becomes as nothing, though indeed always still very real and damaging.

9. Whoever, therefore, desires to overcome and be safe from the devil's poison and evil must rivet his attention on these wonderfully comforting words of the angel, "unto you is born a Saviour." When this conviction reigns in our heart the victory is already won. We can now counter: Though the devil throttle me, deeply imbed sin in me,

and inject me with his poison to bring me under God's wrath and everlasting judgment, yet will I not be overcome with fear and terror to the point of despairing. For great though this evil is, it cannot in any way be compared with the treasure God has given us through Christ. It is far greater than the evil the devil has brought about in us. We don't understand why God did not take charge over the human race in the same way the devil has dominion over people, but instead chose to become a true man himself. That near the devil cannot come to people, to become a human being himself. For although he can possess a human being, man remains man, and the devil remains the devil, two distinct persons and natures. The Son of God, on the other hand, assumed a human nature, so that I can now say in truth: This man is, and is called, true God; and conversely God is, and is called, true man in one person.

10. God thus has drawn much closer to us and entered more deeply into our condemned and troubled nature than the devil could. He can possess and torture a person but cannot personally become a human being, as, conversely, a human being cannot become a devil. The two natures remain distinct not only in essence but in person. But with the Son of God the two are one; he has our flesh and blood, born of the virgin Mary, true, natural man like you and me, except that he was conceived of the Holy Ghost without male semen, and did not partake of the devil's poison, sin and death, but possessed a completely pure, guiltless body and blood. Except for that one fact, that our body and blood are impure and sinful, he is a man like you and me, needing to eat, drink, sleep, wake up, become tired, rest, and carry on as other people need to do because of their nature. As St. Paul says, *habitu inventus ut homo,* "in his appearance he was found in fashion as a man," so that whoever saw or heard him would have to say, he is a true human being in nature, no apparition, for he possesses all the characteristics of human life.

11. This was the gladness of which the angel spoke. I speak now only of the glory over which we should rejoice, not yet about the fruit of his suffering and resurrection. My sermon now is only about the glory with which God honored our nature, that against all dishonor and shame brought upon us by the devil through sin, we came to blessedness in that God drew so near to us by himself becoming man in his

own person like you and me, except that he was without sin. Thereby he adorned the whole human race with this inexpressible honor. This is what the angel wanted the people to perceive with his words, "I bring you good tidings of great joy, which shall be to all people."

12. The dear angels rejoice because of the birth of this Saviour, and they glow and spring happily, completely at peace with mankind. That is the essence of the angel's joyous sermon, "I bring you glad tidings which shall be to all people." His deep desire is that none of us in the human race be excluded from this rejoicing but that all would espouse these glad tidings from the heart, as the angels did, that by Christ the Lord's birth our human nature has been greatly elevated, because the most sovereign Son of God himself, by whom all things were made, has become flesh and blood with us.

13. If there was nothing more for us in the newborn child than that our human nature had been highly honored in that God who created us is now our kinsman, our nearest friend, our flesh and blood (I'll omit for the present to speak of his suffering and resurrection), it would be little wonder, if we, believing it from the heart, would become so dear to each other that, as the saying goes, we would consume each other with love. If our hearts really perceived the greatness of this honor and we could say with firm faith, God is become man, would it be a wonder if we no longer were enemies with any man and surrendered our lives for each other? The fact is you could not even hate or harm anyone in effigy who has body and soul like your God and mine. Should we not, therefore, because of such glory with which God has elevated human nature above and beyond the angels, also love and do good to all people?

14. The angels are much more glorious creatures by nature than we human beings. But God did not consider that; he is not an angel, nor did he become an angel. The angels, moreover, are blameless and holy spirits who have never fallen, as the other angels and we poor humans did, and therefore they are also immortal. That seems to suggest that it would have cost the divine nature less, if God had become an angel. But he sets the course, chooses the lowly, poor human nature, lost in sin and subject under the devil's rule and the power of death, plagued and troubled through and through by the devil and his ceaseless pressure. That meant sinking to the lowest depths. That fact alone ought

to motivate us to ardor, love, kindness, and service toward each other for the sake of this one man, Jesus Christ.

15. Some of the fathers, in particular Bernard, in reflecting on the matter have stated that when the devil, while still in heaven, saw that the Son of God would become man, he became so filled with envy against people and hatred toward God for not becoming an angel rather than man, that out of jealousy and arrogance he fell to his ruin. That may be a pious thought or an actual fact, but in any case the beloved fathers sought thereby to emphasize the great joy, glory, and overwhelming goodness that have come to us, because God took to himself not the angels' nature, but through Abraham's seed our flesh and blood, which had been corrupted by the devil and poisoned through sin and death.

16. People who know nothing of this glory are without hope of salvation, but much worse are those who hear the message of the angels or from the apostles—that God graciously embraces our human nature, honors and magnifies it so highly, that not even the angelic nature equals it in comparison, in fact no creature made by God. But they do not savor it, nor do they have comfort or joy from it. You may be sure they forfeit their salvation. They neither fathom nor possess it.

17. If my father were to become a great and wealthy lord, I would indeed be very happy. When one member of a large family of brothers is promoted they all share in the joy and satisfaction. How great was Israel's joy when Joseph was elevated to prince in Egypt. It is a natural gladness. So how does it happen that we do not rejoice over this inexpressible honor and glory? Why doesn't it grab us in our hearts? and why don't we praise and thank God over the fact that he assumed our flesh and blood and now sits at the right hand of God, Lord over all creation?

18. Whoever rightly perceives this in his heart should, for the sake of the flesh and blood above at God's right hand, hold dear all flesh and blood here on earth and be angry with none of his fellowmen. Simply looking at the manly nature of Christ, our God, should rightly make all hearts rejoice and spread kindness all around, so that no angry thought would evermore occur. By the same token, whoever has really grasped the picture in his heart that God's Son became man can hardly have evil intentions in his heart towards the Lord Christ,

but only good. For I know very well that I don't relish being angry with myself or hurting myself. Now Christ is one with me, having flesh and blood like mine; so how could he possibly intend evil for himself, that is, towards us, who share his flesh and blood? That is why I do not fret over the devil's vexing. When that picture reigns in the heart, then every instance of God's avenging wrath, as with man's fall into sin, or Sodom and Gomorrah, melts away. When we but think of this one man who is God and who has elevated our poor human nature by becoming man, God's wrath vanishes.

19. As stated, are they not a derelict people who, though they hear this, nonetheless, willfully despise and disregard the treasure while they give attention to filling their pockets with money, building nice homes, and chasing after finery? It is, of course, the miserable devil who blinds their hearts so that they don't even give a second thought to these glad tidings. You may be sure that wherever greed, grubbing, jealousy, and hatred are present, there is proof positive that the light of the angel's message does not glow in their hearts but is extinguished.

20. For the present, as I have said, I am not speaking of the benefit and power of our redemption but only of the birth of Christ itself, that he so honored our nature, our flesh and blood, by himself assuming it. By itself that should have melted our hearts and molded us into one cake as in the baker's oven, igniting such ardor within us that we come to each other. But this is a message that goes in one ear and out the other, just as we go into church and come out again little changed. If we really embraced this picture with our eyes and hearts, a kinder, gentler person would result and we would say, How can I do hurt and wrong to that very nature which my God and Lord has so honored by himself becoming man? But the devil seeks to keep that from being preached, and where it already is being proclaimed, attempts to snatch it out of their hearts. The enthusiasts and the radical spirits dispute this with their arguments and ultimately lose the joy through their "wise" cogitations. And so the devil maintains his troops in the world, keeping the light from dawning, or quickly extinguishing it.

21. This is the one fact that ought to move us to great happiness and blessed self-esteem, that we have been so honored over all creatures, even the angels. We can truly boast: My flesh, my blood, sits at God's

right hand and rules over all things by his almighty hand. No other creature is so distinguished as is my flesh and blood, not even the angels. How can I, therefore, but love my neighbor and do good to him? Right there, however is where the devil works his spell, as we have said, spoiling our joy through other concerns, so that we don't hold on to this picture with our hearts as we should. If we possessed nothing else than this privileged station, it would be cause to spring and dance.

22. But there's more to this joy than that we are honored above the angels, for a Saviour is born for us. That really climaxes all. It goes far beyond the distinction and honor to our nature that the man Jesus also wants to be our Saviour. That is the chief point and greatest reason why we ought to be joyful. Those people are lost who neither know nor have heard this. But, as said earlier, much worse off are they who having heard and known still despise it. For these words melt heaven and earth together, make death into sugar, and turn all ills, of which there are plenty, into delectable wine. Where's the man who could have conceived this, that a Saviour would be born to be our Redeemer? For that treasure was valid not only for the mother, the Virgin Mary, for her alone to possess in her motherhood, but for us all. "Unto you," states the angel, "is born a Saviour, which is Christ the Lord."

23. The angel speaks to the shepherds; they were Jews and knew very well the meaning of "Saviour" in their language, that it signified Lord and King. But the greater part of the Jews erred on that point, thinking that Christ would be a Lord and King over a physical realm. That was not the meaning. The angel had something higher in mind, and so stated, "Unto you a Saviour is born." In other words, till now you have been held captive by the devil in sin and death, plagued by him with water, fire, pestilence, and sword; indeed, who can tell all the evil? The whole of poor mankind lay under his tyranny, souls misled by idolatries and lies many more times than our bodies ravaged by the French disease (syphilis). Consequently, the poor, thirsty, weak body also had no rest from the devil; nor was eternal death far behind, with soul and body so afflicted. These are the devil's arts and weapons. However, the angel says to you who now lie captive to this proud, shameless, evil, poisonous spirit, who is this world's prince and god: A Saviour is born.

24. The little word "you" should make us glad. For to whom does the angel speak—to trees and stones? No, to people, and not to one or two, but to the whole human race. So what are we to conclude? Shall we continue to doubt the grace of God? and say, St. Peter and St. Paul might rejoice over the Saviour, but this noble, precious treasure does not pertain to me, a poor sinner. Beloved, when you say he does not belong to me, I will in turn ask, To whom does he then pertain? Did he come for the sake of geese, ducks and cows? You forget who he is. Had he come for the sake of helping other creatures, he would have taken those creatures' nature; but he became the Son of man exclusively.

25. Now then what are you? Who am I? Are we not all human beings? Yes, and who other than people are to receive this child? The angels have no need of him; the devil does not want him. We, however, need him, and for our sakes he became man. It behooves us, therefore, to welcome him with gladness, as the angel here says, For unto you a Saviour is born. Is it not a great wonder that an angel from heaven comes to bring this message to mankind, that many thousand angels thereupon also rejoice, urging and preaching to us people to rejoice over and embrace this graciousness with thanksgiving? We must write the words *"unto you"* with letters of fire into our hearts and welcome the Saviour's birth most gladly.

26. The angel speaks with trenchant, passionate words, Unto you a Saviour is born, as though to say, I am not addressing wood or stone, but you people, you shepherds and people of earth for whom the Saviour is born. This birth is not meant for angels, nor for the sake of the mother's motherhood, but for the sake of poor, lost, and condemned mankind in the devil's bondage, those subject to the devil's derision and mockery. Should we not, therefore, embrace with thanksgiving this Saviour who was born for us? In him we not only have one united with us in nature, with our body and blood, but also a spiritual treasure far greater than physical glory, namely, our spiritual and eternal Saviour. Whoever perceives and believes this understands what it means to truly rejoice, yes, he virtually succumbs because of great joy.

27. Now it is impossible for us here on earth to fully understand and exhaust the meaning of this message. Life is too narrow really,

our heart too small, for us to be able to apprehend, let alone comprehend, this tremendous joy. For one's heart really to be able to embrace it, would cause it to burst and die. Experience tells of how some people even die from fright and sorrow, some because of great joy. In like manner this gladness is so great that were the human heart fully to assimilate it, body and soul would be torn apart and the person would expire.

28. Now even though we are unable fully to grasp and comprehend this joy, we should at least partake of its fruit by becoming kinder, gentler people who bear our neighbor no grudge, yes, do good even to our enemies, remembering the role model that God himself became man. But we see how feebly things go with us, also as regards the fruit that ought to follow, let alone that such gladness should fully reign in our heart and be fully understood. The greater part of mankind continues with the old Adam: envy, hatred, and other evil vices, a sure indication that the [angel's] message is not actually believed, or at best feebly, otherwise some minimal fruit would at least result, even though we did not fully appreciate it.

29. The stronger the faith is, however, the more joyous will be a person's perception of this overwhelming grace. It is impossible for a human heart not to rejoice, if indeed it believes that it has a Saviour from sin, death, and all evil. Surely a person who has found a physician who can cure his fever, disease, and personal ailment, will rejoice; yes, with thanks he will promise the dear doctor that he will never forget his good help. He has heartfelt gratitude for the well-being he feels in his body. Surely rejoicing must be even greater when from the heart he believes that a Saviour, who is Christ the Lord, has been born for him, to provide him genuine security against sin and everlasting death. The greatest number of people, however, seek after another kind of joy, one that provides tranquillity, recreation, and pleasure here and now; but not for one moment are they free from anxiety. It illustrates how like a dream we receive this very joyous message and then snore away. The dear angels preach and sing indeed, but we godless people sleep on, with the treasure before our eyes and ears, but paying it no attention.

30. Now then the smart aleck who hears that word and finds no joy in it may in truth regard himself to be a lost individual. What after

all will cause a heart to be joyful, if it cannot rejoice over the angel's message, Unto you a Saviour is born? Whoever is not changed for the better by this word and made more godly, praising and thanking God; whoever does not relish this heavenly wine, nor have his heart warmed by this fire, to become kinder and gentler to his neighbor, him will the judge and hangman make more pious, for he's beyond reprieve. The fact that he's not set ablaze by this fire nor drawn by this heavenly wine—that Christ is our brother, yes, has become flesh and blood with us—plainly shows that he is a lost and condemned man. Accordingly, let it be a negative rebuff against our coldness and torpid resistance, causing us to pray from the heart for his grace, that by the Holy Ghost he might change our heart and help us.

31. The angel thereupon delineates further what sort of Saviour he is, namely, "Christ the Lord." The sermon is short but it compresses the entire Holy Scripture in one bundle. Were a man to try to delineate it all, it would take him longer and he would need to cite the witness of the prophets about this child's birth. In other words, when the angel says this Saviour born to you is "Christ the Lord," he means that he is the Saviour whom the patriarchs and prophets foretold and whom with all their hearts they yearned to see. They well understood that he was to come, but they did not live to see his coming. But now the Saviour himself, Christ and Lord, has been born.

32. Christ himself states this fact to the Jews (John 8:56): "Your father Abraham rejoiced to see my day: and he saw it, and was glad." What indeed would Abraham, Isaac, Jacob and all the fathers and prophets have done if they had lived long enough to see that Christ had been born? With longing they prophesied concerning him and rejoiced exceedingly about his coming. They were consumed with anticipation, while we are frozen stiff with ingratitude and disdain.

33. This very Christ and Lord has now been born, the angel tells the shepherds. He will put all things in order, freely bestowing the gift of righteousness, everlasting life, and salvation which were lost as a result of sin, and making heaven and earth new and at peace again. The Lord and everlasting Sovereign is born! Be comforted and undaunted, be brave and glad, renewed in courage by him, for it is not Joshua or David whom you have, but the one and only Saviour, who is Christ and Lord indeed. He will not cast you into hell, but rescue

you; nor judge and condemn you because of sin but will forgive you your sins; nor be angry with you, but will greet you with friendly laughter. He is your brother and kinsman, and on top of it, your Saviour, King, and Lord; he dies for you, redeems you from sin, death, and the devil. Whoever believes on him and rejoices in his birth is saved. Whoever finds no joy in his birth, nor thanks God for it, belongs to the devil.

34. So much in brief concerning the angel's sermon. Let each one search his own heart whether he rejoices because of it and whether he loves his neighbor. If he finds no gladness in it, he should know that he is a lost and condemned man. Whoever rejoices over it and loves his neighbor, let him thank God and pray that his joy might increase, becoming ever more complete. Amen.

HOLY CHRISTMAS DAY

*Third Sermon**

THE ANGELS' HYMN OF PRAISE

1. We have heard the angels' sermon summarizing in a few words all that is written in the Scriptures concerning this newborn child, that he is the Saviour, Christ the Lord. Before all else these dear angels want the world to know the precious Saviour, Christ the Lord. All wisdom in heaven and earth reaches its ultimate and eternal purpose in this child. Here God draws near to us, and he is to be found no other way.

2. Now, in order to plumb more deeply into the story of this day, we wish to ponder and reflect on the angels' hymn of praise. It could justly be called the true *SANCTUS*, in letters of gold, even as the message might rightly be called the angel's sermon, because it was an angel, not a human being, that delivered it. So this song is properly the angels' hymn, because angels, a heavenly host sang it, not human beings. These were the words of their hymn of praise: "Glory to God in the highest, and on earth peace, good will toward men."

3. It is brief and, as said, it is known as the angels' song because they sang it for earth to hear, as well as heaven. But it was in human tongue, otherwise the shepherds would not have understood it. It had three parts or themes: first, glory to God; second, peace on earth; third, good will or rejoicing for mankind. In themselves these three themes may appear insignificant, but the fact remains they constitute the angelic anthem. A person may discourse about them, but we really don't fathom what they say, for we can't look, as they continually did, into the face of the Father in heaven. As a consequence, we don't comprehend as well as they. We may warble after them with our eager voices and raspy vocal chords, but we can never equal

*Preached at the parish church in the afternoon on St. Stephen's Day, the day after Christmas, 1533.

them. When they sang, heaven and earth resounded. This was the first part of the song: GLORY TO GOD IN THE HIGHEST.

4. The theme of our song, say the angels is that the Saviour, who is Christ the Lord, has now been born and lies in the manger. God on high will surely be glorified in this. So their hymn was not intended to instruct us about things we are to do, but to indicate rather how with the Saviour's birth God will now have praise and glory given to him. In other words, the dear angels declare that this is how things perforce will be. Because this little child lies in the manger, God will be glorified and praised; everything the prophets foretold will now come to pass. Prior to this child's birth, conditions were very different. Then blasphemy of God and idolatry prevailed, as is always the case apart from or without Christ, no matter how elaborate the religious rites; they are nothing more than sacrilege. If God be God, that is, if he is to be rightly worshiped by people as God, then it can only be through this child. Only here can we learn and be sure that God is a gracious, merciful, benevolent God, because he spared not his only Son but permitted him for our sakes to become man. This was an inexpressibly great work of love and it constrains our hearts mightily to genuine love, trust, and hope towards God, with praise and thanksgiving.

5. Such fruit will follow, according to the angels' song: God will be honored in highest measure, not with outward works—these cannot mount up to heaven—but with hearts that reverberate up to heaven with thanksgiving and confident hope in him, this gracious God and Father. In times past the world dishonored, defamed, and despised God. There were godly patriarchs upon the earth who recognized Christ in spirit, worshiped and praised God in Christ. But there were also people on earth who lived their lives in Christless manner, dishonoring and despising God by their deeds and conduct. Now, however, through this child God's honor and praise will be rightly proclaimed for ages to come.

6. Accordingly, this angel anthem proclaims that whatever is outside of or apart from Christ stands condemned before God as blasphemy, idolatry, and abomination. God can only be honored in and through this child who is Christ the Lord. Apart from him no person can find and worship God, but grossly offends and dishonors him. That

means that everything across the world that is called worship and service of God must end. Truly holy and God-pleasing offerings, genuine service of God, will bear Christ's name or is in Christ; otherwise it is no divine service. God has channeled his worship in this child, and where he is not worshiped in this way, true worship is not present.

7. The whole world, including God's chosen people, the Jews, was replete with idol worship, some going one direction, some another. There were as many worship centers as there were mounds and trees, ceremoniously beautiful, as the prophets testify. That's the way it was also for us under the papacy. At these idolatrous high places people earnestly sought for God, sacrificing and fasting, often at the expense of their physical well-being. This served nobody except the devil and their own thoughts, according them the worship that belonged alone to God. There was no greater blasphemy and abomination toward God in all the world, all of it stemming from people's ignorance of Christ! This should now come to an end (God be praised!) as the angels sing, because people would no longer worship the devil or themselves, but God in the highest only.

8. But there is another, even greater, abomination in that people worship the god Mammon, that is, gold and possessions and the like. Kings, princes, burghers, and peasants alike bow down before and worship this stupid idol, abominable Mammon, who can in no wise help them. Thus in either case God is blasphemed and despised, both by the subtle idolatry of the hypocrites and sanctimonious religionists (as in the case of the Pharisees and Sadducees among the Jews, and monks and Carthusians in our day) who idolize their own righteousness and holiness; and also by the coarse idolatry of the high and mighty, as well as lower classes, who despise God and cling to Mammon. The world is saturated with this despising of God; it doesn't seek him, call on him, or thank him.

9. But now things will be different, sing the dear angels, because God will through this newborn child establish his worship within the world so that people esteem him as true God. Then many will no longer seek after their own piety and righteousness, nor look to father or mother, money or goods. While before they made obeisance to Mammon, now they will embrace this one and only Saviour, cling to him with all their hearts, devote all that they possess to him, and

say, Christ is my Saviour, I will abide by him no matter what God wills for me. From that point onward God will have his glory, while before he was ignored; people will come to know God truly, and will rightly worship, praise, glorify, and thank him. This is our hope and prediction for the future.

10. Accordingly, to worship means nothing else than to rightly know God, praise, glorify, and thank him. Such honoring was lost when Adam sinned in paradise. Now all of us have this damnable trait as part of our nature, each aspiring after his own glory. How else shall we describe the fault of pope and bishops in our day than that they are unwilling to admit they have erred and done unjustly, unwilling to let God have the glory? And is it any different with the high and mighty on this score, or among the common people, burghers, or peasants? None fails to have an appetite for glory, to play his bagpipe looking for praise. If this happens in mundane things—we deem them trash and drivel—that people seek honor and glory, how much truer is it for those who boast of mighty things like power, wisdom, righteousness, holiness, good works, or civic honors? The devil makes it difficult for such people to give God his honor, for in their opinion it belongs to them.

11. The human race is envenomed with this damnable reaching after glory, prompted by the devil in Adam and Eve in paradise when he got them to aspire being like God, and it continues in us till now. When a peasant has money, a scholar has cleverness, a nobleman has territory, a prince has power, a woman has a fashionable veil, a young girl has a fancy sash or skirt, they all want to be fussed over and God does not receive his honor.

12. But the child Jesus, sing the angels, will change all this so that God receives his glory. For all who receive and believe in him will rightly come to know God and say, I am nothing. My righteousness, holiness, wisdom, skill, domain, and power are as nothing; the child Jesus is all in all. In this way God is glorified because he alone is our strength, defense, joy, gold, and wealth; our confidence, comfort, boldness, and joy rest on him alone.

13. God is indeed glorified when I say to Mammon, You are a great god whom all the world worships and serves, but you provide me no consolation except that as long as I live and have you I eat off

of you, clothe myself as needed, and am able to feed and clothe others who have nothing. As long as I have that benefit out of you, that's enough. The same for skill and ability; I have learned, God has given me a good understanding, which I want to use to glorify my God and benefit my neighbor as he has need. My trust, boast, and joy, however, will not be in my money or skills, but in the dear child lying at the Virgin's bosom, my Lord Jesus Christ, God's Son.

14. God's glory, majesty, and divinity are accorded him when we confess: Dear Lord God, all that we have and use is yours; we did not create it, it does not originate with us or by our doing, but you granted and provided us with it. And especially it is of your work and mercy alone that we escape the devil and are absolutely free from sin. For that reason alone you deserve the glory, not I. Such is the incense with which God wants to be praised and that is his highest glory, that we totally bestow it on him, gainsay it for ourselves, and deliver our thanksgiving to him for the least as well as for the greatest gifts.

15. That is the subtle motif of this hymn whereby the dear angels draw everything together that we are or have, stripping us of everything—our wealth, power, honor, and in particular our spiritual gifts and religiosity, that is, our own righteousness, piety, wisdom, and good works—teaching us not to keep the glory here below but raise it up to God alone. This comes about through this child. That is their song.

16. That song turns the world upside down, as we see. Because people do not recognize and esteem this child, there is strife and violence everywhere, everyone seeking to be number one, vying for money, goods, honor, and power. The farmer covets being a city dweller, the common man a noble, the noble a duke, the duke a prince, the prince an emperor, the emperor wants to be God. It demonstrates that they are without Christ and don't care to know him. They turn the angels' song around and sing: Let the glory and honor be here on earth, every red cent, the silver dollar, my power, reputation, skill, gracious rulers, and good friends. So, sing lustily, dear comrades, what does it matter that it turns out to be a jackass's hymn that resounds loudly and turns out to be an evil and monstrous joke? That's what it means to sing glory to human beings and to Mammon, indeed to the devil in hell below, instead of to God on high.

There follows now the other phrase or mandate:

PEACE ON EARTH!

17. This must be understood like the first to be an expression of the angels' desire to forecast well-being, blessedness, and salvation here and now for those who come to know and receive this child. For, if Christ is not there, what is? What is the world apart from Christ other than miserable hell and the devil's kingdom, utter darkness and despite of God, lying, deceiving, greed, gluttony, drunkenness, whoring, knavery, adultery, violence, and murder? As the saying goes, the world knows nothing any longer of openness and trust between people; you have to believe the opposite of what people say if you are to escape people's deception and fraudulent trickery. There is neither love nor trustworthiness; no one can trust his neighbor, brother, son, daughter, even the wife who nestles at his side. Indeed what a beautiful, praiseworthy life when a person cannot trust the next man, when one even has to be on guard with friends as with enemies, and even more so! This is how the devil rules and runs things in the world.

18. People who believe on this child will not only give God his honor in all things but also themselves be "gods" to each other, that is, kind, loving, of irenic spirit towards others. Peaceful government and delightful conditions would obtain among people, with no one wishing ill to another, were the community made up of Christians who have come to know and accept this child. To have a Christian commonwealth one would have to envision a place where people lived in such a way that there was no need any longer for judge or executioner, everyone freely and from the heart doing that which is good. Those would be blissful conditions, everything nicely quiet and peaceful. Of this the angels are here singing and praying. In fact they speak the comforting word that the devil's tyranny over people will come to its end and Christians will live with each other in quiet and peace, gladly helping and assisting each other, eschewing squabbling and disunity, in love preferring their neighbor, happy to grant him the best.

19. Such will be the conditions where God receives his glory and is worshiped as the Lord from whom we have all things. For it is out of such awareness that loving people come to be, no longer hating

and envying the other person, stealing from or doing him harm, or running over him, but rather preferring the neighbor over oneself, looking upon him as being more noble than oneself, petitioning God in his behalf. Peace and blissfulness will then prevail. But if I want to vaunt myself over you, and you over me, each trying to do the thing which vexes the other, then instead of bliss and peace Master Bully muscles in with the sword.

20. A good and peaceful life, the angels sing, will prevail among those who believe on this child. They will not offend their neighbor but will gladly do what pleases him and avoid whatever vexes. Those, however, who act otherwise do not hear the angels' song, but only the howling of the wolf, the devil, whose song is: Gobble away here, guzzle there; steal here, fornicate there; hate here, murder there, and so on—the devil's hymn out of hell.

21. However, among Christians it ought not be so, but rather as the dear angels sing and foretell. They understand service to our Lord God in heaven most excellently: first, to let God in heaven have the glory, worshiping and praising him alone; second, to live here on earth in a brotherly way with each other, refusing to follow the devil's evil input and tyrannical nature. For such conditions in the world the angels earnestly opt. However, with their sharp, eagle-like eyes they discern that most people will have nothing to do with the child Jesus. Glory in the highest and peace on earth will never fully and completely prevail among the children of mankind. There will always be evil rulers, unruly parishioners, rude citizenry in town and country, rebellious children, unfaithful servants. In short, earth remains earth, world remains world, except there where the child Jesus Christ by his power and spirit initiates glory to God in the highest and peace on earth. Accordingly, the angels intone the third part:

AND GOOD WILL TOWARD MEN.

22. Two parts of the angels' song have preceded, telling what the child Jesus will effect, namely, that God on high will be glorified and people on earth will live at peace and benignly with each other. The third part now follows, that people will be content and patient, even if things go contrary to the angels' song. For to preach that God should be glorified and people should become godly, will immediately trigger tyranny and persecution. Even many who do not esteem

or receive this Son will find themselves persecuted. So, in our day the more we preach, cry out, warn, petition, and implore our bishops, magistrates, peasants, and burghers, to leave off blaspheming God and stirring up trouble on earth, the worse they become. The angels perceive how depressing and difficult a thing it will be for a person to regard and endure this. The fact is that if God was not very supportive, pious hearts would likely be crushed with depression over how the Jews crucified Christ, God's Son, and martyred the apostles. Similarly, it would not be surprising were we to die of grief because we had to watch, not only how the pope and his gang, but also how our own people, trample the gospel under their feet.

23. For that reason the dear angels express the earnest desire that God would grant pious believers happy and joyous hearts, that they might endure and overcome such things with patience—comforting, strengthening, and helping Christians to compose their souls with patience and to be of good spirit. It is tantamount to their saying that you who want to be Christians should give glory to God and be kindly, gentle people. So what that bishops, kings, rulers, nobles, and common folks are not! Let it be. Cling to this, that Christ is your Saviour. By his Word and Spirit he will teach you how rightly to worship, serve and receive God, repudiate false religion, be kind to people, and endure evil knaves. So, hold fast to and cultivate patience, albeit that many people remain wicked and godless. And even though for that reason people harm and persecute you, and because of your faith and confession imprison, burn, kill, and despise you, nonetheless, do not become impatient and angry, but find pleasure in this, that no sorrow, suffering, or persecution, no matter how severe and great, can upset or destroy the joy and passion which you possess in the newborn child.

24. That kind of heart is desired by the angels for all believers, to be so level-minded, that whatever the cost, whatever the opposition, they remain unruffled. Let all those, however, who are of one mind join together to sing: "Glory to God in the highest and on earth peace." Whoever will not join and sing with us, let him be; we will not trouble ourselves to death because of him but will sing this third part of the angelic hymn, "good will to men," that is, may good things and good will prevail; prejudice, be gone; sorrow, be gone; melancholy, be gone!

World, we will not allow our joy to be taken from us because of you, but in spite of everything will sing together with all God-fearing believers, "Glory to God in the highest and peace on earth."

25. The dear angels have in effect drawn together a whole service of worship with their hymn of praise: they give God his glory, earth peace, and good will to mankind, so that good things might come to pass no matter what. Indeed, a short but rightly excellent angelic, heavenly, little song! It is not a song that has to do with outward liturgical forms prescribed for the sake of the child Jesus, as when the temple was built and Levitical offerings instituted, but only that God in heaven might have his glory, earth peace, and mankind good will. In other words, if you want to serve God properly, see to it that he receives his glory from you and that here on earth you be at peace with one another. If things do not go well, be patient, hoping for the best with a good heart. Having attained that, then come what may or will, it makes no difference whether you wear red or blue cloaks, are man or woman, boy or girl, whatever station in life given you by God. You have thereby completely shucked off all external pomp and ceremonies, and gotten right to the kernel in angelic manner.

26. Whoever thus knows Christ as the only Saviour, through whom and in whom God in heaven is to be glorified, is a true and genuine priest, even though he wears no cowl, mantle, chasuble, or robe. Moreover, the person who keeps peace on earth will be an excellent, sought after man, citizen, and neighbor. How does it help to have many rules or customs to follow, doing things this way or that, as long as everything is nicely pulled together here? If you have Christ, acknowledge him, in and through him honor God, and are kind and gentle toward people, you are surely on the right path, whoever you are—prince, master, mistress, boy or girl. Then it will not matter if we fail to win people to this mind, no matter how hard we petition, plead, warn, and admonish, we will let it be. If the world accepts it, good; if not, then I answer: Begone, fine world; I will not trouble myself to death over you. If you young Turks, money hungry and wicked peasants and burghers, trample the gospel with your feet, I cannot help you; let us see whether you will fool our Lord God with your shameless thanklessness. For my part I will stand with those who honor God in heaven and live peacefully upon earth.

27. We see from this how the dear angels are minded in their hearts. In this church right now where we preach, pray, sing, praise, and thank God are many angels who sing with us and we with them. Indeed, a worship service in which we preach about Christ pleases them deep down in their hearts. Moreover, they are particularly delighted with us when we live at peace and benevolently with each other; likewise, if we rejoice when things go well, and even then when they don't go as we hoped, and we are compelled to suffer persecution because we worship God correctly and live peacefully. That is the angels' deepest passion, for we are their brothers and sisters, redeemed and called into the kingdom of heaven through Christ. That is why they sing with us and earnestly desire that we join with them, especially if and when we conform to what the hymn teaches.

28. Thus we must perceive of the angels differently than in the theology of Dionysius* where they are treated as though they were separate beings unconnected with us, speculating about things not visible to us. Christ, however, teaches that when the heart is full the mouth overflows. If we are to know a man, we must know him by his words, for with our eyes we cannot know him. For that reason I do not raise doubts about the angels even though I have never tweaked their noses or seen them, because I have their word and listen to what they say. A person can soon enough perceive whether a man is a wise, understanding person or a fool; for what he says will reveal what's in his heart and soul. So also here, if we are to think and write about the angels we must not let our thoughts float on the clouds and speculate, but listen to them as they speak and sing. Then for sure we know what's in their hearts.

29. Accordingly, just as the dear angels here sing about the birth of the child Jesus, so also their thoughts focus entirely on this child, on God's glory, on peace on earth, on patient enduring by Christians. That is their heart and mind. And that is why we should be comforted and rejoice: first and foremost, because the newborn child, our Lord Jesus Christ, is our only Saviour; and, second, because the heavenly host, the dear angels, are so kindly intentioned towards us. We must thank our gracious Lord God for his lovingkindness, and not be fear-

*a 6th-century monk

ful of the dear angels as though they were our jailers or hangmen, but know that they are our friendly neighbors and fellow citizens.

30. The song of the angels, as said, resounds only there where this child is received. There is nothing written here about things pertaining to hell or concerning death. For that would be another song, with other singers.

HOLY CHRISTMAS DAY

Fourth Sermon—1534

Concerning the Account of the Birth of our Lord Jesus Christ.

1. On this festival of the birth of our dear Lord Jesus Christ we should preach and learn about the great and gracious act which God bestowed upon us by allowing God's Son to become a human being. Therefore let us hear what the holy Evangelists write about this event. First of all we are told that the angel of the Lord appeared to Joseph in a dream and announced to him that Mary would give birth to the Son of God. Then they report that Joseph and Mary traveled from Nazareth to Bethlehem and that there Mary gave birth to her first son, in the stall where the cattle milled around them, for there was no room for them in the inn.

Matthew: 1:18–25

Now the birth of Jesus Christ was on this wise: When as his mother Mary was espoused to Joseph, before they came together, she was found with child of the Holy Ghost. Then Joseph her husband, being a just man, and not willing to make her a public example, was minded to put her away privily. But while he thought on these things, behold, the angel of the Lord appeared unto him in a dream, saying, Joseph, thou son of David, fear not to take unto thee Mary thy wife: for that which is conceived in her is of the Holy Ghost. And she shall bring forth a son, and thou shalt call his name JESUS: for he shall save his people from their sins. Now all this was done, that it might be fulfilled which was spoken of the Lord by the prophet, saying, Behold, a virgin shall be with child, and shall bring forth a son, and they shall call his name Emmanuel, which being interpreted is, God with us. Then Joseph being raised from sleep did as the angel of the Lord had bidden him, and took unto him his wife: And knew her not till she had brought forth her firstborn son: and he called his name JESUS.

Luke 2:1–14

And it came to pass in those days, that there went out a decree from Caesar Augustus, that all the world should be taxed. (And this taxing was first made when Cyrenius was governor of Syria.) And all went to be taxed, every one into his own city. And Joseph also went up from Galilee, out of the city of Nazareth, into Judea, unto the city of David, which is called Bethlehem; (because he was of the house and lineage of David:) To be taxed with Mary his espoused wife, being great with child. And so it was, that, while they were there, the days were accomplished that she should be delivered. And she brought forth her firstborn son, and wrapped him in swaddling clothes, and laid him in a manger; because there was no room for them in the inn. And there were in the same country shepherds abiding in the field, keeping watch over their flock by night. And, lo, the angel of the Lord came upon them, and the glory of the Lord shone round about them: and they were sore afraid. And the angel said unto them, Fear not: for, behold, I bring you good tidings of great joy, which shall be to all people. For unto you is born this day in the city of David a Saviour, which is Christ the Lord. And this shall be a sign unto you; Ye shall find the babe wrapped in swaddling clothes, lying in a manger. And suddenly there was with the angel a multitude of the heavenly host praising God, and saying, Glory to God in the highest, and on earth peace, good will toward men.

2. This is the story and history which gives us the account of how our dear Lord Jesus Christ was born. A primary need for our young people, especially now, is to remember this account and adore it with sincerity of heart, so that they will never forget it. It should teach them to thank and praise our Lord and God for this tremendous blessing, that we poor, wretched, yes, also damned people, have been granted this great honor of becoming one in flesh and blood with the Son of God. For no one less than the eternal Son of the eternal Father, who alone created heaven and earth out of nothing, he it is, as we are here informed, who became a human being and was born into this world just as we were, except that in his case this all took place without any kind of sin being involved. That is why we can boast that God has become our brother, yes, part of our flesh and blood.

3. This great honor has been granted to neither angels nor devils but to us human beings. The angels are indeed more glorious creatures than we human beings, and yet God has bestowed greater hon-

or upon us and has joined himself closer to us than to the angels, because he did not become an angel, but chose instead to become a human being.

4. Now if we human beings properly consider this fact, and if we could wholeheartedly believe this, then such inexpressible grace and blessing from our dear Lord God should give us very great joy, and should drive us to thank him with our whole hearts and move us to gladly obey his will and to live godly lives.

5. When we were still under the papacy, they used to tell this story. Once upon a time the devil attended Mass in a church where it was customary in either the Lord's Prayer or in the Creed to sing: *Et homo factus est,* that is, "God's Son has become a human being." While they were singing this, the people just remained standing and did not kneel down. The devil was so incensed, that he slammed his fist into one man's mouth, saying, You boorish bum, aren't you ashamed to just stand there like a post and refuse to kneel for joy? If God had become OUR brother, as he did become YOUR brother, our joy would be so great that we wouldn't know what to do with ourselves.

6. That story may be pure fiction, but if so, then it was invented by someone who was very intelligent and who correctly understood the great honor which was bestowed on us, when God's Son became a human being in a totally different way from Adam or Eve. You see, Adam was formed out of the soil of the ground, while Eve was formed out of Adam's rib. But Christ was even more closely related to us because he was born from the flesh and blood of his mother, the Virgin Mary, in the same way that other human beings are born, with this one exception: the Virgin Mary was single when the power of the Holy Spirit came over her and God's Son was conceived without sin, by the power of the Holy Spirit. Aside from that, he is just like we are, the son of a genuine, natural woman.

7. Adam and Eve were not born but created; God formed Adam from the soil of the earth, while Eve was formed from Adam's rib. How much more Christ is like us since he is of the same flesh and blood that we have! We should truly treasure and cherish this fact. And especially children and young people should treasure this from little on up and have this glorious fact engraved indelibly on their

hearts, that the Son of God has become flesh and that there is no difference between his and our own flesh, except that his flesh is without sin. You see, he was conceived by the Holy Spirit, and God so filled the flesh, body, and soul of the Virgin Mary with the Holy Spirit in such a way, that no sin was present in her conception and carrying of the Lord Jesus. Aside from that, everything was natural in his formation. Just like other people he ate and drank, slept and awoke, was happy and sad. He became hungry and thirsty and got cold, just like other people. He experienced such and similar, natural sensations and emotions, but he remained without sin. As St. Paul says, In all respects he was found to be a human being, exactly like us, a person who ate, drank, arose, walked around, experienced joy and sorrow, cold and heat, and so on.

8. This meant, of course, that he had to humble and humiliate himself a great deal. After all, it would have been a simple thing for him to become a human being just like he is right now in heaven. He has flesh and blood just like ours, but does not do what we do. He could have done this from the very beginning of his humiliation, but he didn't want to do that, so he could demonstrate and prove how great his love for us is. He wanted us to rejoice, to take comfort in and boast of the fact that we have a brother in heaven. And cursed is any person who refuses to accept this brother, thus depriving his heart of this joy.

9. That is the reason why this historical account is the theme of preachers every year. They make it the basis of their sermons, so that every child can impress this mental picture on his heart and thank God for this gift and say: There is no reason for me to live in constant fear, because I have a brother who has become a human being just like me. Why he was willing to let this happen, and what he aimed to accomplish by it, namely to free us from sin and eternal death, I shall not discuss in detail today. Right now I want to tell you only about the honor that has been bestowed on the entire human race, an honor of which we can rightfully boast and celebrate, namely, that the Son of God has become a human being. All people can boast of this honor. However, only Christians can boast of something that is even greater. They will be able to boast of this birth to all eternity. Down here on earth all people have the honor that God's Son has assumed

their flesh and blood. But the spiritual and eternal fruit of this birth belongs only to Christians. That is the primary truth we should learn from this account.

10. Second, we should learn to follow this striking, divine example. For Christ, the Son of God, humbled himself the way he did, in order to transfer all his glory to destitute human beings, and on top of that also transferred to them his divine majesty before which the holy angels tremble in awe, while he himself lives like a poverty-stricken beggar. Up in heaven the angels worship him, while down here on earth he becomes our servant and beds himself in our slimy sins and sinfulness. Now I say, because the Son of God has done this, we should learn from him to gladly and humbly praise and glorify him and his Word, suffering every kind of sorrow in imitation of him, and so follow his example. For what harm can befall us or why should we be ashamed of suffering? After all, our dear Lord suffered cold and hunger and sorrow, but when he came down to earth, his life was especially filled with sorrow and poverty, as we have told you. In the stall there were no bedpans nor any privacy whatsoever, no pillow, no diapers, no bedding. He had to lie in a manger beneath the cows and oxen. Think of it, my kinsman, yes, my brother, the King of all creation in heaven and on earth, and of all creatures in them, lies there in such wretchedness! Shame on me! Why am I so stuck-up? Why do I want to be so high and mighty that I never want to suffer anything? If the King of glory suffers as he does, for my sake, who do I think I am, anyway? Isn't it a fact, that I am a poor sinner who does not even deserve to lie on bristle. But here I am, lying on a bed of ease, while my Lord lies there on coarse straw in a manger for the cows!

11. But isn't this a disgusting deal? Here we see the humiliation and poverty in which our Lord Jesus lies for our sake, while we pretend to be aristocratic landowners who should get off with no punishment or suffering at all! The house-hotel is filled with guests who sit in the seats of highest honor; they also have a separate living room and bedroom, maid service and home health care when needed. Meanwhile the young Virgin and Joseph are rudely shown to the barn where cattle are sheltered. That is where she gives birth to the precious Son of God, the Creator of the entire universe! Those are

the abominable conditions under which he was born! We must clasp him to our hearts and confess: Our Lord was born amid such misery and poverty, and eventually he died on the cross for our sakes. It makes no sense at all that we undeserving louts should enjoy eternal rest and peace; for a servant is not greater than his master. But, sad to say, we don't recognize this; we just go on being troublemakers, twisted and gnarled gripers, always haughty and uppity, even though we see our Lord Jesus lying in such great poverty for our sake. But all we gain by our pride is useless, except to polish our shoes with it.

12. That is why we should learn our lesson well and earnestly ponder the great honor that has been bestowed on us by Christ's becoming a human being. For it is such a great honor, that even if one were an angel, you would do well to wish that you were a human being, so that you could boast: My own flesh and blood is greater than all the angels, and blessed is every creature that is a human being. God grant that we understand this, take it to heart and thank God for this great gift. In addition, we should diligently study the example of Christ, what he manifested with his first advent to this earth in that he suffered for our sake, so that we too do our best to learn from him how to suffer. The Lord of all lords becomes a Servant of all servants. We should follow that example and learn from our dear kinsman and brother to gladly help and serve other people, even when it becomes a burden for us and causes us to suffer a little bit in rendering that service. These two things we should note well: the account itself and the example it sets. To that end may God help us by the Holy Spirit through our dear Lord Jesus Christ. Amen.

HOLY CHRISTMAS DAY

*Fifth Sermon**

Concerning the Message of the Holy Angels and their Song

1. Yesterday we heard the history and account of this festival, how the Son of God became a human being and was born into this world by the Virgin Mary. This Scriptural account is proclaimed in sermons every year throughout Christendom, so that we might take it to heart and learn how to thank God with our whole hearts for this great and glorious blessing and grace which he has shown us through this birth of his Son.

2. Having again heard the Gospel story, let us also listen to how the dear angels preach and sing about this birth. For as soon as Mary had given birth to her son in the stall at Bethlehem, a heavenly sermon began to be proclaimed in the skies by the Lord's angel, who had appeared to the shepherds in the field, in a blinding light, proclaiming that Christ the Lord had been born in the city of David, and that he was wrapped in swaddling cloth and was lying in a manger. It is also an unheard of novelty, that our dear Lord God proclaims the birth of his Son to lowly shepherds. God leaves the mighty and influential "lords" sitting at Jerusalem and reveals the wonderful news from heaven to the "poor beggars," namely the shepherds in the field. The same angel bestows upon the shepherds the honor which their Lord Christ himself has bestowed upon all human beings. Following the example of his Lord Christ, the angel humbles himself, and does not scorn proclaiming this news to the shepherds and the lowly beggars. Glorious though he is, the angel does not vaunt his glory; no, he humbles himself, and delivers this marvelous message which shall continue to be proclaimed among Christians until the end of the world.

3. What wonderful spirits those angels must be, angels in whom there isn't even a trace of pride! For just as the one angel humbles himself and preaches to the shepherds, so also the entire army of the

*Preached on St. Stephen's Day, December 26, at home, 1534.

heavenly hosts—as we shall briefly point out—unite in singing about the birth of Christ, allowing just the shepherds to listen to their song. But what is the Roman emperor with all of his splendor in comparison with just a single angel? That is why all the mighty lords, all the scholars, and all the saints, do not by any stretch of the imagination even come close to being as great, or learned, or holy as the sweet angels are. No, all these human beings should observe diligently this example and learn from it not to overestimate their own knowledge, wisdom, saintliness, and other gifts; nor should they ever despise other people. For if these gifts had resulted in pride, then the blessed angels would have been justified in despising and looking down on the poor shepherds. But they do not do that. The shepherds may be ever so poor and wretched, yet the angels do not consider themselves so high and holy that they lose their joy and gladness while they proclaim this good news to the shepherds.

4. Here everything is done in harmony with the nature of Christ's kingdom, which is a totally different kingdom from the kingdom of this world. You see, in Christ's kingdom everyone is humble and busy in serving others, as Christ says in Matthew 20:25–28: "But Jesus called them unto him, and said, Ye know that the princes of the Gentiles exercise dominion over them, and they that are great exercise authority upon them. But it shall not be so among you: but whosoever will be great among you, let him be your minister; And whosoever will be chief among you, let him be your servant: Even as the Son of man came not to be ministered unto, but to minister, and to give his life a ransom for many."

5. That is what God also expects us to do. He wants us to use our own blessings in behalf of others, comforting them and meeting their needs, not despising anyone. The angels are a fine example for us, demonstrating that just as our Lord Jesus is a faithful Saviour and serves all of us human beings, even so God's angels are faithful servants who gladly and willingly serve us. At the same time, the shepherds of that day must have been pious, God-fearing people who were looking forward to the coming of this Saviour with all their hearts. That is why they all came running, so that they could hear the proclamation of the Lord's angel. The people of our own day, especially the unruly mobs, deserve only to hear what the devil says.

But the message which the angel proclaims to the shepherds is this: "Fear not: for, behold, I bring you good tidings of great joy, which shall be to all people. For unto you is born this day in the city of David a Saviour, which is Christ the Lord. And this shall be a sign unto you; Ye shall find the babe wrapped in swaddling clothes, lying in a manger."

6. Anyone can understand this announcement if he just wants to do so, and then he could pass on this good news, repeating what the Lord's angel proclaimed, "Christ the Saviour has been born in the city of David." He could retell the angel's message: On the night when Christ was born at Bethlehem, there was a blinding light; the Lord's angel proclaimed a marvelous message, followed by a lovely hymn of praise sung by the heavenly hosts. The message was "Fear not!" Anyone can understand that and remember it, provided only that he wants to glorify God in this way and assure himself of eternal blessedness.

7. In this proclamation, the angel summarizes the whole gospel, saying: This Saviour, born in the stall, right next to the manger, will bring great joy to all people; he will free us from sin, death, and the devil, and is Christ the Lord himself. All this took place in Bethlehem. These are not the words of men, nor can such a proclamation even be conceived by the mind of any human being; for not even the most learned people on earth know anything about this, for these are angelic words shouted down from heaven into this world; it is a message which, praise be to God forever, has also been made known to us. It makes no difference whether you are reading or hearing this message today or whether you had heard the message directly from the angel himself. You see, not even the shepherds saw the angels (for they are invisible); they saw only the light and glory. But they did hear the words, and you are also hearing them today. For in these words which I read from the Bible in my sermon, you have a summary of the heavenly, angelic proclamation, provided only that we open our eyes and ears and are willing to hear and comprehend the message.

8. Now then, if you hope to be saved some other way, you ought seriously keep in mind this fact: Here we have the first proclamation about the birth of Jesus Christ, shouted down from heaven, a proc-

lamation that still holds true and will continue to be true until Judgment Day; this infant, born in Bethlehem by the Virgin, is the Saviour, Christ the Lord, who will free us from sin and death and be our comfort to all eternity.

9. After the angel's proclamation, the whole army of the heavenly hosts sings a hymn of praise. A good message or sermon should be followed by a joyful hymn. That's why the dear angels rejoice over the birth of this Saviour of all the world, and follow up the glorious proclamation with a joyful hymn in these words: "Glory to God in the highest, and on earth peace, good will toward men."

10. They divide their song into three assertions or points that form a triad, so that they cite three things: God, earth, mankind; and to each of these they attach an appropriate prayer request. To God be the glory; to the earth, peace; to all mankind, great joy. The word *Wohlgefallen* is bad German. The Greek text says *eudokia,* i.e., "joy and delight."

Their first assertion is: GLORY TO GOD IN THE HIGHEST

11. What the blessed angels wish for God is glory, that is, they sing and wish that we people will recognize in this newly born infant the true God, and they thank God for the great, endless blessing, that out of pure grace and mercy God has sent his Son, and permitted him to become a true human being, in order that he might be able to redeem the entire human race. In effect they were saying: God has sent his Son, for which we should thank and praise him to all eternity. For this grace and blessing we, the angels, want to praise and glorify God, and all people(s) should follow our example by praising and glorifying him.

The second assertion is: PEACE ON EARTH.

12. They also wish that there will be peace on earth, and that the kingdom of Christ, which is a kingdom of peace, will flourish on the earth. The kingdom of the world is characterized by stealing, robbery, murder, clubbing people to death, war, and bloodshed. In short, on the earth there is nothing but lack of peace, or turmoil. Each person harms the next person, no one practices faithfulness toward his neighbor, each one beats the next person over the head. That is the essence of life on the earth! That is why the blessed angels wish for us Christians a peaceful life, so that we will be friendly toward one another, each one demonstrating to the other person

love, faithfulness, and reciprocal service, bearing one another's burdens so that no one will be at odds with anyone else, and that everyone helps and shares good counsel to his neighbor. It is the wish and the prayer of the angels that God will provide these things on earth, so that our life on earth will be friendly and peaceful. That is the second assertion or petition of the angels.

And that is followed by their third request: GOODWILL TOWARD MEN

13. In effect they are saying: It is our sincere desire that all men glorify God in the highest and that they live at peace with one another. Unfortunately it is impossible for these conditions to exist at all times because many people pay no attention whatsoever to the gospel. They refuse to accept this Son of God. Instead of that, they persecute both the gospel and the Son. May God, therefore, grant to the Christians a cheerful, joy-filled heart so that they will say: I have a Saviour, who is Christ the Lord! If people mistreat me and persecute me because of this Saviour, I'll rejoice over that too. I will maintain good cheer and joy in the midst of suffering. That is the kind of heart the blessed angels desire for us Christians, so that we may have joy in the face of hatred and go on singing when the devil goes on a rampage. The angels want us to be proud in Christ and in him to defy all misfortune; and if the devil attacks us, that we mock and ridicule him by saying, Satan, you can only attack my body, my life, my property, and so on. You might as well give up on that, too, Satan, for you cannot harm me since I have an eternal Saviour, who will delight me with joy as a recompense for all my physical suffering here on earth.

14. That is the third assertion: that we will have a cheerful, joyful, defiant state of mind in the face of whatever suffering we may experience, so that we can tell the devil, You do not have permission to make life so bitter for me that it would deprive me of the joy I find in this infant. That is the meaning of *eudokia:* a cheerful, unruffled, joyful, and courageous heart that pays little attention to misfortune and confidently tells the devil, Go ahead, be as mean and poisonous as you wish; I will not let my joy be embittered or destroyed by your wrath. Christ fills me with more joy than any amount of suffering you can impose on me. That kind of heart the angels wish for us sincerely with their song.

15. Now if you reverse this angelic hymn, which is what unfortunately is often the case on earth, you then have the devil's hymn in which God is cursed and blasphemed in the highest, in which great havoc is wreaked, in which murder is practiced, in which government is carried out in such a way that no one can have a happy face, and cannot eat one morsel in peace and joy. That is what those abominable rabble-rousers practice. They are the devil's mouthpiece. The fanatics assist the devil in his crimes, blaspheming and disgracing God with their false doctrine.

16. Then they try to make sure that princes and lords fight against one another, that unfaithfulness and dissatisfaction are created, that "good things" must be said in the presence of witnesses and that the worst possible crimes are proven against them. That's the way I like it, sings the devil. That is glory to the devil in hell: wars on earth, and to all mankind a heart that is filled with timidity and despair. As is often the case, God provides everyone with the basic necessities of life, but that doesn't satisfy them at all, at any time. Even though they have their cellars, rooms to spare, and though their tables are loaded with food, they still walk around with hanging heads, faces filled with grief; though they have everything, they find no pleasure in anything. That is the devil's song and wish. He doesn't want us to have any joy whatsoever in the gifts God has so graciously given to us. Now in sharp contrast to this, the blessed angels wish and request for us a courageous heart that is able to defy Satan and to boast of our Saviour to Satan's face.

17. We had to say this about the hymn of the angels, so that you would learn and properly understand it. You won't find this written anywhere in any books, no not so much as a single letter. For this hymn did not originate on earth but was brought down from heaven to the earth by the angels. May our dear Lord God help us with his Holy Spirit, so that we remember this hymn and live according to it, through Jesus Christ, his Son and our Lord. Amen.

HOLY CHRISTMAS DAY

*Sixth Sermon**

About the Example of the Virgin Mary and the Shepherds

We shall treat this Gospel lesson about the shepherds exhaustively. Yesterday we heard how God allowed his angels, those blessed princes, to become preachers, and how God sent so many glorious, beautiful, heavenly spirits to tell two or three shepherds and lowly beggars about the infant Jesus, and had them sing a beautiful little hymn. After the singing of that hymn, we continue the story from Luke 2:15–20.

And it came to pass, as the angels were gone away from them into heaven, the shepherds said one to another, "Let us now go even unto Bethlehem, and see this thing which is come to pass, which the Lord hath made known unto us." And they came with haste, and found Mary, and Joseph, and the babe lying in a manger. And when they had seen it, they made known abroad the saying which was told them concerning this child. And all they that heard it wondered at those things which were told them by the shepherds. But Mary kept all these things, and pondered them in her heart. And the shepherds returned, glorifying and praising God for all the things that they had heard and seen, as it was told unto them.

1. First of all we learn from the shepherds that the preaching and singing of the angels were not in vain. The most important thing for these shepherds was not their flocks of sheep, for they immediately rush out to go and see the little child, which the angels themselves had called the Lord! That is the first thing we learn from the proclamation of the angels.

*Preached in the *Lutherhalle* on St. John the Evangelist's Day, second day of Christmas, December 27, 1534.

2. The second result is that the shepherds also become messengers, telling everyone what they have heard about this infant. They rush to the innkeeper's building and to other places, telling everyone what they have heard and seen. We should follow their example: seek Christ in the Word, believe in him, and publicly confess him before all men.

3. Another thing we should learn from this account is how the majority of people react to this newly born infant. For the Evangelist writes: "And all they that heard it wondered at those things which were told them by the shepherds." They all marvel at it, but very few of them believe it. For the most part it was a marveling which didn't last. For we know from experience that God has under his regimen people who, no matter how God treats them, be it good or evil, whether he scourges them or brings them good news, forget about it almost instantly. The condition of the human heart is so desperately wicked, that it immediately forgets what is past and keeps on badgering God to provide novel miracles and punishments, when we ought to be stouthearted and remember his blessings; but they immediately forget his benefactions. Therefore this account is to be understood as follows: the Evangelist says that all who heard the account marveled at the news. It was reported, about three months after this account, that a child had been born in Bethlehem, that the angels had preached from the heavens on high, and that the wise men from the east had come to worship the child. But after two or three, maybe even four years had passed, no one remembered it anymore. Then after another thirty years had passed, our Lord himself appeared, preached, and performed miraculous signs and miracles. But by that time no one even remembered that such a child had been born at Bethlehem.

4. And what's more, we are no more godly than anyone else. For you will be hard pressed to find even one person in a hundred—I should have said, one in a thousand—who still remember the distressing misery they experienced fifteen years ago under the papacy, when everyone's conscience was tortured and could find no real consolation or comfort anywhere. People have suppressed their recollection of the endless "good works," the ever increasing financial burdens that were imposed, and the fact that no one had any real

comfort or consolation for his conscience. If we had not deliberately suppressed those memories, the holy gospel, which freed us from that torture, would be far more precious and dear to us, and we would be much more diligent in thanking God for that gospel, and our lives would be far more godly than they now are.

5. The same thing happened to the Jews. While they were in Egypt there was no end to their complaints, their shouted prayers, and their weeping. But what happened later on when, with his omnipotent hand, God led them out of Egypt? Before they had spent three days in the desert they had forgotten all about their suffering in Egypt and wished that they were back there again. The human heart is such a wicked and hopeless thing that the moment it gets tired and resentful about something, it forgets all about its previous suffering and persecution. I won't even mention the fact that the heart should recall God's blessings, something which hardly ever happens. It's like the proverb says: *Nihil citius senescit, quam gratia,* "gracious blessings are soon forgotten." Even though God is filled with wrath and, therefore, sends punishment in the form of a plague and all kinds of illness, though he punishes us with more plagues, it produces no more effect than if you write in the water or the air with a feather. As long as we feel the pain and see the plague's effect on our skin, we suffer pain, but the moment the physical pain is gone, it is forgotten, just as if it had never happened to us. Therefore the Evangelist here asserts, The people wondered at those things. But as we said before, The dance at a wedding reception lasts only until the next High Mass, i.e., until the bride goes home. And yet there are a few pious pupils and children who are not as forgetful and disobedient as worldly people, for the Evangelist says, "But Mary kept all these things, and pondered them in her heart."

6. In the third place, Mary is presented here to us as an example of those who rightly hear and keep God's Word. "Mary," says the Evangelist, "kept all these things, and pondered them in her heart." That is, she diligently searched God's Word, just as all those who firmly cling to God's Word do. They keep on searching and studying God's Word, and the longer they do this, the greater becomes their understanding of that Word, and the greater becomes the comfort they find in it. With each passing day their faith becomes more sure.

However, the wicked people who let the Word come into one ear and go out through the other ear, are the sort of people to whom you could preach as long and as frequently as you wish; they'll remember it only as long as it takes for the waves, activated by a slap of the water, to disappear from sight. That is not what Mary does; she was intent on recalling what she had heard. So she inscribed it in her heart, that is, she kept on asking herself, What does this statement mean? It is a miraculously great thing for me to be the mother of a child concerning whom the angels sing and proclaim, this is the Saviour of the world, Christ the Lord. With reflections like these, the words of the angels sank so deeply into her heart that she could never forget them. And even if the whole world had opposed her, saying that this child was not the Saviour of the world, no one could ever have changed her mind; she would have firmly insisted that her son was indeed the Son of God and the Saviour and Lord of all mankind.

7. We are to follow this example of the blessed mother of the Lord (that's why it was recorded for us) and we are to let this Word of God grow in our hearts until it becomes second nature for us to follow her example, as stated in the Song of Solomon 8:6, "Set me as a seal upon thine heart, as a seal upon thine arm: for love is strong as death; jealousy is cruel as the grave: the coals thereof are coals of fire, which hath a most vehement flame." In that statement God does not want his Word to be only on our tongue, like foam on the water or spittle that sprays from our mouths, but he wants this example to be stamped upon our hearts and remain a lasting impression that no one can erase, just as if it were ingrown and a natural thing that can never be scratched out. That's the kind of heart the Virgin Mary had; these words had been permanently engraved upon her heart. Now, all those who receive these words in that way have the true character of Christ, the right seal and sign. They will not let anyone deprive them of this word, regardless of how many "goons" surround them, not even if the devil himself tries to rob them of it. What they first heard and believed as God's Word is also what they continued to believe and defend. The majority of the people, however, though they heard the message and were amazed by it, soon forgot all about it.

And the shepherds returned, glorifying and praising God for all the things that they had heard and seen, as it was told unto them.

8. In the fourth place, after the shepherds had seen the infant Jesus, they told everyone about this good news, and all who heard their report were puzzled by it. Then the shepherds returned to their flocks, praising and glorifying God. They also sang and said, Praise and thanks be to God who has allowed us to find and to see the newly born child as they had heard and learned from the angels, who were singing: "Glory to God in the highest."

9. Here is another excellent and helpful lesson, namely, that after the shepherds have been enlightened and have come to a true knowledge of Christ, they do not run out into the desert—which is what the crazy monks and nuns in the cloisters did! No, the shepherds continue in their vocation, and in the process, they also serve their fellowmen. For true faith does not create people who abandon their secular vocation and begin a totally different kind of living, a way of life which the totally irrational monks considered essential to being saved, even though it was only an externally different way of existence. They also ate no meat, for they considered the eating of meat a demeaning practice; so they ate no meat except fish. They didn't go to bed or arise at the customary hours; they observed and celebrated on different days, just to show off before ordinary people. And yet all these activities were merely an external matter, consisting of food, drink, persons, and so on. That is the kind of life they led, and they believed that Christianity consisted of such external matters. In reality they were the followers of a different spirit, namely the devil, who is also a spirit, which is why St. Paul calls such satanic spirituality a spirituality of the angels. Colossians 2:18, "Let no man beguile you of your reward in a voluntary humility and worshipping of angels, intruding into those things which he hath not seen, vainly puffed up by his fleshly mind."

10. But Christ did not come to change external things, nor to destroy his creation nor to transform it. Therefore you should clothe your body, provide it with sustenance, and use it to do some honest-to-goodness labor. That is God's creation and order, and he hasn't changed that order; he did not come to change that arrangement. When or if it becomes necessary, we are free to make minor adjustments, of course. That is such an inconsequential matter that it certainly doesn't warrant sending our Lord Christ to make such

decisions, let alone boasting of such changes as worship or piety, especially in view of the fact that even a cow or a sow is quite capable of making such adjustments!

11. The real change which Christ came to effect is an inward change of the human heart, just as I now have a different mind, courage, and perception than I did when we were still controlled by the papacy and before the blessed gospel was revealed anew. At that time I was convinced that God would reject me, and I did not believe that I would be serving God if I continued in my vocation, discharging the duties of my office. As a matter of fact, I did not know God as he really is. Nor did I know how I could ever overcome sin and death, go to heaven, and live in eternal bliss. I had the idea that I had to reach those goals by my own good works; and I became a monk for that reason, and nearly tortured myself to death. But salvation does not depend on caps, robes, not eating meats, fasting, and similar works. Death cannot be destroyed in that way; nor can sins be washed away in that manner. Instead, both sin and death continue to exist under either gray or black hoods, and under red or blue robes. As I said earlier, salvation depends on the heart being enlightened and receiving a new seal, so that it can say, I know that God accepts me just as I am, and that this truly applies to me because he has sent his Son, let him become a human being, so that through him I would be able to overcome sin and death and be assured of having eternal life.

12. That is a real transformation! For my heart had never before known or believed that. But now my heart does know and believe that, and for that reason I have a completely different outlook than before. Our dear Lord Christ is responsible for creating a heart and soul with a new and different mind, will, delight, and love. The result is that, whereas a man previously was only interested in earning money and acquiring property, now, having come to a knowledge of Christ, he would not only sacrifice money or property but also his body and life before he would deny Christ and his Word. Prior to this he would not have sacrificed even a penny for the sake of faith; now, though it would cost a thousand worlds, he would not allow anything to rob him of Christ.

13. Prior to this time many people thought, If I am to be saved, I will have to don a monk's cap or a nun's hood. If anyone tried to force you to wear one now, you would run to the end of the earth to avoid

doing so. Likewise if you previously would have eaten a bit of meat on Friday, you would have thought that the earth would open up and swallow you for sure. But now you tell the pope, the bishops, yes, the devil himself, Go, kiss my hand! Why shouldn't I eat meat? Why should I be afraid to do so? That's what it means to undergo an inner change and a change of heart, a change in which the heart acquires from God's Word a different mind and will, and continues in its vocation and secular life as before, as we learn from the shepherds.

14. It would never have occurred to the shepherds that Christ the Saviour would be born. But now that they've heard it from the angels, they run into the city and go looking for the infant. And when they had found the child they told others about it and kept on thanking God for this gracious revelation. Then they returned to their flocks, having nothing but their cloak and crook, just as before. They keep on working as shepherds, not changing anything in their external way of life. That's what it means to teach and live like a Christian. For Christ did not come to change his creation until that distant day when the soul has already been totally recreated and renewed, a change that merely begins here with the gospel. On that future day, the body will also be recreated in such a way that we will no longer need a warm room, clothing, food, or anything else; on that day we will soar through the air like the angels and will shine like the glittering stars. On that day, the external will also be changed; we will not eat then, nor sleep, nor wear a coat. But prior to that day the entire external creation is to continue as God has ordained it, and no one is to make any changes in that divine ordinance.

15. In accordance with that order, everyone is to conduct himself in his vocation and station in life, being diligent, upright, honest, and godly, and he should be totally assured that such external living does not in any way harm his Christian faith. Neither is Christ the least bit interested in a husband or a wife, emperor or stable boy, mayor or constable. Christ validates all these professions and says, You are to be obedient in that profession and life and not think it unworthy.

16. That is why the shepherds did no more than to praise and glorify God. They do not say, I shall immediately serve God by running out into the desert and totally isolate myself from the entire world. I shall serve God with fastings and prayers and contemplative medita-

tion. No! That kind of action is not serving God; it is self-service, disobedience to God. How so? God has not commanded any of these things. Service to God consists of this: that you continue in the profession into which God has called you. A husband should remain a husband, a wife should continue to be a wife, an emperor should continue as an emperor, a commoner as an ordinary citizen. Everyone should learn to serve God in his personal vocation and in that vocation he should glorify God. Then he will be serving God in the right way. God has no use for your prickly hair shirt, your fasting, or your "beanie"; instead of such things, you should be obedient in your profession and vocation, and you should praise God's Son. Then you will be serving God properly.

17. We also learn from the prophets that God is filled with wrath when the heart remains unchanged. But despite that fact, people think they are pious people because of their external works and service to God. Why do you plague me with your sacrifices? God asks in Isaiah chapter one. Jeremiah asks the same question in chapter 7. God asks the same question in Psalm 50. Go ahead, says God, devour your own flesh and have a bad year as a bonus. If I have need of your sacrifices, I will get them by myself much faster than you can ever supply them to me. After all, I did not command you to make them, but I have commanded you to obey my voice, to praise and thank me. I have provided for you sheep, cows, and oxen for your food, and you try to flatter me by giving them back to me, pretending that I am obliged to beg from you. The prophets always emphasize that the heart must be changed and that we must have a proper attitude toward God. That is what God wants. And he doesn't want any other change. He wants each person to do what his vocation requires of him. Now that is precisely what the shepherds in our text do, joyfully, cheerfully, and thankfully. They do the same work they did before, except that now they also thank and praise God.

18. That is also what we read in *Vitis Patrum (The Lives of the Fathers)* written by Paphnutio. He considered himself to be a great saint, and when he wanted to know to which saint he might be compared, he was told that he was like a piper who lured the farmers to dance with his flute. He immediately rushed to the piper, asking, My dear friend, what is the greatest "good work" you have done? The pip-

er replied, I haven't done anything other than to summon the farmers to a dance, and on one occasion I was present when my compatriots were about to rape a girl. I stepped in and protected her from being raped. On another occasion he was again asked, To whom may we compare you? He answered, To two married women. He addressed the same question to them as he had addressed to the piper, What are your greatest "good works"? They replied, We know nothing of a particularly holy life. We have our house and children, whom we care for the best we possibly can, and we conduct ourselves in such a way that the two of us have never hated the other one and we have never allowed ourselves to be divided. Then the grandfather stepped up and said, Now I see that we should not despise or look down upon any profession or vocation, no matter how lowly it might be. You can always serve God and be a godly person, and God will be pleased with such a person so long as he or she reveres God, and does what is right, regardless of what that person's profession or vocation may be.

19. In my opinion, this scenario of the grandfather, the piper and the two married women did not actually happen, but is a fictitious story created to be a good example to warn all the world to be on their guard against monasticism. For, being a Christian and standing in God's favor is not determined by our external life, but rather by what lies beneath your left nipple, in your heart, namely that you know that Jesus is the true Saviour and he has his delight in you because you thank and praise God for him. Then God is well pleased with your external life or profession regardless of what that is. Therefore we should learn this lesson well and diligently note the fact that we dare not separate Christian faith from the Word, nor mistakenly assume that godliness is determined by wearing a gray cap, or strutting about with our good works as the magpie struts about in her multitude of feathers. In a similar way, the preaching monks have turned the robes inside out, as people do on the night of Shrove Tuesday. Such things run against the stream and basic meaning of the Christian faith, which demands a Christian heart. Externally we should be doing what God has required of everyone and is common practice. This arrangement is to continue until we reach the next life, when our bodies will again be beautiful and pure, holy and sinless. In this present life we must wear our sinful skin, but in the life to come we will be completely holy and without sin. May Christ, our Saviour, grant this to us. Amen.

FIRST SUNDAY AFTER CHRISTMAS

*First Sermon**

Luke 2:33–40

And Joseph and his mother marvelled at those things which were spoken of him. And Simeon blessed them, and said unto Mary his mother, Behold, this child is set for the fall and rising again of many in Israel; and for a sign which shall be spoken against; (Yea, a sword shall pierce through thy own soul also,) that the thoughts of many hearts may be revealed. And there was one Anna, a prophetess, the daughter of Phanuel, of the tribe of Aser: she was of a great age, and had lived with an husband seven years from her virginity; And she was a widow of about fourscore and four years, which departed not from the temple, but served God with fastings and prayers night and day. And she coming in that instant gave thanks likewise unto the Lord, and spake of him to all them that looked for redemption in Jerusalem. And when they had performed all things according to the law of the Lord, they returned into Galilee, to their own city Nazareth. And the Child grew, and waxed strong in spirit, filled with wisdom: and the grace of God was upon him.

1. This course of events took place when the child was six weeks old and was taken to the temple in keeping with the law decrees; for, firstborn sons were to be presented to the Lord and redeemed with an offering of a coin of the realm (gulden) and a pair of turtledoves. Now then, I invite your gracious attention as we hear of the presentation of the child in the temple.

2. At the instigation of the Holy Spirit, aged Simeon came to the temple and took the child Jesus into his arms and preached about him. He had received a revelation from the Holy Spirit that he should not see death before he had seen Christ the Lord. This revelation was now fulfilled. For Simeon saw Christ the Lord and sang about him, that he was to be the Saviour, and a light that would shine not only for the Jews as a dim, little light in a lantern, but as a bright

* Preached at the parish church, 1531.

open light intended also for the whole pagan world. We will hear more about aged Simeon's song in due course.

3. Today's Gospel is based on Simeon's song. He tells how that little child is a Saviour, the one whom God has prepared for all people and a light which would illuminate all the heathen. The child, he says, was not to be a small, limited light, as before when God shone his light only on the Jews, but a far-reaching, brilliant light which, like the sun, would illumine the whole world. Joseph and Mary marvelled at the song and the glorious witness Simeon gave of the child. The Evangelist says: "And Joseph and his mother marvelled at those things which were spoken of him."

4. The Evangelist does not wish to imply that Joseph is the Lord Jesus' natural father, but he spoke of him rather as people of that time understood him to be. Earlier the Evangelist has very emphatically stated that Christ was conceived by the Holy Spirit and born of the Virgin Mary. But Holy Scripture at times speaks of a situation as people are accustomed to speak of it. So the Evangelist here, too, accommodates himself to the language of the people, as did Moses. So did the Virgin Mary as she said, "Son, why hast thou dealt thus with us? Behold, thy father and I have sought thee sorrowing." It was a secret work of God that the Virgin Mary became pregnant, which Joseph himself came to believe after the angel revealed this to him in a dream. Else he would not have known, just as we do not know, but must believe, because Holy Scripture teaches, and the Christian faith professes, that the mother of God is a virgin. One should note this well and not take offense that Luke states here that the father was amazed. He speaks according to the common conception of the people, like Moses did when he spoke of his foster father as father, and as the people in general did of this child.

5. The reason for setting this Gospel on this Sunday lies in the expression of astonishment of Joseph and Mary about what was said of the child. Origen had taught that this was to be grounded upon the message of the angels to the shepherds, about which we heard in the recent festival. However, it is based upon what the venerable Simeon said. The patriarch Simeon steps up, even though by virtue of age he can scarcely see his way, and with penetrating clarity of discernment recognizes and praises this child as the Saviour and Light of the

World. All emperors, kings, and sovereigns are mere darkness, but this child is the Light of the World. All the world is subjugated under death and damnation, but through this child the world will obtain salvation. This child, in short, is the one whom the prophets foretold. The words of the Evangelist are very apt, but Simeon, no doubt, has fine-etched them. It was a sermon, says the Evangelist, that caused the child's father and mother to marvel about the child. The thought that he was to be a light unto the Gentiles was not understood clearly from the words of the angels until Simeon spoke. The other people who were in the temple likely despised Simeon's speech as the words of a fool, or they judged him to be drunk, or eccentric by virtue of his age, a foolish old man. How could this little child be the Saviour and Light of the World when he had nothing but ordinary swaddling clothes and his mother had scarcely a farthing in her purse. No doubt the rest of the people would have disdained the words of aged Simeon as though he were merely beating the wind. But Mary and Joseph marvelled at what was said of the child.

6. Mary had heard much about this child, early on, when the angel brought her the message that she was to be the mother of the Son of God, and later when the shepherds told her what the angels had announced to them. Nevertheless, she had to marvel at what Simeon said, too. She could recall that the angel had said that this child would redeem his people from their sin; but Simeon spoke of something even greater: this child would not only be a Saviour for his people, but also a light to the Gentiles. It was of this that she marvelled.

7. Now what are we to think of this? Did his parents sin and do wrong because they marvelled about it? For it almost seems as though their astonishment was a sign of unbelief. The answer is "No!" The fact that they marvelled is a sign and token of a very great faith and profound understanding. In Genesis 17:15 we read, "And God said unto Abraham, As for Sarai thy wife, thou shalt not call her name Sarai, but Sarah shall her name be." When Abraham heard that, he fell on his face and laughed and said in his heart, "Shall a child be born unto him who is an hundred years old? And shall Sarah that is ninety years old, bear?" Even though both he and his wife were old and Sarah was beyond childbearing age, nevertheless, what God said to Abraham was so great a joy to him that he very firmly be-

lieved and by this faith was justified before God, as Scripture attests, "And he believed in the LORD; and he counted it to him for righteousness" (Gen. 15:6). St. Paul summarizes this in Romans 4:3 when he praises and commends the faith of Abraham, "Abraham believed God, and it was counted unto him for righteousness." Abraham did not doubt the promises of God in unbelief, but rather was strong in faith, giving God the glory, convinced with utmost certainty that what God promised, that he would also do.

8. Just as Abraham, in pure and strong faith, laughed for joy, so too, Mary and Joseph marvelled, not from unbelief but with mighty faith and uncommon understanding. That is the unique nature of faith, that the firmer one believes, the more one marvels and the happier one is. In contrast, when faith is absent, there is neither joy nor enthusiasm. Thus, if this were a certainty in my heart, and I believed without doubt that this child, born of the Virgin Mary, is my brother, yes, my flesh and blood, and that his righteousness is my righteousness, his life, my life (as we have heard these last days about the birth of Christ), I say, if I were to believe this with all my heart, then I would so marvel and be so overjoyed that I could not think enough about this infant child.

9. Thus, St. Luke praises the faith of both the mother and father in the words of our text. He praises the fact that the mother is happy and of good spirit, and that she could not marvel enough that this little child should be a light to illuminate the heathen. In comparison, all other kings and rulers are a deep, dark night, buried in sin and death, and remain silent when it comes to helping others, while she is the mother of this remarkable son.

10. The gospel should instill such amazement in us that we too would exult and proudly assert: I have been baptized in Christ; there is no doubt, that through the Lord Jesus, I become a lord and can overcome death and sin, and heaven and all creation must serve my best interests. If a prince were to give me a gift of a velvet cloak, or an entire village, I would be so very happy and be amazed forevermore. But what is that compared to this? Yes, if I had the Turkish emperor's crown, it would be nothing compared with my being baptized into an inheritance of our Lord Jesus Christ. On the day of judgment he will say to me, even as he already does, You are my

dear brother; everything that is mine is yours, you shall live with me in eternity.

11. But where do you find those who truly believe this from the heart? We can all repeat the words, but whether we truly believe is soon evident, because there is no joy, no amazement, no change in us. If one wishes to call that faith, surely it is cold, half-dead faith; else, we would not be frightened and sullen, but happy and proud. For a Christian is a happy, confident, redeemed person who is sidetracked neither by the devil nor by any trouble. For he knows that through Christ he is master over all this.

12. For this reason, no doubt, the Virgin Mary, in her amazement, had a distinctive holy pride which was based not on herself, but on God's grace and mercy and on the child, Jesus, as Luke beautifully points out with these words: "She marvelled." Not because she was the mother of the child (which certainly also contributed to her joy), but because of what was said of him. Christians, too, do not vaunt themselves by virtue of what they are, but rather exult over that which has been given them by grace.

13. This we preach daily, but there are those among us who think they know it all already. Would to God, however, we believed this with our whole hearts, firmly holding to this truth, that through Christ we have been made lords over all. On the basis of the apostles, St. Peter and St. Paul, we can rightly conclude that they had an inheritance with Christ and would live with him in eternity. But that I should believe this of myself or you of yourself, that is lacking because we do not see it in ourselves. We do not feel it. We do not experience it. In our thinking, St. Paul and St. Peter are lords and sovereigns over heaven and earth. But whether I, too, am a lord and sovereign, that I do not know. But what does it mean to believe? If I do not believe it of myself, that I have become a lord and sovereign over heaven and earth because of Christ, then certainly I cannot believe the same of Peter and Paul. Again, if I do not believe that through Christ I have gained the heavenly inheritance, then I do not believe that Christ became man for me and that I have been baptized into Christ.

14. That is why the Evangelist Luke spoke so highly of the faith of the father and mother. For where there is righteous faith the fruit

follows, that we marvel at and are happy about the great grace and blessing which is ours through this little child. But where this fruit is not present and the heart does not marvel nor is joyous, there either is no faith, or the faith is not as firm as it ought to be. For if such faith is present, which trusts with certainty that we poor sinners have been translated into eternal life and righteousness, a person ought to feel at least a small spark that lifts up one's heart with joy and affords courage against despair, trouble, and persecution. One will then be defiant and say to both the devil and the world, Why should I be dismayed, however much sin, death, devil, world, pope, or emperor rage against and vex me? If the pope or emperor take my life, theirs is a far greater loss than mine. They may take the husk and peeling, but the kernel and treasure remains, that I have been made free from sin through Christ and have been rescued from eternal death and God's wrath. This they cannot take from me. If only this little child remains, the rest may go. For a Christian does not focus on this temporal and transient life as does the world, but rather on the future eternal life.

15. Consequently, we should marvel at what we hear of Christ, and be comforted and undaunted. That we are still frightened and have fear is a sign that we do not believe firmly enough that through Christ eternal life and heaven have been gained for us and have been given us as a gift. Accordingly, let him who knows this hold on to it, and he who doesn't must learn it. There will be some who marvel at and are happy about the unspeakable good which Christ has gained for us and given to us. For them this sermon is an unending feast of which they never tire; as St. Peter says, the angels rejoice as they observe them. But a disgruntled, lazy soul is not at all concerned, but chases after carnal comforts. When he has his god Mammon—wine, bread, food and drink, he thinks he has everything he needs.

Now we want to consider the prophecy of Simeon.

AND SIMEON BLESSED THEM, AND SAID UNTO MARY HIS MOTHER, BEHOLD THIS CHILD IS SET FOR THE FALL AND RISING AGAIN OF MANY IN ISRAEL.

16. This is an unusual blessing. The aged Simeon has just said that this child would be a singular, mighty man, a Saviour who would provide for the welfare of all Christendom, and a light that

would radiate salvation for the Gentiles. As Joseph and Mary marvelled over these words, he added further that this child would be the occasion for the fall and rising of many in Israel. Thus many, not only among the Gentiles, but also from the nation of Israel, would be offended and vexed because of the Lord Jesus when they encounter him and stumble, while on the other hand, many would be greatly blessed, lifted up, and saved because of him. This, then, is the singular significance of this little child, our dear Lord Jesus Christ, over against the world and its relationship to him, that many will encounter him and be offended, while, on the other hand, many will cling to him and be saved.

17. Therefore, whoever would be a Christian must govern himself accordingly. For no one can compel another to believe. God has delegated force to princes, magistrates, and hangmen who must constrain and compel in their exercise of governing and restraining all who refuse to keep from stealing, murdering, lying, deceiving, and other forms of vice. But here in Christ's kingdom this is not the mode of operation. If you are willing to believe, good; if not, so be it; no one will drag you in and force you. In due time another will come, against whose compulsion you will not be able to stand.

18. Yes, you say, since I still have a period of grace, I'll worry about that later. Very well, this is the bottom line: If you wish to be a Christian and be saved, it is imperative that you receive this King who, as Simeon here says, is a controversial King with whom a very large number, both Gentile and Jew, will be offended. But this is no excuse for doubting; there will always be some who accept him, to whom he is not an offense, but rather a means to salvation.

19. This is a very noteworthy lesson, that we consider Christ not only as a stumbling block to the Jews and foolishness to the Greeks (1 Cor. 1:23), but also as the salvation of many in Israel. We must not be troubled by the fact that the vast majority find Christ a stumbling block and treat his gospel shamefully, as we see now at the hands of peasants and burghers who confidently do whatever they please as regards Christ the Lord. It will never be any different in the world, where this King is present with his Word and kingdom; the majority will disdain and reject him. We will have to live with this, while we meanwhile persist in being Christians and are also content to be a part

of that small group which does not stumble, but firmly holds to and stands up for this King. And should it be that many people stumble and fall, we must not be deterred; everything is just as Simeon said.

20. It is a troubling picture in this first part of our text, as Simeon says that the child Jesus is destined for the fall of many in Israel. The pope, and all who are high and mighty in the world, slander our gospel terribly, denounce it as heresy, and oppose it with might, not because they stumble over it—for they know very well that it is the truth—but rather because they rant and rave out of malice and wanton pride, in order to maintain their rank and eminence. They don't ask about Christ and his Word, for their belly is their god. That's why we will not count them among that group that takes offense.

21. Those, therefore, are meant here who in ignorance fight against the gospel, that is, they take offense and resist when they hear that this little child is the sole Saviour and Light of the World. For they simply can't conceive that our works and all that a man does to the glory and honor of God should count for nothing. Well, they say, should all those be damned who for these hundreds of years lived by the old teaching and belief? Do you mean to say that God would permit the church to be in error for so long a time? That is the chief stumbling block of which Simeon here speaks.

22. When that's the situation, you can say that matters are going exactly as foretold. For it is written that this child born of the Virgin Mary who was to be the Saviour of the whole world and a light to the Gentiles was destined for the fall, not of those who know nothing of God, but rather "many in Israel," God's people who have his Word. This child, on the contrary, has been placed as a stone of stumbling for the wise of the world, the intellectuals, and the self-righteous, who will trample, tumble, fall, and break their necks over this child. They simply can't bear to have their wisdom, their righteousness, and their piety count for nothing. If a person is unwilling to accept this child, Jesus, we must simply close our eyes and ears and proceed as though we did not see him fall. For this child's significance will be that his gospel shall be defamed as heresy; this is one of his trademarks, that many will stumble and take offense because of him.

23. It was the same story for the Jews; they were offended by the manner of Christ's preaching when he said in John 8:24, 31–32: "Ye

shall die in your sins; for if ye believe not that I am he, ye shall die in your sins." And again: "If ye continue in my word, then are ye my disciples indeed; and ye shall know the truth and the truth shall make you free." In other words, If you wish to live, you must find life in me and through me. They thought, What is the fool saying? Don't we have the prophets and Moses? We certainly know what is right and what God demands of us, and is this journeyman of a fool going to punish us who have all these elaborate ceremonies and usages which God himself ordained? His preaching and teaching are nothing but base heresy! And so they went their way, knocked their heads against Christ, and fell.

24. The Carthusians and monks today are still the same (I speak of the best of them, for the majority are belly-servers); they disdain our teaching as devil's lies and heresy. They say, I spent thirty years in my order praying, fasting, and making things miserable for myself, and will these Lutheran heretics now say this all amounts to nothing? Very well, if fasting and prayer do not please God, we will pursue after gluttony, drink, and lechery, and seek to please God with our mischief and, thus, enter into heaven. These, too, find the child Jesus to be repulsive, and as a result they stumble, never again to rise.

25. If you wish to be a Christian, know for a certainty that your Lord Jesus Christ, you, your teaching, and all your activity will not be pleasing to the world. For here you hear that the Lord Jesus Christ himself is a stone of contention and a hateful stumbling block for those chosen people of God, and for all those who consider themselves great, mighty, intelligent, and righteous. They find Christ's teaching offensive, then stumble and fall over it. If you wish to be considered a fool, a heretic, and a deceiver by them and their adherents, then accept this Lord and King and be a Christian; if not, if you become lazy and go to the devil, the world will praise and honor you. Therefore, whoever wishes to be a Christian and inherit eternal life must, along with his Lord Jesus Christ, be considered an offense and a pitfall by others, a child of the devil, a heretic, a deceiver, and a fool. That is the first picture.

26. The second part, however, is a beautiful comforting word spoken by Simeon: Jesus has not only been set for the fall but also the rising of many in Israel. These are the ones who accept this King, cling

to him and, if the need arises, give body and life for his sake. They renounce their earthly ways, their own wisdom, their power, their righteousness, and holiness. For they acknowledge that by their own wisdom, work, and merit they cannot help themselves. If they are to be helped, it is only through him of whom it is written that he is the world's Saviour and light. Therefore, to them Christ is the longed for champion to whom they cling, through whom they are saved.

27. So this little child presents two pictures: one of offense; another of beautiful comfort. For some he is a pitfall, as though he were a snag lying on the path over which they trip; but for others a sturdy rock against which to lean and lift oneself up. The proud, the bigwigs, the high brows, and the self-righteous butt against him with their heads, fall back, slander, and curse him. But so-called fools and poor sinners stand by him and believe on him. What lies humbly (before him), stands tall; what vaunts (proudly), falls because of him; what is lost and condemned, through him is saved; what is foolish, becomes wise; what is sinful, becomes righteous and holy. Let us, therefore, learn to be comforted, for that is the significance of this child.

28. For many years I have pounded away at this block with diligence, thought about the matter, how I might preach about the Lord Jesus Christ to please everyone, so that neither pope, nor emperor, nor princes, nor anyone else could be offended at or angered with him. But it can't be done. Therefore, we will just have to live with it and learn how to respond to the papalists who claim there was no heresy or disunity until the time this teaching surfaced; then trouble began and little, if any, good has come about through this teaching. The way to counter such wiseacres and slanderers is with this Gospel and Simeon's prophecy; for the fact is that where the pure teaching of Christ is present, there the result invariably is that some trip over it; or cults, sects, and all manner of misfortune come about. But by the same token, this teaching will bear fruit; some will cling to Christ and because of him will be lifted up. These, as said above, are the poor in spirit, those with a troubled conscience, and they will be saved and comforted through him.

29. The wiseacres and the slanderers are unconcerned; they consider only the stumbling and the offense, which is not a pretty picture; but it cannot be helped, for the fault lies not with the

teaching—it is pure, right, and good—but with the people who will not receive or follow it. Therefore, consider the matter rightly and acknowledge that it was far better that under the papacy, stumbling and offense should occur, even as is true now, rather than that all be quiet and the devil hold sway everywhere with idolatry and false teaching, driving everyone into hell pell-mell. For who would not rather suffer a temporary hurt than an eternal one? Yes, it was an unspeakable and eternal shame that under the papacy, a genuine gospel sermon was nowhere to be found, nor right knowledge of God, nor true worship of God.

30. For many years, it was common experience at many gatherings that preaching was done to please everyone and cause offense to nobody. But the fact is, if you remove the offense and the obstacle, then Christ is lost. For right from the beginning when this man came into the world to show himself, there was opposition and taking of offense. Yes, say the pope, the bishops, the wise, and the mighty of this world, we will not tolerate this. Very well, are you angry? Then suppress it. Christ came to the Jews. He did not ask them beforehand whether or not he should come. This started such a stir in their land that they could not suppress it. Now he has come to us through his gospel, without our knowledge or will, and has also started a great uproar. Are you angered? Then oppose it. Are you wise? Then speak your mind. There are many who want to resolve the matter by human wisdom, but that remains to be seen. If they're going to resolve this, bring an end to division and offense, achieve tranquility and unity, as they suppose, then I will scratch this text. Christ himself says in Matthew 10:34, "Think not that I am come to send peace on earth: I came not to send peace, but a sword." Therefore, it will likely be and remain, as Simeon states, "This child is set for the fall and rising again of many in Israel." On the other hand, many will rise because of him and be saved. Those who try to resolve this matter through human wisdom will accomplish nothing; rather, they will fall, never to rise, and be smashed because of it. For they try to make Christ different from what God ordered and ordained.

31. So, when disunity and other trouble result, it is not the fault of the teaching, but rather of the people who misuse it and of the would-be-wise who want to master and remake Christ. If a boulder

or stump is placed along the way to lean against in time of need, is it the fault of the rock or stump that many people are so foolish as not to brace themselves on the rock or stump, but rather bump their heads running against it? That is not the fault of the rock, but of the foolish, blind people who do not proceed discreetly. So what damage does it do to the cornerstone, Christ, and his gospel that the great majority are offended by him, fall and are thoroughly shattered? He has been ordained and set in place by God, as it is written in Isaiah 28:16, that they who believe on him will never be dismayed.

32. Therefore, let us not look on this Gospel as a teaching that only produces dispute, disunity, and trouble in the world. That's how the pope and his bishops complain, as though they were above reproach and had never muddied the waters. They have caused all manner of strife and misery through their sins and idol worship. If they would permit this teaching to have free course, then disunity and other troubles would soon be left behind. But since the great majority want to impede this teaching and are unwilling to let go of their own interpretation—some even stumble over their own wisdom and refuse to allow Christ to be a stumbling block—they preach about him in such a way that none could take offense. Is it any wonder then that God does not direct the course of events to suit their designs?

33. This, then, is the lesson of today's Gospel. We should especially note what Simeon prophesies of Christ, namely that many in Israel will be offended by him; but also, many will be benefited and rise because of him. Not only should we not be offended by his teaching, but we must gird ourselves against the murderous outcry which blames this dear Gospel for all the turmoil in the world. To this end may God grant us his grace through Christ our Saviour. Amen.

FIRST SUNDAY AFTER CHRISTMAS

*Second Sermon**

Luke 2:33–40

1. This Gospel opens on a happy note as aged, pious, God-fearing Simeon joyously expressed the wish that he might die. As Luke states, he is filled with a keenly perceptive spirit as he holds the child in his arms and acknowledges him not only as his own personal Saviour, but also as the Saviour of the entire world and a light to the Gentiles. This recognition fills him with such joy that he is willing to depart this life, stating, "Lord, now lettest thou thy servant depart in peace." In other words, Lord, I am now happy to die. That is certainly a tremendous mood change for this man, that death is now dearer than life. He considers his death and departure from this world a journey into peace and blessed days. Such a spirit is not of human origin, but the work of the Holy Spirit.

2. The beginning of this blessing is joyous, but note how disconsolate is the ending. Simeon is happy and wishes no longer to live, not even a moment. He knows that his blessedness begins the moment he dies. But he speaks a strange blessing over the child and to the mother, Mary, when he says: "Behold this child is set for the fall and rising again of many in Israel . . . "Yea, a sword shall pierce through thy own soul also." Would you call that a comforting blessing? For Simeon all is well, for he can say, In peace and joy I depart. But for the mother and child, he leaves a taste of life's bitterness: The child is destined to be a stumbling block to many in Israel, the focal point of contention, and a sword would pierce the mother's soul.

3. This blessing was not meant to pertain only to the child, Jesus, and his mother, Mary. It was written also for our instruction that we thereby might understand what the world is like, as Simeon himself said, "that the thoughts of many hearts may be revealed." In other words, the reason that the child was set for the rise and fall of many

* Preached at the parish church, 1535.

in Israel and that a sword would pierce the mother's heart, was to lay bare the thoughts of people's hearts which otherwise would have remained concealed.

4. Through the gospel the world's great maliciousness was revealed, evil that neither I nor even any apostle believed could possibly exist; but by the gospel's coming it was exposed to the light of day. Before this, before the gospel's advent, there were many eminent, upstanding people under the papacy. They conducted themselves honorably and piously, people of exemplary goodwill. One would swear they were pious, trustworthy individuals. The world at its best focuses on people's skill, wisdom, education, and honored station. These are exemplary, smart, honorable, pious, intellectual people as long as the gospel does not expose them. For such people, however, under the light of the gospel, as Simeon said, the Christ child is set for a fall.

5. Accordingly, in the spiritual realm, the devil first of all disguises himself as an angel of light. He initiates so much beautiful pretense, such sanctimonious orders and spectacular rituals that the whole world is mesmerized. Onlookers eat up the pageantry and feigned devotion, acknowledging that those are, indeed, beautiful worship services, most devout, God-fearing people, and exemplary, humble fathers. As a result, common sense was totally captivated by such beautiful pageantry judged either by worldly or spiritual standards, so that if it had not been exposed, the devil had a field day midst beautiful pageantry most glorious and holy. Solomon sums it up in Ecclesiastes 8:14, "There is a vanity which is done upon the earth; that there be just men unto whom it happeneth according to the work of the wicked; again, there be wicked men to whom it happeneth according to the work of the righteous; I said that this also is vanity." In other words, the godless carry on in a godless manner and lifestyle; yet their name and reputation in the world is splendiferous, and they even enjoy the world's gratitude and praise as though they were the best and most God-fearing people on earth. Reason, seemingly, cannot judge otherwise.

6. But once the gospel of the child Jesus takes effect, then those whom the world deemed holy become the greatest sinners; the wise, greatest fools; the sages, foremost dunces; and the quiet, gentle hearts, the bloodiest murderers. The gospel has no more vicious en-

emies than individuals the world deems eminent, sensible, wise, virtuous, and God-fearing, be they man or woman, peasant or urbanite, nobleman or commoner. Indeed, the more endowed with these virtues, the greater and more hostile enemies of the gospel they become. It's the same story among the "religious": the more a monk is steeped in rules and orders, the more fanatical about prayers and fasting, rules and orders, the more antagonistic and inimical towards the gospel does his way of life become.

7. As Solomon says, the world operates in both spheres, the religious and the secular realm, though the latter gets the greater honor. In the secular realm conceit goes hand in glove with virtue and noble, while in the religious there is a multiplying of religious exercises, prayer, fasting, and the like, suggesting that both are perceived to be little short of angelic and beloved of God, the religious because of their great sanctity, the worldly because of their great wisdom and virtue. Who would believe that under such pretense lies hidden a poisonous heart? In the whole wide world there is no rule book nor skill to fathom or judge this hypocrisy except Simeon's sermon about the Christ and the holy gospel. This exposes the poisonous ulcer so that everyone can see the evil and dangerous poison lying below the surface. Once the gospel sounds forth into the world, however, it antagonizes these same fine, pious people. These beautiful "saints" are exposed before the world for what they are, nothing more finally than conceited murderers, liars, and venomous, evil knaves.

8. The world has many a fine prince, well-endowed with intelligence, wisdom, and common sense, who leads an honorable life, sincerely wishes to be a role model for his people, is not greedy, nor a rounder, but a man who sincerely tries to be on top of things in the interest of justice, and is a chaste, faithful husband. In truth, were we to choose an individual to govern in public office we would elect such a person, a man whom we could really trust and praise as being a wise, pious, God-fearing prince, especially when compared with the sanctimonious pretense of the papistry, with its prayers, fastings, devotions, endowed altars, chapels, churches, and elaborate liturgies, all so diligently pursued to the amazed awe of the people. But when the gospel takes hold, you find that it's all nothing but blatant hypocrisy on the part of such "pious" lords, as proved by their deeds. They

are heinous murderers who have shed much innocent blood, engaged in shameful practices and, as they stumble over the gospel, fall into one sin after another, trying in every which way to obstruct and hinder the gospel. We are compelled to say, Who would ever have believed that such a great sinner could be hiding under such a fine pious life? Only the holy gospel exposes such filth and antipathy; the poison comes to light.

9. No one would even have expected to find such godlessness among respected people of the nobility and general populace, such despising of God, such persecution of God's Word. It is only the gospel of Christ which brings this to light. It is when the gospel is proclaimed for all to hear that it becomes evident and people in surprise come to say, Truly, I never would have believed that such devilish murderous poison could be found in such pious, wise, God-fearing people; I would have supposed that anyone who accepted the gospel and posed under the name Christian would be spiritual and God-fearing. Now, however, we find that the gospel has no more vehement, furious enemies than the pope with his cardinals, bishops, academies, doctors, monks, priests—the ones that could be expected to promote the gospel with all diligence.

10. Simeon indicated this to Mary, that the child whose mother she was would cause great hubbub in the world by exposing all of those who pose and parade as living saints. Then people's innermost thoughts would be laid bare and exposed. They would say, That man who appears so pious to the world and who, because of his intelligence, virtue, piety, and devoutness, was given rule over the world and the keys to the gates of heaven, harbors within him a spirit of hostility, in reality, vengeance, hatred, terrible blasphemy, disdain for God's word, idolatry, murder, and evils beyond telling. He cannot bear to hear or defend God's Word and the truth, but fosters idolatry, strangles the people with it, smothers the gospel, and, if he could but extinguish the gospel, would even drown the land and its people in blood. This little child will expose all this evil that dwells in people's hearts to the light of day, Simeon states.

11. I would never have believed that by the precious gospel's advent so much evil of the world would have been revealed; indeed, I assumed that everyone would leap for joy when they heard that they

had been released from popedom's abomination, oppressive burdening, and constraint of conscience, and that now by grace through Christ they possessed treasures for which they formerly struggled at untold cost, effort, and work. I especially thought the bishops and universities would accept this wholeheartedly. But what happened? Because of such preaching they trample over us, and none are more hostile than the spiritual leaders and the universities. If I had known this before I started to preach and write, I would not have opened my mouth or lifted a pen but would have said, Dear sirs, if you can't stand the truth, go to the devil, whose you are. But God did well in that he did not let me know this ahead of time. In his secret counsel, he purposed for me to continue to preach and remain under the assumption that they were pious, devout, God-fearing people, until the time was right to reveal the way their inmost thoughts really were.

12. Through the gospel we rightly learn to know the devil and his cohorts, namely that he is an enemy of God, and so also the world, even where it appears to be most devout and pious. I never would have believed this before, nor that such great despising of God's Word could be found in the heart of any man. Now that the gospel has come, the hearts of men are exposed to show how they despise God's Word and the preachers of God's Word, and how these beautiful "angels" are really nothing but devils. I now see that pope, bishops, princes, nobles, burghers, and peasants are fully of the devil, because not only will they not accept the saving teaching, but also purposefully despise and persecute it. Before the revelation of the gospel, I did not perceive this devilish malice in people, but rather thought them filled with the Holy Spirit. But with his Word, Christ reveals the thoughts of many hearts so that we become aware of what is really in them, namely, that even well thought of, eminent, sensible, honorable people are under the devil's power and that they harbor the worst possible rage and poisonous fury against the gospel and its servants.

13. Why has God made this known? For our instruction, but also for our comfort; for our instruction, so that we don't become frightened when we see that such eminent, wise, excellent, honorable, pious people can be such devils, causing us to say in astonishment, How is it that such an eminent prince, such an honorable citizen,

such a devout spouse can be so blind and harbor such ill will that he or she cannot abide God's Word and becomes a foe of God? The gospel here explains the reason why. Before this the thoughts of the heart were hidden, but now the revealer of hearts and minds, as he is called, has come. He cuts to the quick, so that people's thoughts, things which neither they nor others had previously been aware of, are now in the open, brought to light and exposed, so that one can now say, Once a gentle, friendly man, but now a devil in reality.

14. It is true that the gentle, pious man whom we considered to be so God-fearing was actually in his heart an evil devil; but he was so beautifully camouflaged that his heart and thoughts were not revealed. Now, though, when the gospel spotlights his thoughts, it becomes apparent they have always been vain lies, deception, and murder.

15. Everything about the world from the noblest lord to the most humble servant, is tainted with fraud; the more sensible, the more honorable, the more pious, the more God-fearing these people appear, the greater and more shameful is the hypocrisy. The world doesn't see or understand this. But when the child Jesus comes with his gospel, he reveals that they are filled with poison and blasphemy. Most likely it has always been like this. They appear to be very devout, ornamented with virtue, reputation, and justice, but it's a covering and shield from what's underneath in their guts. But by the gospel, our Lord God opened a window, as Simeon says, for all to see, and now they no longer can hide what's underneath.

16. But such revelation also serves to comfort hearts. Although the world will not abide or tolerate God's Word, and yet wears its hypocritical mask, we are not to be deceived, but straightway conclude that all their good behavior, holy semblance, wisdom, and righteousness are nothing more than hypocrisy, patent sin, and damnation before God. The godless of this world expect to gain heaven the way St. Paul speaks of the Pharisees (Acts 26:5). They were the strictest of sects, assiduously pursuing their code of rules day and night for the sake of the promised eternal life, compelled by this hope of being eternally saved. Our monks and hypocrites do the same today, believing that through fasting, prayer, and the like, they will be saved. Whoever sees this, not knowing and understanding the prophecy of Simeon, perceives them to be holy people and thinks

thus, If anyone is going to be saved, these people certainly will, for look at their great piety.

17. Simeon comforts and warns us with the words, Beware of the hypocrites and be of good cheer. No matter how much they fast, pray, or castigate themselves, the devil is still hidden underneath. He drives them, so that even though for a time they conceal their animosity, finally they break out, blaspheme God, storm against his Word, trample his servants underfoot, steal, rob, and so on. In short, they are steeped in the most venal sins and the greatest malice. For that reason everything they do, no matter how much it glitters and shines, is false and nothing but the devil's hypocrisy.

18. How does this differ from the stealing and robbing that go on today, as tyrants and hypocrites strip away homes and property, and even the lives, of many poor people who cling to the preaching of the gospel and the Sacrament of the Body and Blood of Christ? Of course, they reply, We are not doing it for ourselves but for the sake of God and in the church's name. No matter how you cut it, the fact is that it's nothing more than stealing and robbing the poor of their lives and goods. And yet these hypocrites who rob the poor don't want to be classed as scoundrels, thieves, and robbers, but as commendable princes, honorable nobility, honest citizens, and pious, upright people. Nevertheless, under the skin they are scoundrels, thieves, and robbers. Now then, in the words of this text that's how it would be, and just so it is also happening today. Before the gospel shed its light, they did not act like this; they insulted no one, persecuted no one, robbed no one, shed no one's blood, but were pious, virtuous, holy people. But now that the gospel has come, it has exposed the flaws and contradictions of these same pious, God-fearing people as they now have begun to rage, persecute, rob, and murder. Still they do not want to be known as murderers, robbers, and knaves, but as God-fearing, praiseworthy, honorable, upright princes, nobility, and citizens.

19. Such exposé of men's hearts is for our comfort that we may know that everything that is not of Christ and Christ-centered is false and hypocrisy. It makes no difference if it is a Carthusian monk, or respected, honorable, virtuous princes or nobles, men or women. How does it help that a Carthusian monk endures rigorous disci-

pline, or that a nobleman or citizen is pious, gives many alms, or that a young woman is virtuous when under that guise they mock and persecute God by opposing and refusing to tolerate the gospel? What good does it do if a prince lavishes gifts on the monks in the monastery, builds and endows churches, chapels, and altars, and yet remains God's enemy and a murderer of Christ? What does it help that they expect to go to heaven and yet slander God, murder, and transgress all of God's commandments?

20. As has been said, it took the gospel to expose these sins and malice. It took the gospel to pinpoint the pure hate, envy, and persecution of God and his Word. Previously these thoughts were in people's minds, but they managed to conceal them. Their hearts were lecherous, murderous, and blood-thirsty, but this was hidden. But now it breaks out and they commit the crimes previously lurking there. Yet they say they are not thieves, robbers, or murderers, but pious people who would do no one any harm. All of this revolves around the child Jesus, given by God in order to expose the evil and contradiction. We have to come to understand this for it has been prophesied by Simeon that thus it would be. For that reason we must learn from this and be assured that we can ignore all pretense and say, Everything in the world which is not of Christ, no matter how noble, how excellent, even if it shines like an angel and is designated to be holy—honorable life, virtue, discipline, honor, and so on—nevertheless, it is nothing more than cover-up for shame beneath and is the greatest malice, yes, even the devil himself lying hidden underneath.

21. In itself, it is not bad that the world has wisdom, discipline, honor, and an upright way of life. But if one wants to offer this for God's notice, then it is nothing more than sham cover-up for the most heinous sins of blasphemy against God and persecution of his Word. It is not evil to be sensible, wise, and virtuous; for these are precious jewels given by God. But it is the devil's work that turns these noble gifts of God—lovely virtue, reputation, and upright way of life—into sham cover-ups for malice while God, meanwhile, is blasphemed and his Word persecuted.

22. A virtuous maiden is a precious crown jewel. But if this same chaste maiden were to venture forth to murder her father and moth-

er, her virtue and modesty would only be a veneer for a wicked woman, a murderess of father and mother. So also these people appear devout and God-fearing, but under the camouflage they are wicked beyond all measure. Nothing on earth can expose and bring to light such malice except the gospel of the child Jesus. As Simeon here says, Oh Mary, your son will show the whole world, the best and most upstanding people whom now we regard for their wisdom and piety to be nothing more than rogues, rascals, and murderers. Through the preaching of the gospel, he will prick these individuals so that they burst and prove themselves to be archenemies of God and all true Christians. We are compelled to say, Shame on you, kitten; you have such smooth fur but such sharp claws. You act like all cats; up front you lick, behind you scratch.

23. Therefore, we should be warned that these thieves, robbers, and murderers—when the world's at its best and holiest, the devil himself is present—are far more wicked than ordinary murderers and wicked people. It's a heinous, terrible thing when a murderer kills someone on the street, but it is nothing compared with that of the pope, bishops, princes, and the like, when they become murderers because of the gospel. They employ all kinds of machinations and tyranny to stamp out the gospel, and the whole world, countries, cities, and so on are affected. When a thief embezzles three hundred guilder, that is a great theft. But what is that when compared with the theft of a big thief who, because of the gospel, drives the poor away from wives, children, homes, and property, all the while being regarded as "most reverend father," "esteemed prince," "pious gentleman." The heathen author, Cato, said it well, "Big thieves hang little thieves." Such thieves and murderers maintain the camouflage of sanctity until Christ, through his gospel, exposes and shows them to be enemies of God and murderers of Christians. Before God, all people who are not Christians are nothing more than blasphemers of God, murderers, thieves, and knaves. It doesn't matter that in the world's estimation they are the most devout, the most gentle, the most virtuous, and the holiest of people.

24. These people do not like being labeled thus. But we are not labeling them according to worldly standards, but by God's standards. They cannot excuse themselves before God, but must accept

his judgment. The gospel reveals their malice and testifies that everything of this world is contrary to God and man. When an individual inwardly is a rogue towards God, opposing his words and works, you can count on it that he will soon show openly that he is also a rogue towards mankind. If there is murder in the heart, the tongue and fist will soon get involved, given time and opportunity. If the fist hasn't murdered, it is not by failure of will, but because the time wasn't right or opportune.

25. That's the way the world dealt with the holy prophets, apostles, martyrs, yes, also Christ himself. For the world never lets up, because it is evil by nature. For that reason we have to be aware of the fact that the world is filled with rogues, enemies of God, thieves, murderers, yes, the devil himself. That is how Simeon described them: filled with deceit, blasphemy, enmity, hatred, envious, and cruel, seeking only their own advantage. That is the way of the world, and when the time is right and they have the opportunity, these individuals break out and show people what's really inside them. So when you hear or see something reputedly valorous or great in the world, ask yourself, Is Christ there? Then very well; but if Christ is not there, then surely it is the devil. No matter what the garb—cap, robe, fine or coarse, ornate or bemedaled. Before the world it may look like piety or sanctity, but if Christ is not there, it is only an abomination before God.

26. Simeon adds, "Yes, a sword shall pierce through thine own soul also." This he addresses to the mother, Mary. Simeon has a special word for her because she will see and experience all that he has prophesied. It is not physical ill that mother Mary will have to bear, but rather what St. Peter says of Lot (2 Pet. 2:7–8): "[God] delivered just Lot, vexed with the filthy conversation of the wicked: For that righteous man dwelling among them, in seeing and hearing, vexed his righteous soul from day to day with their unlawful deeds." That was the sword that would pierce Mary's heart. Her heart would be saddened because throughout her life she would see, hear, and experience the malice of the Jews (God's chosen people) against Jesus the Saviour of the world. Before Christ began his ministry they were seemingly pious people and God-fearing fathers, especially the Pharisees, scribes, and high priests. But as soon as Christ stepped forth

with his preaching, the thoughts of their hearts were revealed. Underneath their fine pious exteriors, they were the greatest rogues and villains who denied and rejected their Saviour and King, the very Son of God, and nailed him to the cross. This pierced the heart and soul of Mary, making her heartsick to have to see and endure all this.

27. All Christendom and Christians in every generation share this experience with Mary whenever the gospel radiates its light. The world is a wicked, vicious imposter, appearing pious and good, but under the camouflage and cover-up of piety, it traffics in murder, thievery, and every kind of malice, which only come to light through the gospel. This grieves our Holy God and Christian people. It is pain and anguish to have to see such evil in the world. The sword does not penetrate Mary's hands or feet, nor rip her body; rather it pierces her soul. Heartache exceeds any sorrow, and the sorrow of the soul is greater than any other. When the foot hurts, it does not mean that the hand hurts too, but since the hand is a member of the same body it will feel sympathy. But when the soul sorrows and the heart is sad, the whole body suffers, along with every member of the body. That is why Simeon says a sword will pierce the mother's soul and why St. Peter says that righteous Lot's suffering was so great that his heart was distressed day and night.

28. It is so that the world in general brings sorrow to mother Mary, that is, to the holy Christian church. It is, of course, regrettable that the world continues thus to cause Christians great distress. Surely it is a sign that portends God's great wrath which will soon be kindled. The world, however, does not desist, but continues to provoke heartfelt sighs on the part of devout Christians. St. Paul states in Ephesians 4:30, "And grieve not the Holy Spirit of God, whereby ye are sealed unto the day of redemption." It is a tender, happy situation, he says, as regards the Holy Spirit's pledge that affirms unto us eternal life. Therefore, take care that you do not grieve him. How does that happen? When is the Holy Spirit grieved? He is grieved when pious Christian hearts must sorrowfully observe heart-wrenching wrongs. When that happens, it must certainly portend a large measure of God's wrath. Things will never be any different in the world. A sword will pierce the souls of Christians; they will be tormented, crucified, tortured, driven to fear and suffering. They

preach, sing, speak, admonish, discipline, pray, plead, implore, and do what they can, but nothing changes; their suffering continues to rend their hearts deeply. Be assured, however, the world will suffer a terrible judgment. Mother Mary and the Christian church deserve better and ought to be left in peace, that a sword would not pierce their hearts; but that will not happen, as Simeon foretold, for many a pious Lot will ineluctably have to endure suffering, and so the Christian church likewise. Nonetheless, to its dismay the world found out that the intended hurt was changed to good.

29. I have often said and say it again, that the princes, as well as peasants and average citizens, do wrong when they cause their pastors, preachers, and other devout Christians deep hurt and pain of heart. It is never good to grieve the Holy Spirit and press anguished sighs from Christian hearts. Experience proves that nothing good will come of this. The Epistle to the Hebrews (13:17) states, "Obey them that have the rule over you, and submit yourselves: for they watch for your souls, as they that must give account, that they may do it with joy, and not with grief: for that is unprofitable for you." The example of Lot is a powerful reminder. The Sodomites plagued him, sending a sword through his heart. But what happened? As soon as Lot had left Sodom, fire and brimstone rained on Sodom to sink it deep into the earth. And what of our Sodom, what shall I say? It not only does wrong, and sins knowingly and outrageously against God's commandments, but also grieves the Holy Spirit, forcing a sword through the heart of mother Mary, that is, our dear Christendom. God will not forever remain silent about this.

30. This Gospel lesson, then, has treated two topics which we ought to note well. The first, whatever is not of Christ must be of the devil, no matter how well it is camouflaged with a covering of godliness. The second, people should take care not to grieve the Holy Spirit causing mother Mary to have a sword pierce her heart, that is, causing devout Christians to be troubled by what they do. That it will happen, that a sword will pierce the heart of the mother, Simeon foretold. But blessed are those who are not guilty of that; on the other hand, damned are those by whom that evil comes. So much on this lesson for the time being.

NEW YEAR'S DAY

*First Sermon**

Luke 2:21

And when eight days were accomplished for the circumcising of the child, his name was called JESUS, which was so named of the angel before he was conceived in the womb.

OF THE CIRCUMCISION OF JESUS

1. This is a short Gospel lesson, and we'll make a short "sermon" out of it. We call this day New Year's Day—in the old Roman fashion. As Christians, we actually start our New Year on Christmas Day, as indicated by the way we count years, that is, in the year after Christ's birth, and so on. The Romans began the year on the first day of January, and that's the custom we Germans have followed. After all, we trace back to the Roman Empire, from which we have inherited a lot of other things also. For example: our whole justice system, a large part of the papacy, our time system, or the names of our weekdays: Sunday, Monday, Tuesday, and so on. Now, however, we are not concerned with New Year's Day in the Roman sense, nor with any other traditions from that time.

2. Since New Year's Day has been set aside to celebrate our Lord's circumcision, it's entirely proper that we preach about that today. There are two circumcisions: the old circumcision of the Jews and the new circumcision of our Lord Jesus Christ, quite different from each other. Even though both involved a physical circumcision of the flesh, there's nevertheless a world of difference between Christ's circumcision and the Jewish circumcision, the reason being that the persons involved are very unlike and different. The one circumcised on this day excels all the others. Those circumcised under

*Preached in the morning at the parish church, 1531.

Judaism are of this earth, but the person circumcised today shines like heaven itself, yes, rules over all the heavens!

3. As far as the Jewish circumcision is concerned, it goes back to Genesis 17:9–14, and was to remain in effect up to the time of the child whose circumcision we celebrate today. It began with Abraham, to whom God gave the command that he and his entire household should be circumcised; male children of Abraham's seed, born in the future, were all to be circumcised on the eighth day after birth. According to God's covenant with Abraham every male bearing the sign of circumcision in his body, belonged to God's own community; he wanted to be their God and accept them as his people.

4. Now it's not without special reason that God ordered as he did, namely that not only Abraham and his blood relatives were to be circumcised, but also all of his domestic servants, whether Abraham's seed or Gentiles. This was to forestall any boasting on the part of the Jews that they alone were God's people and they alone had the promise to Abraham. Just as soon as the covenant was established, it included also Abraham's servants, native born as well as those purchased from foreigners; even though Gentile, these also were to be recognized as God's host and as belonging to his children, along with Abraham's blood relatives and legitimate heirs. In fact, these were part of God's people even before Isaac was born—the designated heir of the promise. As soon as the covenant was in effect, Ishmael, born of the maid, was circumcised, together with purchased servants and their children. Isaac, Abraham's designated heir, arrived some thirteen years later, all of which was to remind the Jews not to think of themselves too highly.

5. Of this old circumcision, nothing remains today except the historical fact—and the examples of faith involved. Other events, too, have come and gone and yet survive as faith models. We surely don't want to repeat some of the same deeds which circumcised Jews have done, but we certainly do want to learn the obedience of faith which Abraham displayed. Circumcision ended when the Saviour, Christ the Lord, was born as the angel announced to the shepherds. Had Christ not come, we would still be under circumcision today; we would have no reason for boasting that we are God's people. His command is clear: "Whoever is not circumcised, shall be cut off from

my people!" Christ has abolished this ordinance and instead commands that we believe and be baptized, if we truly want to be God's children and be eternally saved.

6. One lesson we can learn from the old circumcision is this: when God wants to help his people, he sometimes does it in ways that are nothing less than ridiculous as far as human judgment is concerned! Here God established a covenant with a requirement so silly that it's hard to imagine anything more ridiculous! For arrogant Gentiles what could be more laughable than that God—the eternal wisdom!—would order an eight-day-old child and the ninety-nine-year-old Abraham to be circumcised—together with all others in the future who might wish to adopt the Jewish faith? This became so offensive to the Gentiles that they responded with all sorts of spiteful and scoffing nicknames for the Jews!

7. But at the same time, here we also have an example of how God makes the world look foolish! What God proposes does not please the world, and what the world undertakes does not please God! That's how all of God's commandments fare: reason butts its head against them and takes offense, as St. Paul says (1 Cor. 1:21): "For after that in the wisdom of God the world by wisdom knew not God, it pleased God by the foolishness of preaching to save them that believe."

8. If judged by reason, what is more unreasonable than that in the Lord's Supper, under the bread and wine, we are eating and drinking the true Body and Blood of Christ for the forgiveness of sins? The natural mind protests: How can a bit of bread and a sip of wine be of any help? Be patient; you'll know in heaven! But if reason is to judge the things of God, then Abraham, too, might well have said to God, Can't you come up with some other sign for the covenant between us than this ridiculous business of circumcision? Scripture, however, speaks as follows (Rom. 4:11): "[Abraham] received the sign of circumcision, a seal of the righteousness of the faith. . . ."

9. It's the same with holy baptism. Following Christ's order, a child is dipped into or sprinkled with water, and thereby sins are washed away and the child is translated from Satan's kingdom to God's! Immediately reason blasphemously objects: How can water cleanse people from sin? Well, if sin were merely a black or red

splotch on the body, that might be true, but because sin is a matter of the heart, hidden away in man's inmost being, it would take water a long time to soak in and wash it away! So Abraham also, could have said after receiving the circumcision command, Dear Lord, how can this contribute to salvation if on the eighth day after birth a little bit of skin is cut away from the body? That's how reason speaks and thinks when it wants to be really brilliant!

10. As soon as we begin asking why God has commanded this or that, the devil has already won, as is plain from the case of Eve in Paradise! She had the command not to eat from a certain forbidden tree. When she lost sight of that command, and lent an ear to the devil's explanation of God's motives, she was already guilty of that terrible disobedience from which we all still suffer today.

11. That's something we should diligently learn also from this law of circumcision, and govern ourselves accordingly. When God commands, speaks, does something, you should shut your mouth, fall on your knees and, without further objection, do what he has told you, hear what he says, submit to what he does! For God has concluded that all men are fools, blind, deceitful—so evil and corrupt that they can't even perceive their own corruption, as Jeremiah said (17:9): "The heart is deceitful above all things and desperately wicked: who can know it?" How then would or could they understand the word and work of God? And because that's our natural disposition, let's give up our own wisdom and without hesitation believe his Word. In the Lord's Supper, for instance, when Christ says, "This is my Body, given for you; this is my Blood, shed for you for the forgiveness of sins," let's believe these words exactly as they stand. Whoever receives the Lord's Supper in that way, believing Christ's words, has what they say, forgiveness of sins and eternal salvation. Whoever refuses to do that but instead says, Why should I be such a fool? Let God line himself up with my wisdom and do what pleases me—that person is lost!

12. And so this is how the old circumcision gives us an example of a wonderful faith, namely that Abraham and his servants were not repelled by God's command but immediately obeyed. They did not reason, What a silly thing that we oldsters should be circumcised! God surely doesn't mean that literally; there must be some other ex-

planation—some spiritual meaning (as our own "enthusiasts" so often say). On the contrary, they thought like this: God has indeed bidden us do something which seems foolish, but if we really want to be "wise" we'll have to be "fools" and let his word be eternally true. We also perceive here what an excellent bishop and preacher Abraham must have been, and how many servants he had in his household and from neighboring Gentiles who were fellow believers in this God.

13. Now we need also to talk about the new circumcision. The old circumcision was to be valid only as long as the Law ruled up to Christ's time. This is neatly intimated by the fact that children were not circumcised until the eighth day. For in the Law one thing follows upon the other, as taught in the third commandment: Six days you are to work and on the seventh day to celebrate the Sabbath. The eighth day follows the Sabbath and a new week begins. So also a new and different circumcision began when the infant Jesus was circumcised on the eighth day.

14. This is a circumcision different, indeed, from the old Jewish circumcision because with this circumcision our dear Lord Jesus Christ began his office, fulfilling what the angel and Simeon had proclaimed, namely, that he is the Saviour, Christ the Lord, and the true light not only for the Jews in the narrow confines of their land, but also for all the Gentiles in the whole world! This is the ministry he began by this first action, being circumcised on the eighth day according to the Law. Here, so to speak, he grabs hold of the Law and by his circumcision not only abolishes the old circumcision but the entire ceremonial Law! Circumcision, like the Law itself, was given for those conceived and born in sin and, therefore, deserving of eternal death. Neither Law nor circumcision, however, can make any demands on Christ; he was totally sinless and Lord of the Law. The fact that he was, nevertheless, circumcised like any other sinful child means that in his case, the Law overreached itself and Christ silenced the Law and took away its power. He could, of course, have done this with divine power and might, as Lord of the Law, and none would have dared to contradict him, but instead he did it all for us out of love and in humility, so that we might take it to heart for our comfort.

15. Personally, he had no need of circumcision, as little as he needed to obey his mother, or even to die on the cross! He had both right and authority not to be subjected to the Law; he did it for our sakes. But we needed a sinless one to keep the Law in our stead and thus appease the wrath of God, otherwise we would be under the curse of the Law forever. That's why he put himself under the Law, and with his merit and work earned freedom for us from the Law, as St. Paul says in Galatians 4:4–5: "But when the fullness of the time was come, God sent forth his Son, made of a woman, made under the law, to redeem them that were under the law, that we might receive the adoption of sons." The fact that he placed himself under the Law was not done for his sake, for he had satisfied all righteousness and holiness required by the Law without such obedience. But he came under the Law for our sakes; and the victory and righteousness he attained there was granted unto us, as he states, Whoever believes on me, him will neither circumcision nor law bind any longer, for, although I was not beholden to them, nonetheless I subjected myself under their demands and satisfied them; and by so doing, both circumcision and the Law have become subject to me, their Lord who has exhausted their power. Therefore, whoever clings to me in true faith I will assist in being made free from both the Law's and circumcision's burden so that he will not come under judgment.

16. And so mark this difference well; everything depends on it! Abraham came under the Law as a sinner; the infant Jesus, however, came under it not as a sinner but without guilt, as Lord of the Law, who takes away the Law's authority and power; yes, tears the Law to pieces so that it can no longer ensnare and condemn those who believe in him.

17. That's why the observance of Christ's circumcision offers such a rich sermon; there's enough here to talk about for several hours! Circumcised on the eighth day, Christ put himself under the Law to redeem us who were under the Law. And because he has freed us from the Law, we are also delivered from sin and death; for where there is redemption from the Law, there is also deliverance from sin and death, as St. Paul teaches in 1 Corinthians 15.

18. Our need, thus, to be set free from the Law is taught by St. Paul (Gal. 3:13): "Christ hath redeemed us from the curse of the law,

being made a curse for us." But that it is not circumcision, as such, that saves, he teaches (Gal. 5:2–3): "Behold, I Paul say unto you, that if ye be circumcised, Christ shall profit you nothing. For I testify again to every man that is circumcised, that he is a debtor to do the whole law." And (Gal. 6:13): "For neither they themselves who are circumcised keep the law. . . ." These are great passages, especially that last one: of those circumcised, not one keeps the Law. They do, indeed, have the physical circumcision but still cannot keep the Law. What else is that except to say that circumcision enables no one to keep the Law? The false apostles insist that circumcision is necessary for salvation—an impossible thing! For even if one is circumcised and boasts about keeping the Law, God's commandment is still there: "You shall love God with all your heart, soul, strength, and mind." Also "You shall not covet." Name me one man who has ever kept that—or can! Think of the pope himself with his cardinals, bishops, monks, nuns, and virgins; they do indeed say we love and obey God with all our heart and we have no evil desire. But what does God say? You abominable hypocrite, you deceitful saint! You say you love me but there's a wide spread between your saying and doing. I'm asking about your deeds, not your words!

19. Why then drive people to the Law for salvation when the Law can't possibly reach a higher level than to bring us under its curse? That's what Paul plainly indicates in Galatians 3:10 where he cites Deuteronomy 27:26, "Cursed is everyone that continueth not in all things which are written in the book of the law to do them." He concludes, therefore, that all who depend on works of the Law are under the curse; yes, furthermore, (Gal. 3:21): "For if there had been a law given which could have given life, verily righteousness should have been by the law." In other words, if a law had been given which could produce spiritual life, it would follow that righteousness comes from the Law and that before a man is spiritually alive, he must be righteous. But now righteousness does not come from the Law, for according to Scripture all are concluded under sin. For that reason, the Law was not given to make alive, in fact, it has no life-giving power. If righteousness did not come from the Law, the Scripture has concluded all under sin. For that reason, the Law was not given to make alive, in fact, it has no life-giving power. If righteousness did not

come out of the Law, and Scripture had not included me under sin, then I could equally well say, I have kept the Law and will be saved by my works, as the pope and his company claim, who now curse and condemn my doctrine. But no one keeps the Law, as Christ told the Jews (John 7:19); and as St. Paul says (Rom. 4:15): "The law worketh wrath," exposes our sin and condemns us; and (2 Cor. 3:6–7): The law kills, it is a dispensation of death and damnation. To sum up: All mankind is accused and condemned under the Law!

20. That's why we need a greater and better "sermon" than the message of the Law, which can only demand, Love God with all your heart and your neighbor as yourself, neither of which we have done. Or, honor your father and mother. Where in all the world is there a child that has truly kept this commandment? One does not strike an obedient child with the rod, and yet, as Scripture testifies, every father is to discipline his children. Isn't that evidence that no child on earth has ever kept the fourth commandment? If we have no better teaching than the law, we are all lost! Yes, if there were a law I could actually keep, I could say to Christ, I don't need you; my righteousness comes from the Law. But, oh, how far I fall short! And even if we did succeed in keeping the Law, that would not enable us to stand before God!

21. And so a greater and better message did come, namely the gospel proclamation that God's Son, Christ, submitted to circumcision like other sinners, even though he was not personally obligated. Since the Law overreached itself in his case, it lost all authority over him. This triumph he graciously shares with us, saying in effect, Because all mankind has failed to keep the Law—let alone be saved by it—I have subjected myself to the Law on your behalf and redeemed you from its curse.

22. As long as men are under the Law, they have no certainty about their standing with God. No matter what a man does, he forever has to say, I don't really know whether this is God-pleasing. The Law simply cannot bring us peace of mind; yes, the Law has the very opposite effect on conscience. The Law reveals sin and kills. That's why David prays (Ps. 143:2): "Enter not into judgment with thy servant, for in thy sight shall no man living be justified," and (Ps. 130:3): "If thou, LORD, shouldest mark iniquities, O LORD, who shall stand?"

Nobody can say, Lord, I'm in your good graces because I have done this or that good deed; instead, everyone remains troubled and fearful. Because we are thus held hostage under the Law, in the master-slave relationship, there can be neither a good conscience nor a joyous heart! And that's why we need something higher, greater, better, to give us peace. And that, of course, is the gospel of Christ who was made under the Law to redeem us.

23. This Gospel teaches us the following: neither Jew nor Gentile can keep the law, even though Jews are circumcised (Gal. 6:13); and as a result all men are servants and captives of the Law. But now comes Christ and says, Dear people, I will subject myself to the Law for your sakes and let myself be circumcised, so that I can say to the Law: Listen, Law, I personally owe you nothing; in spite of that, however, you have laid hold of me, the innocent one; I am your Lord but you have made me a servant, and robbed me of my innocence and authority. Now then, you must in turn serve me, be my slave and captive, and I will wrest from you your power over all mankind. But because I have no personal need for that authority but have another right—the Law having overreached itself in my case—this is my right I graciously share with all those who believe in me.

24. So now, all who believe in Christ will not be condemned either by the law of circumcision or by any other law; they have Christ who is Lord over the Law. He clothes and adorns them with his works and his fulfillment of the Law. Through that, conscience is put at ease, as St. Paul says (Rom. 5:1): "Therefore, being justified by faith, we have peace with God through our Lord Jesus Christ." Furthermore, it is thus that the law is fulfilled in us (Rom. 8:3–4): "For what the law could not do, in that it was weak through the flesh, God sending his own Son in the likeness of sinful flesh, and for sin, condemned sin in the flesh: that the righteousness of the law might be fulfilled in us, who walk not after the flesh, but after the Spirit."

25. And therefore, when the devil plagues me, distressing my conscience and frightening me with the enormity of my sin, I say to him, With my circumcision, my keeping of the Law, my diligent obedience to God, I accomplish nothing. But my Lord Christ's innocence, that does it! I defy the Law which rebukes him, for the Father himself has spoken from heaven, "This is my beloved Son with whom I

am well pleased" (Matt. 3:17). If I'm thrown back upon my own piety and righteousness I'm overwhelmed with despair, but never in the righteousness of my Lord Christ because he has a testimony from our Father in heaven. When I do that, I build on a sure foundation and will never be put to shame.

26. Yes, clothed in Christ's fulfillment and adorned with his righteousness, I can then also begin to love God and my neighbor. Where I still lack and fail, I have a precious "umbrella" in Christ who shades me with his fulfillment and graciously preserves me. Heretofore, I thought that it was up to me to keep the Law; now I realize that's impossible for me. Therefore I cling to him who kept it so perfectly that not one jot or tittle remains. Because I have him, I can now do what needs to be done: love God and my neighbor. Even though I often fail and fall, that does not damage me as long as I believe in Christ. Under Christ, my "umbrella," I am always covered; and so, I am as pure and innocent as the sun, but always on account of Christ in whom I believe. Because I am in him, I can joyously say both to circumcision and the whole Law, In Christ I am free of you; I am no longer accountable to you because Christ, Lord of the Law, has paid my account. Afterwards, since I still live with flesh and blood, I say with Paul (Rom. 7:23): "But I see another law in my members, warring against the law of my mind, and bringing me into captivity to the law of sin which is in my members." But I do not sin according to the inner man of faith; if the flesh wants to be angry or sin in some other way, faith rises up to protest.

27. And so this is how a Christian's righteousness becomes whole and remains pure, namely, that I confess myself to be a poor sinner who can never fully satisfy the Law. But I do not on that account despair; for I see that my Lord Christ has pitied me, put himself under the Law for my sake, and kept that fully. And it follows that my heart must then say, Listen my heart, you must be obedient! When God, my Lord, out of pure compassion, has done so much for me, giving me his dear Son, should I not in turn heartily love him and diligently do what he expects of me? That's how a man becomes truly happy and friendly with God and his neighbor. He will then also pursue that righteousness with which he is clothed in and through Christ, the real keeping of the Law, not forced, but willing. Even though such a

keeping is not yet perfect because of our sinful flesh, the rest of our fleshly sinning will be swallowed up in Christ, who has redeemed us from the Law in conformity with conscience.

28. Because I now believe in Christ, I could choose to be circumcised with the Jews or remain uncircumcised with the Gentiles, always with a free heart, as a service of kindness to others, as when Paul had Timothy circumcised. But to put my confidence in circumcision, that I cannot do! Also, I will not let myself be forced into circumcision, as Titus was not pressured into it, even though he was a Greek (Gal. 2:3). As with circumcision, so also with all laws: because I'm a Christian and have him who is Lord of the Law, I do not obey any law under compulsion. If you tell me: Yes, but then you are lost, I answer: Not so, because I cling to him who has completely and perfectly fulfilled the Law. I know that whoever believes in him is fully vested with a total keeping of the Law, and so lives not according to the flesh, but in the Spirit! May the dear Lord Christ grant that to all of us. Amen.

NEW YEAR'S DAY

*Second Sermon**

Luke 2:21

And when eight days were accomplished for the circumcising of the child, his name was called JESUS, which was so named of the angel before he was conceived in the womb.

The Name of Jesus

1. Earlier in the first part of the Gospel for this Sunday, we heard concerning the circumcision of Jesus. It marked the end of the old circumcision ceremonial laws, so that they can no longer condemn us. That's why we observe this festival, that we might recognize this fact and thank the child Jesus who saved us from the curse of the Law by becoming a curse for us.

2. We come now to the second part of this lesson, concerning the name of Jesus, which the Evangelist has described with singular care, noting not only that the child Jesus was circumcised on the eighth day but also that he received his name then, a name not imposed by men but given and commanded by God. It came from heaven, announced by the angel and given to Mary, in the words: "Thou shalt conceive in thy womb, and bring forth a son, and shalt call his name JESUS." Thus the Evangelist states that the child was to be so named, even before he was conceived in the womb.

3. Much could be preached concerning the name, no doubt, but we want to limit ourselves to what God, in his grace, gives us. The little babe's name is, and is to be, Jesus. "Jesus" means Saviour. Mary gave birth to a child whose name is "Saviour." That, in plain language, is his rightful name. People try to improve on it by paraphras-

*Preached at the parish church in the afternoon, 1531.

ing it but it can't be done. The meaning of Saviour is good and clear. The angel Gabriel explains to Joseph the reason why this child was to bear this name in Matthew 1:21, "Thou shalt call his name JESUS, for he shall save his people from their sins." He is called Jesus, or Saviour, because he could help the people in every need, here and everywhere, outwardly and inwardly, temporally and eternally. As we translate "Messiah" to mean King or the Anointed One, so we translate the word "Jesus" as Saviour. We are to believe that he is our Saviour who rescues us from the devil's power.

4. Let us diligently learn this name and bear in mind that this child alone, no one else, is named Jesus; we must hold on tightly to the meaning given by the angel Gabriel that he is the Saviour who saves his people from their sins. His help is not for trifling things and little problems, like evil words about one's neighbor or the death of his cow. Such minor matters God entrusts to the secular realm for help: kings and magistrates for country and citizenry, fathers and mothers for their children, masters and mistresses for their servants, and doctors for those with illnesses. Indeed rulers are saviours in a way of speaking, and are even called so in the Scriptures, as in the Book of Judges. But they are but poor imitations when compared with this Saviour, who alone possesses divine power and might, to be and to be called the Saviour who saves his people from their sins.

5. Whoever will accept this child and take him to be his Saviour must look on him as his Saviour and helper not only for temporal things, which as said above, God enjoins upon others, but for eternal life and redemption from sin and sin's effects, death, devil, and hell. For where sin is done away, there also death and devil are done away. So, if you now trust him, you should also firmly believe that after this present life there is another life which is to come. If you don't believe that this is so, then you have enough of a Saviour in kings and magistrates, fathers and mothers, who will help you in matters pertaining to body, money, and property. But if you believe that after this life there is another life, then you need this Saviour and his help. He succors from the sort of misfortune where neither king, father, mother, nor any other person can help. It is all too true that when king, father, mother, and other people are and can be of no help, that then the Lord Jesus stands by and helps his own in bodily needs too.

6. However, his foremost mission is not to help in temporal needs but against sin and eternal death. For that power is needed. That is why it is important that you also believe that after this life there is another life. The person who does not believe this cannot really acknowledge this Saviour. If it is your belief—like that of pope, cardinals, and bishops—that there is no life after this world, then I wouldn't care a fig about your God either; go ahead, do your own thing. For where there is no God, there is no devil or hell either, and it matters not a wit that a man dies, any more than that a tree falls, or a cow dies; that's all there is. Then let's go after things with gusto, eat and carouse, for tomorrow we'll be dead, as St. Paul says in 1 Corinthians 15:32.

7. To perceive this child rightly, therefore, one must pay attention to the angel's words and mark well from what sort of malady he is our Saviour. If you believe that there is a life after this one, then he is the Saviour you need. If yours is an epicurean outlook, so common in the world today, then do what you will. And the fact is that that sort of person fares best of all in the world, in no way believing that there is a God, as I've said concerning the pope and his minions, doing what satisfies their lusts. If I didn't believe that there is a God, I would do the same: robbing, stealing, lying, deceiving, wenching, carousing like the next man, and when I die, that's the end. For this present life a person does not need God, but lives as long as he can, till the jig is up. But when God is in the picture, as he indeed is, then there is more in view than just this present life. This is something the Ten Commandments alone plainly testify to, even if we have nothing further of God's Word. Now, however, since God has given us his Word, where he teaches us human beings plainly what he wants us to have, we know from his testimony that we are to have more than this present life. But where God is not speaking to the people and they do not acknowledge him as God, there is no other alternative than for them to become epicureans and swine, or adopt for themselves some new faith.

8. We have God's Word and do not believe like the world—pope, bishops, rulers, upper classes, lower classes, and virtually the whole of mankind which cares nothing at all about eternal life but focuses alone on this present life, piling up money, striving after fame and

power, living in pleasure's whirl; but we look for another life to follow upon this present troubled existence, and for this reason rejoice that we have this child as Saviour. Meanwhile, in this world, it often seems as though we don't have a God, for he lets us stick in all manner of physical trouble, does not fend off the wicked rascals who persecute and plague us, but allows them to practice their wantonness and get their fill of things in this life. That's why it seems as though he is not of this present world. But he has promised us that we shall have something better than this temporal life. Of this the pope, cardinals, bishops, epicureans, swinish people, who don't believe that there is a God and there is another life beyond this one, know and believe nothing at all. For if they did, they would stand differently and not live so securely. The wonder is that under the Romans, when the Roman empire was at its peak, a virgin or espoused maiden could have remained inviolate and pure. The prevailing faith was (and this was its heaviest penalty): Live today, die tomorrow, and that's the end. If that's the way it is, then every person has designs on his neighbor's goods, wife, etc., doing what satisfies his lusts. We, however, have God's Word which says to us in the last chapter of Matthew (verse 20): "Lo I am with you alway, even unto the end of the world." He does indeed want to rule over us also on earth, give us food, drink, clothing and all that we need; but at the same time it is his will that we bear all manner of adversity upon earth, as he himself says (John 16:33): "In the world ye shall have tribulation; but be of good cheer, I have overcome the world." Therefore, each one should diligently learn that this child is called Jesus, a Saviour, noting clearly what sort of Saviour he is, namely that when we are overwhelmed by trouble, without money, forsaken by father and mother, deserted by good friends, and the time and hour come when the weight of sin presses down, conscience trembles with fear, the devil hurls his fiery darts, and in sum there is no human help or counsel to assist us, then in such predicament this child is a Saviour who can and will help.

9. Except for a brief moment, when a person's got his purse full of gulden and feels neither sin nor death, he does not yearn for this Saviour, nor feel need of his help. For he is not called a gulden-Saviour, but a Saviour who frees his people from their sins and rescues them from death. Money can get you bread, beer, wine, and clothes,

but it cannot save you from sin and death. The same holds for other temporal gifts: human reason, wisdom, arts and science, power, and friends, and whatever else there is upon earth; all of them can help in the things for which they were ordained and created. A mother can provide her children with food and drink, and so on; a doctor can look after the sick; a lawyer can help recover what was lost; but when a person comes to the end of this life and must die, when conscience can no longer disavow its sins before God's tribunal, and on that account must stand in anxiety and peril of everlasting judgment, then is the crucial time for this Saviour, Jesus, to come. If every corner of a house were filled with gold, it would do no good. If all the kings, rulers, fathers, mothers, doctors, lawyers, sages, and experts were to try to help, they could not avail. This child alone is so named and is in fact a Saviour who can and will secure all who acknowledge their predicament and seek his help.

10. The balance of power lies in this: that you give assiduous attention to letting this child be your Saviour alone, over against all religious experts who pervert this name and set up their own false saviours apart from and against the only true Saviour. Monks of various kinds—Augustinian, the barefooted, and the preaching orders—have attributed this name to themselves and purport to be saviours against sin and death.

11. Guard against such notions and see to it that you let this child keep his name untarnished. By God's decree, there will be no other Saviour against sin and death, also no one else to help, in heaven or earth, whether the pope, good works, angels or other creatures, than this singular child of the Virgin Mary, named Jesus. Good works are to be done, but they are not Jesus, do not save, cannot rescue from death. This child, however, saves and rescues from death. The name is not Franciscans, Dominicans, Carthusians, Masses, vigils, absolution, good works, alms, fasts, prayers, but Jesus.

12. The person who under sin's oppression and pangs of death can say, This child, son of the Virgin Mary, named Jesus, saves me from my sin, and him I trust, not on anyone else in heaven or earth, that person will certainly be saved. A person can easily mouth the words, but to believe it truly from the heart, without doubting, that is hard to do day by day. What we need to remember is this: when we're as-

saulted by ordinary earthly misfortunes, we can counter them most likely with the usual human resources; but when we lie at death's door, then let go of all else, look only to this Saviour, and say, I know one doctor, advocate, emperor, king, theologue, namely, the child Jesus. He can and he will save me from eternal death.

13. To try to baptize this child with another name, by whatever scheme or plan, would not have worked or availed. He is called Jesus, because he saves his people from their sins. So it was decreed, and so it will be. His name is not Jesus because he provided enough money for you to become a great lord upon earth. Whatever pertains to bodily life is already allotted, given, and decreed (Gen. 1:28) by God's Word: "Be fruitful and multiply, and replenish the earth, and subdue it: and have dominion over the fish of the sea, and over the fowl of the air, and over every living thing that moveth upon the earth." He is called Jesus because he is a Saviour by God's will against sin, death, devil and hell, and is able to help us precisely where no one else could, when all that we possess must be left behind here on earth and we enter into another life.

14. This meaning of Jesus' name is not men's invention, but is given by God from heaven through the angel Gabriel. This child alone was to bear this name, thereby to root out, repulse, and cast away everything that stood below him as Saviour and helper before God. It means that everything people propose instead of Christ, to serve and assist for forgiveness of sins and everlasting life, is by this name repudiated and condemned. Let each one, therefore, be careful not to give this name to another, nor allow it to be given, no matter who and how great the person be. This art I know but little of, and the world even less, for most people say, My good works must help me; thereby I'll reconcile God to myself, so that he's gracious to me. What else is that but to say that my good works are and should be called my Jesus, and do that which belongs to Jesus. The pope and his theologians teach in that way: Faith does not avail alone; if you want to be saved, you must do good works and be rewarded. That is as much as to say, Good works are and are called Jesus. Well and good, if that's the way you want it, go ahead with your "Jesus" and see where you come out. The point is, that what I think and sketch, that cannot be named Jesus; only the child himself can be called that. Popes, cardinals,

bishops, and the wiseacres of the world think that what they conceive and sketch should be called Jesus. But they miss the mark completely. I confess that I myself, too, in times past wanted to engage my God in calculations, saying, Lord God, I have preached so and so, have done this and that, and now you must let me have my reward. Were I to follow my thoughts in this way, I would eventually conclude that my preaching, teaching, and doing were my Jesus. God keep me from that! But what does this text say? The true, real Jesus does not allow that. He wants his name to remain his completely and alone, so that when it comes to our being helped against sin, death, and the devil, we despair of all holy works, ours and others', and cling to him alone in firm faith, who alone is named Jesus, and who alone should be so named by us. Popes, kings, Turks, and monks rage and venture to rob him of his name, but all for naught. They will have to let the child have his name and get no thanks for it. The enthusiasts, Anabaptists, and Sacramentarians also have misguided intentions, but they, too, will have to allow it—if only we believe it. Let the papists pound, scratch, and defy this name, elevate good works, praise them, and exult that it won't be long and popedom will once again reign. All right, if they are successful in carrying out their boast, then I will blot out this text with the blackest ink that I can find. But before they know it, they will find out what they've done.

15. St. Luke states the case, The child was called Jesus not merely at the time of his circumcision, but by the angel even before he was conceived in the womb. Therefore, your highness, if you want to strip the child of his name—a name chosen neither by his parents nor any person on earth but brought by an angel from heaven for this child alone to be called Jesus and Saviour, and no one else!—may you find out how much success you will have. If you try to make a liar out of the angel Gabriel, you will find out at what price. The result will be that both the papists and the others who want to rob the child of his name will end up with nothing, neither name, nor head, nor leggings. They have gone too far; they must themselves recognize their error; meanwhile they try to get us to deny this Saviour. But their game will end.

16. The child's name shall stand. For God himself has so named him. If the pope and his minions want to rage against this, then I say, Go ahead, dear pope, but you cannot push the child off from the

right hand of the Father, but must acknowledge his place. If you don't want to acknowledge this child with us as Saviour, then may you forever rage, wage wars, and fire your guns. In turn, we will comfort ourselves with this: that the child did not receive his name from men but was so named by God.

17. Whoever esteems this child as Saviour does God the greatest and highest honor, as Christ himself says in John 5:23, "That all men should honour the Son, even as they honour the Father. He that honoureth not the Son, honoureth not the Father which hath sent him." If you receive Christ as your Saviour, God is well-disposed toward you and no wrath is in him. If God is well-disposed towards you, how can it harm you that the whole world rages against you? But if you do not esteem the Son as your Saviour but seek after another helper, or think that your sins are greater than this child can rescue you from, you do God the greatest dishonour and make your salvation most uncertain. For God nowhere says that your good works should be your Saviour. But when you believe on the Son, you have taken God captive in his promise. For he has named his Son to be the whole world's Saviour.

18. That is the significance of the name Jesus, which was given to the child, first by the angel before his conception, and then thereafter by his mother at the time of his circumcision on the eighth day. As we have heard, that name serves for this purpose, that whoever believes that after this life there is another life might know where to find eternal life, namely, in this child alone who is called Jesus, that is, Saviour, and there is none other.

19. Thus, what we have learned from today's Gospel is first, that the child was circumcised on the eighth day and came under the Law, so that he might redeem all who believe on him from the curse of the Law; and second, that the child was named Jesus, because he is the Saviour who can help against sin, evil conscience, death, and every distress that follows from our sin. May God give us his grace to that end. Amen.

EPIPHANY

*First Sermon**

Matthew 2:1–12

Now when Jesus was born in Bethlehem of Judaea in the days of Herod the king, behold, there came wise men from the east to Jerusalem, saying, Where is he that is born King of the Jews? for we have seen his star in the east, and are come to worship him. When Herod the king had heard these things, he was troubled, and all Jerusalem with him. And when he had gathered all the chief priests and scribes of the people together, he demanded of them where Christ should be born. And they said unto him, In Bethlehem of Judaea: for thus it is written by the prophet, And thou Bethlehem, in the land of Juda, art not the least among the princes of Juda: for out of thee shall come a Governor, that shall rule my people Israel. Then Herod, when he had privily called the wise men, inquired of them diligently what time the star appeared. And he sent them to Bethlehem, and said, Go and search diligently for the young child; and when ye have found him, bring me word again, that I may come and worship him also. When they had heard the king, they departed; and lo, the star, which they saw in the east, went before them, till it came and stood over where the young child was. When they saw the star, they rejoiced with exceeding great joy. And when they were come into the house, they saw the young child with Mary his mother, and fell down, and worshipped him: and when they had opened their treasures, they presented unto him gifts; gold, and frankincense, and myrrh. And being warned of God in a dream that they should not return to Herod, they departed into their own country another way.

About the History

1. There is much to preach about in connection with this festival, namely, the stories of the wise men; Christ's baptism; also his first miracle, which was performed at the wedding at Cana in Galilee. For this reason today's festival has also been called the Festival of the

*Preached at the parish church in the morning, 1532.

Epiphany of Christ, for some believe that these three manifestations occurred on the same day, though not in the same year. The first, that the Lord Christ manifested himself to the wise men of the Orient by agency of the star; the second, that the Godhead manifested itself at the Jordan when Christ was baptized by John; and third, that Christ manifested his glory at Cana in Galilee when he changed water into wine at the wedding. Whether or not these manifestations occurred on the same day, they still are very precious stories and wonderful manifestations about which it is well worth our while to preach, ponder, and learn.

2. First, then, let's deal with this Gospel that tells the wonderful account of and manifestation to the wise men of Arabia, or the Orient. Through this story the Lord wanted to make known and validate his coming not only among the Jews, but also among the Gentiles, so that everybody might know that he existed, and none could make the excuse or be allowed to say he had kept himself hidden, so that nobody could have known about him.

3. This event, however, occurred especially for the sake of the Jews as a testimony, so that they would have no excuse or be able to say that they had not known. For since it was determined that he would not come in great pomp as a worldly king, but in wretchedness and poverty, his coming was especially troubling, as the prophet Zechariah foretold concerning him—to be born on earth at a time when he found no room in the inn, be laid in a manger, and so on. The Jews took offense at this then, and do so still today. His coming and his birth were announced and proclaimed so clearly and emphatically that the Jews could not make the allegation: How in the world were we supposed to recognize and welcome him since things went so badly for him? Instead, they had to confess: It is true he comes in wretchedness and poverty, but he is preached and proclaimed gloriously.

4. This magnificent testimony the Jews should have believed. For both time and place agree with what the prophets proclaimed long before, and all details in the account tally. The angels in the sky above the fields, the shepherds at Bethlehem, Simeon and Anna in the temple at Jerusalem, all bear witness to him. Most wonderfully, the Jews are given the word firsthand so that they might be informed.

Especially remarkable and powerful, however, is the witness of the Gentiles. For the wise men come to the Royal City of Jerusalem from a foreign country and spread abroad the story about the newborn king to such an extent that Herod becomes terrified and all Jerusalem is stirred up because of it. For that reason the king asks them where Christ was to be born; and they cite for him Scripture's answer, giving him the name of the city. Accordingly, first from Scripture, then by seeing for themselves, and finally, through the wise men, they knew incontrovertibly about this birth.

5. This example of the wise men serves us Gentiles well also. For it occurred and was recorded so that there might be no confusion for us concerning this event; if we want to seek and find this child, we must believe the Word, stick to it, and not allow ourselves to be diverted from it. If we disregard the Word, the offense has already occurred. For the child is so humble and wretched to look at that it is impossible for one to approach by one's reason, apart from the Word. Reason and worldly wisdom cannot comprehend or believe that this child, who can find no room where he might be born, is a King and a Lord, a King so great that he is the world's Saviour. It is meant to be preached through the Word and comprehended in the Word, and to enter our hearts so that we believe it. And as his birth is poor and wretched, so his entire life is likewise nothing but poverty, privation, suffering, misery, shame, and disgrace. The one who loses the Word and merely with human eyes regards him lying in the manger, in the stable, and so on, has already lost him.

6. Now this occurs, especially, when the devil gets in the act and fabricates for us a false Christ, so that in our thoughts we picture Christ as we would like him to be, just like our fanatics and papists do. They renounce the Word and, as a result, cannot welcome or accept him as he lies there before their eyes, but make him out to be a judge and jailkeeper. That he should be the only Saviour, that is what displeases them about him. For this reason they add to this their own works and acts of devotion, which they propose to have alongside Christ, the Saviour. Also, they pray the Virgin Mary to press her son to her breast and to appease him; they think such prayer and intercession should also have saving power. But this is nothing more than deception; for when a person abandons the Word and gropes about

for Christ apart from the Word, he misses Christ and apprehends the devil. He prattles so much before the eyes of people that they think he is the true Christ, while being only the accursed devil.

7. That was our experience under the papacy when we were engulfed with such thoughts. We taught and proceeded under the idea that whoever wants to stand before Christ must have the benefit of the saints' intercession. I, myself, had more confidence in the goodness and intercession of the Virgin Mary than in Christ's grace and intercession. We viewed him as painters paint him, sitting on a rainbow as a judge. Like the graphic portrayal in oil, so was the perception in our heart! Accordingly, we were led astray; we fell from faith, and fled from Christ, in whom we should rather have taken refuge. We were merely affected by the story that he had come into the world; nothing was said at all about why and for what purpose he had come. That is the way it goes when one does not adhere to the Word. This is a key element especially to the devil, as he seeks ways to tear us away from the Word, and then, apart from the Word, leads us to think our own thoughts. For then he knows that he has won, and we have lost. Accordingly, the wise men come first to Jerusalem seeking Christ. By divine revelation they knew that the King of the Jews had been born. And so their reason leads them to Jerusalem for they think like this: Nowhere but at Jerusalem in a magnificent castle and in a golden room, does one find the King of the Jews; he sits there on a royal throne, and many men clad in armor are assigned there to attend him. Indeed, how else would reason think about a king? However, such thoughts, conceived as they are apart from the Word, do not comprehend Christ aright. That is the reason the wise men go awry in their thinking and do not find this child in Jerusalem, at that time still the Holy City, God's temple and dwelling. However, if they are to find the child, they must follow the Word, which is the right star and the beautiful sun pointing to Christ.

8. Since Christ does not want to be found apart from his Word, even in Jerusalem which still was his seat, we ought to cleave to the word and dismiss all thoughts to the contrary. Our fanatics ignore the Word, baptism, and the Lord's Supper; they scramble up above the clouds and seek him in heaven, but fail to find him. True, heaven is his temple and throne, as the prophet Isaiah states in chapter 66

verse 1; however, to put it briefly, you won't have access to him in heaven, for it is locked, since you are restricted to knowing God and Christ only in the Word. If you do not stick to the Word, you cannot find God or Christ, and you are lost.

9. It is my hope that both I, myself, as well as others will firmly believe this, for the devil's whole deceitful agenda is attuned to tearing us away from the Word. If he does not accomplish it by causing people to refuse to hear the public preaching of the Word, he works on the heart to get it unglued from the Word. I cannot bring our fanatics to the point of discerning God's Word in the Sacrament, likewise to honor father, mother, prince, government, and so on; instead they form inadequate opinions about what they see, just like a cow that looks at a new gate. Are father, mother, prince, better than I, they ask? Also, in their minds, the Lord's Supper is mere bread and wine; for to their way of thinking, the Word is apart from the elements. For this reason they go on to say, What is the benefit of bread and wine? and though it be Christ's flesh, it still is of no benefit. That's why they end up receiving only the husk; but the kernel, the Word, they leave behind. The same thing happened to the Jews; they witnessed Christ's miracles and heard his preaching but because they did not pay heed to the Word, they were not benefited. The same is true for our fanatics; they retain the husk but lose the kernel.

10. True, when one looks at father, mother, men, women, princes, or government, there is no difference between them and other people. They, too, have flesh and blood. Similarly when one assesses the Lord's Supper apart from the Word, reason finds nothing more than bread and wine. However, dear friend, here you must listen to the Word and believe it. It says to you, "Thou shalt honor thy father and thy mother." "Servants, obey in all things your masters according to the flesh" (Col. 3:22). "Submit yourselves to every ordinance of man for the Lord's sake: whether it be to the king, as supreme; or unto governors, as unto them that are sent by him" (1 Pet. 2:13–14). If you say that the flesh is of no benefit, then I respond, Listen to the Word and believe it; it is beneficial to you, for the words which Christ speaks are spirit and life. Everything that Christ does is comprehended in the Word; in and through the word he wants to give us all things, and apart from the Word he grants us nothing.

11. The greatest and foremost skill—no matter who the person is—is to cling firmly to the Word and conceive of the things of God in no other way than as the Word tells us. For this reason we should accustom ourselves to know nothing about God and Christ apart from the Word. If we have the Word, we ought to stand firmly on it and say, You may want to make Christ a judge or jailer, but his Word states, "Come unto me all ye that labor, and are heavy laden, and I will give you rest." I am sticking to the Word. We, therefore, should not try to pry into the hidden things concerning Christ's rule over his kingdom, and so on, but simply adhere to the Word as he deals with us in the preaching of his gospel, in baptism, absolution, and the Lord's Supper. Whenever one abandons the Word and speculates without and apart from the Word, reason becomes a very uncertain, slippery thing.

12. Thus the wise men miscalculated then. The way they think about Christ is that, if he is the King of the Jews, he will occupy the Royal City and castle. And so they head straight for Jerusalem; but when they arrive there, they find that they have erred. What to do? They refer to the Scriptures, according to which the Jews knew that the King of the Jews is not to be born in Jerusalem but in Bethlehem of Judaea, as recorded in the prophet Micah. The Word is a trustworthy star, and it guides them straight to Christ. Without and apart from the Word, they would not have found Christ the King.

13. Now Bethlehem was, so to speak, a cowshed compared with Jerusalem; for Jerusalem was the chief city of the Jewish people and Bethlehem, but a speck on the map. However, it was prophesied that Christ was to come from the family of David. But from the time of the captivity, the people of Israel were now so scattered that no tribe had its own territory anymore. Before the captivity the tribes had precise boundaries, each had its own place. But after the captivity this demarcation was set aside, and the whole populace was mixed into one lump. For this reason the descendants of David were difficult to find. Mary and Joseph were of the house of David, but they lived at Nazareth, in the region of Asher and Naphtali, and yet belonged to Judah; in this way all the people were intermingled. Accordingly, through the mouths of his prophets God had expressed it so precisely that, although the people of the various tribes were now

intermingled, some here, some there, nevertheless, Christ was to come from the region where David had been born and lived, as the prophet Micah states, from the tribe of Judah, and from the town of Bethlehem.

14. All this was conceived to comfort the Jews, because families and tribes were so intermingled, and the time was now at hand for Christ to be born. Consider how troubling and ironic this was: the Jews know the family, the tribe, the place, the city, and they point it all out to King Herod; still they do not believe! For, had they believed, they would have gone to Bethlehem. However, the wise men and strangers from the Orient believe, and believe so firmly that they leave the Royal City of Jerusalem and head for the town of Bethlehem. They might have said, This is ridiculous; if we can't find the King of the Jews in the temple, in the house of his God, in Jerusalem, we certainly should not have to look for him in the town of Bethlehem. Where else should we locate him except where his God, who has sent him, has his dwelling? Now we are being steered away from Jerusalem, from the temple, from God's dwelling, to the shabby little town of Bethlehem. If the King is that badly off, he will be hard to find; if we can't find him in his kingdom and where his God is, we won't find him anywhere else either. They may have spoken this way. But they stick to the word of the prophet, "Out of Bethlehem shall come a Governor." To the Jews this was offensive—as if the prophet were greater than the temple at Jerusalem—that he was allowed to say that in Bethlehem a Governor would be born! Therefore, as far as they are concerned, the prophet had to be the greatest heretic. When the King of the Jews comes, they thought, he will not abandon the temple where God is worshiped and be born elsewhere. But it was not to be the temple and center of worship, according to the prophet. For Bethlehem would produce this Governor.

15. The wise men's faith is thus exceedingly beautiful in that it transcends this troubling dilemma and they are not offended because the King of the Jews passes by his temple and center of worship, and chooses the town of Bethlehem, where the inhabitants were simple peasants, hardly to be compared with the erudite bourgeoisie of Jerusalem. What thoughts went through their minds? Without a doubt, mixed-up opinions and questions, like this: We are

looking for the King of the Jews, and they steer us away from the temple to a cowtown. Do people think that we are fools with no understanding? It was, undoubtedly, natural for them to think this way. However, faith sets aside all such notions, and they do not care whether Christ is to be found in the temple with the entire Jewish priesthood, or in the royal palace with the heads of state; they simply follow the Word and go to Bethlehem.

16. The same phenomenon is true among us too. All the world looks for the Christian church at a council, with the pope and his retinue. But to try to locate the Christian church by a council and pope is like the wise men trying to find Christ in Jerusalem. If you say, The pope certainly possesses Scripture, his office, and authority, how could that be wrong? The answer is: Were not the temple and God himself also at Jerusalem? and still they figured wrong. So, as things go, our experience with a council, pope, and bishops is the same as that which the wise men had with the high priests and scribes at Jerusalem.

17. It was important for them to come to Jerusalem, headquarters both for the government and the priesthood, yes, also God's temple; and yet they would not find Christ there. God purposes things in his own way, because he wants us to cling solely to his Word and learn to disdain the great clamor about church, church! fathers, fathers! and the church cannot err, the church cannot err! Well, then, if the church cannot err, you and I can err and go to where God is and still not find God there. For this reason we must learn to turn a blind eye to church, fathers, temple, priesthood, Jerusalem, God's people, and the like, and listen only to what God says in his Word.

18. The wise men, accordingly, stick to the Word which they have heard from the prophet. This very Word is their light and guide that unravels all their perplexities. So, it is by God's great, overflowing grace that the Gentiles—having neither temple nor priesthood, neither circumcision nor the Law, and being strangers to divine worship and the testament of promise—stumble upon the Word of the prophet and stick to it so firmly that they permit no other thoughts to bewilder them, but remain strictly with the Word and follow it. On the other hand, it is exceedingly incriminating for the Jews, who had the Law, divine worship, and the promise according to which Christ

became incarnate, to be so obdurate that they refuse to believe the Word, even though they apprise others of it.

19. However, after the wise men have heard the Word of the prophet, God gives them also a sign from heaven: the star reappears as soon as they leave Jerusalem pointing out the way to Bethlehem, to the very place where the child was. And they certainly needed such a sign. For, when they come to the town of Bethlehem inquiring after the King, they find Mary and Joseph, who are like beggars, and the child lying in a manger, everything very lowly, miserable, and beggarlike.

20. They might then have reasonably demanded: Is this the King of the Jews? How could he be treated so shabbily? Are the people here nothing but rude clodhoppers, that no one even gives him a drink of water in his own land? Since his own people show him no honor, why should we believe in him? Who knows whether what is said about him is true? If it were true, surely the high priests would come from Jerusalem and embrace him! But the pious wise men allow nothing to dissuade them; they hold fast to what they have heard from the prophet Micah and discerned by the star.

21. That is strong faith: the wise men listen only to what comes from the mouth of the prophet Micah, cling firmly to his Word, giving credence to nothing else. Had I been there, I would have held with the temple and said, This is where God dwells and, if the child is to be found anywhere in the whole world, it would certainly have to be there where the priesthood and divine worship are. For this King, in the thinking of the entire priesthood, intends to establish another kingdom and divine worship, and was in fact to begin it here. For the Jews counted on their kingdom or priesthood, and relied on the temple, because they had Moses, the Law, priests, Levites, and were the people of God. This God could not tolerate and he purposed to do away with it all in one fell swoop: Moses, the temple, the kingdom, and the priesthood. In short, nothing else would be of any help, neither temple nor priesthood, but Christ only.

22. If God has done that, as regards his kingdom and priesthood, which he had ordered, established, and instituted, snatching it all away, much less will he set store by the pope, bishops, monks, and priests with their hoods and tonsures, who have neither been or-

dained nor instituted by him, but contrived and fabricated by men. They do not want God so God says to them, If you do not want me to save you by grace, then I shall not save you according to your contrived spirituality. If you want nothing from me, I want nothing from you, nor anything of what you are and have; if I have not regarded the holiness of my own people under Moses, much less would I set store by you. Therefore, we must get to the point where we cling solely to Christ and cast aside all perplexities, even though pope, Turk, and we ourselves believed otherwise; that to be a Christian we must cling firmly to Christ and his Word and let nothing of a spiritual or secular nature deter us.

23. It was his purpose to let himself be found not at Jerusalem, but at Bethlehem. Bethlehem was not far at all from Jerusalem; nevertheless, God did not want to give recognition to Jerusalem nor allow the Governor of his people to be born in her, purposing thereby to reject false trust in the saints and teaching us that true holiness exists neither in the temple nor in spiritual ceremonies, but in himself. This is what the story teaches us. Let's look now at Micah's prophecy, "And thou Bethlehem, in the land of Juda, art not the least among the princes of Juda: for out of thee shall come a Governor, that shall rule my people Israel."

24. This is a gladsome text, which not only testifies that Christ has come, but also teaches us why we should esteem and cling to him, and what kind of a King and Lord he is. He should be a Lord of God's people, says the prophet, yet be born at Bethlehem and be the most despised man on earth. It is contradictory and shocking that a poor beggar, born in a lowly, poor place should be a ruler and Lord of the people of Israel. The world looks at the matter like this: The one who is to be a king and lord must have money, possessions, land, people, and power. But here the situation is: Bethlehem is small and poor, and yet out of Bethlehem comes a great, mighty King and Lord.

25. From this it readily follows that we must not understand the dominion of this Lord as ruthless, like that of a tyrant who forces and burdens people. For this reason the prophet paints the picture very beautifully, saying, "Bethlehem, thou are not the least." In other words, one need not be terrified by this King as of a tyrant, for there is neither power nor splendor, neither money nor possessions, nei-

ther sword nor firearm, neither horse nor knight, of which we need be afraid. There is only abject poverty, lowliness, meekness, and humility, nothing at all which could cause a person to dread this being or kingdom; for who is going to be fearful of a child and a poor beggar! Of raw power one is rightly fearful, and God's sovereign power, in particular, awesome and to be feared. But here, not majesty and power, but poverty is present. All the same, this poor child is a Lord.

26. So if he is a ruler and Lord and yet is born in poverty and wretchedness in the poor town of Bethlehem, what can his glory be other than that before the world he is poor, but rich in the Spirit, and every kind of spiritual blessing? Before the world he should be as nothing, should not exercise tyranny or power, but be a poor, gentle, and friendly child. But in the Spirit and in spirituality, he is to be a rich King and Lord, who would be everyone's benefactor. But wherein would his riches consist? Nothing other than that sin, death, righteousness, truth, life, and all else lie at his feet.

27. That is the dominion of this child, and from this his people should draw benefit. Materially he does not want to help, unless your salvation and his glory are concerned; for he himself is wretched and poor. Therefore, no one must think of becoming a Christian in order to obtain money and possessions. This we might expect on the part of the pope, who makes his fawning favorites into lords over great estates and divides up countries among them, as Daniel prophesied. But the dominion of this child is to be experienced and enjoyed solely in this: that he redeems us from sin and adorns us with righteousness before God, rescues us from death, and grants us everlasting life.

28. Now then, in the spiritual realm there is another lord, namely, the devil; he is a king and lord over sin and death; he creates timidity, despair, and terror. That is his spiritual kingdom. However, this child is likewise a spiritual King, who drives out the devil, redeems you from sin and death, removes you from the kingdom of the devil so that you become righteous, alive, joyful, and saved. This is his dominion. For since he has no earthly dominion and yet is to be a Lord, he must have another dominion, namely, that in his kingdom he makes a person righteous, pious, joyful, and blissful before God; while the devil, on the other hand, in his kingdom subjects a person to sin, so that he remains dead forever and lost eternally.

29. Now, however, this King and Lord, Christ, cannot govern as one who wants to subject people under sin and drive them to death and damnation. For that very kingdom of sin and death already belongs to its lord, the accursed devil. Nor, on the other hand, can this King govern in a worldly fashion because he is so poor and wretched. It follows, therefore, that this King, Christ, is not a secular king, nor of wicked spiritual nature, but a spiritual Lord who is kind and gracious; and his kingdom is not a worldly kingdom or a spiritually tyrannical kingdom, as is that of the devil, but a merciful and blissful kingdom.

30. That's the kind of Lord he is. Not a lord of sin, death, and hellish fire, but a Lord of righteousness, life, heaven, and salvation. For I need a Lord who is able to make me, a lost and condemned creature, righteous again, redeem me from sin, death, and the devil, and bring me to heaven and everlasting life. This is where faith belongs, that you adhere zealously to God's Word, as stated earlier of the wise men, who correctly understood this passage of the prophet Micah. However, whoever willfully abandons the Word and follows his own thinking will soon lose Christ, because he regards him not as a gracious, merciful Lord but as a judge and flees from before him as from the devil. For that is the devil's bailiwick to represent Christ differently to people, terrify them, and by means of sin finally to plunge them into hell.

31. Our text attests that Christ was born in Bethlehem, is a gracious Lord, who would deliver all who believe in him from sin, death, devil, and hell, and ultimately redeem them on Judgment Day. For on Judgment Day he will not come to condemn his own but set them free from all evil, as St. Paul teaches in 2 Thessalonians 1:7. Much more could be said about how the poor, wretched child is a very mighty Lord over against the devil's great dominion and power. But this is enough for now. We shall save the rest for this afternoon. By means of the star of his Holy Word may God graciously lead us with the wise men to his Son, Jesus Christ, and preserve us forever from every occasion of stumbling. Amen.

EPIPHANY

*Second Sermon**

Micah 5:2

But thou, Bethlehem Ephratah, though thou be little among the thousands of Judah, yet out of thee shall he come forth unto me that is to be ruler in Israel; whose goings forth have been from of old, from everlasting.

1. Dear friends, what you are going to hear today is from the prophecy of the prophet Micah concerning the child Jesus, that he was to be born at Bethlehem and that his kingdom would be unlike the kingdom of the world and the devil, namely, a divine and benevolent kingdom, full of goodness, grace, and mercy, since he was to be a Lord over God's people. Regularly in our preaching we emphasize that Christ's kingdom and rule pertain to the people of God, not the world or the devil's followers.

2. The scribes apprised King Herod, who had made an inquiry of them and pressed them for an answer; they provided him with one text only, and Herod questioned no further. His concern was to remain king in the land of the Jews and eliminate this newborn King of the Jews. For this reason he eventually had Bethlehem's innocent children put to death. Accordingly, the scribes simply answer Herod's question by stating that the King of the Jews would be born at Bethlehem. They were concerned that if they went deeper into the matter they might lose their own heads. So this was their reasoning: Let's lay before him the word of the prophet; then if our reply angers him, it is not we who said it, but the prophet Micah. We must not elaborate more about the newborn King of the Jews before Herod. So, they merely quote the Scriptures, therefore, and leave King Herod to deal with the prophets, pointing out what was written there. Now the prevailing situation at the time was that Herod had

*Preached in the afternoon at the parish church, 1532.

by stint of force managed to build up his rule over the kingdom of the Jews to such an extent that the Jews did not dare to argue with him. So now the scribes simply quote the text from the prophet, no more, and leave their ruthless king puzzling over it.

3. However, the prophet elaborates further, stating what kind of king or ruler this child would be: "The ruler who is to come out of Bethlehem will be a lord over my people Israel." This is spoken relative to the nature of Christ's kingdom, as we have heard, that he is a King over God's people and his kingdom a kingdom of grace. But when he continues, "whose goings forth have been from of old, from everlasting," it describes his person, who precisely the person of this King would be. He is to be a king and ruler over God's people, originating in Bethlehem; however, his going forth has been from days immemorial, that is, even before the world existed, from everlasting.

4. This the scribes did not tell King Herod; indeed, they themselves did not understand or believe it, for it was somewhat more obscure than what was first stated: that he was to be born at Bethlehem and govern the people of Israel. It was important to know this, for it was a sure indication that he had to be a man. But when the prophecy further states, "his goings forth have been from of old, from everlasting," this is not so easily comprehended, for that is tantamount to saying that he also is everlasting God and did not originate first at Bethlehem but existed from eternity.

5. He is to be Lord and go forth from Bethlehem. This can mean nothing else than that this ruler is true man. For Bethlehem is a city, a worldly, geographical location, visible to the eye and a place to be lived in. Since this ruler is to go forth from Bethlehem, he was to be born there, like anyone else born in a city. If Bethlehem is his birthplace, then he is a natural, true man. Moreover, if he is to be ruler over the people of Israel, he certainly must be a human King and Lord, have flesh and blood, body and soul just like any other man, otherwise he could not be Lord over the people of Israel. The prophet states further, "His going forth is even before the days of the world came into existence," that is, his going forth is from eternity. This King does not first originate with his birth at Bethlehem. That is indeed his birthplace, his place of origin; but in addition to this origination, he has yet another going forth, namely, before the world

began, from eternity, before days were counted. So when we acknowledge that he issues forth at Bethlehem, we must also acknowledge his going forth before the beginning of time, from eternity.

6. The words, therefore, of the prophet have to stand as given. In the first place, he says, *Ex te egredietur*, "out of thee shall he come forth." With this the high priests and scribes themselves attest that "come forth" means as much as to be born. It's like we say in German, From where do you come? From Wittenberg, Leipzig, meaning, I was born at Wittenberg, or Leipzig. So also here: The ruler was to hail from Bethlehem, that is, was to be born at Bethlehem. But then he also says, *Cujus egressus ab antiquis diebus*, "whose going forth is from everlasting," before time, day, or hour ever existed. The one who was to be born at Bethlehem is also born from eternity.

7. If, therefore, you want to know where this child came from, then listen to the prophet Micah, who says that he is from Bethlehem. From where else? From Bethlehem only? No, he was born before there ever were days, before the world, before heaven and earth, before sun and moon were created. Words fail us here. He originates from Bethlehem through his mother. But he is from eternity, before day and night, minutes and hours of time were ever counted. This Herod and the Jews were not likely to believe, nor did they deserve to understand it. They were left merely with what is related of his physical birth; about the other they knew nothing, which is as much as such fools deserved.

8. Now then he is the King and Lord over all the people of God, our Lord Jesus Christ, who during the reign of King Herod was born at Bethlehem, a true man, of a natural mother, without a human father's seed, conceived by the Holy Spirit. And the very same true man also bears the name and is called: *Egressus ab antiquis diebus*, "the ancient of days," who existed before the world or days existed. Thus we must acknowledge him to be true man, born in time at Bethlehem, and also true God, born in eternity before time began.

9. Over such a person the world is inclined to become indignant and irritated, because it cannot reconcile the fact that this child had his beginning or birth at Bethlehem, was born a human being of the Virgin Mary, and that he, nonetheless, had his going forth, or was born, before the world, before woman, the estate of marriage, sun or

moon, were ever created. Of whom then was he born if he was born before the world? Of no one but of God. For this reason he has to be eternal God. For before the world nothing existed but God. As long as people believe that God created heaven and earth, they have to conclude: If his going forth or his being born was before the world, he must have proceeded from, or have been born of, God and be God himself. For before the world there was nothing but God. Now all creatures were created or made by God. But God is uncreated; he is himself the Creator. Outside of God, and the things he created, there is nothing.

10. This is the King who is capable of doing all things. Now if Christ had been only a mere man, he would not have been able to deliver us, and the devil would have devoured us all. For death would have slain him just as it has all other men. Nor would it have helped that he was born of a virgin. For it is much more astounding that God fashioned Eve from a rib, than that a virgin should give birth. For a virgin is a female who by nature has been constituted to bear children. Therefore, neither the devil nor death would have cared a rap that he was born of the Virgin Mary. But it does matter that the Virgin gives birth not only to a son, but to a son whose origin is before the world began and who now is born in the world. As a result, the devil and death and the devil's entire kingdom were vanquished, simply because of this man who had his beginning or birth before the world ever existed. If that were not the case and he had originated only at Bethlehem, death would have devoured him just as surely as you and me, the Virgin Mary, John the Baptist, and other great saints. But his going forth is from eternity. Therefore death, which up till now had slain all men, was forced ignominiously to deal with this child, the Lord Jesus, who was God, and the Godhead cannot die nor be condemned by the devil.

11. However, since he had his origin in time by being born at Bethlehem, like any other child, he had to die; and since he was sent for that purpose, he had to become sinner in our stead and let himself be condemned. Now that is how the devil and death got themselves entrapped. They lay claim to him and could see no farther than that he originates at Bethlehem. And in accordance with these roots, this child allows himself to be slain. But then, when he lies in the grave,

he declares: I was born before the world began; and with all his might he bursts through grave, sin, death, and devil; and they were unable to contain him.

12. What the prophet wants us to understand from this declaration concerning this ruler is this: he has two points of inception, or, as we say in German, two births. For this reason he is a person who is, at one and the same time, true God and true man, but still one person, not two; and we have to say: Christ is the son who nursed at the Virgin Mary's breast and, like any other human being, developed physically. However, besides that, he was born also of the everlasting Father in eternity, before time began in the world. Now therefore, these two natures, divine and human, are inseparably united in one person, one Christ, who is true God and true man. The one whose origin and place of birth was at Bethlehem is precisely the same one whose roots, or beginning, are laid in eternity. Mary calls him her son, the same one who is the Son of the everlasting Father. The Virgin Mary's son, born in time, and the everlasting Father's Son, is the selfsame son, not two sons, only one person, not two persons, only one Christ, both God and man, not two Christs.

13. These things the high priests did not tell Herod; nor, as stated, did this tyrant deserve to know or understand it. And, what's more, even they did not understand it. But our greatest comfort and consolation is that we have such a King and Lord, who is not only true man but also true God, Creator and Lord over all creatures, with whom neither sin, nor death, nor devil can find any fault.

14. The one who wants to follow this person and not be on a collision course with him must, first of all, understand that he was born at Bethlehem and then, also, that his going forth is from eternity. Precisely this is how the prophet presents the matter, in this order. First he tells of the fleshly birth, stating much more about this than about the other birth which occurred in eternity, although this occurred first, before the world began and before his fleshly birth afterward in the world. So, let me repeat what I said above: The person who wants to know God, free from unsubstantial speculation about him, must begin at the bottom and learn first to know the Virgin Mary's son born at Bethlehem. Thereafter he will learn, as the text itself states, precisely who the Virgin's son is, namely, the everlasting

King and Lord. This then will not be a dread-filled reality but a most beloved and comforting truth.

15. Solomon says in Proverbs 25:27, *Qui scrutator est majestatis, opprimetur a gloria*: "For men to search their own glory is not glory." The one who wants to begin there, probing questions like: How does God govern the world? Why did he predestine some and not others? Why did he not prevent the fall of man since he knows all things? I say, whoever wants to know God by prompting such questions (human reason is impertinent and conjures up such thoughts), will come to grief—just as the evil spirit, Lucifer, who had high notions like that, foolishly, and as a result fell horribly. It's a fact: we must not start on top, on the roof, until the infrastructure has been laid.

16. If you want to be on the safe side and know God aright, then, following the prophet here, hold to this, that you do not want to know first about his beginning before time and the world, but come to know his birth at Bethlehem, even as Christ himself teaches in John 14:6–7: "I am the way, the truth, and the life: no man cometh unto the Father, but by me. If ye had known me, ye should have known my Father also." Also, verses 9–10: "He that hath seen me hath seen the Father . . . Believest thou not that I am in the Father, and the Father in me?" The one who does not want to begin there, but at once has high notions of probing into the Godhead and speculating as to how God governs—why he is such a stern King, why he punishes and destroys—that person will be overwhelmed by God's majesty, as Solomon says, as indeed he deserves to be.

17. Therefore, the right approach is this: If you want to know this child aright, go first to Bethlehem, that is, learn that this child is born of the Virgin Mary, true man, flesh, blood, and bone like yours and mine, yet without sin, with a mission to fulfill and discharge in the world, namely, as Micah says, to be a ruler who would redeem his people from sin and eternal death. Then, after these things are well learned and the child is found, seen, and touched in the manger, the light will dawn, too, that this son of Mary is also the Son of God, born of God before time and from everlasting. He has two goings forth or births, and yet is only one person. Consequently, when you lay hold of this man, Christ, you have laid hold of God; when you touch him, you have touched God; when you pray to him, you pray to God; when

you blaspheme him, you blaspheme God. That is the reason why the Evangelist has such high regard for this passage of the prophet. The fact is, it was held in high esteem also by the Jews, but they understood it in a fleshly way and looked only at Bethlehem.

18. We are told here, further, how shamefully the high and mighty treated these precious, excellent words. The proud, arrogant high priests and scribes hold this child in contempt, and wretched Herod persecutes him. This is God's modus operandi; he holds this great text under the people's noses, yes, puts it into their mouths, so that they speak and sing about it, and yet they do not understand a word of it. It is the same today: emperors, kings, princes, nobles, burghers, and peasants think they know all about the gospel, but all that they know is the fire of hell. The high priests and scribes know this text very well indeed, talk about it, and even Herod accepts it when it is shared with him, and because of it he sends the wise men to Bethlehem, even saying to them, "Go and search diligently for the young child; and when ye have found him, bring me word again, that I may come and worship him." Indeed, he is a Righteous Branch, very worthy of such attention! But what does it help the shameful, miserable people to have and know the Word and yet really understand none of it?

19. It is a singular thing that our God should give his Word to people, even though they, in turn, neither smell nor taste of it. I must sing his praises for so doing because, in their pride, they despise God's Word, as though they already know it all. I have often said it, and I say it again: I wish that I did not have to preach anymore. I say this because those to whom we preach and who now have the gospel do us the greatest injustice. They hold office, possess power, wealth, and property, yet vex everyone, but especially us who preach the gospel. Well and good if you mistreat us, we repeat it once more: You will get nothing from the gospel, though we preach it for you, yes, even though you hear, see, and comprehend it, as Christ also says in Luke 8:10: "that seeing they might not see, and hearing they might not understand," just like the scribes and Herod who had the prophet's words: "Out of Bethlehem shall come the Governor." They know what is said, and yet their minds will not accept what they know.

20. So our Lord God must deal with shameful, ungrateful people, with despisers and persecutors of his Word, with those who hear and

yet do not hear, who even preach it and yet understand nothing of it. Even if our people, whether urban or rural, understood the gospel, I would still not want to preach it because they so shamefully misuse it. But now I am preaching to myself and to those of my people who feel need of it. The rest get merely the husks; yet it is the kernel they need to have. They hear the sound but not the melody. Our Lord God is a preacher who broadcasts his Word so clearly that all the world is able to hear it, and yet none but the believers understand it. These high priests, scribes, and Herod have the prophets in their mouth and ears, but understand about as much as does a cow!

21. Therefore, let no one smugly think: I have the gospel, I cannot lose it. Just a minute, let us see whether or not you really have the gospel. If you believe the gospel with all your heart and are changing for the better, then you really have it. But if you become arrogant and scorn it, then you do not have it; but like Herod you hear it and talk about it just like the high priests and scribes. The wise hear it correctly and understand it; but Herod remains a rogue, and the high priests and scribes, scoundrels.

22. Christ's wonderful kingdom has singular disciples. Some hear his Word and understand it; but others hear it and yet do not understand it. We can take comfort in this, that the world—pope, bishops, the wise and intelligentsia, and the like—are far superior to us in money, power, possessions, wisdom, honor, and all that pertains to the world; but in this respect they are far inferior to us, because our treasure, our beloved gospel, they will neither smell nor taste, even though they most diligently hear, read, study, yes, even speak and teach it, for by their lives they plainly demonstrate that like the hardened Jews, they have ears and yet hear nothing, eyes that see and yet are blind.

23. May God by his grace grant that we may be among the wise who hear and understand his glorious gospel and are kept from hardness of heart and blindness unto eternal life. Amen.

EPIPHANY

Third Sermon—1534

Matthew 3:13–17

Then cometh Jesus from Galilee to Jordan unto John, to be baptized of him. But John forbad him, saying, I have need to be baptized of thee, and comest thou to me? And Jesus answering said unto him, Suffer it to be so now: for thus it becometh us to fulfil all righteousness. Then he suffered him. And Jesus, when he was baptized, went up straightway out of the water: and, lo, the heavens were opened unto him, and he saw the Spirit of God descending like a dove, and lighting upon him. And lo a voice from heaven, saying, This is my beloved Son, in whom I am well pleased.

1. It is truly a great and wonderful happening about which we are to preach on this festival, that Jesus was baptized in the Jordan. Young folks today, especially, should learn to thank God for his grace in revealing that Christ, born at Bethlehem, came also for the Gentiles.

2. The Gentiles were not part of the Jewish people, but were strangers. But God commenced to draw this people who were not his chosen people to himself, so that the Gentiles might not despair because of Christ, as though they did not belong to him. Closely coupled to this drawing of the heathen to himself was the revelation of Christ's birth to them, so that the Gentiles might comfort themselves with the knowledge that Christ belonged to them, too, and that they, as well as the Jews, should receive him, even though they were not the chosen people like the Jews.

3. The wise men, after all, were Gentiles, who had no priests like the Jews, no divine worship, no Word of God, were uncircumcised, without the temple, churches, or prophets; yet notwithstanding they come as alien, blind, and thoroughly undeserving people to the light, to the Lord Christ, and receive him on bended knee, worshipfully, presenting their gifts to him. And he receives them, and is most pleased with their worship and gifts.

4. This is written for our consolation, that we might thank God, because we Gentiles are not totally cast off by God but are as acceptable before him as were the Jews, and because God through Christ established his kingdom on earth, in which he deals with us not by merit but by grace.

5. But the very highest and most comforting thing about this festival is the manifesting that occurred with the baptism of Christ at the Jordan. I would prefer to call this festival the Lord Christ's baptismal day, the day on which the Lord was baptized, presenting himself publicly, being now thirty years old.

6. In truly artless manner, the Evangelist explains how this came about. Christ, who till then had kept in the background and had not yet entered upon his office, now proceeds from Galilee to the Jordan, in order to be baptized by John, in company with sinners who acknowledged their sinfulness and yearned for forgiveness. Before such a one, John demurred because he felt himself unworthy to baptize him. "I have need to be baptized of thee," he says, "and comest thou to me?" But Jesus reassures him, "Suffer it to be so now, to fulfill all righteousness." In other words, in order that poor sinners might come to righteousness and be saved, you must now baptize me. For I have for the sake of sinners become a sinner and must fulfill that which God imposed upon sinners, in order that they might become righteous through me.

7. That was to be a comforting paradigm for us, that God's Son lets himself be baptized—though he was without sin—and performs what he was not obligated to do. We in contrast never do anything above and beyond what is necessary, for we are such wicked louts who don't even do what is our duty. Christ, God's Son, is holier than baptism itself, and yet he allows himself to be baptized. He institutes and ordains holy baptism, and moreover commands that such baptizing, henceforth, continue within Christendom, so that all who desire to be saved might be baptized.

8. That is the reason why wicked people come into the abyss of hell, because they despise or disdain baptism. Satan has ravished and blinded them, so that their eyes and ears are closed and they don't see or hear what is happening here. Why aren't you baptized, or your children? If Christ permitted himself to be baptized, how can you be

so haughty, so blind and foolish, as to despise baptism? Even though baptism were worth nothing, ought you not regard it with respect because of what this text is saying, that the Son of God himself was baptized, and that you, too, should be baptized, if for no other reason than to honor him, even though it were of no benefit to you?

9. To this, however, we must add baptism's promise and benefit. For we see how God in heaven pours out his grace through his Son's baptism. Heaven which before was closed, is opened by Christ's baptism and a window and door now stand open for us to see through. No longer is there a barrier between God and us, since God himself descends at the Jordan. The Father lets his voice be heard, the Son sanctifies baptism with his body, and the Holy Spirit descends in the form of a dove. Is this not a great manifestation, a truly great sign of how very precious baptism is to God, that he does not abstain from it?

10. That is why this day is called Epiphany, the Festival of the Manifestation, because the Father, Son, and Holy Spirit manifest themselves. The Holy Spirit appears in the lovely form of an innocent dove. Among all birds, a dove is known for its gentle nature, peaceful and not aggressive. So the Holy Spirit reveals himself in the friendliest of forms to show that he is not wrathful toward us, but wants to help us become holy and rescue us through Christ.

11. The Son, who does not require it for his person, nonetheless, allows himself to be baptized, revealing himself not only as example, but also for the sake of grace, that we might gladly receive baptism and be sure that by it we have a gracious God when we follow Christ's example and command, allowing ourselves to be baptized.

12. The Father's voice resounds, "This is my beloved Son in whom I am well pleased." It is a new voice, the likes of which no one had heard from heaven before. It would not be surprising if heaven and earth had trembled at the sound of God's speaking. I would have fallen on my face if I had heard God's voice. But this voice is different from the voice at Mt. Sinai where God also spoke from heaven. There his voice was so terrible that the earth quaked, the hills trembled, and the people feared for their lives. Here, however, it was all friendliness, grace, and compassion.

13. It was as though God said, You people, turn your eyes and open your ears in this direction. Note carefully this man who is here bap-

tized. Do you want to know who he is? He is my beloved Son, in whom I delight with deepest pleasure. You need not fear him. He stands here stripped, like any other man, brandishing neither sword nor worldly might. Nor do you have to be afraid of me either. I do not now come with thunder and lightning, with the rumble of drum and trumpet, as at Mt. Sinai, but with friendly mien and gracious demeanor.

14. Is there any unfriendliness here at all? The Son of God, who is without sin and guilt, stands in the Jordan and lets himself be baptized, doing more than he in any way was obliged to do. The Holy Spirit comes in the gentle form of a dove upon Jesus, right before the eyes of John. The Father speaks with us in most kindly manner, making known to us that he does not send a prophet, an apostle, or an angel, but his own dear Son in whom he is well pleased.

15. That meant, to my way of thinking, that when God directs us to look upon the Son, it is not because he is annoyed with us in some way as he reveals his Son to us and says, This is my beloved Son in whom I have highest delight. If you desire that I be a gracious Father, you may rest assured. Only hold fast to my Son, with whom I cannot be at enmity, and you will be beloved of me also because of him. So hear him and do what he says to you.

16. A person ought to be locked in and absolutely riveted to this voice, never letting this manifestation out of sight or earshot, how the Lord God tore heaven open, sending the Holy Spirit down in the form of a dove and he himself speaking gently with loving words, Here you have my Son, my dear and highest treasure, and me, too, in fullest measure. Here the Son presents himself as a poor and needy sinner, letting himself be baptized by John at the Jordan.

17. Thus the Godhead in all fullness, Father, Son, and Holy Spirit, was manifested on this day in profoundest graciousness and friendliness, each person of the Trinity clearly distinguished, so that everyone might know what and how to believe concerning God, especially what his stance towards Christ should be. For whoever holds to Christ, accepts his Word, and trusts his work cannot be an enemy of God. The bottom line is this: What the Son is called, what he says and does, is perfectly attuned to the Father's heartfelt good pleasure.

18. Oh, how blessed we would be if we accept this and cling to the Son with our whole heart. Contrariwise, people who allow that voice

to sound forth and pass it by as though they didn't hear it are without salvation and under the curse. The accursed papalists slander and persecute his voice, asserting that Christ is not the only beloved of the Father, but so also are monks, priests, masses, pilgrimages, and the like. If a person has thought this through correctly, that the friendship of God and his fatherly heart deserve the highest honor, he would rather die ten times over than give quarter to such slanderous, godless people and their notions.

19. So, my dear children, learn while you can, when you hear this voice sound forth. A few years ago we knew virtually nothing about it, heaven was shut and we heard things in the devil's name, as the monks preached of purgatory, hobgoblins, and other falsehoods. Now, praise God, preaching focuses on this inexpressible grace of God, and all that is lacking is for people to hear and learn! Since there's no help from the side of the thankless and blind world, let us be thankful to God for his goodness in today showing us his heart and his treasure: the Holy Spirit in the form of a dove, the Son by his baptism at the Jordan, and the Father in his own glorious and loving voice.

20. Who would not execrate an unthankful and joyless person who is unwilling to take to his heart the Son who here stands at the Jordan and lets himself be baptized as a sinner? The one upon whom the Spirit lights in the form of a dove? and the Father's voice in closest proximity? No doubt there were also countless holy angels present. For where the Father, Son, and Holy Spirit reveal themselves, all the heavenly host must also be present. This was the ultimate manifestation.

21. Therefore, learn to esteem this festival highly. The star given to the wise men was a manifestation, too, but this was much more wonderful. For here the three preeminent Kings—God the Father, God the Son, God the Holy Spirit—are all present as Christ was baptized. And how wondrous that this glorious manifestation occurred at Christ's baptism at the Jordan! Had God so willed, it might have been in the wilderness or in the temple. But it happened at the baptism, in order that we might esteem baptism highly and regard ourselves as nothing other than newly created, holy people by our baptism.

22. The Anabaptists and fanatical spirits today say that baptism is nothing more than ordinary water. May the devil take these slander

mouths! Dogs, sows, and cows also see nothing in the water but its taste. But a Christian ought not go by the taste, but by the Word. For it is not just plain water but God's Word and power. Just see what Christ's baptism portends: God the Father, the Son, and Holy Spirit are all present, along with the holy angels! Therefore, it is not powerless water but water in which God's Son is washed, over which the Holy Spirit hovers, and upon which God the Father preaches. For that reason baptism cannot be insignificant, but a gracious water sanctified and consecrated by God the Father, Son, and Holy Spirit. That is shown by the words which Christ spoke when he commanded baptism, "baptizing them in the name of the Father, and of the Son, and of the Holy Spirit." Without these words it is poor water, but when these words, "in the name of the Father, and of the Son, and of the Holy Spirit," are connected with the water, then it is not impotent water, but baptism.

23. That is why when I today am baptized in the name of the Father, and of the Son, and of the Holy Spirit, the Son is there with his body, the Holy Spirit with his presence, and God the Father with his voice, to hallow it. One cannot, therefore, say that it is powerless water in view of the fact that the entire Godhead is present. By the same token, it must not be looked upon as a human work since, although it is done by a human being, it nonetheless is not done in his name but in the name of the Father, Son, and Holy Spirit. They are present and give their full support, otherwise baptism would be a long time accomplishing what it does.

24. Who, now, would despise the word of the Father, Son, and Holy Spirit? Who would call the baptism of the Father, Son, and Holy Spirit powerless water? Do we not see what seasoning God throws into the water? When a person adds sugar to water then it no longer is mere water but a delectable claret, or something like that. Why then would we want to separate the word from the water here and call it poor water, as though God's Word, yes, God himself were not in and with that water? Not so, for God the Father, Son, and Holy Spirit are in and with that water, as at the Jordan where Christ stood in the water and the Holy Spirit hovered overhead, while God the Father preached withal.

25. Accordingly, baptism is water that can take away sin, death, and all evil, and help us come to heaven and eternal life. So it has be-

come a priceless sugar water, fragrant nectar, and medicine because God has interposed himself. God is a God of life and can make alive. Because he is in this water, it must be a true *aqua vitae,* "water of life," which drives death and hell away, and makes eternally alive.

26. We should, therefore, learn to know baptism well and esteem it highly, since we are not baptized in the name of angels or men, but in the name of God, the Father, Son, and Holy Spirit; or, as Acts 2:38 puts it, "in the name of Jesus," which is tantamount to the same. For whoever confesses Jesus Christ must also confess God the Father and the Holy Spirit, inasmuch as Christ clearly says that he comes from the Father and will send the Holy Spirit. Whoever believes on Jesus with his heart will not belie his Word but acknowledge that the Son is not alone but with the Father and the Holy Spirit, even though one may not in the same breath mention the Father and the Holy Spirit by name.

27. These are things a person ought to learn well, so that the word is not separated from baptism, or from the water with which one baptizes, but we confess that it is ordained of God to cleanse us for Christ's sake from sin and save us from eternal death. What else is there that God, the Father, Son, and Holy Spirit desire? Each and every sinner needs baptism, so that his sin might be washed away; whoever is in death needs baptism that death might be swallowed up, for baptism has God-given power to cleanse from sin and to bury death.

28. Upon this we are baptized; and even though we have fallen into sin and have done wickedness, yet will our baptism and its promises remain firm and sure. Only, we need to repent and not persist in sinning. For these two things are mutually exclusive: to yearn for forgiveness and then cling to our sins and refuse to leave them. We need to repent and say in true faith, God has plunged me into the baptism of the Father, Son, and Holy Spirit; to him I return, and I trust that my sins are taken away, not for my sake or any other creature's, but for the sake of the man, Christ, who commanded and ordained baptism and let himself be baptized as a sinner.

29. Accordingly, this manifestation far exceeds that of the star to the wise men. Under the papacy, however, the lesser is viewed as the greater and is celebrated on the eighth day. But this festival should rightly bear the name connected with baptism and be called the day

on which Christ was baptized. Then we would be justified to preach about it over against the fanatical sects and the devil, who would gladly divert us to all manner of other things rather than our treasure; he would gladly thrust it from before our eyes and out of our hands, as he has done in popedom, where little preaching has been done about this revelation at the Jordan.

30. So learn diligently how God this day manifested himself in a lovely sermon about his Son, how he deals with us and we with him, all in accord with his godly pleasure. Whoever is his disciple and holds to his Word will also be his dear child. The Son manifests himself in his fragile humanity as he allows himself to be baptized by John. The Holy Spirit reveals himself in the form of the dove. Thus God pours himself out upon us in all friendliness and grace, especially so the Father, whom we hear speaking in great kindness: Here you have not an angel, prophet, apostle, but my Son and myself. How, indeed, could God reveal himself more wondrously! When he himself preaches, there could be no greater preacher! How could we better serve him than to listen to his Son, our Saviour, and accept what he preaches and tells us? Whoever does not believe this for the sake of his salvation, does not deserve to hear it; instead he should listen to the devil and his apostles for his everlasting damnation. God give us his grace so that we may thank him for it and pray that he will preserve us in it and save us. Amen.

FIRST SUNDAY AFTER EPIPHANY

1534

Luke 2:41–52

Now his parents went to Jerusalem every year at the feast of the passover. And when he was twelve years old, they went up to Jerusalem after the custom of the feast. And when they had fulfilled the days, as they returned, the child Jesus tarried behind in Jerusalem; and Joseph and his mother knew not of it. But they, supposing him to have been in the company, went a day's journey; and they sought him among their kinsfolk and acquaintance. And when they found him not, they turned back again to Jerusalem, seeking him. And it came to pass, that after three days they found him in the temple, sitting in the midst of the doctors, both hearing them, and asking them questions. And all that heard him were astonished at his understanding and answers. And when they saw him, they were amazed: and his mother said unto him, Son, why hast thou thus dealt with us? behold, thy father and I have sought thee sorrowing. And he said unto them, How is it that ye sought me? wist ye not that I must be about my Father's business? And they understood not the saying which he spake unto them. And he went down with them, and came to Nazareth, and was subject unto them: but his mother kept all these sayings in her heart. And Jesus increased in wisdom and stature, and in favour with God and man.

1. This is a striking, poignant Gospel lesson for us to consider, if we bear in mind that the Virgin Mary had lost her son. Just think what it would mean if we lost the child Jesus from our hearts! But we will leave this analogy for another time and now consider the simple and plain facts of the story, which for the ordinary person are the most needful.

2. You have heard that Epiphany is Christ's manifestation. The newborn child's birth was not to remain a secret, but was to be revealed; otherwise his coming would have been of no use, if we were to know nothing of it. This is why in preaching during this season of the church year, we use texts from the Gospels which tell how Christ

manifested himself as Lord with power over all things, for example: when the star appeared to the wise men in the east; when he was baptized by John the Baptist at the Jordan River; when he performed his first miracle at Cana. For this reason the early church fathers chose the Gospels in which the manifestation is described, so that the Lord Jesus would not only be known among the people, but would be esteemed and renowned as more than an ordinary human, namely, as one born to a truly majestic lordship over the whole world, and that we recognize him as our Saviour, cling to him in every need and temptation, and learn to find help through him.

3. Today's Gospel also serves this very purpose. For it is a manifestation in which the Lord Jesus shows that he is not an ordinary but an extraordinary child, as he secretly withdraws from his parents and oversteps the discipline which all children owe their parents by God's command. The Evangelist explains that it happened in the following manner: His parents, like the rest of the Jews, were required to present themselves at the temple in Jerusalem at the Passover. The child Jesus had accompanied them, but then he tarried behind in Jerusalem. Because a child often joined the company of relatives, the parents did not miss him. For as a boy Jesus was not an eccentric misfit, but rather a well-adjusted boy among his peers, with whom he also played; but he was without sin, as he grew in grace and wisdom. So, naturally, Joseph and Mary assumed he was with friends and let it be. That evening when they arrived at the first night's lodging, they looked about where their son might be. After checking among friends and acquaintances, and not finding the child, they became frightened, for the child had been especially entrusted to his mother. Joseph also had received a solemn mandate to care for the child. But Mary was his mother, uniquely and alone. So it was a great fright and an especial heartache when they could not locate the child. There was no sleeping, no eating, no resting, only tears. We assume that they ran back that same night several miles, but the child was gone.

4. Just imagine what their hearts were telling them. The first day the child was lost and they were unaware of it; the second day they looked and failed to find the child; finally, on the third day they found him. Many thoughts went through their minds those three nights when they were unable to sleep. Especially the mother may

have thought, God has taken his son back; he no longer wants you as the mother because you have been negligent of his care. Joseph, too, could well have thought, God no longer wants you as a foster parent since you have been negligent in the care of this child who is God's Son and was entrusted to your care by God.

5. This is a unique situation in which the child Jesus, our dear Lord God, wishes to let it be known that he was not subject to his mother by necessity or authority; for what he did was done freely and with good intentions to show he was not under obligation. For he was not only his mother's son, but also her Lord and God. Therefore, he stands before his mother here not as a son—we shall be hearing of this pointedly next Sunday in the Gospel lesson when he says, "Woman what have I to do with you?" (wedding at Cana). So here also he shows himself to be not only a human who, of necessity, must be obedient to father and mother, but very plainly as one who has another Father who is greater and commands greater respect than Mary and Joseph. So he says, "How is it that ye sought me? Wist ye not that I must be about my Father's business?" In other words, as much as to say, I am your son; but more, I am the Son of my Father who is in heaven.

6. He revealed himself thus for our sakes that we might know with certainty that he is not only true man, but also true God. Accordingly, as the mother addressed him with the words, "Son, why hast thou thus dealt with us?" he responded with the following explanation: I have not been disobedient, nor have I despised you as you may think. He wishes to justify himself before his mother. Mary and Joseph thus had to add wrongful misjudging to the pain and anxiety they suffered. Do you know that as the Son of God in heaven I have authority over you? his response implies. He also reminds them of what the angels, the shepherds, the patriarch Simeon, and others had said about him. In other words: Have you forgotten all that? You should have known that even though I remained behind, I was not disobedient, but that I owe primary obedience to my Father in heaven.

7. As said, all this happened for our sakes to enlarge our faith, that we might learn to know Jesus correctly, that he is more than a man, namely, also true God. That is why he withholds obedience here from his parents, tarries behind in Jerusalem, and wishes to be justified be-

fore his parents, so that by this revelation he wishes to teach us, by example, that we must obey God rather than men, even though that be our parents. One of the products of our depraved nature is that in our ignorance and blindness we are much more inclined to serve men rather than God. Therefore, we should learn from this example of our dear Lord Jesus that if a situation arises where we must choose whether to be disobedient to God or to our parents, or those in authority, we must answer with Christ: "I must be about the business of my Father in heaven." Other than in such a case, I will with all my heart, be obedient to father, mother, emperor, king, lord and lady of the house. But in this instance there is no other way than this: Dear father and mother, I have another Father to whom I owe greater esteem than to you. This is what Mary and Joseph had forgotten; therefore, he had to remind them and teach them.

8. Now this has been written for our sakes, as stated, because of the bad habit, which we have by nature, that when we should obey God above all else, we excuse ourselves before the world and say, I cannot, for God has ordered me to be obedient to the government. This is how the enemies of the gospel now act—they learned it from us—saying, We are obligated to be obedient to the powers that be, for whoever is obedient to the ruler is obedient to God. Such obedience they praise highly. They put off the obedience which they owe God and say, We know very well from Scripture that it is not wrong to receive both kinds of elements in the Sacrament; but we have to be obedient to constituted authority. That is our father and mother, our sovereign, and he forbids it; therefore I cannot do it. Thank you, dear sir!

9. Who then is your magistrate? It is my sovereign, my father, my mother. Right! But what is the primary authority? Do you have no other authority here on earth beside your sovereign, your father and your mother? Whom do you consider him to be who says to you in the first commandment, "I am the Lord your God"? Should it not apply here, also, when he says that it pleases him that, with all due respect for your sovereign, king, emperor, father and mother, you say with Christ, "I must be about my Father's business"? For God's Word must have precedence. After that is complied with, then we must do what is demanded by father, mother, emperor and king. Thus one does not put the cart before the horse.

10. In this Gospel, our Lord Jesus Christ manifests himself not only for the sake of our faith and comfort, that he is our God and Saviour, but also as example of how in those matters that pertain to God, no one should take precedence, be it father, mother, sovereign, or whatever. For there is another Lord, a higher authority, that says, "I am your God." Him you should obey, do as he directs, and above all, serve. When you have fulfilled this obedience, then do what father, mother, sovereign, or government wish; but they may not hinder you in this higher obedience which, as said, must be carried out before anything else.

11. I don't wish to touch upon here the great anguish people feel when they lose Christ out of their hearts, but simply concentrate on the child who here reveals himself. We see that he is of much higher station than men in general, in that without special permission he exempts himself from obedience to his mother and does not follow her, but she must go running after him; thus the word is fulfilled which she received from the angel: "He shall be called the Son of the Highest!" She had to be reminded of this here, so that she wouldn't forget it.

12. So this manifestation corresponded well with the other revelations. For here we see that Christ is an extraordinary person, as the shepherds and Simeon also testified concerning him. That is why here he did not want to be regarded like other children, though indeed he also romped and played with them.

13. The Evangelist explains very nicely what took place in the temple. The lad did not inquire about the price of wheat, or what's to eat or drink. Rather, he discussed with the Bible scholars the Law and Word of God, first of all listening to them as they expounded the Scriptures, then chiding them if their interpretation and teaching were wrong, though in a way that a young boy would do it. For example, if I may take something suggested by Matthew: When the Bible scholars spoke of the fifth commandment's meaning and limited it to striking someone dead with the hand, he would have interposed as follows. Killing someone does not occur only with the hand, but also with the heart, with the eyes, and with the tongue, as when a person rages against his neighbor, scorns, speaks evil about or curses him. For the fifth commandment requires us to have a caring heart toward our neighbor.

14. This was his manner of listening and questioning these scholars, like a young child would do. As a result of what was here manifested, the scholars were impressed and wondered in themselves about how this lad came to these thoughts. For when they erred in any way in what they were saying, he chided them for it, but in childlike manner.

15. It all had to do with what he said, "I must be about my Father's business." Which was? God's Word, the Law, and his will! So just as he inquired of them concerning God's Law, so also, undoubtedly, he raised questions concerning the promises of God, what they thought concerning the Messiah, whence he would come, and what his mission would be. And in all of this he would have acted humbly, piously, and respectfully, as a son who had learned these things from his mother; it would have left everyone thinking, This lad is filled with the Holy Spirit; he will become a Wundermann. For as the saying goes, even apart from this era: Our young people must be shown how they ought to strive in order to amount to something.

16. This then is a short summary of how the child Jesus revealed himself to his mother and Joseph; he was no ordinary child, nor was he subject to their obedience and to be scolded for failure to obey.

17. Now St. Luke concludes the lesson. Jesus returned with his parents to Nazareth and was subject to them. So this child who, because of his Father in heaven, separates himself from his mother, is once again obedient to her and to Joseph, even though he was not obligated to be, as St. Luke indicates when he says, "and was subject unto them." He did this of his own free will, not of necessity, for he was God and Lord over Mary and Joseph. He was obedient to them not for their sakes as father and mother, but rather as an example. This, therefore, is what we ought to consider, how he performed chores about the house, whatever was asked of him, picking up shavings, fetching water and food, whatever was needed, without being disgruntled.

18. Young folks, especially, should note this example how the Lord, our God, behaved in his youth, without a whimper of complaint doing whatever his mother asked, no matter that the tasks were insignificant, trifling, or small. Our youth should do the same and cultivate obedience and humility, which is pleasing to God. God

expects this of all children as the fourth commandment states, that they be obedient to their parents and of willing spirit.

19. I remember well in the monastery how the young monks puzzled over the question of what Christ did in his childhood. The monks even produced a book about Christ's infant years that contained much clumsy foolishness. They told this fable, too, about a bishop who had a deep desire to know more about this time in Jesus' life. He dreamed he was a carpenter trimming a plank, with a small boy next to him picking up the shavings, when a young woman in a blue cloak carrying a pan called to the two, the man and his little son, to come and eat. In his dream he crept quietly and hid behind the door, so that he might see what they were eating. Now when the young woman poured porridge into a bowl, and then some into a smaller bowl which she handed to the child, the child spoke up and said, Thank you, mother, and what should the man behind the door eat? The bishop, frightened, awoke at these words. Such was the inane stuff they fantasized about!

20. If you really want to know what Christ did in his youth, listen to what the Evangelist says in the Gospel, "and was subject unto them." That means he did as his father and mother asked and was never sullen or out of sorts. Every child and every servant should feel shame within his heart when he hears this account of the child Jesus and still fails to give the same sort of obedience, either to parent or to employer, but as a matter of fact lives in shameful disobedience. People, in general, think and say, If I knew what the child Jesus had done, I would do likewise. The monks say, What St. Francis did—his garb and his vigils—we want to do too. Even more emphatically, they say, If I knew what Christ had done, I would do the same. But who can know what Christ did? People love to fantasize and talk about this, and to use it as an excuse. It is as clear as day what Christ did, for we have it written, "He was subject to his parents." With these words the Evangelist summarizes the entire youth of our dear Lord Jesus Christ.

21. But what does it mean that "he was subject to them"? Nothing more than that he carried out the obligations of the fourth commandment. That would include all tasks a father and mother require around the house, doing everything asked of him like any other child.

So, our dear Lord Jesus too. When his mother said, Son, get me a bucket of water, fetch some beer, some wood, some straw, or whatever, he ran and got whatever she asked.

22. Now, because we know how Jesus behaved, it seems reasonable to expect that all pious children would consider themselves unworthy to be compared with the child Jesus, our glorious Lord, and to do as he did. Likely he picked up shavings, perhaps herded the cattle, gave them their feed, and anything else requested by the parents, things of no special significance. My, what exemplary children we would be if we would follow his example and do our parents' bidding, no matter how trifling and insignificant it might be.

23. There is no need for great volumes to be written about what the child Jesus did in his youth. One need only observe what father and mother require around the house, the tasks they ask their children to perform as they say, Come here, do this, run yonder, do that! For it is very evident that Jesus did not enter a monastery and become a monk, but went back to Nazareth, remained among the people, was obedient to father and mother, and, like other children, permitted himself to be directed, but never transgressed the Ten Commandments.

24. The monks, in their crude imagining, had the child Jesus making new little birds, fawns, and other small animals. They ascribed to him such deeds as did not serve obedience nor belong to the fourth commandment. Father and mother would not have asked him to make new birds, for childhood obedience required other tasks connected to the household, the kind almost no one wants to do. The Evangelist implies such things as fit with the household routine and the fourth commandment, thus simply attesting his childhood obedience toward his parents.

25. This we should diligently note, so that we not only know what the child Jesus did in his youth and follow his example, but also that we do not doubt but believe that such works, like obedience to parents, have been sanctified and blessed through the child Jesus. Because he, through his person, sanctified these tasks, we should quietly strive to do the same. But you can't tell the world anything. That is why we have disdained such tasks and obedience, and have rushed into the monasteries. Everyone thinks he can do it better and

more excellently than the dear child Jesus. Do they not see that such household chores and obedience to father and mother have been sanctified through this holy person, God's Son, who in his youth gathered wood, picked up shavings, started the fire, fetched water, and did other household chores? Truly we are not worthy even to follow his example.

26. Accordingly, we should study this bit of Scripture with diligence and consider ourselves blessed when we see that in being obedient and performing such works, Christ did not permit himself to be vexed. Surely these routine tasks are a thousand times better and more blessed than those performed by monks in the monastery. The child Jesus did not rush into a monastery, but remained at home and served his mother and Joseph, providing us with an example, so that we might learn what precious, excellent, holy deeds these are which Christ, our dear Lord, himself did.

27. This, then, is a summary of this Holy Gospel: first, that Christ is not only the son of Mary, but also her God, and Lord, yes, a Lord over all, and that he is to be found doing what his Father wills. Second, that even though he is Lord over all, nevertheless, as an example for us, he humbles himself, is obedient to father and mother, so that we in our lives and in our tasks might learn two things: first, obedience to God, and second, obedience to father and mother and all authority. Godly contentment and blessing will be ours as we fulfill our duty on both counts. May God help us thereto through Christ, our Lord. Amen.

SECOND SUNDAY AFTER EPIPHANY

1533

On every holy day we are to worship our Lord God, listen to what he has to say, and learn from what he is telling us about Christ. So, let us read and learn from today's Gospel lesson.

John 2:1–11

And the third day there was a marriage in Cana of Galilee; and the mother of Jesus was there: And both Jesus was called, and his disciples, to the marriage. And when they wanted wine, the mother of Jesus saith unto him, They have no wine. Jesus saith unto her, Woman, what have I to do with thee? mine hour is not yet come. His mother saith unto the servants, Whatsoever he saith unto you, do it. And there were set there six waterpots of stone, after the manner of the purifying of the Jews, containing two or three firkins apiece. Jesus saith unto them, Fill the waterpots with water. And they filled them up to the brim. And he saith unto them, Draw out now, and bear unto the governor of the feast. And they bare it. When the ruler of the feast had tasted the water that was made wine, and knew not whence it was: (but the servants which drew the water knew;) the governor of the feast called the bridegroom, and saith unto him, Every man at the beginning doth set forth good wine; and when men have well drunk, then that which is worse: but thou hast kept the good wine until now. This beginning of miracles did Jesus in Cana of Galilee, and manifested forth his glory; and his disciples believed on him.

1. As John states, this is the first miracle which our dear Lord Jesus performed on earth, a miracle whereby he wanted to manifest his glory to his disciples. They are to recognize from this miracle that he is the Son of God and the true Messiah, since he is able to do what no other human being is able to do, namely, alter the nature of cre-

ated things by changing water into wine. Such power belongs solely to God, the Lord of creation.

2. This miracle, therefore, serves chiefly to teach us who Christ is, and to seek his help and mercy with confidence whenever in need. He will supply it at the proper time. This is the principal point in today's Gospel.

3. However, inasmuch as we find that sort of comfort and instruction in all of Christ's miracles, we wish now to deal particularly with the miracle that the Lord performed at the marriage, so that the teaching concerning matrimony might also be upheld among Christians. For there is much here that is timely.

4. The Lord performed his first miracle at a wedding in the little town of Cana, when he was thirty years old. He had already been baptized by John and had then begun his pastoral, preaching ministry. According to the pope's viewpoint on sanctity, it would have been better for the Lord to have done it prior to this. But he did it afterwards, at the time he entered his priestly office and was baptized, anointed, and called by the Holy Spirit to be a preacher. In keeping with this holy calling, ordained and consecrated by the Holy Spirit to preach and perform miracles, he came to the marriage.

5. We have here a pertinent object lesson for use against all false practices, fanatical spirits, and sects, not only against those existing before our time—now mostly dead and gone—but also against those arising in the future, whose so-called piety has been characterized by little more than opposition to marriage and other civil duties, and wandering off into wilderness solitude. All heretics have denigrated matrimony and have sought for and begun some newfangled and bizarre way of life.

6. However, it was particularly under the papacy that matrimony came to be looked at with contempt, and only virginity and chastity were extolled. If you want to live in a state of holiness and serve God, the word was, then forsake the world, enter a monastery, and become a monk. What they mean by forsaking the world is to have better and more tranquil days than are common to matrimony. The fact was that not only simple souls but also intelligent people were caught up in this misguided zeal, not wanting to be entangled and troubled with a wife, children, servants, maids, evil neighbors, preferring instead to live in

peace. Then came the monks, who considered their mode of life holy and perfect. In reality, however, it was an indolent, easy, undisturbed, sensual, epicurean life. It was a common saying: My son is becoming a monk or a priest; they have it good. How true it was, tragically. While they had everything, they neglected the world's poor whose miserable crumbs turned rancid and bitter; nonetheless they got the reputation of living a good and sanctified life.

7. Although the object lesson which Christ has pictured for us here is really very pertinent, it has not helped the godless. To be sure, people have listened to it in church, but they have not really understood it. They ask, If it is such a good idea to enter wilderness solitude or a monastery, how come Christ attended the marriage? If it is wrong to live in the world and to marry, why does Christ honor the marriage with his presence and perform such an extraordinary miracle?

8. Now, had it been his opinion that such monastic life or seclusion be undertaken for two or three weeks, or for a year or two, it might have made some sense. But that a person not only avoids matrimony but repudiates it permanently, is to despise and dishonor the marriage estate to the nth degree and is not really seeking for a holier estate but a life of tranquillity, of quietness and pleasure, contrary to God's command and ordinance.

9. Therefore, let us learn here how greatly our Lord God esteems the fourth commandment. For where people are married, there a household is constituted with father and mother, wife and children, hired hands and maidservants, cattle and fields, all laboring for daily bread. The Lord wants to teach us that this is a holy and blessed life, that we should not disdain marriage but esteem it very highly as created and ordained by God, even as Christ did.

10. Accordingly, this Gospel is a good sermon for young people since they need to learn how they can serve our Lord God in the home; also, how unnecessary it is to undertake something special, in the manner of that unctuous and tonsured monkish rabble. For a father who rules his home in the fear of God, who rears his children and servants in the fear and knowledge of God, has a good, blessed, and godly life. Likewise, a woman who provides her children with food and drink, and washes and bathes them, need not aspire to a holier and more godly vocation. Household servants and maids, who

do what the master and mistress require, are also serving God; and if they believe in Christ, they please God much more by simply tidying up the room or cleaning shoes than by all the praying, fasting, saying of Masses, and whatever else the monks regard as constituting divine service.

11. For this reason one ought in no way regard domestic life with contempt, nor denigrate it, like the monks, as being a worldly, unholy estate. For we see here that our Lord himself attends a marriage. Indeed, this applies not only to the wedding but to the whole business of maintaining a family. God wants family life esteemed, just as the fourth commandment, which stands first in the second table, points out.

12. If you are a father or a mother, continue in your position and know that God is very pleased when you do what your station requires of you. If you are a servant, male or female, know that God is pleased with your vocation. God indeed blessed and honored matrimony, accepted the invitation to the wedding, and honored the marriage by his presence and by performing the first miracle of his pastoral office. He might have said, I do not choose to come; I shall attend to my priestly office; it is a worldly affair; I am committed to a spiritual office; I must act in accord with it.

13. However, even as the very highest of bishops, he does not allow the office to which he is especially committed to interfere. He does not disdain the wedding which is the beginning of domestic life; instead he honors, extols, and upholds the functions of this estate, so that everybody ought to say in agreement, Since God has ordained that through marriage and the household I be a servant, a child, a husband, a wife and mother, I shall gladly do it and serve God in my position with joy. For I realize that the High Priest, my Lord and God, Christ Jesus, not only identifies himself with and esteems this estate highly, but also supports and sustains it.

14. We need to cite this truth and example against the false teacher and the pope, and today especially against fanatical spirits, like the Anabaptists and others, who say, There is nothing but trouble in maintaining a household; it's always one thing or another going wrong; servants prove unfaithful; neighbors are bad and quarrelsome; there is no end to problems involving wife and children, just a whole lot of grief, toil, and worry connected with a family; on top of

everything there's the burgomaster to obey, and also the prince. Amid so much unrest—and there's neither limit nor end to it in married life—how can you be mindful of God and serve him? For this reason I do not want to marry and set up housekeeping; I'm going to enter a monastery where I am free from all such disturbance. And so they run off, in the name of the devil, the one into this order and station, the other into that.

15. Let's take special note, therefore, of this instruction and object lesson, so that, if some such crazy spirits appear again, we are well forewarned and persuaded that marriage and looking after a household are extolled and endorsed by Christ. For we clearly see here how the Lord himself, by his presence at the wedding, did not disengage the bride from the groom but let them be together, let them manage their household, and let their servants serve; meanwhile he himself even assisted them, so that the wedding could be celebrated all the more fittingly. By this beautiful example he wanted to teach us that he is very pleased when people faithfully assist and serve in maintaining the home. For even though deficiencies may abound, you must not be dismayed. Just make sure you have Christ at your side and that you live a godly life. He will turn water to wine, and so bless your estate that you will always have enough and things will work out for you, even though you may be in want for a while. At the proper time, help and comfort will be forthcoming.

16. This is what experience teaches. When husband and wife live together as Christians, our Lord God sustains them so richly that they receive more than they ever imagined or believed possible. And I fully believe that, if you were to heap the total amount of money he could earn in a year in front of him on a table, a laborer, who is otherwise very diligent and fears God, would still not believe it was sufficient to support him and his family. But here's where God's secret blessing is at work: today you spend twenty pennies and tomorrow another twenty pennies, and thus day for day you experience God's blessing as you quietly manage your household. Our dear Lord, you see, today still changes water into wine, in my home and in yours (if we are but godly and pious and let him do the caring). Again, it is his doing which multiplies one piece of bread into ten, and causes one coat to wear as long as three otherwise. If we would but open our

eyes, we would be forced to say, Lord, it is by your will that our household is provided for; when we establish it, we do so in service to you; you have honored it and continue still to honor it with your blessing. For this reason I shall not disdain it, but make it my calling to look after it.

17. The Evangelist makes special mention of the fact that Jesus' mother was there also. She could well have acted as the bride's mother. It was a wedding feast, where nothing was lacking except bread and wine. But she is a mother; she takes charge of matters, as though they are her concern when she sees what is needed. Here again we need to keep something in mind. Were marriage not pleasing to God, would not Jesus have said to her, See here, mother, you are too noble and great a person, among all women the Virgin-mother of the Son of God, and, therefore, you should devote yourself simply and alone to the church and spiritual matters. But now you concern yourself with wedding details, so that things go right, assigning people to their tasks and seeing to it that they perform them. Certainly it seemed ridiculous that the holy mother should resign herself to such menial work, like being a maid at the wedding, and caring for the people with foodstuffs, and otherwise attending to their wants. However, that's the way it was, as I have now repeatedly stated, so that we might rightly learn to understand this estate which Christ and the Virgin Mary so highly honored.

18. Nevertheless, this object lesson made no impression in the papacy, nor does it have any effect on the disobedient, unfaithful servants in the home. It is the devil's doing that no one wants to learn, believe, or regard as true that it is service to our God when we faithfully and diligently do our duties in the home; otherwise servants and maidservants, children and domestics, would keep a cheerful attitude in all their tasks, and cause the household to become a Garden of Eden as they work, saying, I am happy to do what I am given to do and leave undone whatever they wish, in order to please my master or mistress. And even though I am reprimanded from time to time—that's bound to happen—I am sure, nonetheless, that my position is a service and my life pleasing to our Lord God. For my Redeemer, Christ himself, went to the marriage and honored it with his presence and the services of his mother Mary. Should I not gladly now

render honor and service to such an estate? But we find very few domestic servants who behave like that. Most are hard, harder than steel. Even though they hear this story, they still do not choose to ponder it, nor be persuaded that they are able by faithful performance of duty—even though it's hard work—to serve our Lord God better than a nun or a monk in a convent or a monastery. However, since no one takes it to heart or believes it, everything is done grudgingly and unwillingly, and it is impossible for a good and wholesome spirit to prevail among such unwilling servants.

19. Now, ought not a God-fearing and pious maidservant, who must cook and do other things, take consolation from, and be pleased by, the example set by the mother of God? Shouldn't she say, Are not the cooking I must do, and the other things, the same duties performed by dear mother Mary at the marriage? She kept busy, saw to it that everything was being done well, and so on. And even though what I am doing in the home is menial and insignificant, I still am doing it to the glory of God, who has commanded and wants me to be obedient and diligent, and I know that when I am being obedient I am pleasing him. Let the world place whatever value it wants on such obedience. Those who want to be Christians ought to regard it as fundamental and true worship of God and resolutely render obedience. Thus a servant can be very happy in his position in the home and do what is pleasing to God, saying, Thank you, Lord, for placing me into this position and service, because I know that I am pleasing and serving you more than all the monks and nuns who have no mandate for their service. However, in the fourth commandment I have God's command to honor father and mother, to serve my master and mistress with all diligence and faithfulness, and to help care for the home. Therefore, I want to do it willingly and with love.

20. Whoever approaches things in this spirit will have pure joy and delight in his position and service, and were it already in paradise, our Lord God with all his angels would be rejoicing over it too. Similarly, a master and mistress will also be pleased by it, and for their part gladly and richly reward such faithfulness and willing service. For a faithful, pious servant is thought of very highly everywhere.

21. However, that's not the way it is today. People would much rather enter a monastery, supposing to serve God better there than

by serving masters and mistresses in performing domestic duties. Since the fourth commandment is thus trod underfoot, and marriage and caring for a household disdained, it is God's just judgment—and our God does deal justly—when he permits such despisers of his estate and ordinance to become monks and nuns, and lets them continue in that calling where they torment themselves and, in addition, commit the greatest disobedience and disservice to God. For since he has not commanded such estate, they have not served him, but the devil.

22. Therefore, let's learn this object lesson well, so that each of us willingly and contentedly serves and supports the estate of marriage which our Lord himself ordained and honored and created to be a wellspring and source of all other estates on earth. For every king and ruler must support the establishing of households, or marriage (they themselves have stemmed from the estate of marriage), because there would be neither people nor means to support government were people not to marry. For the householder, father or mother, must lay the foundation upon which all estates in the world, from the loftiest to the lowliest are sustained. For this reason our Lord God has caused the marriage estate to be a wellspring of every gift that belongs to our life and existence, as Scripture states, "Eve is the mother of every human being."

23. We should acknowledge and be most ready to give honor and support to this estate, so that every servant might come to say, Lord, it is pleasing to you; you were at the wedding at Cana, and your mother, esteemed as most blessed among all women, performed at the wedding the things which I do in my master's home and service. Since she was not ashamed to perform such menial service but volunteered her service, why should I, poor worm-bag, be too proud to perform such work in the home? For compared with the pure Virgin Mary, what am I but dirt?

24. However, married people, if they are pious and God-fearing, ought to take comfort from the fact that God does not want to abandon them but is eager to overwhelm them with his blessing and relieve them of all want, just as he does here. For it will never be otherwise: married people have to face many difficulties in order to sustain the family. But if a person invites Christ to the marriage and

is God-fearing, blessing and help will be near. So let us learn this lesson well today, that we should be most willing to perform our household duties and not allow ourselves to be seduced by those who say, Performing household tasks and getting married are things of the world; if you want to serve God, you must strive and do things in another way.

25. As the Anabaptists, those deluded people, do and say, one must desert wife and child, and boast that such leave-taking is a great cross to bear but augments holiness, and this is painful. However, this is pure villainy, the reason being, that whatever cross one loads on himself does not trigger pain. What one suffers because of wife and child, or neighbor, hurts much worse, and everyone, therefore, is fearful of being bound by more than twenty ropes. Wicked scoundrels free themselves from such cords and live as they please. But you cannot call this hurting yourself. What is really painful is, according to God's injunction, to be bound to wife, rulers, neighbors, servants, while on every side one's hands are busy showing Christian love and patience. For then we must hear, see, and endure a lot of things which are unpleasant; nevertheless, we must stay the course and not run away. We must say, We shall gladly endure, for we know that God will bless our home. Yes, we thank God, who has placed us into this estate so pleasing to him, from the bottom of our hearts. If troubles arise, he will help, just as he did here at this marriage.

26. May we learn this from today's Gospel and call upon God for his grace, so that we may retain what he has taught and in a Christlike way perform the duties of our calling. Amen.

THIRD SUNDAY AFTER EPIPHANY

1533

Let us hear today's Gospel in praise of our dear Lord God:

Matthew 8:1–13

When he was come down from the mountain, great multitudes followed him. And, behold, there came a leper and worshipped him, saying, Lord, if thou wilt, thou canst make me clean. And Jesus put forth his hand, and touched him, saying, I will; be thou clean. And immediately his leprosy was cleansed. And Jesus saith unto him, See thou tell no man; but go thy way, show thyself to the priest, and offer the gift that Moses commanded, for a testimony unto them. And when Jesus was entered into Capernaum, there came unto him a centurion, beseeching him, and saying, Lord, my servant lieth at home sick of the palsy, grievously tormented. And Jesus saith unto him, I will come and heal him. The centurion answered and said, Lord, I am not worthy that thou shouldest come under my roof; but speak the word only, and my servant shall be healed. For I am a man under authority, having soldiers under me: and I say to this man, Go, and he goeth; and to another, Come, and he cometh; and to my servant, Do this, and he doeth it. When Jesus heard it, he marvelled, and said to them that followed, Verily I say unto you, I have not found so great faith, no, not in Israel. And I say unto you, That many shall come from the east and west, and shall sit down with Abraham, and Isaac, and Jacob, in the kingdom of heaven. But the children of the kingdom shall be cast out into outer darkness: there shall be weeping and gnashing of teeth. And Jesus said unto the centurion, Go thy way; and as thou hast believed, so be it done unto thee. And his servant was healed in the selfsame hour.

1. There are two marvelous works told in this Gospel: first, the healing of the leper; second, the account of the centurion whose servant Christ restored to health.

2. However, the first and foremost thing in this story, which Jesus extols and commends so highly, is the faith of the centurion, a heathen, of whom Jesus says that he has not found such faith in Israel. It

was indeed a wonder that a heathen, who did not have the promises as the Jews had, should nonetheless have had such great and excellent faith as to surpass all of Israel. The Lord welcomes such faith gladly and, as he longs to do, says to the centurion, "Go thy way, and as thou hast believed, so be it done unto thee."

3. We see from this what is the best and most acceptable service before God, namely, nothing pleases our Lord God more than that we believe and trust in him from the heart. The Lord, our God, does not ask for beautiful temples or splendid, shiny works, but rather for inner devotion of the heart, that is, for faith, as the prophet Jeremiah (5:3) asks, "O Lord, are not thine eyes upon the truth?" We should, therefore, know that when we serve God from the heart, with faith, we are then his servants, priests, children, and heirs, who will be with him in heaven.

4. It is an especially beautiful sermon as the Lord Christ singles out the centurion and lifts him higher than the whole people Israel. He leaves out Annas, Caiaphas and all the priests, the Pharisees and scribes, and makes out of the heathen centurion an example of holiness for all of the Jews. It is like having someone in our day say, I have found a Turk of such splendid faith that neither pope nor bishops, neither spiritual leaders nor secular, neither learned nor unlearned, have a faith to compare, or as Christ says, I have not found a faith like it in Israel. The Jews were the native citizens, with the rights and status of children and heirs, under the covenant and the Law, having the temple services and the promise; also, Christ originated from them according to the flesh (Rom. 9:5). They heard Christ preaching daily and saw his miracles; yet did not believe in him. The centurion, on the other hand, was a guest and stranger, outside of the citizenry of Israel, alien to the testaments concerning the promise (Eph. 2:12). In short, he was a pagan, and this same heathen comes without circumcision and the Law, and clings to the Lord Christ with such faith that he obtains more from him than he could ever have wished or hoped for.

5. The Evangelist informs us that the centurion's faith manifested two excellent features. First, with his faith there is great, deep humility, as he says, "Lord, I am not worthy that thou shouldest come under my roof." This amounts to saying, O Lord, why would you even

bother with me? I am wicked, you are holy; I am a sinner, you are righteous. Indeed, I have heard that you do great miracles in Israel, that you restore health to the sick, and I dearly wanted to have my sick servant helped; but I consider myself unworthy for you to come into my house.

6. Second, there is an effulgent magnificence to his faith in that he understands that Christ is true God, and attributes to him such power and might that, even though absent, he could still heal his servant. He confesses not only his unworthiness that Christ should come into his house, but also that it would not actually require so much trouble, for Christ could effect that for which he petitioned merely by his word, even though not personally present. The centurion had heard that the Lord had previously raised the dead, and from the same report he had concluded within himself that it was not necessary for Christ personally to come to his servant. He need but speak the word and his servant would be well. So firmly does he believe this that he draws an example from his own life, "I am a man under authority, having soldiers under me; and I say to this man, Go, and he goeth; and to another, Come, and he cometh; and to my servant, Do this, and he doeth it." I am a man, he says, who is under authority. I am not a ruling magistrate with supreme power, but under authority. Yet I can with one word cause things to be done. If my word, then, is so powerful, your word is many more times so, because you are not mere man but the Lord God over all creatures, who demonstrates power and might everywhere by great signs and wondrous works.

7. That meant not only having faith, but also to speaking and teaching about the nature and way of faith in the best, most vivid manner. For it is faith's rightful art to be moved to trust the word with the whole heart, as the one and only treasure and hope, never doubting the "Yea" and "Amen" to what the word promises. The centurion rested upon the word without wavering, fully confident of it. For that reason he said to Jesus, "Speak the word only, and my servant shall be healed." This was tantamount to his saying, If I but have the word, I have everything, and nothing is lacking for my servant; he will be safe and sound.

8. This is such wonderful, excellent faith and such beautiful, deep humility on the centurion's part that Christ marvels over it, and

bursts forth with joyful heart to say, "Verily I say unto you, I have not found so great faith, no, not in Israel. And I say unto you, that many shall come from the east and west . . ." The Jews, in other words, are unwilling to believe; the Gentiles are beginning to come to faith. The tables are being turned. The Jews, the children of the kingdom who had the promises, will be cast away because of unbelief, while the heathen, who lack the promise, will be received into the kingdom because they believe.

9. The Lord is so pleased and so impressed with the centurion's humility and faith that he is ready straight on to do what the centurion desires. "Go thy way," he says, "and as thou hast believed, so be it done unto thee." The centurion has no need to petition further, nor explain anything more about his servant's illness. So deep is the Lord's love for him, that everything is "Yea" and "Amen" even before he petitions further. Even though the centurion was a heathen and unworthy, his fine faith pleases Jesus so very much, not because the centurion vaunts his unworthiness, but because of his recognition of unworthiness, because he feels and confesses it. Such humility and faith prompts the Lord not only to heal the servant, but also to praise and commend the centurion's faith.

10. That is one part of this lesson and it is recorded for our learning, to goad us, so that we may learn to believe, to regard ourselves as unworthy, and be led to say, Though I am not worthy of it, I accept it being unworthy; though I have not merited it—for I know nothing in myself by which I deserve it—yet will I take it as gift. That, indeed, is true faith and genuine humility when a person fears because of his unworthiness and yet does not despair. As Psalm 147:11 states, "The Lord taketh pleasure in them that fear him, in those that hope in his mercy." This is today's lesson, a glorious one, really too sublime for a house sermon; it really belongs in the church's pulpit.

11. The leper is cleansed from his leprosy by the Lord and sent to the priests. Jesus does not deal with the centurion's servant in this manner, nor with others whom he healed from their diseases, as he does here with the leper. He himself explains the reason why, when he says, "Go thy way, show thyself to the priest, and offer the gift that Moses commanded, for a testimony unto them." They have to give certification, and that I won't contest. Theirs is law and they

have the authority to examine the lepers and to offer gifts for them; that prerogative I won't take from them. In the case of the centurion, however, he did not say, Go, let yourself be circumcised and become a Jew. Even less does he say now, Give up your vocation, run to the monastery and become a monk, or that the servant be given his freedom; rather he lets the centurion remain a centurion, the servant, a servant.

12. In this way Christ shows us that his kingdom does not overturn secular rule and the world's vocations. All stations in life, given and established by God, are good, and to become a Christian a person is not required to have a specified external station. A husband and wife need not part and run to the cloister in order to be Christians and serve God. They can be Christians and serve God where they are, yes, be better Christians and serve God more than by leaving their vocations and running from each other. It is the pope who labeled all other vocations worldly, calling his alone spiritual, as also that of his monks and clerics. That is a perilous line for the world, and indeed false and fabricated. We see how the Lord lets the Jews retain their law and authority; and if they had received him, he would have let the whole of Jerusalem, with Moses, the temple, the kingdom, and the priesthood stand and remain; even though they were wicked rascals, yet he would have let them abide.

13. That God later destroyed Jerusalem with the temple, its worship, and the kingdom, came about because they refused to receive him. This is his usual way: If they will not allow him to abide, he will tear them to pieces. He was willing to let the Jews have their temple, if only the people would acknowledge him and serve him. But because they were unwilling, he let it all be smashed. It is similar to a great king and lord who storms a city, not intending to destroy, devastate, and demolish it totally, but wants it to give up, yield, pay tribute, and be subject to him instead of to his opponent and enemy. But if the city refuses to yield and tries to destroy the king, he will demolish it. In like manner, Christ with his gospel does not wish to tear apart the government, family life, and external estates of the Jews, but simply said to them, Receive me as your Lord, follow me, and I will let you go on. But they did not want to receive him as Lord nor follow him. He warned them earnestly, admonished, entreated, and im-

plored them, saying, I did not plan for you to oppose me; I will be tolerant, but let me continue to be your Lord. But they refused, saying, We don't want this one to rule over us. In fact, they did their utmost to destroy him. But what happened? Indeed, they killed him on the cross, but they could not be done with him, and he destroyed them.

14. The same thing happened with the Roman Empire. Christ came to them, implored them to receive his gospel and follow him in true fear, acknowledgment, and faith, willing to let them have their rule and government. He did not want to strip the Roman emperor of his authority, even teaching that people were to give the emperor his due (Matt. 22:21). Indeed, as he stood before the governor of the land, Pilate, he deigned to give worldly rule its honor (John 18). But the Roman emperor set himself and his empire against Christ, persecuted the gospel, crucified some Christians, killed others with the sword, and sought to destroy Christ and his followers. As a result, his government and empire fell, and Rome lay crumbled in the dust.

15. In short, we must receive Christ and his gospel ahead of everything else. When we do this, all else goes well; and even if for a time we lose sight of it, we shall not finally lose it. But if we do not accept Christ and his gospel, but persecute it, we will not hold anything else for long. If ever the dire necessity comes when I must choose either to deny Christ or leave behind my wife and children, the way out is clear. If I may continue to hold to Christ and retain my wife and child too, well and good, but if it's a choice between having wife, child, rule, power, and the like, and denying Christ, then I must forsake wife, child, rule, power, body, and life before I deny Christ.

16. Nowadays we are ready to grant the pope and his henchmen their power, glory, and honor, doing them no harm, if only they will not lord it over the church but will acknowledge Christ and allow him alone to be Lord in the church. And if they do not themselves want to receive him, we would ask them only to allow us and others who want to trust in him to do so, and not entice people to idolatry and blasphemy, nor kill people because of it. But the pope with his tonsured hordes are unwilling; they try to push Christ from his seat and set themselves in his place, throttling and killing those who want to belong to Christ. Bring on the fire, is their cry, burn the heretics, and their Christ be damned. For that reason Christ rebuffs them and

says, Dear sirs, pope, bishops, lords, you intend me evil, to push me from my seat and set yourselves in my place; that will not happen. I will keep my throne, and all who want to unseat me, pope, bishops, prelates, princes, lords, and all evil rascals, will lie in a heap anon.

17. To sum up, Christ wishes to let each man abide, but instead of serving Satan he wants him now to serve him. Those who accede to his wish shall not only abide but they will also be built up (Jer. 31:28): "As I have watched over them, to pluck up, and to break down, and to throw down, and to destroy, and to afflict; so will I watch over them, to build, and to plant, saith the LORD." Whoever refuses will be destroyed. For God cannot and will not permit those to go unpunished who will not have him to be Lord but serve Satan, as Moses testifies (Deut. 18:12:) "For all that do these things are an abomination unto the LORD: and because of these abominations the LORD thy God doth drive them out from before thee."

18. The world cannot and will not have Christ as Lord, nor serve him. As a result land and people are destroyed and laid waste. If our town does not want to have him who saved them as Lord, no injustice will be done to her when the same Lord and Saviour destroys and lays her level with the ground, saying to her, Is this what you want? Will you not only forget all the benefits shown to you, but on top of it all drive me out of the land and serve another master for having rescued you? Very well, let it be so, since you are so disloyal. No injustice is done those who cast Christ aside when they are punished and destroyed.

19. That is what Christ has in mind here, as he sends the leper to the priests. We are not to understand the Christian faith as the fanatics do, who straightway overthrow constituted authority; nor as the papists, who define spiritual life in distinction from worldly life in terms of an outward discipline. On the contrary, we should know that a Christian and believer is one who has gotten another Lord. As far his outward life goes, it remains as before, as St. Paul says, (Gal. 3:28): "There is neither Jew nor Greek, there is neither bond nor free, there is neither male nor female; for ye are all one in Christ Jesus." It does not follow that for the sake of Christian faith a person's external life itself is altered; rather it remains as before. Whatever you were when you were called to faith—husband, wife,

servant, maid—continue so, as St. Paul teaches in 1 Corinthians 7:20–24. We must rightly distinguish one's status as a Christian from the external existence, so that we properly spell out what it means to be a Christian, namely, to acknowledge Christ alone to be true Lord, who redeemed us and whose debtors we are.

20. This the pope and his minions have not understood, nor do they want to; but they mix and mingle together the outward way of life with the Christian station and make no distinction between the spiritual and worldly. The bishops and clerics have become worldly lords, ruling over land and people, and not least, have called their over-lordship, properties, and possessions spiritual holdings, even though spiritual goods are those things which properly are not seen by the naked eye, nor taken in hand, like forgiveness of sins, righteousness which avails before God, life, and salvation. These are treasures which neither eye can see nor hand grasp, but faith only, which takes them in the Word.

21. It is gross blindness when a person is unable to distinguish Christian life from mere outward, worldly existence. As I have said, we need to learn this well, so that we can rightly define it verbally. A Christian life consists in this: that we receive the unseen Christ and believe that he is our only Lord and Saviour, who rescued us from sin, death, devil, and hell. Then, once we have acknowledged him as our Lord, we ought also serve him with our whole life and pay tribute to him, saying, Lord, previously I was under the devil's power and in his service, shamefully misusing your gifts which also then I possessed, in part; but now I have learned and know for sure that you alone are my Lord and God. I believe in you, and therefore I also want to serve you in this faith, trusting you from the heart, that you are my Lord and Saviour, and want to be obedient to you in my station of life and do what pleases you. That means we must rightly distinguish Christian life from routine existence. Yet, both are to be and remain subject under Christ, even though a Christian according to the body is subject to worldly rulers; for we would gladly yield body and life, goods and honor, in fact everything we have, rather than let go of Christ.

22. To this the Lord points as he says to the leper, "Go, show yourself to the priest." Along with evidencing his glory through miracu-

lous healing, he does not want the impression in any way to be drawn, not even in slightest measure, that he taught and agitated insurrection against the Jewish rule and priesthood. It was as much as to say, The Jewish Law and rule given to them by Moses would in no way displease me, nor be a hindrance, if they would only receive me as their Lord. To let themselves be circumcised, to deal with leprosy according to Moses' Law, to bring sacrifices and to do other works of the Law, would be pleasing enough to me, if only I might remain their Lord. But when they will not allow me to be their Lord, then the friendship is at an end.

23. We see this everywhere in the Gospels how Christ did not assail the Law of the Jews, had they only permitted him to teach and do miracles, and received him. But when they refused to accept him, and on top of it reviled his teaching and his miracles, grounding their scolding and punishing of him on their Law, then he responded by smashing through their Law like through a spiderweb, saying, "The Son of Man is Lord also over the Sabbath." It is so yet today, as he says, Let everything be as it is, plain and honest, as long as the world receives me as Lord. But if men will not receive me, they shall be plucked up. For my Father will not tolerate my being despised and scorned. If men despise and reject me, my Father will utterly destroy them, as Psalm 2:8–12 states, "Ask of me, and I shall give thee the heathen for thine inheritance, and the uttermost parts of the earth for thy possession. Thou shalt break them with a rod of iron; thou shalt dash them in pieces like a potter's vessel. Be wise now therefore, O ye kings: be instructed, ye judges of the earth. Serve the Lord with fear, and rejoice with trembling. Kiss the Son, lest he be angry, and ye perish from the way, when his wrath is kindled but a little." It is as though God were saying, The world will have good days, with body, life, and every good thing as largesse from God, if it will only acknowledge him as Lord, receive him, and serve him. If it will not, its judgment is sealed.

24. We, who have learned this and been obedient, have pleased God and possess salvation. But the world has not responded in this way. Yes, the world says, If I were to receive Christ as Lord and serve him, everything would be turned topsy-turvy and thrown into confusion. Indeed, God responds to the world: It will be as you say, total

destruction, but not through fault of my word, but because of your stiff-neckedness for not receiving my word and acknowledging my Son as Lord. The Jews reasoned to themselves, If we let this man go, the Romans will come and take our land and people. Indeed, the Romans did come and, as the Jews themselves foresaw, left no stone upon another. And the Romans, too, later on said, Because these two beggars, Peter and Paul, have come, we've had nothing but trouble. And they were true prophets about their own necks! Our opponents today speak in the same way: Were we to accept the Lutheran gospel and believe on their Christ, everything—land and people—would be undone. They say this quite openly, knowing full well that it isn't true, for our gospel would allow them to be and remain, if only they are filled with fear. Put them and Christ together, however, and then see who is the stronger.

25. To the centurion Christ does not say that he should go to the priest, nor does he put him under the Jewish Law, but allows him to remain a centurion under Roman imperial authority. The centurion's office was sanguinary business, and yet Jesus allowed him to keep the sword, lets him carry on in his bloody office, and does not forbid him from engaging in war and pursuing his bloody tasks. He, on the contrary, upholds the centurion in his post, and with his miraculous word heals his servant. Just as he did not take from the Jews their Law and governance, so neither from the pagan Romans their offices and stations, not even from their military men. This is not to say that everything which their soldiers did pleased him, but he permitted these stations and offices to remain. For one has to distinguish between the office and its abuse, as John the Baptist also taught when he said to the soldiers (Luke 3:14): "Do violence to no man, neither accuse any falsely; and be content with your wages."

26. This is the nature of Christ's office and work, and for this reason he came, that the devil's kingdom might be taken off of us, and that the people who formerly served the devil might now serve him. So we teach too: Whoever under the papacy served the devil with idolatrous practices, Masses, vows, and the like, should now take his stand against these and serve God, believing on Christ, that through him alone, without worthiness of his own works, he is righteous before God and saved. If that remains sure and solid, then we rest at

peace. If one tonsure is not enough, then let there be two; it makes no difference to God. But without and apart from Christ, to rely on caps and tonsures, God will not tolerate, but will smash it to smithereens. That's why Christ says, I will not take things from you; take nothing away from me either; you remain you, and I will remain myself. If then you die, you know where you will go. In short, Christ wants only to destroy the devil's kingdom, and beyond that he lets things be. God give us his grace to keep and hold on to this. For that we pray and beseech him.

FOURTH SUNDAY AFTER EPIPHANY

1531[*]

Matthew 8:23–27

And when he was entered into a ship, his disciples followed him. And, behold, there arose a great tempest in the sea, insomuch that the ship was covered with the waves: but he was asleep. And his disciples came to him, and awoke him, saying, Lord, save us: we perish. And he saith unto them, Why are ye fearful, O ye of little faith? Then he arose, and rebuked the winds and the sea; and there was a great calm. But the men marvelled, saying, What manner of man is this, that even the winds and the sea obey him!

1. Today's Gospel presents an episode from which we learn not what things we are to do—for there is no mention of deeds—but rather, what one ought to believe in time of need and tribulation, and how we may be comforted. It is, therefore, a lesson on faith, the cardinal article of Christianity. We all like to think of this as a simple thing, within each person's capacity; but no one except a genuine Christian and truly sanctified person really understands it.

2. We wish to divide the discourse as follows: first, we will speak of the cross and suffering, how it affects those who preach of Christ and faith; second, of faith's nature and form; third, of the Lord Jesus Christ and his person; fourth, of the fruit and benefit which issue from faith under trial. These points will illustrate well what a comforting discourse the Evangelist is presenting here in a few words, something we are not likely to match.

3. The first section is about the cross, for Christ, and then for his disciples. When the Lord stepped into the ship with his disciples all was quiet; there was no storm. Instead the sun was shining and the sea was calm and friendly. But soon after they had shoved off from land and were on the sea, the sky became dark and a great storm

[*]Preached at the parish church.

arose, so that the little ship was swamped with waves and seemed ready to sink. The wind did not buffet the other ships so violently, only the ship in which Christ and his disciples were seated.

4. Let us note this incident well, for it seems that as soon as the teaching about faith is in the picture and Christ steps into the ship, then, as the saying goes, It won't be long before there's threatening weather; the sun won't shine any longer and the sea will rage and storm. Christ himself says in Luke 11:21–22, that a strong man, well-armed, is able to hold his castle in peace and quiet until a stronger comes; then violence starts, with fighting and slashing. It is a story oft repeated in the Gospel accounts. Where before all is quiet, as soon as Christ permits himself to be heard with his preaching and to be seen with his miracles, there pandemonium breaks out on every hand, as the devil angrily stirs up and agitates the rogues—the Pharisees, the scribes, and the high priests—who want him dead. Christ himself said it long before in Matthew 10:34–37, "Think not that I came to send peace on earth; I came not to send peace, but a sword. For I came to set a man at variance against his father, and the daughter against her mother, and the daughter-in-law against her mother-in-law. And a man's foes shall be they of his own household."

5. This all works together, if you want to be a Christian and follow this Lord, and step with him into the ship, resigning your heart to him and composing your soul in patience. For as soon as you commit yourself to this Lord and come with him into the ship, wind, storm, and buffeting will surely ensue. This is how Jesus Sirach warns all believers in Sirach 2:1–2, "My Son, if you come forward to serve the Lord, prepare yourself for temptation. Set your heart right and be steadfast, and do not be hasty in time of calamity." In other words, if you don't want to be God's servant, just coast along, the devil will leave you alone. On the other hand, if you desire to serve God and be a Christian, resign yourself willingly and say goodby to good days, for you will not escape persecution. But don't despair! Even though the waves beat over the ship, and the sea becomes wild and turbulent, do not be afraid because of that, but think rather: I didn't get into this to gain the world's favor; and I'm not going to give it up because of its rancor and raging. That's what the Evangelist wishes to teach us, namely that the storm first started after Christ stepped into

the ship and launched into the sea, as though the conclusion was: If you want to be a Christian, then you must expect that the wind, the sea, and storms will make mischief. Do you wish to preach Christ and acknowledge the faith? then expect the world to turn ugly.

6. This also serves to show us how to answer the malicious, no good slanderers who have nothing else to do than to mock the gospel and say, Formerly, before this teaching surfaced, all was quiet, and everything went along merrily and in abundance; now, however, conditions are miserable, with indescribable distress everywhere—riots, war, violence, hard times, the Turk, and all manner of trouble. To stuff the craws of such miserable slanderers who ascribe all misfortune to the gospel, you should say, Dear sir, have you never heard the gospel tell that as soon as Christ entered the ship and it was launched, a storm arose?

7. This, however, is not the fault of the Lord Jesus, but of the devil who is his enemy and cannot abide him. For he also hates the gospel, and because of it wanted to instigate as much unrest and misery as possible, in order to smash it. But blind and stubborn folks don't perceive this. They see only the trouble and the distress, and wrongfully blame it on the gospel. But it is blessing that comes from the gospel, for by the gospel one comes to know God, comes to forgiveness of sin, and gains eternal salvation, which they refuse to see.

8. And this is not the first time this happened. For the unthankful, stubborn, intractable, whining people of the Jews, and their leaders, did the same in the wilderness, murmuring against God and Moses, and asked, Why did you lead us out of Egypt? We are going to die of hunger in this wilderness. While they were in Egypt their sons were thrown into the water and each man was burdened with two men's labor. They pleaded with God then to deliver them from this misery, promising they would be the most pious of children. But what happened? As soon as they were delivered from their misery and were safe in the wilderness, they forgot everything: how they had to slave and suffer in Egypt, how pharaoh killed their children, how men were murdered in front of their wives. They thought only of the fleshpots and the bread. They picked out the good they had had in Egypt, forgetting the misery, and wished themselves back in Egypt. They had manna in the wilderness, but in their minds this did not

compare with the fleshpots. They were able to make all manner of dishes from the manna—pasta, porridge—but that didn't help. They were only aware that in the wilderness there were no fleshpots, neither did pomegranates and figs grow there as in Egypt. Therefore, they complained and said to Moses and Aaron, You did not lead us out of Egypt in God's name, but in the devil's name. So they blasphemed, even though God gave them angel-bread and food in abundance. But God did not smash them pell-mell, for it is his nature to be patient and forebearing. No human would have tolerated such peevish behavior. So also today we have many renegade loudmouths who have the talent of boisterously blaming all misfortunes in the world—famine, war, affliction—on the gospel. They pick out in detail all the good they had under the papacy, but keep silent about what they suffered.

9. Twenty years ago, if one had asked these slanderers whether they would not rather have a year of scarcity in place of the conscience pangs of auricular confession (not to mention the countless torments and satisfactions the monks and priests load upon the people), without doubt they would have answered, We will gladly suffer a year of scarcity to be rid of the unbearable and unceasing torments of conscience. For they would have hoped that what didn't grow one year would be produced the next. But the torment and oppression went on and on, and increased from day to day. This and other bitterness we have completely forgotten; we only consider the temporal well-being of what we have had; but as regards the spiritual misery and anguish under the pope's regime we fail to see how this "peace" deprived us not only of money and goods, but also of body and soul through false teaching and idolatry, and failed to address the external misfortunes as well. Meanwhile, the Elbe inundated its banks; there were also hard times, pestilence, war, and other maladies that struck. Now all misfortune, no matter where it happens, is blamed on the gospel.

10. Thus the devil confuses the hearts of people, so that they do not recognize the precious treasure and the great benefits which the gospel offers, namely, that they are redeemed from sin, death, the devil, and the pope's tyranny and power. They slander horribly and blame the gospel for every misfortune, just as the Jews did in the wilderness. How will such slander be punished? Indeed, eventually fear

will fall upon them. Now they say, Since this gospel came to light, nothing good has happened in the land. Hold on, sir, you're going to eat your words. For it's in the nature of the gospel that, if it is despised when it is preached, all manner of evil will follow.

11. Now this is not the fault of the gospel, but of the ungrateful people who despise the gospel and who, because of their thanklessness and disdain, merit such punishment. Even where the gospel is not preached there is all kinds of trouble in the world. The Romans had war and problems galore before the gospel was preached to them. After the gospel was preached to them, and they despised and persecuted it, the punishment became more severe. When Christ preached the gospel in the land of the Jews, and did many great and mighty miracles, the high priests and Pharisees said, "What will we do? This person does many signs; if we let him be, all will believe on him, and then the Romans will come and take land and people." Indeed, what they feared also happened, as they said; the Romans came and devastated the country. Such reward is mete for those who persecute and despise the gospel—that it happens, as they said.

12. Nevertheless, God rescues his believers from distress, no matter how great it may be. At the time Jerusalem was destroyed, God sustained his apostles and the believers, although the people were crushed and destroyed, with the priesthood and the kingdom. God can do the same also in our time: rescue his own and punish the godless, thankless world. The first lesson of this Gospel, then, is that if you want to be a Christian and want to have the gospel, you must anticipate rough weather, for it is inevitable.

13. The second lesson concerns the right form of faith, its rightful work and readiness for action. The word "faith" seems like an insignificant thing to our ears, just as our adversaries, the papists, laugh at and ridicule us when they hear us preach about faith. Oh, they say, what is faith? They, on the contrary, make much of free will. I might wish that they had been in the boat with the disciples and experienced free will's capacity in time of extremity and need.

14. The disciples had an excellent object lesson here of how free will does not stand up very well. Even though their faith was weak and small, nevertheless, if there had not been this weak, small faith, but only free will, they would have sunk into the depths of the sea. But be-

cause there was a flicker of faith present, as Christ himself witnessed when he said, "O ye of little faith," they had recourse, so that they did not despair; they ran to Christ, awoke him, and begged for help.

15. If now those with faith, however weak and frail, could not survive in time of need—as the apostles found out under duress when the chips were down—how could free will and human wisdom prevail? I grant that you have a free will to milk the cow and to build a house, but that's it. When you live in security, exercise your freedom, are free of danger, and have no needs, then you may think that with free will you can do anything. But in time of need, when there is nothing to eat or drink and you are without provisions or money, where is your free will then? It's lost, and fails you when it comes to the test. But faith stands and seeks Christ. Accordingly, faith is a different matter from free will; yes, free will is nothing, faith is everything. Free will is a powerless thing, faith a mighty thing. We see this very clearly in the disciples' case when they were in danger. They found rescue and happiness; and all was well. As the saying goes: "Man's extremity is God's opportunity." What the disciples tried to do, each of us will experience in time. Try to venture—if you are rash enough—with your free will to confront pestilence, war, and hard times. In times of pestilence you are afraid to begin any new task. Then you think, O Lord God, would that I were somewhere else rather than here. If you could wish yourself a hundred miles away, your will would much prefer it. When times are hard you think, Where will I get something to eat? These are the "great" deeds free will accomplishes. Free will does not comfort the heart, but causes more and more despair, to the point where even a rustling leaf triggers fright.

16. But, in contrast, faith is the regal lady, the queen. Even though faith be weak and small, it nevertheless exerts and does not permit itself to be frightened to death. It has great potential as we see here in the case of the disciples. The waves, the wind, and the sea all work together to bring about death; the little ship is covered with waves. Who wouldn't despair in such desperate straits on such a deadly voyage? But faith, no matter how weak, stands firm like a wall, and fortifies itself like scrawny David against Goliath, against sin, death, and all peril. A strong, fulsome faith rides like a conqueror. But even

weak faith fights well though not as valiantly. The disciples in the ship had a weak faith; nevertheless, they sought help where it was to be found, namely, with the Lord Jesus; they awoke him and cried, "Lord, save us, we perish."

17. The Lord described them as men of little faith; but he acknowledged that they had faith, though small and weak. If they had had no faith, they would not have awakened Christ in their need. But the fact that they did awaken him is evidence of faith. For no one can call upon God, especially in a crisis, unless he has faith. Even though there was but a spark of faith in the disciples, it shone forth and clung to the person who could overpower death. Their call, "Lord, help!" was the expression of faith. If their faith had been strong, they would not have been frightened by the wind and the sea but would have thought, We will ride out the wind and the sea just like Jonah who survived in the whale's belly. For we have the Lord of the sea with us, and even if we did not have him with us, we would find a vault in the depth of the sea where we could rest, remain dry, and not drown. Our Lord can help us and rescue us not only on top of the sea, but also under it.

18. Therefore, it is God's great mercy if even with a weak faith we do not despair of God's help as do the vast majority. Free will sees only the present moment, faith looks beyond the transient. Faith is a replay of all comfort, salvation, and joy. It may see death's fangs and hell's jaws; nevertheless it calls to mind and clings confidently to the hope of being helped, just as the disciples clung to the Lord for help and comfort. In the same breath it cries both, "We perish!" and also "Lord, help!" But the "Lord, help!" finally wins and brings the victory.

19. That is the characteristic of faith, which everyone assumes he understands very well. But the person who truly understands it and has experienced it, knows how in time of need the world is pretty narrow. On the other hand, those that pride themselves on having a strong faith are likely to be bold, impudent, proud souls as long as the sea is calm and the weather good; but when disaster strikes and all is amiss, then courage and comfort forsake them and they are ready to despair. So much for "glorious" free will then!

20. The third lesson treats the person of the Lord Christ. It tells of Christ's sleeping on the boat. His was a real, natural, deep sleep,

for the Lord had spent the day working and preaching, and at night had prayed and watched, becoming very weary; as a result he at times slept during the day while others were awake.

21. We must not assume that Christ had only halcyon days here on earth. Were the record complete, we would read of many temptations he suffered from the devil, as he laments in Psalm 88:15–16: "I am afflicted and ready to die from my youth up: while I suffer thy terrors I am distracted. Thy fierce wrath goeth over me; thy terrors have cut me off." For that reason he was never carefree. Burdened heavily, his mind was deep in thought. He was filled with misery and sadness, watching many nights without sleep, seldom laughing, as verse 4 of Psalm 88 indicates: "I am counted with them that go down into the pit: I am as a man that hath no strength." Though his sleep was necessary and natural, he gave attention to the faith of his disciples, to exercise and strengthen it, as was always his purpose.

22. This is still so today as the Lord deals with his Christians. It seems that he doesn't see them, knows nothing of their trials, is indifferent about them, yes, as though they were not his worry—like here in the ship. He lies there sleeping and pays no attention to the weather, his disciples, or the ship. But he is with the ship even though he sleeps. Even though we think that Christ does not hear or see the thunderstorm, the wind, and the sea, he hears and sees it nonetheless. Therefore, we should make this a maxim: Even though he sleeps, Christ is in the boat.

23. These, then, are the trials which regularly befall us, namely, that our dear Lord Jesus permits the waves to swamp the ship, that is, permits the devil and the world to rage against the Christian to make him concerned that the ship will sink. This past year we experienced some of this at the imperial diet in Augsburg when the emperor, the pope, the bishops, and the princes opposed us.* Then our state of mind was no different than that of the disciples in the ship. Our minds respond, Where now? Who are we against such mighty rulers and princes? For human reason, with its free will, cannot think otherwise. Even to this hour, the pope and his followers seek how

*Luther was not able personally to be present at the Diet, because according to the Edict of Worms (1521) he was an outlaw and, therefore, his safety could not be guaranteed by his prince, Elector John Frederick; but he kept in touch with the proceedings through couriers.

they may upset the little boat. We feel their waves, their anger, their might, and the devil strikes, too. Then the worldly-wise say, What do we do now? Here we are sitting in the ship, with nothing ahead of us but certain death. Meanwhile, the Lord rests quietly and gives no indication that he will help us.

24. At such a time we must remind ourselves that there is no dire crisis, for the Lord is with us in the ship. Even though he sleeps and acts as though he does not see us, nevertheless, we should proceed as though we see him, and believe with all our hearts that he is Lord over the emperor, Turk, pope, devil, pestilence, and all misfortune, come what may.

25. So it is also in our own life's journey where trials affect each one individually in some personal way. For every Christian finds out for himself that the devil buffets him, just as the waves beat against the ship. When such temptations come and the devil reproaches you with your sin, frightens you with God's anger, and threatens you with eternal damnation, do not despair, but firmly believe that Christ is with you in the ship and, even though he sleeps, will certainly hear and rescue you when you petition and implore him. When distress strikes and he does not help immediately, no matter, just hold fast, do not waver, but firmly believe that Christ is with you in the boat. For in his own good time he helps. In the meantime you must persevere, let the devil drown, and recognize the power of faith, how it fights and fends for itself. Then, too, consider what free will accomplishes, if Christ withdraws his hand and does not help. Faith is exercised and strengthened when one stands firm and endures temptation, happily and confidently venturing all because of Christ, no matter how great the extremity may be.

26. Beside this beautiful, comforting doctrine, we have a portrayal of Christ's person. First of all, the text tells us that Christ slept in the ship. The Lord was not pretending, but rather was sleeping a true natural sleep. As the Gospel relates how Jesus slept in the ship, it seeks to portray Jesus as a true natural man who had body and soul and who required food and drink, sleep and other natural functions, the same as we, but always without sin. This keeps us from succumbing to the crazy notion that Christ was merely an apparition, not a true man.

27. The fact is that when he threatens the sea and the wind, and they obey him, this proves his almighty Godhead, that he is the Lord over the sea and wind. With one word he can quiet the sea

and cause the wind to abate. This is not the work of mere man. The power of God is needed to control the violence of the sea with one word. Christ, therefore, is not only a natural man, but truly God. That he sleeps is certain evidence that he is true man, the natural son of the Virgin Mary; but at the same time that he awakens, arises, and rebukes the sea is certain evidence that he is true God and God's own Son.

28. Even though he is both true God and man, Scripture, nevertheless, speaks of him as one single person; for the two natures, divine and human, are united in the one person of Christ. Wiseacres speak of this person according to his human nature alone and not according to his divine nature. This is very dangerous. Holy Scripture and St. Paul do not do this, but assert strongly that Christ is one person, at one and the same time both true God and true man in this one person, the only Saviour of the human race, promised to our forefathers (Gen. 3:14–22) and sent into the world.

29. We must suffer trials, but there will also be happiness and salvation for us. For Christ, true God and true man, helps all those who believe in him and call upon him in every time of need and danger. This comfort, protection, and shield, all believers have, and even though because of this they must suffer and endure much, it is of no account. The godless also have their enemies and adversaries, even though they may seem to fare better in the world than believers. But why shouldn't we be patient in our tribulation and suffering? Even though our tribulations are greater than the troubles of the godless, yet in comparison we have greater gifts and blessings than they. The devil does not pursue them as vigorously as he does us Christians. But of what do they have more? They have a bad conscience and must finally expect eternal damnation.

30. The fourth lesson is about the fruits which result from faith, that is, others become aware of these miracles, are converted, and say, "What manner of man is this that even the winds and the sea obey him?" Likely until now they had considered him a poor carpenter's apprentice, Joseph's son, and an ordinary man, and did not know or believe that with him one could seek for and find help when in peril of life. Now, however, they learn to know him as the best and greatest helper at times when human help could not avail.

31. As always, the greater the trial, the greater the antidote. That is why affliction is very necessary and useful for the Christian. Let me relate a personal example. If it is God's will, as a result of the recent diet at Augsburg, the fruit of our faith and the power of our prayers will be that we happily thank God because he once again has hon ored our teaching of his gospel in place of the shameful slandering, bitter hate, and rancor of our adversaries. Then the truth which we openly confessed will be acknowledged. What we have suffered because of this, what each of us has borne personally, will not run its course without bearing fruit. For that reason we should not become frightened when it looks as though everything were collapsing around us.

32. This, then, is a most wonderful lesson for those who earnestly desire to be Christians. From it we should learn that when storms rage, Christ will not only be there ready to help us, but great blessing and glorious fruit will also result. That has been so for us, and from personal experience we have learned the power and virtue of the word and faith. Psalm 50:15 states, "Call upon me in the day of trouble: I will deliver thee, and thou shalt glorify me," and Psalm 91:15, "He shall call upon me, and I will answer him: I will be with him in trouble; I will deliver him, and honour him." If you wish to be a Christian, you will certainly experience trials. However, if you call upon Christ in time of need, he will hear you, rescue you, and cause your trial to bear blessed fruit and great glory. For the present every necessity is met; and later, eternal life will follow. It bothers the old Adam greatly; he does not willingly submit to wind and waves on the sea, and would rather remain on shore. Indeed it's always the same: time of need must always come first, then follows rescue and glory.

33. Dear Father in heaven, grant this to all of us for Christ's sake, through his Holy Spirit. Amen.

FIFTH SUNDAY AFTER EPIPHANY

*1528**

Matthew 13:24–30

Another parable put he forth unto them, saying, The kingdom of heaven is likened unto a man which sowed good seed in his field: But while men slept, his enemy came and sowed tares among the wheat, and went his way. But when the blade was sprung up, and brought forth fruit, then appeared the tares also. So the servants of the householder came and said unto him, Sir, didst not thou sow good seed in thy field? from whence then hath it tares? He said unto them, An enemy hath done this. The servants said unto him, Wilt thou then that we go and gather them up? But he said, Nay; lest while ye gather up the tares, ye root up also the wheat with them. Let both grow together until the harvest: and in the time of harvest I will say to the reapers, Gather ye together first the tares, and bind them in bundles to burn them: but gather the wheat into my barn.

1. In this parable our dear Lord Jesus Christ advises us not to be offended when, as the word of the gospel is sown, seeds of noxious tares are also sown among the good seed, so that as a result, bad and good, counterfeit Christians and genuine Christians, are mingled together. His special concern, however, is over those who aspire to be bishops and teachers in the church, but who really are tares and enemies of Christ, willfully intending to silence Christ and his gospel. His purpose, therefore, is to emphasize that whoever possesses the gospel should be forewarned and spiritually forearmed. For alongside the true, pure doctrine of the gospel many fanatical spirits, heresies, and offenses will sprout up, over which we must not fret unduly.

2. There is a commonplace that goes as follows: Where God builds a church, the devil builds a chapel next door. And from olden

*Preached by Luther at the parish church, December 9, 1528, in a series of sermons on the Gospel of Matthew.

times a story was handed down which went like this: When God formed man out of a clod of earth and breathed into him the breath of life, so that man became a living soul, the devil, seeking to emulate God also took a lump of earth, in order to form a man out of it; but instead it turned out to be a toad. The point of the story was to show that the devil is forever and a day trying to ape our Lord God, presuming to cloak himself with divine mien and appearance, pretending to be God.

3. We see this today, as the devil through the fanatics and sectarians pretends to elevate the Word of God by his dissembling references to it, meanwhile pouring out his venom and deceiving the world. Likewise, he disguises himself cleverly as he assumes a pious mien and an austere countenance causing people to believe that he is a trustworthy spirit; yet under the guise of such slick humility and spirituality there is nothing but hellish deceit and lies. Actually, what else is the papacy but mere empty show of sanctimonious holiness, under which the accursed devil lies concealed? The devil thus constantly tries to mimic God. He cannot bear to hear God speak. If he cannot prevent it, or forcefully obstruct God's Word, he counters with a beautiful representation, using God's very words but twisting them to peddle his lies and poison.

4. This offends very many people, often misleading those who possess and know God's Word. For example, when we preach about the freedom of conscience, the devil comes through his sectarians, Anabaptists, Sacramentarians, and radical spirits, speaking the same Word of God, but perverting its sense. Thus the freedom which God has granted for the consolation of a poor conscience held captive under the Law's accusation and curse, the devil interprets as freedom of the flesh, thus giving rise to dissolute behavior that seeks to be free of all restraints and to openly resist constituted authority. Thus the devil decks himself out under the guise of the gospel and Christian freedom, meanwhile striking down both the gospel and Christian freedom. When we preach that faith alone saves, he lays hold on the same word and inverts it, falsely applying it against holy baptism, thereby supporting the Anabaptists in their belief. Since faith alone saves, he asserts that baptism cannot achieve it. Baptism, therefore is useless water and does not benefit the soul. Under this

pretext of preaching faith, the devil in this way destroys faith. Truly a satanic artifice!

5. When now these satanic henchmen who distort and pervert everything and spawn fanatical sectarianism make their appearance among Christians, the gospel is scandalized before the world, turning people's eyes, ears, and hearts away from it. For human reason, wise in its own conceits, straightway pontificates; who wants to accept a teaching about which the teachers themselves cannot agree? Such reasoning scores so impressively against the gospel that there is no way to counter it. Even we ourselves, if weak and ill prepared in our knowledge of God's Word, can be intimidated with overwhelming odds by the devil. God's Word, for example, teaches that we are to believe in the one Christ; Christians are to be joined in one faith, with one heart, one mind, and one spirit. That is a principle that reason cannot criticize or debate. However, when reason sees someone boasting that he is a Christian while living like a non-Christian, or claims to have the true faith and yet teaches contrary to the true Christian faith, and so on, the scandalizing offense piles up; and human reason cannot help being offended by this, even though unable to find fault with the doctrine itself.

6. In particular, however, since the Word teaches that Christians are to be united, and yet greater discord, dissension, and division exist among those who boast of their Christianity than under the papacy; or again, since the Word teaches that Christians are not to condemn one another, and yet those who claim the name of being true Christians condemn one another more than happens under the papacy, human reason concludes that the doctrine is of the devil and, because it is so beautifully conceived, it's the cause for so much misery and distress in the world. And despite human reason's readiness to overlook such faults and offense, it concludes that in the final analysis, truly valid doctrine will prove itself by its fruits; but since the opposite is the case, how can it then be true doctrine? As a result our adversaries remain more firmly entrenched in their own righteousness, while the doctrine of faith, as we preach it, suffers, and is hated more than ever, and denounced. The sectarians frighten people away from the gospel and become ever stronger and more hardened in their hypocrisy.

7. Accordingly, sectarians give offense on both sides, to us and to others, doing greater harm to the gospel than its avowed opponents and persecutors. For ultimately even tyrants will feel shame, grow weary, and cease to persecute if unity were to exist among us. But since there is discord, dissension, and division—meanwhile those who cause it purporting to be good Christians and evangelical tyrants—conclude that they are fully justified in persecuting and killing us. In this way sectarians and fanatics do nothing but make our enemies and tyrants more determined. That's what happened in the case of the betrayer Judas against Christ and his disciples. When the scoundrel defected from Christ and allied himself with the Pharisees and the high priests, they became boldly defiant. It's the same story today also.

8. This parable refers to, and warns us to be careful not to attribute such difficulties to the word of the gospel and the Christian church, but to our adversary, the devil, who through his apostles sows tares among the wheat. For the text states that the tares are sown by the enemy, not in a separate area of the field but with the wheat. Therefore, be alert, be on your guard, and do not say, The field contains tares and, therefore, the field is worthless; or, because the field is dense with tares, no grain or wheat are present. No, you should rather say, The devil likes nothing better than to sow his tares among the wheat; and there is no one else whom he would rather trouble than true Christians. We must not hope or expect, therefore, that, just because the evangelical doctrine is good and completely in harmony, all who hear it will also be nicely united. Rather, things will proceed as before: mingled in with the wheat there will also be those who are not wheat, but tares.

9. I would only be too happy to see the wheat stand in a field completely free of tares, just as the landowner's workmen also wished. But it simply does not happen. Where the wheat stands, there you will also find tares. Where Christians are, there you will also find fanatical spirits, false teachers, and false Christians. We do not have to look very far from home; as you know, we have plenty of them all around us. Here at Wittenberg, praise God, there is now a small stand of wheat, although we have not been totally spared the tares. Everywhere, with but few exceptions, we find tares. Whoever wants

to be a Christian will have to put up with his worst enemies calling themselves Christians and with finding false teachers and false Christians in the midst of orthodox teachers and Christians.

10. The same is true of the human body; it is never totally pure and without blemish. It is not in the nature of our body to be flesh, blood, and bone in all purity. The body harbors certain impurities which it does not retain but expels. The mouth contains saliva; the stomach is full of waste matter; eyes, ears, nose have their discharges, and so on. But it is not at all proper to look at a little child and say, This is not a human being, but a snot-nose. Were a child's mother to hear this, she would retaliate, You scoundrel, what kind of a fool are you? Can't you see beyond the snotty mess? Can't you see the child has a sound body, a fine neck, beautiful eyes, and all the members of a natural sound human being?

11. So, just as it is true that the human body cannot be totally free of impurities, so also with Christendom, which is a spiritual body, it can never be without corruption and impurity on earth. Were we to eliminate waste matter, sweat, saliva, and impurities from our natural body, it would become weak. Better for the body to get rid of such impurities itself in normal cleansing manner than for its flesh and blood to become totally corrupt by retaining it. If the Christian church here on earth, therefore, were to be completely pure and without tares, without fanatics, sectarians, and non-Christians, that would not be a good omen. In fact it would be a sure indication that it is not a true spiritual body, that is, not the true church, just as the body cannot be a true natural body if it is without corruption; that the church is mere filth, just as the body putrefies when it no longer expels waste.

12. We must, therefore, pay close attention to this parable and learn correctly to identify the Christian church, and not take offense when we see tares sprout and grow in the midst of the wheat. For wherever Christ scatters the seed, there the devil also sows his tares. Christ does not sow noxious corn cockles and weeds, but pure wheat. The devil, however, sows the tares. Therefore, we must not blame Christ or the wheat, or say that the wheat seed was contaminated with corn cockles and henbane. But we should acknowledge that the devil also wants to be in that company among the Christians. Wherever there is a stand of pure wheat, there he also seeks to have his stand of corn cockles, henbane, and tares.

13. Look at Christendom as it stood in its prime during the days of the apostles. When Paul was preaching at Corinth, Christ through him sowed good, excellent wheat there. But how did things go? Read the Corinthian Epistles and note how he complains about the tares. As soon as he turned his back, false prophets, aroused by the devil, came and sowed their seed amidst the wheat and corrupted everything. After the apostolic age, during the days when bishops ruled, matters got much worse; there were but few bishops and teachers like Cyprian, Hilary, Athanasius, and others, through whom Christ sowed good seed. On the other hand, the devil had many thousands of false bishops, Arians, and other heretics through whom he sowed nothing but tares. Then it could have been said (undoubtedly the blind, obdurate heathen did), There is nothing but dissension and division; how can there be any true doctrine? Can they be Christians, where so many offenses and so much wickedness prevail? I shall remain in unbelief rather than become a Christian and join those who, while they preach a good story about Christian unity, demonstrate anything but Christian unity and love among themselves.

14. There is where the devil has a special hankering to be, and there he labors day and night, in order to accomplish what he wants. Today his best argument, whereby he girds himself, attacks our doctrine and in odious manner casts it into our teeth, is the charge that Lutheran doctrine has given rise to so many sects; so how can it be true doctrine? Christ girds and strengthens us to fend off such malevolence, so that we don't do as the heathen have done and as the papists still do today, taking offense at the tares which are found among us and choosing not to be aware of the wheat. Let's realize, therefore, that we are in position to reply, Haven't you read in the Gospel that wheat and tares grow at the same time in the same field, not isolated from each other but intermingled, and that the tares want to be marketed as good wheat? Fanatical enthusiasts want to be numbered as Christians, but they are not Christians.

So much by way of introduction. Let's now look at the text and deal with it verse for verse.

The kingdom of heaven is likened unto a man which sowed good seed in his field.

15. The good seed are the righteous Christians. For later that's how the Lord explained it when he said, "The good seed are the children of the kingdom."

But while men slept, his enemy came and sowed tares among the wheat, and went his way.

16. These are the children of wickedness, who are found among the children of the kingdom, the true Christians. As also St. Paul says in 1 Corinthians 11:19, "There must be also heresies among you." Those, therefore, who think that all who are attentive to the gospel are as pure as is the evangelical doctrine have another think coming. For there are many who hear and receive the gospel who still remain unclean.

17. Note well, however, that the enemy sows the tares during the night, when people are asleep. After he has done his sowing, early in the morning he turns on his heels and acts as though he knows nothing about what has happened. This sleeping occurs when people are secure or when Christians preach diligently but pay little attention to what the Word says. Today, for example, we preach in all sincerity and earnestness, but we cannot see or determine whether those who listen believe our gospel or not. That is hidden from us. When I see that people listen to the Word or read it, I think to myself that they accept it, and yet they can so easily deceive me by such appearance. Therefore, I must contravene the man who hears the gospel while his heart is asleep. Otherwise I, too, would be dozing just like people who because they are asleep are unable to prevent the enemy from sowing his tares in the field by night. That means that when I have preached, I cannot, nor should I, judge whether the hearer is a true disciple or not. But when they who were not of us went out from us, as St. John states, they struck us a blow, and that's when we knew something was amiss. Christ complains very much of such companions (Ps. 55:12–14): "For it was not an enemy that reproached me; then I could have borne it: neither was it he that hated me that did magnify himself against me; then I would have hid myself from him: But it was thou, a man mine equal, my guide, and mine acquaintance. We took counsel together, and walked unto the house of God in company." And Psalm 41:9, "Yea, mine own familiar friend, in whom I trusted, which did eat of my bread, hath lifted up his heel

against me"; also verse 6, "And if he come to see me, he speaketh vanity: his heart gathereth iniquity to itself; when he goeth abroad, he telleth it."

18. Today we, too, lament about such people. For those who give the appearance of being our true brothers cause us the greatest heartache. When we are happy and buoyed up by hope, as though everything were pure and tranquil, these same false brethren and fanatics raise themselves up against us. We do not detect that they have a depraved heart. The devil plants them in our midst before we are ever aware of it. Who can discern them?

But when the blade was sprung up, and brought forth fruit, then appeared the tares also.

19. The tares sprout up first; thereafter the grain sprouts and blooms. From the leaves one can tell whether it is wheat or tares. Then finally comes the fruit. False preachers can be identified by their petals, that is, by what they are preaching. In time also the fruit appears by which to identify the plant. Since they, meanwhile, still listen—though they themselves do not believe the Word—we cannot tell them apart. But as soon as they begin to preach, it becomes evident. Then our doctrine is rejected as of no account, but their doctrine alone is valid. Thereupon they begin to preach against us, and we against them, until ultimately the fruit also is evident and the tares become more patent.

20. But we must not for this reason trample the field, nor reject it, even though tares are growing among the wheat, nor be unduly concerned about the fact that blades of wheat or blades of corn cockle are simultaneously seen growing in the field. If nothing but corn cockle and tares and no wheat were standing in the field, we might then trample and judge it to be useless. But since not only tares but also golden wheat are growing there, we must not reject it. We should reject the preaching of the pope, for there tares are growing; there we see nothing but corn cockles and no wheat. But we must not scorn the field where the gospel is being preached, for there golden wheat is growing, even though it is overgrown with tares. For the sake of the wheat, a Christian should value the field and not despise it because of the tares. Often for the sake of one righteous man we must spare seven villains. When the tares are sown, one cannot rec-

ognize them immediately, for the enemy makes off, wipes his mouth, as though he had never been there. But when the plants begin to grow, the tares become evident.

So the servants of the householder came and said unto him, Sir, didst not thou sow good seed in thy field? From whence then has it tares? He said unto them, An enemy hath done this. The servants said unto him, Wilt thou then that we go and gather them up? But he said, Nay; lest while ye gather up the tares, ye root up also the wheat with them. Let both grow together until the harvest.

21. Where I know a Christian to be, I would much rather put up with an entire country of unbelievers than to root out one Christian with the non-Christians. But what does the Lord mean when he says here, "Let both grow together"? Are we not to root out the tares? But this is not the way to go, nor should it be. But are we to do nothing and let the tares flourish uncontrolled? Here is where the papists for once were shrewd. They set this text before us charging that we, here in Wittenberg, have done wrong by abrogating private Masses; we should have retained both Masses and monasteries. That would be to misunderstand the text. For the Lord does not say we are to leave the tares unchecked, but that we are not to root them out. But they press the text farther, and since many monasteries were destroyed by God's anger during the Peasants' War, they seek to prove from this text that the destroyed monasteries should be rebuilt.

22. They are desperate scoundrels. They themselves acknowledge that their clerics, both priests and monks, were wicked; yet they want the whole system not only to remain intact but to be rebuilt and bolstered up as though it was a very precious thing. For by saying, Let our priesthood and monkery continue on because Christ has commanded that we are to allow the tares to grow, they admit it's all tares, and yet think it to be wheat, simply because that's what they wanted to have planted and produced. But Christ did not say that weeds were to be sown and produced, but that while people slept, tares were being sown by the enemy. It does not follow that we are to allow the tares to be sown right before our eyes, so that we can hold them in check. Rather, the meaning is that when they have been sown and are growing amongst the wheat, we must let them be. The papists latch on to the words "let them grow" and do not see, indeed,

do not want to see, that what the words mean is "let both grow together." They want their doctrine to prevail and do away with ours. The word "both" to them means no more than the word "theirs." For they refer the term solely to their own, and say, Let our system grow and remain. Were that the meaning, then the Jews might also have said to the apostles, Put away your gospel and let Judaism alone prevail. The Gentiles might have done the same thing also.

23. Second, Christ is speaking of the growing and not of the sowing, setting, or planting. "Let both grow together," he says, and he does not say, Let them both be sowed and planted together. The tares are not to be sown or planted. However, if they are sown or planted, while we have been sleeping, and grow amidst the wheat, we are not to weed them out but let them grow with the wheat. The papists thus violate this text on two counts. First, they twist Christ's words "Let both grow together" to mean, Let this one system, ours alone, grow. Second, they make Christ's words, "let grow" to mean let it be sown or planted.

24. But the Lord's intent is this: He wants to show what his kingdom is and how it is to be distinguished from the kingdom of the world. Christ's kingdom has nothing to do with fist and sword. God has commanded the secular realm to use the sword and to root out wickedness, adulterers, thieves, murderers, and killers. But in Christ's kingdom there is neither sword nor rule of force. We, preachers and Christians, are to engage in combat solely with the Word. Just as Isaiah 2:3–4 clearly states, "Out of Zion shall go forth the law, and the word of the LORD from Jerusalem. And he shall judge among the nations, and shall rebuke many people: and they shall beat their swords into plowshares, and their spears into pruninghooks: nation shall not lift up sword against nation, neither shall they learn war any more." Again, Christ says (John 18:3), "My kingdom is not of this world: if my kingdom were of this world, then would my servants fight, that I should not be delivered to the Jews: but now is my kingdom not from hence." Also, verse 37, "To this end was I born, and for this cause came I into the world, that I should bear witness unto the truth." The Lord here intends to say, Christians are not to weed out the heretics or combat sectarians with the sword, as the pope is doing. He exterminates, hangs, drowns, burns,

strangles, and kills those who oppose him, and his princes do the same. So, too, Thomas Muentzer, who took the sword in hand and with violence attempted to enact the parable of the mustard seed, which, as Christ says, is the smallest of all seeds; however, when it has grown, it is the largest of the garden plants and grows into a tree so large that birds roost among its branches. Muentzer explained this by saying that we must, with might and main, spread the gospel. But he did not consider this parable of the tares, that we are to let them grow together with the wheat until harvest time.

25. There is a lot at stake here, and there seems to be just cause for exterminating heretics and fanatics by the sword. In order to counter what appears to be reasonable, Christ says, "Let both grow together until the harvest." In other words, let things be as they are; you are not to set things right by using the sword; simply continue on with the Word and preach it resolutely, against heretics and sectarians. You cannot stop the tares with the Word, for they were sown while you were asleep, so let them be with the wheat until the harvest. Then surely they will be rooted out. St. Paul teaches that very thing (Titus 3:10), "A man that is an heretic after the first and second admonition reject." He does not say that we are to slay such a heretic, but that we are to admonish him once, and then a second time. But if he will not accept admonition, we are to avoid him as one who is corrupt and self-judged.

26. This parable, therefore, is given to us for our consolation; we are to know that we are not sinning when we allow sectarians and fanatics to exist. That is what the Lord means, "Let both grow together." Concerning the use of the sword, Christians are to know that they must not resort to the sword, nor with the sword root out the tares.

27. The pope lays blame on us, as though we were the insurgents. But he is doing us an injustice. For insurgents are people who take sword in hand and use their fists, contrary to what they ought to do. But we do not resort to the sword, nor use the fist; we fight solely with the Word. Therefore, we are not rebels. But the pope and his bishops are the insurgents. They boast that they are the church and yet wield the sword, slaughter, and kill with the sword. By such fruits we can see whose children they are. Muentzer wanted to be a part of us, and yet he belonged more to the pope than to us, even though

early on he extolled the gospel. But we preach that people should let the sword alone and respect secular government to which God has entrusted the sword. We do not wield the sword as does the pope. As a bishop, the pope is commanded to nourish people with the Word of God. Yet he heads straight for the sword and takes it right out of Caesar's hand, smites him with it, and still wants to be primate of all Christendom. Surely he demonstrates full well that he and his bishops are the real bloodhounds and insurgents in the world.

28. Christ well foreknew that the bishops would use the sword in dealing with the matter. For this reason he so earnestly warned against it, both in this parable and elsewhere. But it did little good. Indeed, it is very exasperating to sow good seed and have to tolerate tares growing in the midst of the wheat; to preach the gospel pure and undefiled and see all kinds of fanatics and sectarians arise and not to lash out against them but simply contend with the Word. Everyone is anxious, just as were those farmhands, to pull out the tares. But Christ says, No, "let both grow together until the harvest." In other words, since you cannot win the fanatics over by what you are saying or convert them by the Word, you must also not exterminate them by use of the sword.

29. But why are we not to take action with the sword? "Lest while ye gather up the tares," says Christ, "ye root up also the wheat with them." This is what he's saying to me, Were I to restrain the sectarians by means of the sword or gather an army against the pope in order to exterminate the papacy, what would I be accomplishing? I would be doing away with many who, under the papacy and among the fanatics, are still to be converted, and I would thus harm the wheat. For the sake of the elect, therefore, Christ will not suffer a single hair of the pope's or the sectarians' heads to be hurt. In our day many are being slain because some of them are possibly Anabaptists or fanatics who have again made their appearance. Were I to have acted, as did Muentzer, no doubt there would have been many in various places who might yet have come to confess Christ. By being precipitous, I would have kept that from happening.

30. In order to prevent such a thing, Christ speaks this parable and says, Once more I tell you, you will find tares among the wheat; fanatics and sectarians among the true Christians. But how are you

to handle this? "Let both grow together until the harvest." Wait and see; in time it will turn out all right. Therefore, this parable is relevant also against the insurgents, as against the pope and Muentzer who reach for the sword, which they are commanded not to do.

31. However, this we may do: If two kinds of sermons are being preached at a given locale, a prince or municipality may show good sense by not tolerating two kinds of preaching in their area, in order to avert disunity and turmoil. They might examine both and judge them according to the proper norm, namely, according to Scriptures and the Word of God. Then whichever party taught in accord with Scripture and the Word of God would be allowed to remain. Whichever party, however, was teaching contrary to Scripture and the word of God would be given permission to leave. But to exterminate, never.

And in the time of harvest I will say to the reapers, Gather ye together first the tares, and bind them in bundles to burn them: but gather the wheat into my barn.

32. "Let both grow together," says Christ, so that I retain my wheat, lest it be pulled out or be destroyed; I shall ordain that at the proper time the reapers will gather up the tares so that they may be thrown into the fire. Here you see that the tares are already condemned and sentenced to be burned in the fire. Why should you want to pursue after a heretic? Listen, don't you understand that he is already condemned to suffer severe punishment? Who are you to try to punish the one who already has been judged by a mighty Lord? What charge need I bring against a thief who has already been condemned to the gallows? If a thief has been condemned to death and stands there bound, and then along comes someone who wants to kill him while in the pillory or in chains, wouldn't that person deserve to have his head chopped off as having committed a crime against justice, since he is without official mandate? Thus today our bishops and princes are slaying heretics. God has already ordained that at his own time his angels will be the executioners of the heretics. Yet these haughty lords presume and pretend that they want to serve God and punish those whom God has reserved for himself to punish. Verily, if anybody refuses to renounce the pope, for any other reason, let him at least renounce him for the shedding of blood, by which act the pope along with his henchmen has compromised himself and dipped

into God's jurisdiction and judgment. They are bloodhounds, and yet they think that they render God a service by killing people and shedding blood.

33. But Christ says here, At harvest time my workmen will gather the tares and tie them in bundles, just as a farmer gathers tares and bundles them, indicating they are ready to be burned. In like manner, the angels of God will separate the tares from the wheat and tie them into bundles, that is, they will condemn the evildoers to eternal death and unending fire. You who murder heretics ought to be praying for these poor people, that they might be converted and not be judged and condemned in this fashion. What you are doing is rushing in and condemning them before the time.

34. This is the other reason why Christ does not want the tares eliminated by the sword, for they are already condemned to be burned. As St. Paul says (Titus 3:11), A heretic has a distorted mind and stands self-condemned. A man should be moved to pity such a person rather than to desire to kill him. This is the way for God-fearing preachers and Christians to act. The ungodly and the hypocrites can do nothing else but slay and kill, just like the pope, Muentzer, and the fanatics.

35. Christ thus teaches in this parable that in his kingdom here on earth there will also be tares—heretics and fanatics—among the wheat, amidst the apostles and the Christians, and how we are to behave towards them. May God give us his grace and Spirit, so that we may be genuine wheat and at all times do God's will. Amen.

SEPTUAGESIMA SUNDAY

1534

Matthew 20:1–16

For the kingdom of heaven is like unto a man that is an householder, which went out early in the morning to hire labourers into his vineyard. And when he had agreed with the labourers for a penny a day, he sent them into his vineyard. And he went out about the third hour, and saw others standing idle in the marketplace, And said unto them; Go ye also into the vineyard, and whatsoever is right I will give you. And they went their way. Again he went out about the sixth and ninth hour, and did likewise. And about the eleventh hour he went out, and found others standing idle, and saith unto them, Why stand ye here all the day idle? They say unto him, Because no man hath hired us. He saith unto them, Go ye also into the vineyard; and whatsoever is right that shall ye receive. So when even was come, the lord of the vineyard saith unto his steward, Call the labourers, and give them their hire, beginning from the last unto the first. And when they came that were hired about the eleventh hour, they received every man a penny. But when the first came, they supposed that they should have received more; and they likewise received every man a penny. And when they had received it, they murmured against the goodman of the house, Saying, These last have wrought but one hour, and thou hast made them equal unto us, which have borne the burden and heat of the day. But he answered one of them, and said, Friend, I do thee no wrong: didst not thou agree with me for a penny? Take that thine is, and go thy way: I will give unto this last, even as unto thee. Is it not lawful for me to do what I will with mine own? Is thine eye evil, because I am good? So the last shall be first and the first last: for many be called, but few chosen.

1. This is a rather subtle Gospel lesson; young folks and mean-spirited people will learn very little here. Nevertheless, since it's read on this Sunday, we'll go through it quickly and say something about it.

2. It's the parable about a householder who went out early one morning to hire workers for his vineyard, agreeing with them on the

usual wage, one denarius for a full day's work. Afterwards he hired others who worked nine hours; still later, some who worked six, and others three hours; and finally some who labored only one hour. But in the evening, he paid these last ones the same one denarius that he had promised those whom he hired early in the morning. The hours worked varied greatly, but the wages were the same! Except in the case of the very first ones hired, the householder had not promised any specific wage. The paycheck was the same—those who had labored twelve hours receiving no more, and those working only one hour receiving no less; each worker received exactly the same amount! That's the parable.

Now obviously, such a standard would not be acceptable in ordinary labor relations; it just wouldn't be fair. In the marketplace, there's a different measure and rule: He who labors hard and long gets higher wages; he who works less gets, comparatively, less pay. And yet, even here, if a worker does receive his agreed upon wage, he really has no reason to grumble if his employer—out of the goodness of his heart—wants to reward some other worker with a little extra. In principle, however, it is not right to pay equal wages for disproportionate labor.

3. The Lord told the parable in this fashion so as to distinguish clearly between his kingdom and the worldly realm, and thus to remind us that his kingdom operates with principles different from the standards of the world. On the worldly scene there can be no equality simply because people themselves are so diverse. That's why, as a general rule, he who has labored more, also receives more pay. It does happen that one who has worked less, nevertheless, gets more; but when this happens a different interpretation is being followed. What one person gets as a free gift, cannot be claimed as a right by the next party. Case in point: the owner of the house has much more property than his servant, even though the servant puts in more physical labor than his employer. Such disparity exists of necessity in the worldly realm. In Christ's kingdom, however, there should be no such difference. All are to be equal, one the same as the other; each to have and be "worth" as much as the next one.

4. Outwardly, then, there is a difference; inequality will and must remain in the public domain simply because of the diversity of pro-

fessions and occupations. A farmer's lifestyle is different from that of the townsman, a prince occupies a different role than a nobleman; here there's a lot of inequality—and it needs to stay that way! In Christ's kingdom, however—be it king, prince, lord, servant, wife, maid, or whatever—all of them are equal! None has a different baptism, gospel, faith, sacrament, or a different Christ and God. Together they all go to church; servant, townsman, farmer all hear the same Word as the lord, prince, and nobleman hear. The baptism I have is the same one that any little maid receives; the faith Peter and Paul had is the same faith Magdalene and the thief on the cross had; as Christians you and I also have it. John the Baptist's God and Christ is the same one every repentant sinner has! Here, then, all are the same, even though the one is higher or lower as far as his worldly status, office, or talents are concerned.

5. All this we need diligently to learn, so that we can rightly distinguish Christ's kingdom from all worldly realms. This is surely a very comforting Gospel for us Christians, that all of us are so wonderfully equal in Christ! As far as the world is concerned, differences remain: a father is more than the son; the lord more than the servant; the king and the prince more than his subjects. That's the will of God; he himself has created and arranged all this diversity. Whoever now wants to "equalize" everyone, so that the servant counts for as much as his master, the maid has as much authority as her mistress, and the peasant as much as a prince, that would indeed be a spectacular accomplishment—as we recently saw in the case of the rebellious peasants! And so let the world operate with its inequality as best it can. We will continue to take comfort in the fact—our station being high or low—that we all have one Christ, one baptism, one gospel, one Spirit. No one has a better gospel, a better baptism, a different or better Christ, or a different or better heaven—we are all equal!

6. Again, all this we should carefully note so that everyone may serve God sincerely and cheerfully, whatever his station in life, always thinking, I'm not an emperor or king, I possess neither cities or castles as great princes have, but I do, nevertheless, have the same holy baptism, and he who died to earn eternal life for me is the same Christ who saved the emperor. All of these good things we have in Christ ought to make us justly proud, so that we may have the proper

perspective toward worldly goods, riches, and glory, taking courage and comfort alone from the fact that we are baptized in Jesus' name, who died for us and ascended to heaven, where he sits at God's right hand, ready to help us out of sin, death, and every misfortune.

7. Whoever, then, has this conviction that we are all equal in Christ can go about his daily work with joy, whether he occupies a lesser place and position than someone else will not trouble him during his brief sojourn here on earth. He will understand that in his daily life there must needs be inequality—one having much, another little; one a lord, the other a servant. A Christian will not let this disturb him; instead he will go ahead in the name of God, knowing that here on earth it cannot be otherwise. Even if I have a more arduous station in life than the lord or lady of the house, even if I'm not as powerful as a prince, king, or emperor, I'm not going to grumble about it, but instead will gladly and willingly remain in my place until God himself promotes me to be a lord or lady. Meanwhile, I have the comfort of knowing that neither emperor or king, pope or bishop, have a different Christ, or more of him, than I. In truth, the pope doesn't have what I have! I am cleansed by the blood of the Christ who sits at God's right hand—something the pope disavows.

8. Knowing that in Christ's kingdom there is no inequality, we have courage and comfort, and in Christian "pride" we go forward to do what needs to be done. In this way everyone can go about his daily work in a joyful and godly manner. A Christian can truly say, I have no real reason to grumble about my station in life; it is a good and precious one, even though it be unimportant and even boring. It may not be a princely position but it is a Christian one; what more could I have or desire?

9. That, however, was not the attitude of the "first workers," who grumbled and were envious because they weren't getting more than the others. Our monks and nuns and clerics are no different. They want our Lord to reward them according to their works as he sees how much more they have done than others; because of the overtime they have put in, they expect a higher place in heaven and a bigger and better Christ. Also they have taught that a virgin in the convent has a better faith than a married woman; and if someone in our day teaches otherwise, he's condemned as a heretic. All such are repre-

sented by those "first ones" in the parable, who thought they should have more than the others. Piously they reported to our Lord how long they labored and how much they endured. But what did he tell them? As far as civil, public life is concerned, he says, You are unequal; whether you are a better man or work harder than someone else is not the point. But no one has a better gospel, baptism, or a better Christ than the next man.

10. When monks and nuns, for example, exalt themselves over married folks, saying that these have only an ordinary gospel and commandment, while they have a superior gospel and they observe more than ordinary Christians are commanded to do, this is simply not true; in fact, it's entirely contrary to the gospel! They insist that the gospel implies a diversity even though, as he has pointedly taught in this Gospel lesson, Christ has made all equal in his kingdom, every individual counting as much as any other. In and by itself it's not evil, nor should anyone discourage or forbid any young woman to remain a virgin, granted she has that special grace. But that she could then boast about this before the Lord God, claiming that she's better than others and deserving of special reward, that is wrong and evil! And this is also why the pope takes offense and accuses us of forbidding good works. Here he distorts our position and belies us. We certainly do not forbid good works! What we say is this: In Christ's kingdom all are equal; God deals with all of us not on the basis of merit but solely and alone according to grace and mercy—for the sake of his Son Christ Jesus.

11. Accordingly we say, if you have such equality in Christ—whether you are a teacher or preacher, lord or lady, servant or maid—then labor and act according to whatever your station in life obligates you to do. Here you function in diversity, because of different stations and vocations. In Christ, however, we are not different but equal! This is, indeed, obnoxious to the world; the Jews particularly become mad and furious when they hear that we Gentiles are to be saved—we who are not circumcised and do not keep the Sabbath and other burdens of the Law, whose weight they bear with grievous toil and sweat. Our Lord refers to that in the parable when he says that the "first hired" expected to receive more and grumbled about it when each got his denarius—even those who worked only one hour. To this very day, this is still

what scandalizes the Jews. They lived under the almost beyond telling burden of the Law! Because of that they reasoned as follows: We Jews are circumcised and assumed the burden of the law; Gentiles do not submit to circumcision and are likewise under no burden of law; now are they to be equal with us who have done so much good under the Law? By no means; if God deals thus with Gentiles, then he owes us Jews much more!

12. But Christ will not countenance any such difference. "Friend," he says, "I am doing you no wrong; take what belongs to you, and go"; or to put it another way: You already have your reward, namely the land of Canaan; but I am now establishing a new and different kingdom, in which all are equal. After all, the property is mine; I have the right to do my business as I think best; you have no right to lecture me on how to deal with my servants. It is thus that the Jews, in their spitefulness, are apt to lose eternal life itself, refusing to be on the same level with us Gentiles and accusing our Lord of unfair dealing in saying to them, Take your agreed upon wage and leave; it's my vineyard, not yours! What business is it of yours how I run my affairs? The pope and his company do the same, refusing to be considered equal with us Gentiles in Christ's kingdom, and, insisting on special treatment, they risk eternal life itself.

13. That's why it is so important that we truly understand this difference between the worldly and the spiritual life, or between earthly realms and the kingdom of Christ. In his kingdom we are all to be equal, since we all have one and the same God, Christ, Holy Spirit, gospel, Holy Sacrament and faith. On account of such equality, each one of us is as good, pious, and holy as the next person.

14. Because we are thus privileged, we should thank God for such gifts, truly recognize them as such, and praise him by saying, Let men regard me as they wish, consider me as inferior as they want, I, nevertheless, have as much as all emperors and kings, yes, as much as all the saints and angels in heaven! How? Through Christ! And so I'll go my way, being a father or mother, servant or maid, and doing everything my station in life requires with joy, courage, enthusiasm, and love—all because I have such a great treasure in Christ my Lord.

15. And so, to sum up, this is the teaching of today's Gospel, that here on earth there will always be inequality, even as people and sta-

tions in life are different. A prince is a different person and has a different office than a preacher; a maid, a different person with a different position than her mistress; and a schoolmaster is a different man with a different role than the mayor. Obviously then, they neither should nor can function with the same kind of lifestyle. Here in this world, then, of necessity, such differences remain. But Christ operates under a different principle in his kingdom: I will give as much to one as to the other. The reason? No one has ever succeeded in earning the kingdom of heaven—salvation from death and sin—and because of that I am not under obligation to anyone; always the kingdom comes by grace to whomsoever I will. Let's, therefore, beware of murmuring about his ways; instead, thanking God always for his undeserved mercy from which we can draw comfort no matter what dangers, troubles, and labors we must bear because of seeming inequalities. This will always ease and lighten our loads. May our dear Lord Jesus Christ provide that for us all, Amen.

SEXAGESIMA SUNDAY

1534

Luke 8:4–15

And when much people were gathered together, and were come to him out of every city, he spake by a parable: A sower went out to sow his seed: and as he sowed, some fell by the way side; and it was trodden down, and the fowls of the air devoured it. And some fell upon a rock; and as soon as it was sprung up, it withered away, because it lacked moisture. And some fell among thorns; and the thorns sprang up with it, and choked it. And other fell on good ground, and sprang up, and bare fruit an hundredfold. And when he had said these things, he cried, He that hath ears to hear, let him hear. And his disciples asked him, saying, What might this parable be? And he said, Unto you it is given to know the mysteries of the kingdom of God: but to others in parables; that seeing they might not see, and hearing they might not understand. Now the parable is this: The seed is the word of God. Those by the way side are they that hear; then cometh the devil, and taketh away the word out of their hearts, lest they should believe and be saved. They on the rock are they, which, when they hear, receive the word with joy; and these have no root, which for a while believe, and in time of temptation fall away. And that which fell among thorns are they, which, when they have heard, go forth, and are choked with cares and riches and pleasures of this life, and bring no fruit to perfection. But that on the good ground are they, which in an honest and good heart, having heard the word, keep it, and bring forth fruit in patience.

1. Dearly beloved, today's Gospel teaches us that Christ our dear Lord gathers to himself four kinds of disciples. They all hear God's pure Word, yet only the fourth and last group retains it and brings forth fruit. We should very carefully study this Gospel so that each of us may examine himself to determine to which group he belongs. Hopefully we belong among those who spring out of the good soil, among whom the Word bears fruit.

2. Those who belong to the first class, the Lord says, are like the seed which fell by the wayside. It does not bear fruit, because it is either trampled on or the birds eat it up. Those belonging to the second class are the people who hear the Word and not only discuss it but also believe it, growing quickly and nicely like seed that falls on soil that is stony. But as soon as a hot summer's day comes along, the plant withers since it has neither roots nor moisture. At first the Word is precious for these people. But when trial and persecution come, and they have to endure a little suffering, they fall away and do not bring forth fruit with patience. Those who belong to the third class are the most easily recognized of all: they are the Christians who are like seed that falls among thorns. Even though it grows vigorously at first, it fails to come to maturity because it is choked by the thorns. But those of the fourth group are the righteous, those whose hearts receive and retain the Word until it brings forth fruit with patience. These are the righteous who suffer for the sake of the Word, who are very faithful and obedient servants of God and show love to their neighbor; they persevere and bring forth fruit, some a hundredfold, some sixtyfold, some thirtyfold.

3. So, let each of us examine his own heart and determine to which class he belongs. The first three classes of disciples hear the Word without being benefited or bearing any fruit. But particularly troubling are those who belong to the first class. "Those by the way side are they that hear," says the Lord, "then cometh the devil and taketh away the word out of their hearts, lest they should believe, and be saved." Mark these words well.

4. I never would have dared to presume that the hearts of those who hear the Word and yet pay it no heed, ignore it, and give it no further thought, were possessed of the devil. We would like to think that there is no particular danger involved in heedless hearing and not retaining the Word, and that those who act thus are simple, inattentive people, with a natural trait of forgetting what they heard preached. But Christ assesses things differently here, stating that it is the devil who takes the word out of their hearts.

5. Here we have the verdict upon people—young and old—who hear the Word preached and walk away as though they had never heard it, with no intention of giving it heed. These people cannot say

that they have the Holy Spirit; they are the devil's own. He is their master. He reaches into their hearts and plucks out the Word. The result is other perversities: they are disobedient, dishonest, self-centered, proud, implacable, and greedy; they want everybody to be subservient to them, while they are unwilling to serve anyone. In contrast, where the Word remains in the heart and people diligently ponder it, there it fashions hearts which are pure, obedient, faithful, selfless, ready to help, humble, and gentle.

6. The first group is the worst, and their behavior displeases the Lord very much. He reproaches no other class as he does this one. The devils, Christ says, who are always around, take the Word from their hearts so that they do not espouse it; they are of the opinion that nothing much is lost when they let the Word in one ear and out the other. But if we want to know what that loss is, then listen to what Christ has to say, for his judgment is better than that of the world, and he states that it is the devil who instigates this.

7. When, therefore, you meet such a person, or you yourself are no more responsive to preaching than a log (just like our greedy burghers and peasants, also our adversaries, the papists, for whom all preaching, singing, and exhortation has as much effect as striking water with a rod), you may conclude that none other but the devil is in control of their hearts. He does not allow the good things they hear to enter their hearts but at once frisks it away so that they do not believe, nor are they saved. For were the devil not there or were this forgetfulness natural and innate—some indeed are more easily taught than others—there at least would be desire there, and they would say, O God, how thickheaded can I be! Grant me your grace and open my heart so that I may be attentive to and retain what I hear when your Word is preached. Among such folks, who long for the Word and want to retain it, there the devil finds neither room nor abode, else the longing would be lacking. But the former do not change; to them the loss of a penny or some other trifling thing would be a greater loss. You can be sure the devil is present there, and let no one think differently.

8. This group that hears the Word and pays it no heed is the largest. The Word goes in one ear and out the other. Furthermore, along comes the devil and snatches the Word right out of their hearts. Now

we must note very carefully the judgment which Christ pronounces upon this class, and be forewarned, for he gives it over to the devil.

9. The other two classes are not quite so wicked, but they are nonetheless very weak. There is a little beginning; they take note of some things, even start to believe. For this reason, the Lord does not give them entirely over to the devil as he did the first class, even though they as yet do not bear fruit. The second group is composed of those who do not persevere under persecution and remain steadfast. Instead, they are like wormy fruit that continues to hang on the tree while the air is calm but falls off as soon as the wind blows. "For a while," the Lord says, "they believe." But as soon as tribulation comes along, they grow terrified and are unwilling to endure suffering. As a result the fruit of eternal life will also remain beyond reach, along with all other fruits which proceed from the Word and faith.

10. The third class consists of those who neglect the Word because of the great cares and the pleasures of this life. For whoever is obsessed by worldly cares, whose sole concern is how high he can climb and how rich he can become, will have a heart that is encumbered, as Christ says (Luke 21:34), and as a result the Word is choked within him, like the seed among the thorns. Work we must, and each of us is to work most diligently and industriously in his calling. This is not forbidden but commanded. But to scratch and scrape and to be concerned merely with temporal cares, with money and possessions, these are the thorns which choke the Word of God in the heart so that it cannot grow and bear fruit. Such a person is concerned more with other things, giving no thought to anything else.

11. For these three groups the Word is of no effect. Certainly this is no minor loss, but a great and frightful loss which the heart cannot fully comprehend.

12. Consequently, the Lord admonishes us earnestly (as St. Matthew writes): Take heed therefore how ye hear: "For whosoever hath, to him shall be given . . . whosoever hath not, from him shall be taken away even that which he hath" (Matt. 13:12). By such Word, Christ gives us to understand that he is not talking about ordinary things but about the Word of God; those who have it in their hearts will be saved and those who do not have it will be damned. A person should, therefore, be steadfastly devoted to it and not trifle with it as

though it were an indifferent thing. It is not a trivial matter. It does no good for a person to think he would like to become interested for a while, thinking to himself, I shall study and believe God's Word after I've tried other options and have accumulated all other things that I consider important. Take care; do not deceive yourself.

13. So let's rouse ourselves to diligence and be found among those who belong to the fourth class, also earnestly praying that we may with ready hearts accept and retain God's Word, and bring forth good fruit.

14. Now this little band constitutes the precious saints, not the pope's saints with their hoods and tonsures, who read Masses, fast, wear strange garments, and the like; but those who hear God's Word, whose worst enemies and most violent persecutors are the pope and his "saints." They hear the Word and bring forth fruit a hundredfold, that is, bountifully, beyond measuring, or, as Matthew puts it, some bring forth fruit a hundredfold, some sixty, some thirty, meaning that some produce more fruit than others. For just as people's callings or offices differ, so also do the fruits. A preacher serves the church to a greater degree than a workman who devotes himself only to his domestic affairs. And yet both are Christians, redeemed from sin and death through Christ and heirs of eternal life. May we be found within this class, despite it being the smallest.

15. However, to this, as Christ says, we must add a good and honest heart, that is, a heart which, in the first place, is not listless but really intent on the Word of God. Such a heart must, above all else, have fidelity, if the devil is not to come and snatch the Word away. Second, the heart must be firm and steadfast, not weak and timid, allowing itself neither to be led astray and become frightened, nor swayed by people's favor or disfavor. For if we do not fear and love God above all else, his Word will not continue long, since it is constantly being assailed. The devil can neither endure nor tolerate it. He is a taskmaster who never lets up, forever and ever driving his servants, never allowing them to be idle, as we see things going on all the time among the papists. Third, the heart must be purged and swept clean so that no thorns remain in it, that is, we must no longer love possessions, money, fame, and pleasures more than God's Word and the life which is to come, nor be more concerned with secular

affairs than with God's Word, as Christ says, "Seek ye first the kingdom of God."

16. So, where the heart is circumspect, focused, steadfast, and swept clean, there you find a heart that is good and honest, producing good fruit without fail and with patience. To be sure, trial and tribulation, adversity and temptation will not be lacking, as St. Paul says (2 Tim. 3:12): "All that will live godly in Christ Jesus shall suffer persecution." May we be ready to meet such eventuality and, as Christ says, possess our souls in patience, and in the meantime take recourse in prayer. For it never fails, we must confess, that we are, unfortunately, assaulted on all sides, with no letup in sight. And naturally it is quite out of the question for us earthlings ever to be able to turn our backs on the temporal. Nor does the devil rest. He tries in various ways to take the Word away from us and also to burden us with cares, greed, pride, anger, and all manner of mischief. As we know, there have been many good people whom greed, ambition, fornication, and the like have not overcome and deterred from the Word.

17. We need to be on guard against the weaknesses and infirmities in our nature, against succumbing to false security, but petitioning God for his Holy Spirit (we have the clear, comforting assurance of Luke 11:13: "How much more will your heavenly Father give the Holy Spirit to them that ask him?"), to remove such obstacles, to sweep out those thorns and thistles from our hearts, so that we can continue to hear and retain God's Word, and bring forth the good fruit, by faith in Christ, through which faith we not only live in obedience to God but also become God's children and heirs. The main reason this seed is sown, that is, that the gospel is proclaimed in all the world, is to create and work fruit in us which endures into eternity.

18. Now, then, this parable also tells us not to be surprised if we see that the Word does not bring forth fruit in every case. For we learn that it is the Lord himself who sets up four divisions of which only one, the smallest group, is truly upright. The other three classes are actually worthless; we must let them go and not become disturbed when we see that there are more who despise than accept the Word. It is in the nature of the gospel that wherever it is preached, there three types of unworthy hearers appear, while the fourth is good and upright. And yet the fault lies not with the Word nor with

the one who preaches, as the blind papists charge, like the ranting crazies that they are. They think they can defame us and make our gospel all the more offensive by charging us with the offenses the devil has stirred up ever since the gospel first was proclaimed.

19. In evidence thereof, isn't it so that when Christ himself, along with John and his apostles, preached, weren't there also great offenses and weren't great sins committed? When John the Baptist stood up and preached, people came running. They listened to him again and again, saw that he was a holy man, and yet he had to hear himself defamed as out of his mind and possessed of a devil. And King Herod who delighted in listening to him, as the Evangelists report, not only did not bring forth fruit but also finally had him put to death. Yes, they heard Christ, God's Son, in person, they saw him raise the dead, perform great miracles and yet they nailed him to the cross. Why not clamor there too, Ah, John, Christ, the apostles, they did not have the true gospel, or, they were not true preachers, since the people remained wicked and should have mended their ways if the teaching was pure. But here is where they must remain silent if they don't want to expose themselves as foes and blasphemers of Christ, indeed as antichrists. But they go on thinking that they have just cause to reproach us and our doctrine.

20. However, we want to let the matter involving our doctrine rest without apologizing for why we hold to it and why we will not be driven from it. We simply call attention to the words of our dear Lord Jesus, who says that the seed is the Word. Now, there is not a single papist so senseless and foolish who would dare say that the Word about which Christ is speaking here is an evil word or is false teaching. What, however, does Christ say about the good, pure seed? What does he explain? That only a fourth of it takes root and bears fruit! Who then can deny that the world is evil, even though the Word and its preaching are upright and good, and that they will bear fruit?

21. As I said above, we do not want to talk about our doctrine and explain why we hold to it. But the papists must acknowledge—who knows whether or not they will—that, although preaching is pure and the preacher pious, the world, nevertheless, remains evil and does not improve itself through use of the Word. Christ's Word

plainly states that only a fourth part of the seed bears fruit, and his own experience (to say nothing of John's and the apostles' experience) exhibits the fact that not everyone was ready to believe and accept the Word. The majority of the people are and remain evil and without fruit; only a limited number, a fraction, repent and come to faith.

22. If this now was the experience of Christ, God's Son and the greatest preacher, is it any wonder that it was the experience of John the Baptist, the apostles, and ours today as well? Therefore, to fault the doctrine and say that it is no good, amounts also to saying that the seed which falls by the wayside, on the rocks, and among the thorns is also no good. But we must turn this around and not blaspheme God. His Word is the seed which is being sown. This Word in truth is pure and good, and by its very nature can do nothing but bear fruit. The fact, however, that it does not bear fruit everywhere is not the fault of God and his Word but the fault of the soil which is not good, and in which, as a result, the seed must remain unproductive and decay.

23. The papists, therefore, have no ground on which to fault our doctrine and call it false because so many are offended by it. They ought rather reproach themselves and all others who do not possess a pure heart. For the blame does not lie with the Word but with people's hearts. They are unclean and impure, and either despise the Word or fall away from it under duress, or are choked by the cares, riches, and pleasures of this life.

24. So, let everyone learn from this parable that it will always be this way with the gospel: Some will be converted but there are probably three times more who will take offense. There are, therefore, not only all manner of gross sins and offenses, but also, as the Lord says, a mischief which is punished with such blindness, that these hearers of the gospel, who have eyes to see, but do not see and ears to hear but do not understand, are unable to discern and pass judgment as regards the gospel.

25. Finally, we should note that as the Lord concludes this parable, he cries out loudly, "He that hath ears to hear, let him hear." In other words, Listen to God's Word while you have it; the time may come when you would like to hear it, but it may not be there for you.

Therefore, give ear to it diligently while you have it. For he who despises it is overcome by darkness. As the Lord says (John 12:35): "Walk while ye have the light, lest darkness come upon you." May our dear Lord Jesus Christ grant us his grace so that we may diligently hear his Word, retain it in a pure heart, and bring forth fruit in patience. Amen.

THE DAY OF THE PURIFICATION OF MARY

1534

Luke 2:22–32

And when the days of her purification according to the law of Moses were accomplished, they brought him to Jerusalem, to present him to the Lord; (As it is written in the law of the Lord, Every male that openeth the womb shall be called holy to the Lord;) And to offer a sacrifice according to that which is said in the law of the Lord, A pair of turtledoves or two young pigeons. And behold, there was a man in Jerusalem, whose name was Simeon; and the same man was just and devout, waiting for the consolation of Israel: and the Holy Ghost was upon him. And it was revealed unto him by the Holy Ghost, that he should not see death, before he had seen the Lord's Christ. And he came by the Spirit into the temple: and when the parents brought in the child Jesus, to do for him after the custom of the law, Then took he him up in his arms, and blessed God, and said, Lord, now lettest thou thy servant depart in peace, according to thy word: For mine eyes have seen thy salvation, Which thou hast prepared before the face of all people; A light to lighten the Gentiles, and the glory of thy people Israel.

1. Dearly beloved, today's Gospel tells the story of how the child Jesus, when six weeks old, was brought to the temple. Following the custom of the day, the Evangelist calls these six weeks the purification, as does Moses. This was not a requirement of natural law; therefore, the heathen did not observe it. But God had so ordained for his people requiring the obligation of each mother, that after giving birth of her child—six weeks if it was a boy, twelve weeks if a girl—she must go to the temple to bring a sacrifice.

2. The pope has set the regulation in the church that mothers after giving birth must be reconsecrated before the congregation, as though they were unclean, otherwise they may not enter the church or go about among the people. But this is wrong; the uncleanness

which this decree attributes to mothers who have given birth is not a natural but a fabricated uncleanness that goes beyond the Law; so no one should be thus burdened.

3. Further, the Law required that the firstborn son at six weeks of age was to be presented as a gift to the Lord, as it is written in Exodus 34:19, The first offspring of every womb belongs to me, including all firstborn males. That meant that every firstborn male was to be surrendered sacrificially to the Lord; this was not true only for children, but also cattle, oxen, and sheep. The first fruits belonged to the Lord. Therefore, the firstborn had the peculiar distinction of being lord of the house, a priest and house father, king and spiritual father among his brothers. If all the firstborn were the Lord's and remained at the temple, there would have been too many because of the large populace. God, in his kindness, allowed parents to redeem the male child with a payment in coin, or a yearling lamb, or a pair of turtle doves, depending on whether one was rich or poor. So Jesus' parents redeemed their son, who at the same time was the Son of God.

4. It seems as though the Virgin Mary was poor and of little means, because she brought the sacrifice of the poor, a pair of turtle doves. With this sacrifice, she redeemed her son and acknowledged that, though she is his rightful mother, the son is not hers, but God's, because he is the firstborn.

5. That was the decree of Moses concerning firstborn sons. Parents came to the priest in the temple and said, Reverend sir, the child is my firstborn, but he is not my son, but the son of our Lord God; therefore, I am bringing this sacrifice and gift for him, as required. The Turks have a similar practice; of every ten sons they claim one, the most gifted and train him. That is the reason why they have so many well-trained troops.

6. But our Lord God was more gentle with the Jews by allowing the firstborn son to be redeemed from his claim on him, to be a constant testimony and remembrance of how God had brought the people out of Egypt and in a single night had slain the firstborn in every Egyptian family. In token of this deliverance, God designated that the firstborn male of men and cattle be presented in sacrifice at the temple. This has now been abrogated and is no longer binding on Christians, as also other ceremonies and laws which had appertained exclusively for the Jews.

7. There is, therefore, nothing of especial significance for us here, except that we should see that Christ placed himself under the Law even though he was not obligated. There is consolation for us on this festival of Christ's presentation at the temple and his gracious compliance under the Law. We, too, should cultivate such obedience that even as his example serves to increase our faith, so may it also serve to promote good works in our daily life. For here the obedience of the child Jesus and that of his mother are extolled and held before us, to reprimand and goad us on. Now the mother's and child's obedience under the Law are held before us here as praiseworthy, and as an object lesson to our shame, because God cannot get us to do even half of what we would owe for our salvation and rescue from the everlasting damnation of hellfire.

8. Our disobedience and miserable bad habits do not comport well with the example of the child Jesus who is Lord over the Law. In comparison, Moses is a mere man and beggar. He, nevertheless, did what Moses, his servant, required of other children who are sinners. The Virgin Mary did likewise. She well knew that she was a virgin and, therefore, was not obligated under the Law, for Moses was speaking of women who became pregnant in the normal manner. She, however, did not draw on immunity, because others would not understand her situation and might take offense, so she did what other women were obligated to do under the Law.

9. These two examples, that of the child Jesus and that of Mary, his mother, shame us and highlight our sinfulness and for this reason they are preached and written about, so that we might blush red with shame when we realize we do not do the things required of us by the Lord from whom we have everything. He did it all for our sake when he complied with the Law of Moses, his servant, even though by rights he was not obligated. Really, we ought to spray ourselves full of red paint and say, I am not worthy that the sun shines on me since my Lord and Saviour has subjected himself under the Law and by his example has so shown our disobedience to be so blameworthy that it could not possibly be shamed to greater dishonor. When he lowers himself and endures such an unnecessary obedience, he thereby heaps censure and disgrace upon us who are not obedient to the Lord who has power to throw us into hell or to bring us into heaven.

10. The whole of mankind should, therefore, feel shame in their hearts and say, What now, poor bag of worms? Should I not be obedient to my Lord and follow his example who for my sake became man, permitted himself to lie in a cradle, be carried to Jerusalem, and be obedient to his servant Moses to whom he owed no obedience? For he is the Lord. Moses is scarcely worthy to be called his servant. Nevertheless, he does what he was not obligated to do. On the other hand, I do not do what I am obligated to do, and thereby deserve damnation. This is the very first, basic lesson taught in childhood, that we learn to feel shame because, in spite of the example of our Lord Jesus Christ, we are so mischievous and disobedient.

11. The second lesson has to do with the glory of this firstborn son whom God esteemed so highly, because he was God's own, and was to be called his Son. That was a glory and a privilege which the Jews readily presumed to claim for themselves, looking askance at others, as though God had no concern for them, while they alone were the beloved children. We don't have to be told how a firstborn often turns out worst and acts in a shameful manner. Pride gets the better of them, prompting them to think, I am the Lord's holy property, you are nothing; and they arrogantly despise others. We have some glaring examples of this in the case of the monks. They would love to claim this prerogative and say, I am the Lord God's holy child, by his Word and ordinance. Can't you hear them bragging because of the insipid cap they arrogantly wear?

12. It was pride that jolted Lucifer, the first and highest among the angels, causing him to fall. Cain was the firstborn son, and what a precious thing it was that Eve named him, THE man, the one who would crush the serpent's head. As soon as he was born, she pictured him with a holy ray or crown above his head, and called him the man, the Lord! But just as the first angel Lucifer was a devil, so was Cain an evil rogue.

13. Ishmael was Abraham's firstborn, but he was so proud that he could not abide his brother Isaac in the house and considered himself the master. We read in Genesis 21:9 how Ishmael scoffed. The firstborn are often so steeped in pride that they consider themselves God's sacred, chosen ones, to the exclusion of everyone else. That is why God has caused them to tumble. Esau, too, was of the opinion

that he would unfailingly remain topmost and that he could not lose his birthright, but our Lord God arranged things differently. Because he complacently thought that as the firstborn he could be proud and despise and oppress his brother, God said, Do you think just because you are the firstborn you can be so arrogant? God arranged events in such a way that he lost the blessing and was overthrown like Cain and Ishmael. Such wantonness has been characteristic of the firstborn throughout time.

14. The Jews, too, thought they were the rightful and chosen firstborn in God's kingdom and in Christendom, and we Gentiles were the "other child." It is true the apostles, who were the first believers, were Jews, too, but the rest of the Jews were haughty. Therefore, our Lord God said, No, you are not mine; I did not consecrate you to be my people in order that you should be proud and despise others, but rather that you were to be more thankful and more obedient. But since you do not wish to do that, give way, and let the Gentiles come forward; they shall be preferred, you shall be last. In fact, you will be locked out.

15. David also had to do the same thing when his sons began to fight and quarrel among themselves. The firstborn, Amnon, raped his sister, Tamar, and was murdered by his brother, Absalom (2 Sam. 13). When David saw all this terrible violence, he abrogated the legitimate rights of the older sons and designated Solomon, the youngest, to succeed as king. This was our Lord God's will because he cannot abide arrogance.

16. The same thing happened in the case of David and his seven brothers. When the Lord sent the prophet Samuel to anoint a son of Jesse as king in Saul's place, the eldest stepped forward. He was a proud blusterer, as we can see from the way he shamefully dealt with David in the camp, addressing him like a servant, Why did you not stay home with the sheep? But the Lord God said to Samuel, Anoint the youngest to be king for me over my people. All the brothers were presented and paraded by. But what did our Lord God do? He rejected the seven brothers, the firstborn and all the rest, too.

17. Why does God do this? Weren't they all older than David? Why does God not proceed justly according to his own ordinance and make the firstborn king, rather than David who was the young-

est? He does it so that no one takes things lightly, becomes proud, and presumptuously assumes that according to the Law his blessing and gifts cannot be withheld. He wants humble, not proud children. The man who idly boasts because of his elevated station can easily be humbled and set down. Cain, Ishmael, Esau, Eliab, the Jews, and the angels themselves became haughty and considered the advantage given them through grace as their right and for that reason despised and looked down on others. Therefore, they were consigned to the devil in the chasm of hell, as Psalm 113:5–7 states, "Who is like unto the LORD . . . in heaven, and in the earth! He raiseth up the poor out of the dust, and lifteth the needy out of the dunghill." Again, the Virgin Mary in the Magnificat, "He hath put down the mighty from their seats, and exalted them of low degree."

18. That is our Lord God's mode of operation as he tumbles the haughty. For he cannot tolerate haughtiness and defiance, nor allow his gifts to be dealt with as though we had them on our own. For that reason he often elevates a despised pauper, and on the other side knocks a king off his throne and into prison, death, and all manner of misfortune. This is our Lord's mode of doing things.

19. Primogeniture is a case in point. It was highly regarded by the Jews, because according to it, by God's ordinance, the firstborn took precedence in worldly and spiritual matters. But because this honor was misused to further personal pride and arrogance, God abrogated this right and regulation. Reuben was the firstborn son, yet Jacob decreed with a curse that he should have neither the kingdom nor the priestly office, both of which were his right by birth. Abraham, as we assume, was the youngest son, but God gave him the privileged station that was reserved for the oldest and firstborn.

20. Throughout time it seems the firstborn sons seldom turned out well; this is likely because in their arrogance they thought, I am the first son, master of the house, the Lord God's chosen one, his very own. My brothers are nothing; God doesn't notice them. Such boasting annoyed God to the extent that he knocked them down.

21. Therefore, let no one presumptuously presume upon God's grace or gifts. If one has a talent or some other gift, let him not exalt himself over someone who does not possess them, but let him use the same to the glory of God and the welfare of his neighbor. If a per-

son is comely, pious, holy, or rich, let him not flaunt this over a neighbor who is awkward, unholy, and poor. For God has amply proved in the lives of the first and noblest patriarchs that he will not brook pride. Almost all the firstborn turned out badly. John the Baptist turned out well, but he is almost an exception. Christ turned out well, but he was without sin.

22. Other firstborns, as a rule, misused their distinction and were, therefore, because of haughtiness and arrogance brought down, until finally the entire Jewish nation was cut off, and we have succeeded in their place. For Christendom is now the Lord God's own and his firstborn, but not because of outward might and ceremony, as the pope boasts that he is the foremost bishop, while actually he is nothing but dirt compared with the Word and Holy Sacrament. Even though we vary greatly among ourselves, as far as our physical lineage is concerned, yet because of baptism, we are all equal. For we have all been given birth by the Christian church which is an immaculate virgin in spirit; for she (the church) has the pure Word of God and the Holy Sacraments through which she becomes pregnant and again and again gives birth to Christians who are the true firstborn and the Lord God's very own—I as well as you, you as well as I. Now it is a true reality, where before it was merely prefigured for us.

23. If God had made something special, and graced you and me with a special baptism, and given us our own special word and our own sacrament, we, too, would have gone to the devil through arrogance. But because God made nothing for anyone to have alone, but all must say and confess that we have one baptism, one mother—the Christian church—one faith, one Word, one Sacrament, even so no one can despise another, you must permit me to be a firstborn son, and likewise I, you, as well as, myself. So all are alike, one the same as the other, kings and priests, but only in the spiritual realm. In the secular world differences will remain.

24. The pope thinks he is of greater importance in the spiritual realm, but he has no ground for this other than through the tiresome devil. For among true Christians no one is better than another, simply because no one has a better baptism than the next. There must be preachers, pastors, and other church workers, but these are offices. They make no one into a child of God. But baptism, the

Word, and faith in the Word cause us to become children of God and the firstborn.

25. So now, let everyone learn that by these Old Testament examples, the Lord God wants us to understand that he will not tolerate arrogance and that he puts down all who vaunt themselves, sparing only those that humble and lower themselves. The world simply will not believe this and even today misuses simple and trifling gifts in arrogance. For that reason God knocks them down, one after another, so that they tumble like Lucifer and his angels from heaven.

26. That's the significance of today's Gospel as it treats the story of the sacrifice in the temple. May we ask God for his grace, so that he will keep us from all arrogance and through his Holy Spirit awaken in us pure hearts for rightful and earnest obedience, and graciously keep us in the same to our end. Amen.

ESTOMIHI SUNDAY (QUINQUAGESIMA)

1534

Luke 18:31–43

Then he took unto him the twelve, and said unto them, Behold, we go up to Jerusalem, and all things that are written by the prophets concerning the Son of man shall be accomplished. For he shall be delivered unto the Gentiles, and shall be mocked, and spitefully entreated, and spitted on: and they shall scourge him, and put him to death: and the third day he shall rise again. And they understood none of these things: and this saying was hid from them, neither knew they the things which were spoken. And it came to pass, that as he was come nigh unto Jericho, a certain blind man sat by the way side begging: And hearing the multitude pass by, he asked what it meant. And they told him, that Jesus of Nazareth passeth by. And he cried, saying, Jesus, thou son of David, have mercy on me. And they which went before rebuked him, that he should hold his peace: but he cried so much the more, Thou son of David, have mercy on me. And Jesus stood, and commanded him to be brought unto him: and when he was come near, he asked him, Saying, What wilt thou that I shall do unto thee? And he said, Lord, that I may receive my sight. And Jesus said unto him, Receive thy sight; thy faith hath saved thee. And immediately he received his sight, and followed him, glorifying God: and all the people, when they saw it, gave praise unto God.

1. Today's Gospel has two parts. First, there is the Lord's very pointed foretelling to his twelve disciples privately of his impending suffering. His words were similar to those which the angel addressed later to the women at the tomb on Easter, namely, "Remember how he spake unto you when he was yet in Galilee, saying, The Son of man must be delivered into the hands of sinful men, and be crucified, and the third day rise again." Even now the Lord Jesus was on his way from Galilee to Jerusalem, where he then remained and was crucified. The second part treats of the miraculous healing of the blind man.

2. So, then, in the first part the Lord gathers the Twelve to himself and tells them, "Behold, we go up to Jerusalem, and all things that are written by the prophets concerning the Son of man shall be accomplished. For he shall be delivered unto the Gentiles." He spoke this while still in Galilee, before he had come to Jerusalem. But the Evangelist repeats three times that the disciples did not understand what he was prophesying. They thought he was speaking in a strange, convoluted sort of way, and that his words had a special meaning. That he would endure suffering in Jerusalem did not ring a bell with them. It was as though they were listening to a foreign tongue and didn't understand a word. For that reason the Evangelist purposely repeats it again, that "they understood none of these things: and this saying was hid from them, neither knew they the things which were spoken." In their hearts they were thinking, this man Jesus Christ performs so many miraculous signs, wakes up the dead, gives sight to the blind, and so on, that we must simply conclude that God is with him, no matter what. In time he will be a great lord, greater than Joseph in Egypt and Daniel in the land of Babylon. And we, his disciples, will also become princes and lords with him. After all, who would wish to do him harm, a man so mighty that even death and all kinds of illness are healed and done away by him? So, in their hearts they thought, God is with him that good may come, and will not permit him to suffer. The fact that his words sound as though he would suffer and die must surely have another meaning. Such was the simplemindedness of the dear apostles.

3. This is the way with all of God's words and works; at first speaking, before they happen, people don't comprehend them. But once they have happened, then people know and understand. That's what St. John (2:22) points out: Once Jesus was risen from the dead, his disciples recalled that he had said this, and they believed the Scripture and the words which he had spoken. Faith is the natural, divine correlative of the Word of God. For God's Word speaks of, indeed cannot but speak, things which human reason cannot understand or conceive by itself. We should believe it, and that it is so, we will in due time find out that it is indeed true and that we rightly understand it.

4. Let me give an example. God's Word teaches us concerning the resurrection from the dead, something human reason doesn't under-

stand. Accordingly, one sees that the worldly wise mock and hold us to be fools for believing that there will be a resurrection of the dead and a life after this life. Again, that God should become man and be born into this world of a virgin, human reason cannot admit, saying "No" to it. Therefore, it must be believed, until we come to where we see and say, Now I understand and see that it is true, what before I believed. Again, that a person should have the forgiveness of sins, God's grace and mercy, without having earned it, through the water of baptism and through absolution, seems like an utter falsehood to human reason. It argues, Christians who believe that are balmy and off-the-wall; if God is to be reconciled, there must be something higher and better, namely, good works, which demand pain and sweat from us. This harmonizes with the pope's example, which we have before our eyes, and by his preaching he directs people to their own merits.

5. It does not even occur to human reason to believe that alone by baptism and faith in Christ, everything necessary for salvation is done. Reason holds that to be a falsehood. For it does not know what faith is, deeming faith in Christ a trifling thing. In the same way the Word is seen as a paltry thing and the one who urges and preaches it as a poor, miserable, and sinful creature. That one should trust and wager body and life for eternity upon faith and the Word, both such insignificant things, is ridiculous to reason. That's the reason why, even though God's Word is plainly spoken to people, human reason does not comprehend, does not believe, declares it to be untrue; and the precious gospel, the meanwhile, is labeled as heresy and a teaching of the devil by which people are misled, teaching them not to do good works. Human reason knows no other verdict.

6. For that reason we should learn to believe with ingenuous faith and say, If it's God's Word, I cannot doubt it in any way; and, even though I cannot see, touch, or feel that it is true, nonetheless, I listen because God is speaking. He is so great and mighty that he can make it true, so that in his good time, or in the life to come, I will be able to comprehend and understand it, yes, see and grasp it, even though I don't understand it now.

7. We know this from other examples. Before David attacks Goliath, he believes that he can beat and kill him, for he has God's Word,

as he says to Saul, "The Lord that delivered me out of the paw of the lion, and out of the paw of the bear, he will deliver me out of the hand of this Philistine" (1 Sam. 17:37); likewise, "This uncircumcised Philistine shall be as one of them, seeing he hath defied the armies of the living God" (1 Sam. 17:36). So firmly is this set in his heart that, although his strength cannot compare with the Philistine's, he confronts the Philistine confidently and says, "This day will the Lord deliver thee into mine hand; and I will smite thee, and take thine head from thee" (v. 46). They all heard these words from David's mouth, but deemed them an idle boast and mockery. And it's true, had it been David's word only and not God's, all would have come to nothing. But it is God's Word, and David believes it before he experiences it. And although Goliath storms and curses David, saying, "Am I a dog, that thou comest to me with staves. . . ." nonetheless, as things went, David is vindicated. Reason did not see that David with sling and stone would strike down that huge, powerful giant. But David believes and does it. And after he had done it, then people could see and understand that it was indeed true and no misrepresentation.

8. But earlier, when only David's word was there, "This day will the Lord deliver thee into my hand," it was a gross exaggeration, indeed an impossible thing. For reason figures like this: David is but a youth, a shepherd, with no battle experience, a Johnny-come-lately, with staff and sling, whereas the giant comes in full battle dress with cuirass and spear. Was that not an unequal sort of harness and battle dress, a spectacle ridiculous to see, the youthful marksman, David, assaying to go forth, something no one else in the encampment dared to do? That is why his oldest brother, Eliab, bristled angrily at him and said, "Why camest thou down hither? . . . I know thy pride, and the naughtiness of thine heart; for thou art come down that thou mightest see the battle." Also, King Saul said to him, "Thou art not able to go against this Philistine to fight with him; for thou art but a youth, and he a man of war from his youth." David, moreover, did not see, or know for sure, how God would punish the blasphemy of his opponent and help him. Yet that's what he judged would happen, because he believed God's Word.

9. This is the way it always is. God's Word and work always are judged impossible before coming to pass. But once it does, then we

see how easily and beyond all expectations it was done. Yet prior to its happening, we need simply to believe it, not know or understand it. For how sins are washed away through baptism and how we shall be raised from the dead at the last day, reason will never understand, especially when we see how many a saintly man has met his end eaten by the birds, torn by dogs and wolves, even burned to ashes and then strewn upon the water, as the pope did to the saintly Hus at Constance. Reason then asks, How will our Lord God restore the body again? But God has said that he will waken and raise our bodies again. Because it is but his Word, human reason, therefore, considers it not only incredible but also impossible. But we are to believe it, and know that it will be so. For this is the man who is almighty and can make all things out of nothing.

10. Who, or what were we a hundred, or sixty years ago? Just as little as the child who will be born twenty, thirty, or forty years after us! Since God has the know how for creating all things out of nothing, he can again reconstitute something that once upon a time existed. One ought not be concerned, therefore, whether a thing is possible but should rather say, God has said it; therefore, it will happen, even though it seem impossible. For although I cannot see or grasp it, God is the Lord who makes the impossible possible, and creates something out of nothing.

11. Pope Clement, Cardinal V. M.,* and his henchmen are exceedingly vexatious fools when they measure the Lord God's Word and work in terms of their reason. For they draw the conclusion that because they cannot make a dead man alive, God cannot either. They reckon God's Word and work in terms of their own thinking and capability. If that were true, that God's Word and work could be measured according to our reason, the Lord God might just as well have kept silent. But because he speaks, it is clear that our reason does not know and understand all, and that God's Word is above and beyond reason, as experience teaches.

12. This is the way with God's Word. I preach the forgiveness of sins and absolve you by Christ's command. You hear the Word, you

*A reference probably to Albrecht, Archbishop of Mainz.

hear that you are released from sin, and yet you do not feel that God and his angels are laughing with you, that they are your friends.

13. Accordingly, when now you are baptized, you still have the same flesh and skin after baptism as before. Do baptism and absolution, then, amount to nothing? Oh, no! That's why you should learn to say, God has baptized me, and God has absolved and released me from my sins through his Word. Therefore, I believe firmly, though I don't see and feel right away that God is smiling at me and calling me his son, that Christ, my Lord, is called my brother, and that the dear angels are rejoicing with particular happiness over me. This, I say, is what I believe; whether I see or feel it, I don't doubt it. It doesn't matter whether or not the pope believes; I do, because God does not deceive me in his Word.

14. The disciples had not yet mastered this, otherwise they would not have disputed or puzzled long, but would have concluded that it would happen just as he said; because this man cannot lie, it will certainly occur when and how he wills. The blind man, on the other hand, of whom the Evangelist next reports, has learned the art well. His eyes are totally sightless, utterly unable to see the slightest thing. But as soon as the words sound, "receive thy sight," he believes, and it comes to pass, just as he believes. That word, although it stands alone, tells of something that does not yet exist, for the eyes of the blind man are still shut; but straightway upon that word, which he believes, it is enacted as he believed, and now he grasps and experiences it. This is the way it should have been for the disciples. Although they could not see how it was possible, they still should have believed because it was his Word. For faith is the Word's only correlative. But what happened? Christ tells them plainly what will happen to him in Jerusalem, but they don't understand, and for that reason they don't think it true. It wasn't because they held him to be a deceiver; but they thought his words must have another meaning.

15. That is the first thing which we are to learn from today's Gospel, namely, to believe God's Word with our whole heart and mind, without doubting. The pope knows nothing about such faith, doesn't teach it, and really no papalist knows the meaning of faith and Christ. But you should be capable of understanding it. A Christian heart not only hears the Word of God concerning the forgiveness of sins but

also firmly believes it, never doubting, even though it does not feel or see it. Such faith and heart God's Word seeks for. When we have firmly believed that and when God besides brings it to the light of day in actual fulfillment, then we shall say, Oh, happy me, that I believed! But the pope, his cardinals, Erasmus, and others, who have not believed, will see, marvel, and say, Who would have thought it? Oh, murder, that we did not believe! In the end they have to believe anyway, but it will be too late and a lost cause, for it will not help them; they delayed too long.

16. This, then, is the lesson, that we should not trip over God's Word, even though it sounds extraordinarily incredible, even impossible, but firmly take our stand: God has spoken it; it must happen. One should not ask whether it's possible but only be concerned about God having said it. For if God has spoken it, he is mighty and truly able to bring it to pass. For that reason believe it! Whoever will not believe, slanders God in the worst way. Therefore, let us do God the honor, in accord with the first commandment, that we do not doubt that, however incredible it may sound, God will also grant and effect it precisely as promised. Wherever God's Word is, whether in baptism, absolution, the Sacrament, or in the preaching of the gospel, God is speaking with us. In absolution, he himself is releasing us from sin; in the Sacrament, or Lord's Supper, Christ himself nurtures us with his body and blood. Similarly we have God's Word in the church, yes, in the home. When the pastor speaks God's Word to us in the church, or the father at home, God himself is speaking to us. We should be concerned, therefore, to receive and esteem it as God's Word.

17. The second part of today's Gospel treats of the blind man. The Evangelist is teaching us the true beggar's art of how we should learn to gambol happily before God, be unashamed, and come near. For whoever is timid lets himself be easily shunted aside and has no use for begging. It happened to me once, as a young student, as on New Year's I was begging. With a friend I came to a house and we sang for a bratwurst. The master of the house stormed out of the door with a shout, saying, Where are you rascals? and brought out two bratwurst. But my friend and I ran pell-mell from the place thinking that he wanted to beat us, until the master of the house called after us to

come and get the bratwurst. People don't take to begging. But we have to doff our bashful hats and realize that the Lord God wants to have it so, that we happily come near. For it is his desire and honor to be generous and it pleases him when people look to him for every good thing. Therefore, we should be as importunate as he himself wishes us to be. For if a man is going to wait until he's worthy for God to give him something, he's never going to ask for anything. Therefore, it's best that we take off our bashful hats, open our mouths pronto, and say, Lord, I am in great straits of body and soul, and I need your help and comfort. Again, I have need of this or that, and for that reason I beseech you graciously to grant it to me.

18. The monks and beggars in the streets and lanes know this art well. But the people don't like it; they are fed up with such capers and send the beggars shipping with harsh words. But our Lord God holds dear such eager beavers who keep on persistently, refusing to be sent away, as in the case of the blind man, who dearly wanted to have seeing eyes. That is why, when he heard the great commotion, he straightaway asked what it was. When he heard that it was because of Jesus, he began to cry, "Jesus, thou Son of David, have mercy upon me." Those that were in the forefront threatened him, shushing him up. But he paid no attention; the more they warned him, the more insistently he cried.

19. Here was a real alms seeker and genuine beggar, the kind our Lord God covets. We should note this example well and also come before our Lord Christ petitioning, O Lord! I am a poor sinner; grant that your kingdom come to me; forgive me my sin; help me. . . . Whoever begs like this, unashamedly, is doing right, and our Lord God loves it. For he is not as sensitive as people are. Such clamoring makes us tired, disinclined, and turned off. To him, however, it is a great honor that people think of him as tenderhearted, not giving up, but saying, Lord, all glory and worship be thine, all honor and praise. I beg of you, dear Lord, do not look upon me as unworthy but as one who needs your help. It is to your glory that I, an unworthy and poor sinner, beg of you; I cannot presume upon your help, but I know that you can and will help those that beg of you.

20. Such bold petitioning, which holds on firmly and is not scared off, pleases God well, as we see in the case of the blind man. As soon

as he begins to petition, Christ summons him to himself and moves everyone out of the way. The blind man does not feel ashamed but allows himself to be led to him. Thereupon Jesus asks him directly, "What wilt thou that I shall do unto thee?" We see how the Lord's hands stand open, as though to say, Pray, tell me what you wish, and I will give it to you. The blind man does not hesitate at all but says, "Lord, that I may receive my sight." And the Lord answers, "Yes, receive your sight." That's praying boldly, yet courteously. We should learn from the blind man so to bring our petitions and our needs to Christ, confidently trusting that he will hear us and grant our petitions.

21. Under the papacy we held such praying in low esteem, thinking, If others do not pray for us, we will get nowhere. That's exactly what a Christian ought not do. Rather, as soon as trouble presses him, he should go directly into the church or his closet, fall on his knees, and say, Lord, here I am; I have need of this or that, although I am unworthy; however, look upon my misery and need, and help me for thy honor's sake. So, learn to petition boldly and do not doubt that God will for Christ's sake give you what is for your good. The promise is clear and sure: What you ask in Jesus' name shall be yours! Only see to it that you don't grow weary in prayer because God does not grow weary in giving. The more you persist in prayer, the better God likes it. He does not grow tired of your clamoring, yes, even when you petition him with strong insistence that he should hear and answer you this very moment in what you desire, as though he was delaying too long. He answers quickly because of importunate prayer. I hope that the last day will not be long delayed but will soon come—earlier than we expect—because of the earnest prayers of Christians. The Lord gives us an example in Luke 18:1–8 of the widow who would not give up, until the judge, who feared neither God nor men, said, I cannot endure it longer; this widow is making me deaf. I'll help her, so that I get rid of her and am done with this constant demanding. "And shall not God," says Christ, "avenge his own elect, which cry day and night unto him, though he bear long with them? I tell you that he will avenge them speedily." In other words, prayer speeds God's answer, that he not delay.

22. Prayer, therefore, serves to hasten something which otherwise would have been delayed longer. This example teaches us that we

should be bold, clamoring beggars who do not grow weary but say, Lord, it is true, I am a poor, unworthy sinner, indeed; but nonetheless I have need of this and that. I have wife and child, and have nothing to feed them; Lord, give us food. I am desperate, and need your comfort, Lord, help me. It is not a question of whether I am a saint; only one thing matters, that I am in need, and that you gladly give what is needful for my body and soul.

23. When you pray in this manner, and firmly, then he will certainly say to you, as to the blind man, "What do you want me to do for you? Receive your sight! Your faith has helped you." To pray and not to believe is to mock God. But faith rests alone on this: that God for the sake of Christ, his Son and our Lord, hears, shields, rescues, and saves. May our dear Lord and Saviour, Christ Jesus, help us! Amen.

INVOCAVIT SUNDAY—FIRST SUNDAY IN LENT

1534

Matthew 4:1–11

Then was Jesus led up of the spirit into the wilderness to be tempted of the devil. And when he had fasted forty days and forty nights, he was afterward an hungred. And when the tempter came to him, he said, If thou be the Son of God, command that these stones be made bread. But he answered and said, It is written, Man shall not live by bread alone, but by every word that proceedeth out of the mouth of God. Then the devil taketh him up into the holy city, and setteth him on a pinnacle of the temple, And saith unto him, If thou be the Son of God, cast thyself down: for it is written, He shall give his angels charge concerning thee: and in their hands they shall bear thee up, lest at any time thou dash thy foot against a stone. Jesus said unto him, It is written again, Thou shalt not tempt the Lord thy God. Again, the devil taketh him up into an exceeding high mountain, and sheweth him all the kingdoms of the world, and the glory of them; And saith unto him, All these things will I give thee, if thou wilt fall down and worship me. Then saith Jesus unto him, Get thee hence, Satan: for it is written, Thou shalt worship the Lord thy God, and him only shalt thou serve. Then the devil leaveth him, and, behold, angels came and ministered unto him.

1. In this Gospel we learn that the Lord Jesus after his baptism was tempted three times, after having spent forty days and forty nights in the wilderness without food. Or, as Luke reports it, these three temptations continued throughout the forty days, and Jesus was harried by one or the other for a period of days, and perhaps not in the same order recorded by Matthew.

2. However, this is a comprehensive Gospel, particularly when applied to all Christendom, which also experiences trials, like Christ, by hunger and persecution, by heresy and finally by the kingdoms of this world, as the histories devoted to the subject also well document. But

on this occasion we shall not deal in a far-ranging way with temptation but as it is commonly understood. So, first, we want to note and learn from the example of our dear Lord Christ that every Christian as soon as he's baptized, is marshaled into an army in confrontation with the devil, and from his baptism onward is saddled with the devil who harasses him as long as he lives. If this bitter enemy cannot by his onslaughts get the better of Christians and bring about their downfall, he seeks to hang them on the cross and kill them as he did Christ.

3. All Christians face such attack, for the adversary never relents but continues to try to wrench us away from Christ and our baptism, by means of hunger or persecution, by worldly fame and wealth, or by heresy or false interpretation of Scriptures, so that we give way to despair and vain glory. If such tricks fail, the devil tries to get us by the throat and strangle us to death. We can learn from Christ's encounter with Satan how to deal with and overcome this adversary, so that he's forced to let us go. However, this happens only through true faith in God and his Word. Whoever thus arms himself properly will be able to withstand the devil; but whoever fails to do so will certainly be helpless against this deadly adversary.

4. It is the bounden duty, therefore, of every Christian to earnestly hear God's Word and its preaching, diligently learn and become well-versed therein. We also should persevere in earnest prayer that God would let his kingdom come among us, not lead us into temptation, but graciously deliver us from all evil.

5. Now, the Evangelist says that the Lord Jesus was led away by the Spirit into the wilderness. For since there was no master over him who could demand things of him, the Holy Spirit directed him into the wilderness. The Evangelist wants especially to caution us to be on guard against self-imposed devotion, since Christ did not go into the wilderness by an act of his own will or resolve to wrestle there with the devil, as many and sundry people do with mandate of God's Word or Spirit. In no way ought this happen. No one should seek after self-chosen avenues of service to God unless so enjoined by God, either by God's Word or by persons whom God has placed in authority over him. Whoever undertakes things like this without a proper call, as do the monks and nuns who run the cloisters, not only does God a disservice but also contravenes genuine obedience to him.

6. It is well, therefore, for us to reflect on this example of Christ. He did not go into the wilderness of his own accord but was led there by the Holy Spirit. Accordingly, we should respond in similar manner, not prompted merely by our own ideas of religion, but in faithful conformity and obedience to the Word of God in all that we do. This is a teaching you have often heard repeated, to be sure that God has commanded whatever you do and to do nothing extraneous to his Word.

7. With respect to ordinary duties and works of love, no new command is necessary. We have these expressed in the Ten Commandments. There the Lord enjoins everybody to hear his Word, to love him, to pray and call upon him. Doing these things is God's will, as he requires in the first three commandments. God also commands obedience to father and mother, not to kill, and not to commit adultery but to marry. All this is by God's ordering and command. For this reason we need not look for the Holy Spirit's prompting to be a father or mother, to enter the estate of matrimony, and so on, for such commands already exist. But to initiate something special as service to God, like entering a cloister, or fasting by foregoing meat, eggs, and butter, or refraining from singing hallelujahs while fasting, there are no commands in God's Word. Therefore, such things are really nothing but sacrilege in God's sight and not true worship.

8. But now let us consider in turn each of Christ's temptations. The first occurs when the devil, seeing the Lord Jesus hunger, says to him, "If thou be the Son of God, command that these stones be made bread." This temptation does not appear to us to be so very serious, for we reason like this, How could that have harmed Christ? He could easily have made bread out of stones. He had already done much greater miracles! But the reason he does not want to do it is this: He knows very well what the devil is after and that he is not particularly interested in Jesus performing a miracle. Rather, as we see from Christ's reply, Satan wanted very much to rob him of faith and reliance on God's lovingkindness and to prompt the thought in his heart, God has forgotten you; he's indifferent to your needs; he's willing to let you die of hunger, begrudging you even a piece of bread. That is why the Lord answers, Away devil, not so! "Man shall not live by bread alone, but by every word that proceedeth out of the

mouth of God." So, the devil's prompting is this: Your only concern is for bread; forget about God's Word; bread is what you need.

9. This sort of temptation is still with us today. The devil still puts such thoughts into people's hearts like: If you are a child of God, God cannot be angry with you. Let us keep on hoarding and being covetous. Let's meddle to our heart's content into the affairs of the world; no harm is done; you are not sinning if you do. For if God does not want to give nourishment and bread, he must be a bad God and a merciless Father. By such promptings, the devil makes scoundrels out of burghers and peasants, convincing them to go on hoarding and being greedy, and to thinking that God will not become angry about it since after all it has to do with daily bread and sustenance. I must, everyone thinks, take care of wife and child and provide for them, and so on. Thus by saying that "You are a child of God," the devil puts a lid over sin, by implying that as such you cannot sin or do what is wrong. Everywhere in the world we see that people are not conscience stricken; they do not pay attention to the Word, but are only concerned with bread and sustenance. So, this temptation is still very much in the world. The devil makes the Word appear of little value and forces people to pay more attention to bread than to it.

10. We must recognize this and learn to overcome this temptation by saying, Satan, you would like very much to tear me away from the Word, but you will not succeed. Before I starve for want of the Word of God, I would rather do without bread and die of hunger. For it is better for the body to perish than for it to be kept alive by food and the soul to die and be lost forever. The devil is not happy to have us think that way and so maneuvers things by seeing to it that we always have a full stomach, tempting us to despise God's Word and to think, No want exists; God is my Father; will he begrudge me bread and sustenance?

11. If you want to guard yourself against such temptation, learn from Christ here that there are two kinds of bread. The first and best bread, which comes down from heaven, is the Word of God; the second and of lesser benefit is the temporal bread, which comes forth from the earth. If I now have the first and best bread, the heavenly bread, and allow nothing to deter me from partaking of it, I am confident that temporal bread will also not be lacking, even if it takes stones to be made into bread. Those, however, who are overcome by

the devil, give up the heavenly bread, and feed only upon the temporal, will find that having filled up their stomachs they must lie down and die; having refused to feed on the good bread here, they must leave it behind and suffer eternal hunger there. But it does not have to be this way. If the devil is assailing you through persecution, want, hunger, and affliction, suffer it and fast with Christ, since it is the Spirit who directs you, and do not let up on your trust in God's grace. In time the angels will come and wait on your table, as the Evangelist says in his concluding word.

12. The first lesson as regards the initial temptation is that we must learn to value God's Word as highly as we do eternal life. For it is the kind of food and nourishment that bestows eternal life upon everyone who eats of it, that is, believes it. Just as Christ says to the Jews (John 6:27): "Labour not for the meat which perisheth, but for that meat which endureth unto everlasting life, which the Son of man shall give unto you." Mark this well. Temporal bread, on the other hand, after which the whole world scrapes and scratches, endures only until the last crumb is eaten, and then everlasting hunger sets in.

13. In the second temptation the devil leads the Lord Jesus into the holy city of Jerusalem, sets him on the parapet of the temple and says that he should throw himself down, suggesting that no harm would befall him, for he is the Son of God, and surely the angels would come to his assistance before he would ever strike his foot against a stone.

14. This is a very severe, spiritual temptation for faith, in which faith is assailed with regard to God's grace in the same way it was assailed above as regards sin and God's wrath. For if the devil cannot cause us to despair of God's benevolence, he brazenly tries next to see whether he can make us proud and reckless enough to rely on our own righteousness. It is as though the devil were saying to Christ, If you want to argue with me from the Word of God, hold on! I am able to do that also. Listen, here's the Word of God: He will put his angels in charge of you, ordering them to provide a chute for you, and carry you in their arms. So jump off, and let's see whether you believe that promise of God!

15. Here you must look upon Christ as a human being, who kept his Godhead concealed in his humanity. Just as on the cross he shows

that he is a real human being, grieving and crying for help and deliverance, as the one whom Satan has filled with sorrow, so he shows himself here also as a true man. For this reason the devil believes he can bring him to the point where he can tempt God to perform an unnecessary miracle. He cites Psalm 91:11 in testimony, yet he leaves out the most relevant part—*in viis tuis:* The Lord will keep you "in all thy ways." With this passage the scoundrel tries to perplex Christ and to lead him to do what God had not ordained. For Christ is now in the wilderness as a human being, not for the purpose of performing miracles but to suffer. Thus the devil tries to direct him from the way God ordained for him to walk, namely, to be a human being facing temptation, and induce him to perform an unnecessary miracle.

16. But Christ repulses him and says, "It is written, Thou shalt not tempt the Lord thy God." For there is a good staircase there and no need for me to hurl myself down. Because I'm able to descend via the steps without danger, it would be wrong for me unnecessarily and without command of God to endanger myself and jump down.

17. This is also a needful and beneficial lesson, for it is called tempting God when a person renounces the ordinary command and, in defiance of the Word of God, contrives something new and different, as monks and nuns do. They are motivated by their self-chosen notions and propose to live a special kind of life, claiming on the basis of Scripture that Christ ordained it when he said, "Forsake all and follow me." Both reason and Scripture lend support for their argument. But you see here that the devil, too, is able to quote Scripture and deceive people with it. But he becomes guilty of prevarication when he does not quote all of Scripture, but quotes only what serves his devious purpose. He leaves out what doesn't serve and remains quiet about the rest.

18. The Anabaptists do the same thing. They quote a lot of Scripture to the effect that one should not trust in anything that is created. Then they argue, Baptism is also a created thing, for it is nothing but water; therefore, one should not put any trust in, nor rely on, baptism. They refuse to believe that God's grace is in baptism but blindly feel their way about. It's not that they don't have the Scripture, but they fail to interpret it correctly. For if the Word of God did not state as follows (John 3:5): "Except a man be born of water and the Spirit,

he cannot enter into the kingdom of God," it would be wrong to seek God's grace in baptism or in the water. But God's Word stands firm (Mark 16:16): "He that believeth and is baptized shall be saved." For faith and baptism, Word and water must abide together. This, however, the blind don't want to see.

19. Accordingly, Christ contests what the devil has said, When I walk the way God has commanded me, I know that angels are with me, and that they will wait upon and keep me. Thus, also, in the case of an obedient child, or a father, mother, or domestic servant going about the routine tasks of their calling, if a mishap befalls them, God will, through his angels, help and deliver them. But if they depart from the right way, the angels will not be there, and the devil can then at any moment break their necks, if God permits. And it will serve them right, for they should not be creating new self-designed ways, for that is called tempting God.

20. This is a temptation which no one understands except the one who has been there and been tempted. For just as the first temptation leads to despair, this one leads to audacity and to rash actions that contravene God's Word and command. A Christian needs to take the middle road so that he neither despairs nor becomes arrogant, for both are contrary to the Word of God. He should instead continue in all sincerity with the Word in true faith and trust. Thus the angels will be with him, otherwise not.

21. The third temptation involves *traditio humana,* "setting human traditions and doctrines above the Word of God." It is a vile temptation by which Satan impudently offers temporal honor and power, trying to lead us into idolatry contrary to the Word of God. It helps that outward, human righteousness has such a tremendous appeal to reason and glitters far more enchantingly than does obedience to God's Word, obedience to father and mother, and doing what God commands him to do. This still will not gain him the kind of respect he gets when he dons a monk's drab garb, adopts a lifestyle different from other people, eats no meat, and so forth. Briefly, such man-made show of piety has such strong appeal that emperors and kings reverently bow down before it.

22. With this self-centered and self-conceived spirituality, the pope has become presumptuous to the point that he and his crowd

do not want to act and be like other people, because that is too contemptible. That Joseph obeyed his father Jacob does not dazzle the senses, for other upright children do the same thing. Thus it is too ordinary and common. But there is something spectacular to it when a person enters a cloister, when a monk or a nun and our Lord God become, as they boast, mutual co-workers, as they disdain gold and possessions and withdraw from the world. Monastery life has been extolled, but the fact is, as everyone knows, that there's another side to it. Christ calls it a severe and devilish temptation, and he shows us what such *traditiones humanae* and doctrines of men are, namely, doctrines of the devil, stating that they are serving and worshiping the devil with their misguided self-righteousness. "Get thee hence!" Christ says to the devil, for people are not to serve you but God only. If a person does not serve God only, he must be serving the devil.

23. But what does it mean to serve God? Serving God means to do what God has commanded in his Word. If you are a child, then you must honor your father and mother; if you are a domestic, you should be obedient and faithful; if you are a master or mistress, do not provoke your servants by either word or deed; do what your calling requires of you and walk in the fear of God. This means that we are to serve God and his Word and not our own person. For we have his Word and commands on this. Let the world call serving masters or mistresses, father or mother, neighbors or children, whatever it wants, it is still true worship of God. For God has written it into his Word relative to my neighbor, You shall love your neighbor as yourself.

24. That the pope now disregards this commandment and attributes a special type of holiness to it when a man puts on a gray hood, when he fasts and eats no butter or meat but only oil and fish, that is sheer deviltry pure and simple. They think they thereby are serving God, but actually it is serving the devil, for it is not supported by God's command and Word. In fact, this harmonizes with the righteousness that avails before God as little as does a house constructed by children out of a pile of cards become a building constructed of stone. The fact is that you cannot serve God unless you have his Word and command. If his Word and command are not there, you are not serving God but your own will. Our Lord God's response to this is, Then let the one whom you serve reward you, for what devil

has commanded you to do this? I command you to serve father and mother, your superiors and your neighbor. But this you disdain and, in the meantime, do what I have not commanded. Am I to tolerate such disobedience? No, it is out of the question.

25. Therefore, the pope and his followers, by reason of their attitude and life, are idolaters and servants of the devil. For he does not trouble himself about God's Word; yes, he condemns and persecutes the Word and by his diabolic artifices leads people away from true faith in Christ. Under the semblance of divine worship, which he has embellished with hoods and tonsures, with fasting, eating of fish, reading Masses, and whatever else, he displays great sanctity; but basically it is diabolical doctrine. You wonder perhaps why the pope and his followers hold so strictly to such devilish doctrines? The Gospel lesson answers this for you. Satan has promised them the kingdoms of this world. This shows how he scorns our preaching and worship of God, for as a result of it we are beggars and have to suffer much. But the worship of himself, the pope elevates to the heavens, for from it he has achieved wealth, property, honor, and power, and has become a lord mightier than emperor and king. We see here how by this temptation the devil has embedded himself so solidly among them and driven them to the point where they have abandoned God's Word, and have fashioned and introduced a self-fabricated righteousness. Yet amid this satanic specter God has preserved a remnant few. We must face up to the devil and tell him in the words of Christ, "Get thee hence, Satan: for it is written, Thou shalt worship the Lord thy God, and him only shalt thou serve." In other words, we should look solely to God's Word, follow it, and pursue no other worship than what the word teaches.

As long as we live, we can expect all three of these temptations. We must, therefore, gird ourselves well with God's Word, in order to protect and sustain ourselves. May Christ, our dear Lord, who himself overcame these temptations for our good, give us also the strength through him to overcome and to be saved. Amen.

REMINISCERE SUNDAY— SECOND SUNDAY IN LENT

1534

Matthew 15:21–28

Then Jesus went thence, and departed into the coasts of Tyre and Sidon. And, behold, a woman of Canaan came out of the same coasts, and cried unto him, saying, Have mercy on me, O Lord, thou Son of David; my daughter is grievously vexed with a devil. But he answered her not a word. And his disciples came and besought him, saying, Send her away; for she crieth after us. But he answered and said, I am not sent but unto the lost sheep of the house of Israel. Then came she and worshiped him, saying, Lord, help me. But he answered and said, It is not meet to take the children's bread, and to cast it to dogs. And she said, Truth, Lord: yet the dogs eat of the crumbs which fall from their masters' table. Then Jesus answered and said unto her, O woman, great is thy faith: be it unto thee even as thou wilt. And her daughter was made whole from that very hour.

1. This is a wonderful Gospel lesson. Like others, it was chosen for this Sunday because it deals with driving out the devil, and by it they (our opponents) wanted to show that people were to strive to be pious, go to confession, and partake of the Sacrament because the pope required these things. But this is a miserable, papistic piety, which lets a whole year go by until now, and then is satisfied—without Scriptural warrant and without people's hearts being in it—by wretched fasting, involuntary confession, and compulsory attendance at the Sacrament.

2. We must, therefore, first of all realize that this Gospel is not treating of a trifling, insignificant matter, but of a very important and crucial teaching concerning faith's life and death struggle before God. From it we are to learn that nothing, not even the throes of death, must deter us from calling upon God in prayer—even though he has already said "No." The devil always needles us with thoughts

of how God's face is turned away from us, that he wants nothing more to do with us. This is a terrible situation, and thick black clouds seem to cover and extinguish the lovely, bright sun—a wretchedness beyond telling.

3. That's the struggle pictured for us in the case of this woman. Not only her person, but all other circumstances, are so miserable that it's hard to imagine things being worse. First of all, she is a Gentile, a difficult situation under the circumstances, for that means that she is not of Abraham's seed and, therefore, an outsider with no right to ask for help. The thought must have bounced around in her mind, Why should I implore? It's of no use. I'm a stranger here, and in addition a Gentile woman, and he is a Jew, sent to the Jews.

4. If such a staggering blow had hit our hearts, we probably would have succumbed and given up on prayer. For it is no joke when conscience tells us, You have no right to pray; you don't belong to Christ. Let St. Paul and St. Peter pray, but our Lord God won't listen to you; you have no faith, are probably not among the elect, and not worthy to be eligible for and deserving of stepping before God to ask for anything. With such thoughts and troubling doubts, the devil assaults and jabs at us.

5. But look at the woman now and learn from her how you ought to proceed under similar circumstances. She blinds her eyes and shuts her mind to the fact that she is a heathen, a Gentile, and he a Jew. Her heart is so full of trust in Christ that she is convinced, he will not turn me away. By such faith she has wiped away the thought that she is a Gentile and he a Jew. Another person without faith would not have withstood but would have thought, You are of the devil, and it's useless for you to petition; let his own people do the imploring, but it won't do you any good. Thus prayer would never have been uttered. But this woman lets nothing deter her, refuses to dispute within herself, You do not belong in the house; you are a locked out Gentile, not worthy that the earth carry you.

6. There is no more severe and malicious trial than when the devil shatters the heart, saying, Why do you keep on praying? You belong to me! Go to it, curse God, it doesn't matter, you won't be saved. Such devil inspired thoughts can derail the unpracticed heart, so that it no longer prays and succumbs to doubts.

7. This incident, therefore, was recorded for our sakes to keep us from stumbling when the evil foe confronts us with the charge: You are no Christian; your prayers won't accomplish a thing. No, not on your life, pay no attention, but say, I'm in charge here, there's no question about that; and even though I am a wicked sinner, I nonetheless know that my Lord Jesus is not a sinner and wicked, but forever righteous and gracious. Yes, the more sinful and wicked I perceive myself to be, the more passionately and earnestly will I call upon him and let nothing deter me. I haven't the time now to debate whether I am among the elect, but I do know that I need help and therefore I come humbly seeking for it.

8. Then you are following the woman's example to the letter, when with firm faith you counter the thoughts that would keep you from prayer and affirm: The Canaanite woman was a Gentile and not among the chosen people and yet she prayed and let nothing keep her from praying, nor will I, for I desperately require help from my various needs. Where else can I look for help, but with God in heaven, for the sake of his dear Son and my Redeemer, Christ Jesus? That's the kind of heroic, soldier-like faith the woman had, truly remarkable!

9. Now the text states how she cried, "Have mercy on me, O Lord, thou Son of David; my daughter is grievously vexed with a devil." In those words she explained her anguish, and Christ certainly heard her cry, but answered her not a word. Thus Christ added another blow on top of her dilemma. She is a Gentile, an outsider, without any share in the inheritance of the chosen people. She runs after Christ and begs him, but he remains impassively silent, as though he had nothing to do with her. Before a double onslaught like that, a tower, yes a will made of iron would crumble. Through her mind the thought raced, Where is the man whom everyone was praising for his compassion, being quick to listen, eager to help? But all I see and meet with is that he hears only when he wants to and not when we need him. But the poor woman does not let herself be scared off. But what else happens to her yet?

10. In the third place, the disciples become weary of her crying and are more compassionate, to their way of thinking, than Christ himself. In fact they judge him to be too hard and insensitive. So,

they get into the act and beseech him in behalf of the woman, O Lord, give in and help her, otherwise she won't let up. Thus we have a priceless object lesson never to give up when we pray.

11. Tauler* offers an example of when it's time to stop; but it is wrong to suggest that in our preaching, for giving up praying is all too common among us already. So this is a wholesome example why we should on no account cease but continue to pray, and like this woman we ought to affirm: I will not now argue the question whether I am good or bad, worthy or unworthy. I have no time for that. There's something more important than that: my daughter is grievously vexed by the devil, and I need help and advice now. Her need was pressing her so heavily that she was ready for the hard cuffs and rebuffs she was encountering.

12. The third blow or shocking rebuff comes when Christ says, "I am not sent but to the lost sheep of Israel." And by so saying he also knocks the disciples on the head, disdaining to hear the woman or them as they plead for her.

13. They must have thought, This is a cruel man who won't even listen to other people who of their own accord, and unsolicited, plead in behalf of someone. And that is true. Christ is nowhere pictured as pitiless as in this Gospel. Nonetheless she doesn't relent, but keeps right on, even though she's had to swallow three direct hits.

14. Since her cries and the entreaty of the disciples have not helped, she now follows along into the house, as Mark tells the story, like some ill-mannered woman crying and running after Jesus. But even in the house he is not free of her, for she prostrates herself at his feet begging him. It's a lesson, indeed, recorded for our learning and comfort, teaching us that Christ is pleased at heart when we persist in prayer and do not give up.

15. Even then the Lord does not open himself up to the woman's entreaty to help her, for listen to what he says, "It is not meet to take the children's bread, and to cast it to dogs." If he had said such words to me, I would have charged out of there, convinced that it was useless and that my efforts were all in vain. It was surely the hardest blow of all that as she lies there at his feet he doesn't just let it rest with her being an impudent child and a Gentile but also calls her a dog. This was worse,

* A German mystic and eminent preacher of the Dominican order, in the 14th century, from Strassburg. Wrote: *The Book of Spiritual Poetry*.

much worse than if he had said, You are a heathen and belong to the devil; now get to your feet and stop throwing yourself around; you have nothing to gain here. That certainly was a most traumatic trial. If he had spoken in this manner to me, I would have been scared off—words spoken not just by St. Peter, St. Paul, or some other esteemed person, but by Christ himself! I would have been frightened to death.

16. What a superb and wonderful object lesson this is, therefore, to teach us what a mighty, powerful, all-availing thing faith is. Faith takes Christ captive in his word, when he's angriest, and makes out of his cruel words a comforting inversion, as we see here. You say, the woman responds, that I am a dog. Let it be, I will gladly be a dog; now give me the consideration that you give a dog. Thus she catches Christ with his own words, and he is happy to be caught. Very well, she says, if I am a dog, I ask no more than a dog's rights. I am not a child nor am I of Abraham's seed, but you are a rich Lord and set a lavish table. Give your children the bread and a place at the table; I do not wish that. Let me, merely like a dog, pick up the crumbs under the table, allowing me that which the children don't need or even miss, the crumbs, and I will be content therewith. So she catches Christ, the Lord, in his own words and with that wins not only the right of a dog, but also that of the children. Now then where will he go, our dear Jesus? He let himself be made captive, and must comply. Be sure of this: that's what he most deeply desires.

17. It is a true masterpiece, an especially vivid example that is recorded for our sakes, in order that we might learn not to be rebuffed by this man whom God permits to oppose us, as it were, and to call us dogs and Gentiles. As the woman said, Also dogs must have masters and crumbs, and also the Gentiles must have a God.

18. By such tenacity and unflinching faith the Lord is taken captive and pressed to answer, O woman, if you can tolerate and survive such blows to your heart, so may it be granted to you, even as you believe. Yours is not the typical pattern that I find. The Jews are soon offended in me and fall back at the slightest pretext, even though I have shared with them a salutary teaching. You, however, cling firmly to the hope that I will help you and you don't let go of me.

19. We see here why the Lord presented himself so unyielding and refused to hear her, not because he wanted to present an un-

friendly image as not wanting to help her, but rather that her faith might be so evident, that the Jews who were the children and heirs of the kingdom might learn from the Gentile, who was not among the children and had no inheritance, how they were to believe in Christ and place all confidence in him. Her faith pleases him so much that he can no longer hide his compassion and kindness, and he states, "O woman, great is thy faith: be it unto thee as thou wilt." Thus he gives her not merely a dog's rights, but is constrained to give her what she petitions for, healing her daughter, and places her among the descendants of Abraham. Her faith brings her to such a state of grace, that she is no longer a dog or a Gentile, but is welcomed as a beloved daughter and a blessed woman.

20. This example serves us well in that, when our Lord God puts off answering, we do not let up but firmly trust that he will finally say "Yes," and even though he does not say it loudly and publicly, still says it privately in our hearts, until the time comes when we see and experience it in fact, provided that we don't meanwhile become lazy and lax in prayer and perseverance. We learn this from other examples as well. Joseph cried out in persevering prayer for more than twelve years before God willed to help him. In his case, the longer he waited the worse the situation got; the more he prayed, the worse things became. Christ himself cried out urgently for help and deliverance at the time of his Passion, but God held back, as we read in Psalm 22:2, "O my God, I cry in the daytime, but thou hearest not; and in the night season, and am not silent." It is the same for Christians today. They very urgently and repeatedly call upon God and see no improvement, but like Joseph find that the longer and harder they have prayed the worse things have become. If God had answered Joseph sooner and rescued him, then no doubt Jacob, his father, would have been happy but Joseph would have remained a sheepherder. But because God's answer was long delayed, he became ruler over all Egypt and the greatest among his brethren; and God through him accomplished much good both in the secular realm as well as in the church.

21. This is also the manner of God's dealing with us. For a long time he denies our petition and the answer always is "No"; but if we hold fast to the "Yes," it will finally be "Yes," and no longer "No." For

his Word does not lie (John 16:23): "Whatsoever ye shall ask the Father in my name, he will give it you." Because the Word is true, his promise will not fail.

22. But our mind is greatly agitated by such delay and we would much rather that God would answer without delay. But we must not become aggravated. We must let our Lord God say "No," as he holds up our petition for a year, two years, three, or even longer, being on guard lest our hope and faith be wrenched from our hearts. We will in the end find that God will do far more for us than we asked for, just as in the case of this woman. Had she asked for even more, he would have granted it.

23. Our Lord God thus wishes to teach us that it is not always good to be heard immediately. In urgent need his answer is there, as for example, should we fall into the water, or be involved in warfare; the answer will not be long delayed. The same is true for great, difficult spiritual trials. But where the waiting and delay can be endured, we should learn that he usually holds back for our own good. It is as the prophet Habakkuk says (2:3): "For the vision is yet for an appointed time, but at the end it shall speak, and not lie: though it tarry, wait for it; because it will surely come, it will not tarry."

24. That is also the situation now as he lets the pope and the Turk rage against us. We cry out woefully but he does not hear us, acts as though he doesn't know us, and lets us go on in our misery as though we had no God. But it won't go on like this forever; God will requite us. Let us, therefore, never doubt that we have a "Yes" in heaven, imbedded in the heart of our Lord Jesus Christ, and his Father's, and that in his time it will be revealed. Now he builds four or five iron walls in front of it, and the devil shoots off his futile "No" too. But we must learn to say, I will cling to the "Yes," that God will be merciful to his church and rescue all who cry to him for help. The "Yes" is deep in his heart, in keeping with Christ's promise (John 14:13): "And whatsoever ye shall ask in my name, that will I do, that the Father may be glorified in the Son." Therefore I will not dispute whether I am among the elect, or a Gentile and unworthy, but firmly persist that the "Yes" is there.

25. This episode, accordingly, is an especially beautiful example of true faith, that it needs to be practiced, that it will finally prevail and

win out; also of how we, therefore, must not despise the Word, but cling firmly to its promise, never doubting that our prayer will be heard, even though for a time God delays. So, in the case of this woman, she cries and implores, and will not let the "Yes" word be plucked from her heart—that Christ, the Lord, is friendly and will help.

26. May our dear Lord God help us to learn this lesson well, so that with our whole heart we firmly believe his Word and promises, and through Christ, with the Holy Spirit's help, are eternally saved. Amen.

OCULI SUNDAY—THIRD SUNDAY IN LENT

*1534**

Luke 11:14–28

And he was casting out a devil, and it was dumb. And it came to pass, when the devil was gone out, the dumb spake; and the people wondered. But some of them said, He casteth out devils through Beelzebub the chief of the devils. And others, tempting him, sought of him a sign from heaven. But he, knowing their thoughts, said unto them, Every kingdom divided against itself is brought to desolation; and a house divided against a house falleth. If Satan also be divided against himself, how shall his kingdom stand? because ye say that I cast out devils through Beelzebub. And if I by Beelzebub cast out devils, by whom do your sons cast them out? therefore shall they be your judges. But if I with the finger of God cast out devils, no doubt the kingdom of God is come upon you. When a strong man armed keepeth his palace, his goods are in peace: But when a stronger than he shall come upon him, and overcome him, he taketh from him all his armor wherein he trusted, and divideth his spoils. He that is not with me is against me; and he that gathereth not with me scattereth. When the unclean spirit is gone out of man, he walketh through dry places, seeking rest; and finding none, he saith, I will return unto my house whence I came out. And when he cometh, he findeth it swept and garnished. Then goeth he, and taketh to him seven other spirits more wicked than himself; and they enter in, and dwell there: and the last state of that man is worse than the first. And it came to pass, as he spake these things, a certain woman of the company lifted up her voice, and said unto him, Blessed is the womb that bare thee, and the paps which thou has sucked. But he said, Yea rather, blessed are they that hear the word of God, and keep it.

1. As you have heard, today's Gospel treats of the casting out of a devil and, like last Sunday's Gospel, teaches how people today are able by contrition, repentance, and confession of sins to drive Satan

*Preached at the castle church in the presence of Elector John Frederick.

out. It is a timely message always, today or tomorrow, all through the church year, as it portrays our dear Lord Christ's work, not only then, but also until the world's end, as long as his kingdom remains on earth.

2. It is written and to be preached for our sakes, therefore, so that we might learn from it and be comforted. We need to know that Christ's work of driving out the devil never ceases but continues to go on in the Christian world until the Last Day. Wherever Christ's kingdom is, his wondrous work continues, causing the dumb to speak, the blind to see, and the deaf to hear. When Christ came into the flesh he set this work going, and it continues in Christendom day for day till the world's end. For this task Christ left us designated instruments: holy baptism, the blessed Sacrament, the Word and absolution, and whatever else belongs to the ministry of preaching, in order to enable us to destroy the devil's kingdom, to take from him his captives and cast him out of people. That promise is written in Isaiah 55:11: *Verbum meum non redibit vacuum*, "[My word] shall not return unto me void." Just as rain fructifies the dry land, causing it to become green and alive, so God's Word produces fruit wherever it comes. The Holy Spirit accompanies the Word, to enlighten, kindle faith, cleanse, and free people from the devil's power and rule.

3. So what that the world takes no note of it! That was true then when Christ personally accomplished it. For the world is not worthy of seeing the smallest spark of God's wondrous signs and works, but deserves to be blind, senseless, and deaf; for it dishonors, reviles, and slanders the Lord Christ as we see here. We Christians, however, who have and believe the Word should see, know, and be comforted in our hearts that God has vested us with the power here upon earth to continue to drive out the devil also now—indeed it is our duty!—both spiritually and physically.

4. Every child that comes into this world is born into the kingdom of the devil, the lord of death, who exercises his sway through sin's tyranny. But upon Christ's command we bring a child to holy baptism, speak the words of promise which he commanded, and the child is born anew into God's kingdom; and the devil must yield and get out. God's grace, through Christ, is spoken by God to the child, inasmuch as he or she is baptized into Christ's death. When a person

whom the devil has greatly overwhelmed and seared with many accusations comes to me with heavy heart and troubled conscience seeking comfort and instruction, I have the mandate, as does every Christian, to comfort my brother and pronounce God's grace, for Christ's sake, upon him. The devil must yield, not to me, a poor and wretched sinner, but to the Word which the Lord Christ left us upon earth. When your conscience is weak and terrified, therefore, and you are unable to grasp tightly enough the comfort that God graciously wants you to have, the forgiveness of sins, then know that Christ has given the Lord's Supper, his true body and blood to eat and to drink, so that you have no reason further to doubt that his body was given for your sins and his blood poured out for your transgressions. Where such faith and trust are present, there it is impossible for the devil to dwell and hold sway.

5. This work, therefore, must continue apace in Christendom, in order to drive the devil out by the finger of God. Christ began it, as St. Paul states in Acts 10:38, "[Jesus] went about doing good, healing all that were oppressed by the devil; for God was with him." The Christian church continues this work until the world's end, indeed more and greater works than those Christ did, as he himself promised (John 14:12): "Verily, verily, I say unto you, He that believeth on me, the works that I do shall he do also; and greater works than these shall he do; because I go unto my Father."

6. The fact is that the Christian church carries forward its ministry even further than Christ did. He preached in only a small corner of the Jewish homeland, driving out Satan, converting but few through his preaching. The Christian church, in contrast, is spread throughout the world and pursues its office of preaching and administering the sacraments with the help of the Lord Christ, who is the church's Head and sits at the right hand of God, punishing the devil and his wicked works continuously, now at this place, tomorrow at another.

7. This is very damaging to Satan, and for this reason in turn he persecutes. Christ's casting out of the devil went on continuously until Satan turned the land against him and hung him on the cross. It's the same story with the Christian church until the end. We punish Satan because of his false and wicked dealings, casting him out and rescuing ourselves and others from his errors, lies, and ungodly ways

by means of the Word; and we do this unceasingly, until the devil succeeds to throttle many among us and drive them out of the land, the Lord God allowing it.

8. But he will burn himself because of us, even as he burned himself on Christ. As the devil pursued him, Christ came upon him from behind and cast both the leader and his servants, that is, the devil and the godless Jews, out of the land, leaving them dispersed throughout the world, never to return. This is exactly what the Lord had foretold would happen (Matt. 22:7): "[The king] was wroth: and he sent forth his armies, and destroyed those murderers, and burned up their city." If Satan seeks to drive us from the land, we will in turn drive him from heaven and earth at the Last Day.

9. Accordingly, we should have the highest esteem for God's Word because it has the power of God to drive Satan out. The devil must yield not only at all places among us where the Word is preached, but also under the papacy where the devil himself is in charge; he will be driven out through holy baptism when administered in accord with God's ordaining. We must thank God from the bottom of our hearts for such grace, given us by our dear Lord Christ, to empower us poor mortals to drive out such a great and evil spirit. Though he protests openly and fights back vehemently, he must nonetheless yield. We vanquish him with no other power than opening our mouths, preaching and teaching God's Word. Against it Satan must give way, this Word of God which we believe, as does the whole of the beloved Christian church, otherwise it wouldn't be Christian. When spoken with faith and the Spirit, God's Word accomplishes mighty things.

10. For that reason we should never speak in a derogatory or careless way about God's Word and the Holy Sacraments. True it is that the preached Word is but an ordinary Word and the people who preach it are but ordinary people. But when it emanates from Christ's command to preach it and is coupled with faith, then it possesses the kind of power that can make the devil flee. God has set his almighty power in a very lowly instrument and a very fragile vessel. Against Satan we human beings are but straw, so that were he able to unleash his power against us he would demolish us in a flash. So what does God do? He kindles a little flame against this arrogant,

mighty spirit, that is, he puts his Word into the straw's mouth, and that selfsame word is a heavenly fire which, wherever it goes, scorches the devil, so that he doesn't know where to run.

11. That is indeed an almighty power, as St. Paul calls it in Romans 1:16, able to save those who believe on it. It has the power and might of God and is able to bring people out of sin to righteousness, from death to life, from hell into heaven, out of the devil's kingdom into the kingdom of God, to save them. Surely there is no more wonderful, mighty power than that of the Word, which empowers the poor straw with such potency that it can drive Satan away and free those who believe it from sin and death, and bring them righteousness and everlasting life.

12. With thankful hearts to God, we Christians must learn this, esteeming his Word and the Holy Sacraments very highly as our greatest treasure. Unbelievers and the papists know nothing of this, nor do they deserve to see or know the glorious majesty and might of God's Word, as the proverb states: *Tollatur impius, ne videat gloriam Dei*, "the godless must be removed lest he see the glory of God." Isaiah (6:9) says of the Jews, "Hear ye indeed, but understand not; and see ye indeed, but perceive not." In other words, they hear and receive the Word, but do not actually understand its power, for they are unworthy of it.

13. We must thank, praise, and glorify God because we do understand and appreciate the exquisite, glorious majesty and power of the Word; though we are still poor beggars and sinners, yet are we wealthy and holy, possessing all things and seeing the Word's power, which others neither have nor see, as St. Paul says in 2 Corinthians 6:10, "As poor, yet making many rich; as having nothing, and yet possessing all things." Of course it is not our power, but God's, by which the devil is driven out. He tries with might and main to control us, so that we might destroy one another. But in the end he will be driven out, so that he cannot any longer destroy us.

14. In this way the Word continues to prevail in the church. In other words, Satan is driven out, as the blind are made to see, the dumb to speak, the deaf to hear, with power equal to that at the time of Christ, indeed with even greater power, if not in physical dimension, then spiritual. For it is many times more wonderful that the

devil is driven out of the soul and heart than out of the body, since he sits more securely in the soul and heart than in the body. If, therefore, he is to be torn from the soul and heart, there is need for superior power and strength. If Satan is to be extracted from the place where he sits the tightest, this can only happen, as said, through these lowly things like the Word, absolution, baptism, and the Blessed Sacrament. Christ has given this power to us. May he also grant us grace to recognize this gift, rejoice, and be thankful for it.

15. There follows now in the Gospel the account of how the hypocritical, cocky world looks upon Christ's work. Here there are three schools of thought as regards Christ's driving out the devil and causing the dumb to speak. In the first group are those who do indeed stand in awe of Christ's work and thank God for such miraculous happening. These are the pious minority whose eyes have been opened to perceive the glory and the power of this miracle of God. It is indeed such a truly glorious thing that they cannot wonder enough over how it is possible simply through Christ's Word to convert so many people and drive out Satan. God's Word is so wonderful to them that they can never see, hear, and wonder over it enough. Theirs it is to know the mystery of the kingdom of heaven, namely, to recognize what the Word, absolution, Sacraments, and the keys can accomplish. For the rest this is not so; their eyes do not see and their ears do not hear because their hearts are hardened so that they do not understand. But the godly do understand, are thankful to God, and stand amazed over such great divine power, as indeed it was that the deaf, dumb and (as Matthew writes) blind man was made well through the Word alone, and now he speaks, hears, and sees like any other person, calmly now and composed, while before he raved and was violent.

16. The second group feigns piety but, as already pointed out, not only does not see or understand the miracle but also mocks at it. What a contrast between them and the small remnant of the faithful! The latter were awed by Christ's work, saw it as an excellent wonder, and thanked God for it from the heart. But the former were so blind, hardened, foolish, and stupid that they were unable to see anything wonderful about the miracle, in fact just the opposite. While they should have been astounded, they reviled it instead and attributed it

to the devil. Such blindness, callousness, and madness is beyond words to express.

17. If only they would say, Now hold on! He drives out the devil; surely God must be with him. But they do not do that; rather they proceed like confident smart alecks to say without hesitation that what he does is against God and with the devil's power, nothing but pure deception and hocus-pocus, the work of a fool, like the stuff done by the sleight of hand artists and wizards. After all they have sharp eyes, they think, and sharp wits that cannot fail them! In this way God's Word and work, so patent to human eyes, perception, and understanding are mocked at by these smart, super intelligent people.

18. Moreover, they are so strong and "holy" that they give the devil a very contemptuous name; they call him "Zebub," which in German indicates a bumblebee or big fly; and the prince of devils they call "Beelzebub," that is, a master or lord of flies. They think that they are saints, so great and filled with the Holy Spirit that they call the devil, yes, even the prince of devils, not a mighty, powerful spirit, as Scripture describes him, but an impotent fly. Just like our ghouls—bishops, princes, tyrants, including our fanatical spirits—do not care in the least or give a rap about the devil. They have set themselves way above him and deem him to be but an insignificant fly, quickly killed with a slash of the knife or flick of a feather. These saints, therefore, are so secure, strong, and superior over the devil that they regard him as an impotent gnat and harmless fly. For this reason they consider this work of Christ to be but that of a fly or bumblebee. Were they able to depict and shape it with more derision and disdain, they certainly would do so.

19. They are indeed "pious" people, who stand opposed to the plain truth, because it shines too brightly for their eyes, and yet they knowingly revile our Lord's work and call their own lord, the devil, who rules over and drives them to such mockery, a powerless bumble bum. They don't realize that they themselves are possessed by a thousand devils, are full of envy, blasphemy, murders, lies, and deceit, doing the devil's will to the utmost, meanwhile boasting of their holiness and proceeding as though the devil has no claim on them.

20. That's just the way it goes nowadays also. The beloved gospel is preached—heaven be praised!—pure and unadulterated, in a very

godly and peaceful manner. This being so, we certainly ought to take comfort in the fact that a number of upright people are accepting this preaching with all their hearts and taking pleasure in understanding the power of the Word, being amazed at it, and thanking God for it with all their hearts. On the other hand, the pope, with his hangers on, indeed confesses that it is God's Word, yet blasphemes it, calls it heresy and the doctrine of demons. So great is their depravity, obduracy, and blasphemy that it would not be surprising at all if on account of such sins the sun would lose its brilliance and light, heaven turn black, and earth swallow up these blasphemers. And yet they are so secure, irresponsible, and without a care in the world, as if they were sitting in the lap of our Lord God, to say nothing about the fact that they are fearful of the devil just as I and other Christians are.

21. We Christians know the devil's power and might. For we have learned from experience that he is able in a moment to recast and pervert a godly man who has a strong faith, and beguile a pious husband, who today is living chastely in his marriage, to become an adulterer tomorrow. Yes, he can (were he permitted) block the advance of God's most beautiful works. He is, therefore, no bumblebee but, as we see and experience, a strong, powerful spirit who sets upon us everywhere, against whom, with all our wisdom and strength, we are much too weak. Besides, once he determines to lead someone into error, heresy, unbelief, and sin, he holds on so tightly that the individual cannot free himself. Similarly, I believe that when he propels a man into fornication or adultery, into greed, anger, hatred, envy, arrogance, or some other vice, he holds on tightly. Sure, he permits a person to flutter like a bird, but he soon restrains again so he cannot get away from him. That's the devil—a lord, prince, and god of the world, who can strangle people, lead them into sin, propel them into despair, heartache, fear, anxiety, grief, and all manner of affliction, if God does not prevent it.

22. For this reason we Christians are not so overly confident and so scornful of the devil as are the work-righteous; nor do we call him a bumblebee, but a powerful lord, prince, and god of the world, who is able to accomplish more than all princes of earth, yes, over against whom all kings and lords on earth, with all their power and might, are but bumblebees and powerless flies.

23. However, our nobility, the pope and his band, think of him as Beelzebub, that is, as lord of flies, whom they long ago devoured in mustard. They, likewise, are as blind and obdurate as these Pharisees, who, although they are not bodily possessed like this poor man, are still seven times more intensely and dangerously possessed spiritually, since they not only do not know God's Word, but also blaspheme and scorn it and God's work in really dreadful manner and without compunctions as if they were doing something good.

24. Now, then, this is written for our encouragement, as we seek out the devil and preach God's Word. We can expect the same reaction here, namely, that some were astonished; others, however, blasphemed and reviled it as false and seductive. For they regard their teaching to be far superior to our gospel, that their teaching leads people to God, while our gospel merely snatches people away from God. This should not offend or annoy us. True it is, it hurts very much that the pope, bishops, and their gang so shamefully blaspheme our gospel. It couldn't be blasphemed any more shamefully! Yet they are so secure in doing it that they have no more fear of the devil than they have of a bumblebee. That is what we have to see and hear, and it hurts. But Christ himself, our Lord and Head, experienced the same when he, by the finger of God, performed that wonderful miracle and cast out devils. They blasphemed then, too, as though the lowly bumble bum could do it as well and better than Christ.

25. The third group also postures piously, asking for a sign from heaven. Indeed they see the miracle, but they do not count it a true sign. They say, Yes, it is, of course, a wonder that he drives out the devil, but it is a small, insignificant sign, a terrestrial phenomenon. If he gave us a sign from heaven, then we would believe. To cast out the devil, that's nothing. If he would make a new sun, or moon, or stars, or something of that order in the heavens, that would be something. Such are the know-it-all scholars who want to instruct our Lord God on what sort of signs he should produce. They want him to be a sort of magician who with his dunce cap performs wondrous tricks in front of them, at their command, just as if our Lord God had nothing more to do than satisfy their curiosity. That's how Herod looked upon him, as some sort of magician who would perform tricks for him.

26. Nowadays you will find many such people in the world, quite a few among the masses, but most of all among the "big shots." For these, the worldly-wise, influential people of our day are usually saying, What! Am I to give credence to the preaching of such poor beggars who are like worn out monks and untrustworthy priests? I would believe it if the pope, a bishop, the emperor, king, prince, or noble lord would preach and endorse it! They also adumbrate in what way our Lord God is to become a wise, pious, and shrewd manager of things, who will send them preachers after their liking, the kind who tell them what they like to hear. Yes, indeed, it shall be so ordered, as you say, dear lords!

27. For that matter we, who pretend to be so evangelical, act in nearly the same way. For our country plowboys and urban rogues are beginning to demand what and how they want their preachers to preach. They know very well that they ought to respect those in charge. This they misinterpret to mean that people should not be admonished, but be allowed to do as they please. However, if a pastor, in keeping with his office, rebukes vices—public offenses whose perpetrators are known by all, even though their names are not mentioned—a hue and a cry go up that this causes an uproar which the government will have to put down. Preaching the gospel is tolerable, in other words, as long as we do not single out and rebuke people so publicly—as though government will be reviled and disparaged when one speaks the truth. What indeed should one make of these devout people? Don't you think they are somewhat similar and akin to those who are witnessing these miraculous signs here, but do not want to regard them as miracles, unless he produces some magical illusion to their liking? So they want to be lords not only over country, people, and things in general, but also over the Word and the church. They purport to be upright children in whom God should still have delight!

28. And lest I remain silent about it, what are the bigwigs in the villages doing? They are not improving matters much; they want to force the village preachers to preach what they want to hear or they will pull the purse strings shut. That's when I say, dear squires, come up here and preach. Believe me, for two cents I would just as soon walk away from the pulpit and no longer preach to you, since that

seems to be what you want. Come on, try your hand at preaching; we can play the game as well as you and ask you whether you are listening, dear squires! Your preaching is very offensive to me; you should not do that. Yes indeed, sirs, it is especially nice that you want to be lord over Christ's Word and church. This we have to grant you.

29. This does not mean that if we grant that temporal government should be respected and not spoken evil of, for this reason it has authority over God and his Word. It is equally true that people are to be under God and his Word, and acknowledge and honor God and his ministers, as God's Word teaches, and be its subjects. The gospel must have free course and should be heard. If they refuse, and want to be tyrants and bloodhounds, then we preachers should candidly reprove and set them straight. If they refuse to listen, we nonetheless have done our duty, for if, in the process, they want to relinquish the gospel and abandon the pulpit, let them answer for that. Temporal government should thank God with all its heart for the preaching of the gospel. For thereby it has recovered honor, in that people now know what government is and how they should esteem government, something which under the papacy no one understood. But they go right on and are willing to trample the gospel, for which rightly they ought to be thanking God, and they harass the preachers' consciences by demanding that they preach what they want to hear.

30. Long ago a solemn charge was given to us preachers to fulfill the duties of our office conscientiously, since we must give account on Judgment Day. Why then would we, for your sakes, burden ourselves still more and preach what you would like to hear? Remember, the Word is not ours and we are not in office because of you, as if you had appointed us and had to preach what you want. If, for this reason, you want to be angry and draw shut the collection bag, then all right! On Judgment Day the Lord above will ask me why I was more awed by your collection bag than by his anger. For this reason I want to give you a sign from heaven, just as you desire, and preach to you what you want to hear: yes, hellfire!

These are the three sorts of persons who are wont to concern themselves with God's Word in accord with their own desires, just as our squires nowadays say to us, You are to preach what I want you to preach. To which we say, We won't and cannot do that. If you do not wish to listen to it, then in God's name go out through the gate the stonemasons left, and let others hear. We, indeed, want you to be washed clean. If this displeases you, then may the devil smash you to pieces. These things, you see, are written for our instruction, not so that we follow such thinking, but that we might know that the gospel is true when we see how people divide into three types of hearers.

31. The first group praises it, is pleased with it, and stands in wonderment over it. The second group is openly hostile, mocks, and ridicules it. The third set of people want very much that God would do, not what he wills, but what they want. That's the story of how the gospel has been received time and again in the world. Some hear it and love it; others persecute it openly; still others trample over it with their feet inwardly.

32. God grant that we are not swayed thereby, whether they believe, mock, or trample it under foot. When we preachers proclaim the saving gospel, we know that souls are safe. Whoever does not wish to follow, let him find out for himself who it is that he has despised, mocked, and reviled.

33. The Lord answers those first of all who revile him. The rest who want to tell him how to preach and do wonders are borne with till the time is ripe. Even though it is to no avail, he is very longsuffering as he deals with their poisonous mouths.

34. Because they (the revilers) accused him of casting out demons through Beelzebub, giving him a bad name and creating a stir among the people, as though his preaching was of the devil, Jesus declines any longer to refrain from replying, defends himself against their reviling, and states (John 8:49): "I have not a devil."

35. We must endure the same sort of mockery, persecution, knocking, and disdain. But if our silence under revilings and opposition suggests that the doctrines of these who rail and revile are correct and our teaching is of the devil, that's not so. We must rather witness openly for the truth, for the sake of others, just as against our opponents we have shown the ground and basis of why our doctrine was not of the devil, as was our duty to do. We did not try to force them into believing us, nor were we commanded to do so. For we are watchmen only, as the prophet Ezekiel (3:17–21) states, who warn the ungodly to turn from their evil ways. When the ungodly turns,

well and good, we have won him over; if he does not repent, he will die in his sins, but we have saved our souls.

36. The Lord defends his teaching with persuasive arguments, saying, You charge that I drive out the devil through Beelzebub; how can you say such a preposterous thing? Use your head and think it through logically. Have you ever seen a kingdom, if divided, able to stand? When in a given council one member disagrees with another, or in a city government three magistrates disagree with each other, or in a princedom three rulers stand opposed to each other, don't you see what evil will result? So if one devil drives out another, the result is that there is chaos in the ranks and their kingdom cannot stand.

37. Here is a picture from everyday life, which human reason very readily understands. When a husband and wife are at odds, with him living in the front of the house and she in the rear, with him breaking the pitchers, as the saying goes, and she the pots, such a household cannot long survive, let alone the family's finances. Experience teaches that disunity destroys and lays waste lands, people, households, and all else. That's why the Pharisees and scribes like mad, crazy people, are here talking out of their heads saying things contrary to their own reason. In like manner our opponents today, the papists, speak like stupid, irrational people who lack not only Christian understanding but just plain common sense and reason, making no more sense than a seven-year-old child.

38. Christ himself testifies that Satan is a king with a kingdom, a very united kingdom, tightly held together, so that whoever provokes one devil provokes them all, whoever attacks one attacks them all. Satan is not divided against himself, otherwise, were he not so intimately tied in with the bishops and princes' courts, we would have succeeded to win more people away from the pope. One devil stands by the other, and the devil's kingdom is stronger and mightier than all the kingdoms of the world. It is this kingdom which you have to take on when you are baptized, hear the Word, and receive the Sacrament.

39. However, just as the devil's kingdom is united and fiercely compact, so on the other side is Christ's kingdom, likewise united and closely bonded together. When the devil assails a Christian he assails Christ himself and the whole heavenly host, as Christ himself

said to Saul who persecuted the Christians (Acts 9:4–5): "Saul, Saul, why persecutest thou me?" "Who art thou, Lord?" he asked, and the Lord answered, "I am Jesus, whom thou persecutest." Two champions stand opposed, Christ and Satan, and each has a strong, united kingdom. Whoever provokes a devil provokes Beelzebub, chief of the devils, and all devils with him. Contrariwise, whoever attacks a Christian attacks Christ and all the angels with him. In this we should take comfort and also learn well that a Christian's stance is not a matter of child's play, because there is a strong kingdom against us, and every moment we are in constant danger, were it not that God stands by us with his grace.

40. Here someone might ask, How does it happen that wicked scoundrels, charlatans, sorcerers, and exorcists often cast out devils? This the devil does, God never. I have personally seen a man who was filled with devils, yet the priest who exorcised him was so sure he was on safe ground that he put his finger into the man's mouth and said, I dare you, bite! How can it be other but that one devil casts out another? St. Paul gives the answer (2 Thess. 2:9) that in the last days the devil will work signs, but they will be false signs. Therefore, the exorcism of the exorcist is false and not like Christ's exorcism. For even though the devil does come out, he does not do it in order to further the gospel but that he might strengthen people in idolatry and lead them away from faith, so that they fall completely from Christ. The devil possessed both of them, the poor man and the exorcist, and it can well be that the poor man was more upright and pious than the exorcist who cast out the devil, even though God admonished the poor man to discipline the flesh. When a devil comes out, he does it in order to aid another devil, to promote error, idolatry, and other abominations in people's hearts. For example, possessed individuals were brought to St. Cyriacus, St. Anstadt, and other saints, for the purpose of casting out a devil. However, the devil did not come out because he was compelled and was forced to retreat, but willingly and gladly, in order thus to strengthen the person's idolatry. Moreover, he has pretended at times to be very fearful of consecrated candles, consecrated salt, water, and other things, while his only interest in such pretense was to strengthen people in their superstition, so that there might be less likelihood of

their coming to true faith and trust in God's Word and grace. Accordingly, these signs were, as Paul calls them, *mendacia signa*, "fictitious, lying wonders and signs," and pretense.

41. In order, therefore, really to distinguish the genuine and true signs from the false, lying wonders, as when Christ and his apostles cast out devils by means of the Word, we must look at the devil's ultimate intent for exorcising himself and for positioning himself to do this sort of thing. Where the exorcism is a truly serious matter, that the devil should come out in order to verify the divine Word, to the glory and strengthening of Christian faith, he will then balk and resist being cast out. It's the same with the pope and the fanatics, and their conjuring with the cross, consecrated water, salt, and other things; the devil in fact remains unexorcised there; he does not yield unless he does it voluntarily. He indeed cannot tolerate God's Word being attested to, truth being comprehended, and Christian faith being strengthened.

42. But when it's to his own advantage to come out, in order to promote his lies, so that the ungrateful world which refuses to call upon Christ can be persuaded to intercede with the saints and fall deeper into superstition, he then may allow a wicked rascal to be exorcised. Thus he can make the blind again to see, the deaf again to hear, the lame again to become whole. For this is not happening for the glory of Christ and his gospel, in order to confirm the truth but in order to confirm his lies, that people might place their trust in monkery, intercession of the saints, pilgrimages, vigils, Masses, and the like as being holy things. For this reason he is so favorably disposed toward them. In short, the devil is never at loggerheads with himself; for if his lying charade is to continue, he is very ready to let himself be exorcised. But it is a deception played out under cover in order to deceive and seduce the world. When, however, exorcism progresses to the point where the finger of God is manifested and the kingdom of heaven draws near, there he resists as long as he can, as Christ states in the parable about the strong man who was fully armed.

43. Let us, therefore, thank God for his grace, because he has sent his Son for help against the devil, to drive him out, and has left us his Word through which today yet he performs this work, destroying Satan's kingdom, building and extending the kingdom of God. God keep us in such grace through his Son and the Holy Spirit, Amen.

LAETARE SUNDAY—FOURTH SUNDAY IN LENT

First Sermon—1532

John 6:1–15

After these things Jesus went over the sea of Galilee, which is the sea of Tiberias. And a great multitude followed him, because they saw his miracles which he did on them that were diseased. And Jesus went up into a mountain, and there he sat with his disciples. And the passover, a feast of the Jews, was nigh. When Jesus then lifted up his eyes, and saw a great company come unto him, he saith unto Philip, Whence shall we buy bread, that these may eat? And this he said to prove him: for he himself knew what he would do. Philip answered him, Two hundred pennyworth of bread is not sufficient for them, that every one of them may take a little. One of his disciples, Andrew, Simon Peter's brother saith unto him, There is a lad here, which hath five barley loaves, and two small fishes: but what are they among so many? And Jesus said, Make the men sit down. Now there was much grass in the place. So the men sat down, in number about five thousand. And Jesus took the loaves; and when he had given thanks, he distributed to the disciples, and the disciples to them that were set down; and likewise of the fishes as much as they would. When they were filled, he said unto his disciples, Gather up the fragments that remain, that nothing be lost. Therefore they gathered them together, and filled twelve baskets with the fragments of the five barley loaves, which remained over and above unto them that had eaten. Then those men, when they had seen the miracle that Jesus did, said, This is of a truth that prophet that should come into the world. When Jesus therefore perceived that they would come and take him by force, to make him a king, he departed again into a mountain himself alone.

1. This miracle of the feeding of the five thousand men, which our dear Lord Jesus Christ performed in the wilderness with five barley loaves and two fish, is recorded in Scripture for our sakes, so that people in the church might hear it again and again, and learn from it that we must trust that God will provide for us. For in this world, faith is under constant siege either by Mammon and wealth on the

one hand, or by poverty on the other. The rich "Haves" throw God's Word to the wind and trample it with their feet, like those in the Gospel account (Luke 14) who were invited to the great banquet but disdained to come because of their concern for property, oxen, a new wife, and so on. The "Have Nots" are ready to sell their souls to the devil in order to surmount their poverty in this world. Neither side does right; both are wrong. The rich despise God's Word and opine that they need neither God, nor his Word. The poor ask, How can I accept the Word, follow and be obedient to it when I am so poor and need something to eat and to drink? If I expect hand-outs from other people, then I must fawn upon them and do what they want, whether I like it or not. Those who grovel this way before others, prostitute themselves, become godless louts, and do what others want them to do. As a result, whether it's riches on the right, or poverty on the left, God's Word and faith are under constant threat.

2. Against these two extremes, both of which become obstructions to the intended purpose, the Lord here exhorts a middle course teaching that we must come to rely on God, trust him in every need, and learn to be content with what he daily provides us. No matter that you are not rich, you will not starve or suffer want. God will see to it that you have as much as a king, who really has no more than a common Christian. For even though he has a great kingdom, what more does a king have than sufficient food, drink, clothes to wear, a place to stay warm, and a bed to sleep in? By himself he cannot drink up all the wine his land produces, nor squander all its wealth by himself. When he dies, his eating and drinking cease, and that's no more or less than is true for the average Christian too, who, though he may not have as much as a king, still has his needs met like a king.

3. Through this miracle, therefore, Christ, our dear Lord, teaches his disciples and us Christians not to fret nor be greedy for great wealth, because what we need will be provided. Only believe that the heavenly Father will sustain you. And just see what a paradigm he sets here before our eyes to prompt our faith. I, too, am poor and possess nothing, he is saying, and my seventy-two disciples and twelve apostles also have nothing more than five loaves of bread and two fish, plus two hundred pence in cash. On top of that, there are five thousand men with me, not counting a large following of women

and children, all of whom would like to eat. You wonder whether I am poor, with but five loaves and two fish, and no bread to be had here in the wilderness that I might buy some? And yet it is imperative that I feed them all, and with such bounty that there will ultimately be four times as much left as was originally required. Now then that's the sermon the Lord wants us to hear.

4. His point is very plain and easy for us to comprehend and learn. It is very true that in poverty and want people begin to argue among themselves and say, I have only one, two, perhaps five gulden; only one keg of home brew, and so and so many bushels of grain; when this is all gone, that's it, there is no more. When such thoughts arise we should think of this miracle and ask: Is there not something more I have? Whether I have much or little, I will trust in God to sustain me according to his good pleasure, and I will let him worry if and when I require more; for I have heard the Gospel lesson preached, how Christ fed five thousand with five loaves and two fishes in the wilderness, and why should I then worry or be in doubt!

5. We should, therefore, use this incident for the sake of exercising and strengthening our faith. It was not just written for us to read (the devil can do that also), but should remind and prompt us to say, What Christ did in the wilderness he will and can do again, if only I trust him; he will provide food for me to eat, if not in super-abundance, yet sufficient to care for my necessity.

6. The fact is that what the poor have, be it ever so little, suits them better and tastes better than that which the rich have in superfluity. A sovereign and a great lord with ten kingdoms will hardly find a piece of meat that will taste any better than a poor man's chunk of dried bread and barley beer. For the former has a jaded appetite and indigestion, while the latter enjoys pure contentment. The rich man's fare feasts his eyes and not his belly, whereas the poor man fills his belly till he's satisfied. It is better, therefore, to have less and enjoy what one has with anticipation and pleasure because it tastes good, than to have much to look at with jaded appetite and aversion, unable to enjoy it. As St. Paul states (1 Tim. 6:17): "The living God, who giveth us richly all things to enjoy." That it tastes good and that we enjoy it is God's to grant. If God does not give the enjoyment, it does not help to have an abundance. Kings and princes, great lords

and rich people may have super-abundance, but nothing tastes good if people are unable to relish it.

7. With this miracle, therefore, Christ wants to draw us to faith, so that we trust him. In gist he is saying, I will indeed sustain you, only believe. If you do, I will cause two fish to become three thousand in my hand, and one loaf of bread a thousand. Year for year I cause this to happen. In winter the trees are bare, having neither leaves nor fruit; but as soon as summer arrives the trees put forth leaves, cherries, plums, apples, pears, and so on. There is no dough, or glue, or wood from which one could whittle these, only useless dry twigs. The same is true for the grain; it grows from the earth in the field and is gathered into huge piles. Who clothes the trees with leaves and fruit? Who causes the grain to grow in abundance? Is it not he who with two fish and five loaves of bread fed five thousand men?

8. But now human reason remonstrates: Of course that's true of the trees, the fields, and other things every year, but hardly something unusual or a wonder; but this happening, to feed five thousand men with two fish and five loaves was unusual and a miracle. And the devil thanks you for this observation. Where does the fault lie that this is looked upon as something unusual and a miracle, while producing manifold return from a single kernel of grain does not seem unusual and miraculous.? The fault does not lie with God and his providence but with our incredulity, because we are so blind and obstinate that we cannot recognize God's miraculous works. And that same sort of incredulity causes us not only to be blind but to become clods with stony hearts, otherwise we would always be learning and daily comforting ourselves with God's great miracles. Christians should recognize God's wonders and from them learn to rely upon him. Why would we even want to despair? The cherry tree doesn't, even though in winter it stands bare without leaves or fruit. It trusts the word God has spoken, Burst forth in summer and blossom! and relies on it. With summer's advent it leafs out and blossoms. The field also does not despair even though in winter it lies frozen and covered with snow, without one blade of grass for us to see. We ought to learn from these everyday wonders to trust in God and not despair. Even though at times our circumstances are meager, it is no cause for worry; our necessities will be provided for, if we but trust our God.

9. And what more would we want? If our needs are met, and we're kept from freezing to death or dying of hunger, it suffices. For if we have the necessities, our hearts and bodies can rest content and we can be of good spirit and happy. On the other hand, when we have overly much, our hearts and bodies are weighed down with worry and with greed. We should, therefore, rest satisfied with God's provision, as we read in Psalm 145:16, "Thou openest thine hand, and satisfiest the desire of every living thing," because we have all that we require. Along with wealth come worry, fretting, and discontent, as we see in the cases of kings, princes, and lords. Their worries are more and when the Last Judgment comes they will be required to give an accounting and reckoning: the emperor more than a prince, the prince more than a duke, the duke more than a lord, the lord more than a peasant, a magistrate more than the average citizen. We should, therefore, learn contentment and not become impatient and angry with God because we are not wealthy. Were we rich we might well become meaner and more sinful.

10. This miracle, then, has been recorded for our benefit and consolation, in order that we might keep it in mind and affirm: I believe and am sure that my needs will be met, even though it be in meager manner. For the Lord here had only two fish and five loaves of barley bread with which he fed five thousand men, not counting women and children, and all were satisfied. And what he did here he demonstrates year in, year out, and day for day, with the trees, fields, meadows, bodies of water, and all creatures, so that apples, pears, wheat, barley, grass, fish, and all other things necessary to sustain life are produced. He does it that we might believe that he will sustain us. It is his will that we have enough to eat, be it but one fish multiplied to ten thousand, or one loaf to a hundred thousand. Therefore, we must be unafraid in poverty and await his benevolence. If a man die of hunger, it is because of his unbelief. But for him who believes, however, the whole world would more likely die of hunger than that he should die by starvation.

11. The second lesson of this Gospel is to see how our dear Lord Jesus commanded that the fragments be gathered up, so that nothing went to waste. This also is a very necessary lesson. Experience teaches that when God gives little, people despair, thinking that they will

die of hunger; when they are given an abundance, they become profligate and despise God's blessing. This is what happens in lordly circles where the leftovers are shamefully wasted and pitched away as useless. Our Lord desires waste as little as he wants despair and worry, desiring that we opt for the middle course, that is, trust him and carefully husband what is left over. The well-known proverb still obtains: Waste not, want not!

12. This applies not only to bread, but to all the gifts of God, bodily or spiritual. These are good times. Today God's Word is in style and the economy flourishes. But how many people are there who lift up their hands in thanks to God? People despise both God's Word and their own industry, carelessly trampling over both. The wise man will gather and carefully store away supplies for the time of need. For God will not always provide a new supply of bread when the surplus was allowed to go to waste instead of conserving what he created and bestowed.

13. We all know the common proverb: Lay in store for the rainy day and conserve, for eventually it will fill a need. It is a miserable, dysfunctional household where a tippler runs through everything and nothing remains for an emergency; likewise where a housewife is not frugal. We're reminded of the man who said to his wife, Careful, Elsa, careful, lest we become rich and prodigal. The same principle applies in other situations as well. It becomes intolerable in the church when it has lazy pastors and satiated, discontented people weary of hearing God's Word; and in the school when students are indifferent and forget more than they learn.

14. In these days we have industrial pursuits that are richly productive, if we only had sufficient buckets to gather it all. Likewise, Holy Scripture is available everywhere. The bounty overflows and becomes like crumbs which the dogs are not inclined to eat. Look, you young folks, you ought be like baskets to gather it in. The time will come when people will wish for one page where now there's an entire library. After these plentiful times will come such impoverishment that people will wish for one single sermon where now there are hundreds. This was my experience under the papacy; I would gladly have traveled to Rome to hear one honest-to-goodness gospel sermon, but there was not even one.

15. When our Lord God gives, he gives so bountifully that it is overwhelming. On the other hand, when he takes away, he takes it away so completely that not a single kernel remains. Under the papacy there was none to be found who understood grammar and rhetoric. It was the same with the gospel. No doctor of theology could be found who knew the difference between the Law and the gospel. Now we have it in rich abundance; we can read and hear it everywhere, but no one pays any attention to it. If our Lord were to snatch it away, there would be nothing. Moses told of how God threatened the children of Israel, warning them that he would make their "heaven as iron and their earth as brass" (Lev. 26:19). And when this punishment came upon the people, they died like flies. It was so also under the papacy. When God withdrew his gospel, people no longer knew anything of the Holy Scripture. Indeed, the Scripture was locked and had become like iron, impenetrable to men's understanding.

16. Hence the exhortation, "Gather up the fragments that remain, that nothing be lost." A good housefather should conserve carefully for the future that nothing be wasted. In temporal affairs a good governor will see to it that nothing goes to waste, as Joseph did in Egypt. He stored up the grain during the seven plentiful years, so that there was a supply during the seven years of drought. So also in the school a student is to be diligent, because by the skills he learns he will earn his bread; and in church we should listen attentively to the gospel while the light shines (John 12:35). To summarize, redeem the time before it is gone. Once it's gone, there's no way of recovering it, no matter how one tries. Deal carefully and circumspectly with the bread God supplies, laying it in store for the future. He will not always give a new loaf, but wants you to conserve carefully what remains. If you, however, are going to be a prodigal, carelessly wasting the bread so bountifully provided, you may some day starve when you need it most.

LAETARE SUNDAY—FOURTH SUNDAY IN LENT

Second Sermon—1533

John 6:1–15

1. The keynote of this Gospel is that our dear Lord Christ wishes to teach his Christians to trust him and know that they will not die of hunger, but by his blessing will be provided with all that they need. On the other hand, such a message is meaningless to greedy people, peasants, or townsfolk who think only of what is to their advantage. They don't think it's worth their time to listen to such a sermon, much less believe it. To be sure, they hear how the Lord granted his blessing and performed a great miracle. But they would never admit that he could also do it for them. In their self-centered greed, therefore, they act as though Christ couldn't perform such a miracle for them. They think that if they don't plan and look out for themselves, they will be left wanting. For people like them Christ means nothing.

2. Those, however, who cling to his Word, he teaches how they ought to trust him. He doesn't use many words, but rather by action and deed shows that he can create what we need to eat, so that we do not doubt or think that provision is up to us, but rather place our heart and trust on him. Such faith will not be disappointed nor permit us to suffer want. That is the situation here with his disciples and the people listening to him. He provided for their need and fed all of them. Even though there were only five barley loaves and two fish, he, nevertheless, fed five thousand men, not counting women and children. They all ate and were satisfied; in addition, more was left over than they had to begin with. At the outset as he began to feed the people, there was scarcely a half basket of bread, but when he finished and all were satisfied the remaining fragments filled twelve baskets.

3. Such preaching was coupled with dynamic action, and it meant: Trust God, be God-fearing, cling to God's Word with diligence, and be confident that God will provide food and sustenance. These peo-

ple, even though not all were God-fearing, still include some pious hearts who were more concerned with being in God's Word than eating and discovered that there was no need to worry about food; for the Lord provides for them so that they had food to eat without their fretting about it. With this the Lord wishes to say, My dear man, first of all search for and learn about the kingdom of God, hear my Word, believe on me, and with diligence carry on in your appointed station. If you do that, let me worry about the rest. Even if you aren't rich, even if you haven't many thousand gulden, I will still provide you with sufficient bread. For you can't eat gold, silver, or precious stones—it must be bread which grows from the earth. Even though you do not get your bread from the earth, because you have neither house nor farm, neither acreage nor garden, only believe and follow me; you will have bread and all necessities. No one has ever been forsaken.

4. Experience teaches us this day for day. God makes a great doctor of a poor little student who is diligent and pious. God rewards a poor servant girl who is God-fearing and serves her master and mistress faithfully with a pious husband, a house, and farm. One daily sees such examples of how God helps poor people. On the contrary, those who do not fear God, do not trust in him, do not obey his Word and are generally unfaithful and lazy must remain poor beggars. If it should be that these die of hunger, very likely it serves them right.

5. An incorrigible lad who doesn't attend to his studies and is otherwise wicked, wanton, and unfaithful should know that our Lord God will permit him to go to war, perhaps to be stabbed or shot, or to become a hangman or an otherwise unworthy individual. Likewise a servant or a maid who is not God-fearing, insubordinate, disobedient, or otherwise unfaithful and lazy, will become a wicked rascal or a loose woman. This serves them right and is their desert and empty reward. Why do they not piously hear God's Word, believe in Christ, and become obedient? Were they to do that, Christ would be at their side saying, Let me do the worrying as I exalt you, bring you honor, make you rich, and so on.

6. So this Gospel teaches us to believe that Christ will sustain and provide for us in all our needs if we are God-fearing and attend to his Word. This is our emphasis with people, that for the gospel's sake they be willing to suffer in its behalf, even if it involves a risk. The

miracle that the Lord performed is in reality a sermon, as though he wished to say, If you are God-fearing and devout, holding my Word dear, then I will provide you with food; you will never be forsaken, and I will surely make something of you. On the contrary, if you are not devout, if you despise my Word, and are otherwise dissolute, and end up a beggar, remember that the fault is no one else's but your own; even if you become rich, you, nevertheless, will end up in hell with the devil where your earthly possessions will be of no help. This, then, is the bottom line: Whoever despises God's Word and does not wish to do what God enjoins, for him God will not do what he dearly wishes and will not provide what he requires.

7. What the Lord, therefore, wishes to teach us is how with five loaves and two fish he fed five thousand men who had followed him into the wilderness. In addition, he fed the women and children, likely another five thousand. Everyone had sufficient to eat, with plenty left over. This was not preaching with words, as Christ says (Matt. 6:33), but with action: "But seek ye first the kingdom of God and his righteousness; and all these things shall be added unto you." It was tantamount to Christ saying, I am rich and can certainly feed you; just take heed that you are God-fearing, cling to God's Word, and follow his precepts; then let me do the worrying as to where you will find something to eat. Today's miracle presents a lesson concerning faith. May God grant his grace that we from day to day grow more God-fearing. Also may we experience God's blessing as he provides sustenance and alleviates our every need through Jesus Christ our Lord. Amen.

JUDICA SUNDAY—FIFTH SUNDAY IN LENT

First Sermon—1533

John 8:46–59

Which of you convinceth me of sin? And if I say the truth, why do ye not believe me? He that is of God heareth God's words: ye therefore hear them not, because ye are not of God. Then answered the Jews, and said unto him, Say we not well that thou art a Samaritan, and hast a devil? Jesus answered, I have not a devil; but I honour my Father, and ye do dishonour me. And I seek not mine own glory: there is one that seeketh and judgeth. Verily, verily, I say unto you, If a man keep my saying, he shall never see death. Then said the Jews unto him, Now we know that thou hast a devil. Abraham is dead, and the prophets; and thou sayest, If a man keep my saying, he shall never taste of death. Art thou greater than our father Abraham, which is dead? and the prophets are dead: whom makest thou thyself? Jesus answered, If I honour myself, my honour is nothing: it is my Father that honoureth me; of whom ye say, that he is your God: Yet ye have not known him; but I know him: and if I should say, I know him not, I shall be a liar like unto you: but I know him, and keep his saying. Your father Abraham rejoiced to see my day: and he saw it, and was glad. Then said the Jews unto him, Thou art not yet fifty years old, and hast thou seen Abraham? Jesus said unto them, Verily, verily, I say unto you, Before Abraham was, I am. Then took they up stones to cast at him: but Jesus hid himself, and went out of the temple, going through the midst of them, and so passed by.

1. This is a beautiful Gospel lesson, its content too great to be treated in a single sermon. We shall, therefore, focus our attention only on its central theme, namely, that Christ says we should gladly hear God's Word; that whoever hears the Word belongs to God; that whoever does not hear it is not of God.

2. These words are spoken in such a simple fashion that no one gives thought to their rich meaning. But when we look closely at

these words, carefully think them through, zealously ponder and meditate upon what it means "to be of God" and "not to be of God," we must admit that Christ is speaking about something very important here. For it is true and beyond cavil that you cannot say anything more ultimate, and to judge a person more severely, than to say that he is not of God. To have someone call me a knave and a villain, or to cut my throat, is nothing compared to the horrible and terrible verdict of having the Lord say, as he does here plainly to the Jews, "Ye are not of God." Therefore, everything hinges on our gladly hearing and keeping God's Word.

3. Wherever the gospel is proclaimed we find that those who do not wish to hear God's Word follow the devil so persistently that he ultimately takes total possession of them; and the longer he holds onto them the more wicked they become. This is exactly what we see occurring in today's Gospel. First, the Jews are very annoyed when Christ begins to preach. Then they upbraid him, call him a Samaritan, and say that he is possessed of the devil. By saying this they have already fallen four or five fathoms deeper into hell than before. Thereupon, they become still more foolish and ask, "Whom makest thou thyself?" In short, the longer they talk, the more depraved they become, until finally they take action and like murderers pick up stones in order to kill him. In their contempt for the Word, they fall into the horrible sin of blaspheming God and his Word and in the end become raving mad.

4. Thus you can see what it means not to be of God and to be of the devil, that is, not to hear God's Word but to revile and blaspheme it, cursing God and finally engaging in murderous violence. The fact that also in our day children are generally so disobedient and insolent to their parents is because they do not listen to God's Word; or if they do hear it, they neither comprehend nor keep it. Once they, contrary to God's command, begin to despise father and mother, the sin does not stop there. It grows worse, they curse their parents, and finally bring them to death's door. Even though they may not take them by the throat or strike them dead, they, nevertheless, wish their parents dead; or they lead such a shameful life that their parents grieve themselves to death.

5. That is exactly the way things are. Whoever will not hear God's Word, or after hearing it will not adhere to it, becomes a liar, blasphemer, and persecutor. We see this in the papists. The longer they persist in what they are doing, the more wicked they become. And they will not desist from their blaspheming and persecuting, but finally resort to violence, take the sword in hand, and become murderers.

6. There is nothing worse than this. When a person inclines toward sin and doing what is wrong, it is still possible to convince him of his sin and to desist from it. But the person whose sin is refusing to hear God's Word and blaspheming it instead, cannot be dissuaded. Such people do a beautiful cover-up job and allow themselves to think they are doing right and are thereby serving God; in contrast a sinner involved with other wrongdoing can, to his shame, be shown his sin and be led to repent of it.

7. It is, therefore, the accursed devil who himself is at work when a person despises God's Word. For in such a situation it is inevitable that he will finally cast stones at Christ, yes, will also bring him to the cross, consider what he is doing as being completely right, and will want to get off scot-free when perpetrating such a great sin.

8. For this reason it is a stern, earnest word which Christ speaks here to the Jews when he says, "Ye therefore hear them not, because ye are not of God." For whoever is not of God is of the devil. If he now is of the devil, he is totally corrupt and subject to all manner of hellish, moral turpitude; he has more misfortune than we could invoke upon him. The most dreadful thing you can say to a person is, You do not hear God's Word; therefore, you are not of God.

9. When you admonish such a person for a long period of time, he becomes more and more furious and says, What do I care about what is preached? You may indeed keep on pleading with him and say, This is not good; you will have to adopt a different attitude if you wish to be saved; but he will let fly with these words: In the name of a thousand demons let me alone; and he may even come to blows.

10. Therefore, the one who refuses to hear God's Word is not of God but is a child of the devil. This is particularly true when he adds to his evil conduct by insisting that he is in the right and seeks to justify his corrupt acts, just like the Jews here who say, "Say we not well that thou art a Samaritan, and hast a devil?" This emanates from that

wicked devil who wishes to be God and holy. Despisers of the Word are like this; they will not admit being in the wrong, nor will they listen to reason.

11. The point, therefore, is that the one who refuses to hear God's Word is not of God but of the devil. However, this is not to be understood as though it was the devil who is the creator of these people and had given them their mouth, eyes, ears, mind, and other members. No, all these things are God's creation and gifts. For this reason we must distinguish between what a person is and what he does. The essence of the tongue, eyes, ears, mind, and so on, is of God. But the use of such tongue, eyes, ears, and mind is of the devil when man uses them in the service of the devil. The man who lies has received a good tongue from God. But the use of the tongue to deceive is of the devil. Also, when the eyes are disposed to look at the unchaste thing, the eyes are of God, but the misuse is of the devil. Similarly, when the heart dwells on unchastity, deceit, lies, and the like, the core of one's person, as far as its essence is concerned, is good and is of God, but the acts are evil and of the devil.

12. On the other hand, "to be of God" is to use one's ears willingly to hear the preaching of the Word, willingly accept reproof when wrong has been committed, and also to pray, preach, instruct, comfort, reprimand, and give consolation with the tongue. Such ears and tongues are of God and good, not only as far as the essence but also as far as the use is concerned, for they are engaged in doing things pleasing to God. When the heart, therefore, is disciplined and is concerned with helping the neighbor, and not being irritated with him, such a heart is of God. Thus the things created by God, as eyes, ears, mouth, and heart, are said to be "of God" when they are guided by God's Word and do not wish to do, see, hear, speak, or think anything contrary to God. Although it happens from time to time that they err and say things that are profane when they ought to pray, and the heart is irritated when it ought to be cheerful, such things are, indeed, wrong. However, when we give up our evil ways and confess that we have done wrong and ask for mercy, this is what is known as stumbling or falling, but it is not called having the devil or being of the devil. For we are in the process of turning back and have resolved that we never want to commit the wrong again.

13. However, they are children of the devil who obstinately go their own way. And when to their own good, one reproaches them, they say, Why should I give a rap about that? When a disobedient son is rebuked by his mother, he purses his lips, walks away from the situation, and says, What is that to me? This is what it means to be of the devil: to have no concern for the Word of God and refuse to be accountable. The longer people have this attitude the worse they become, for the devil will not leave them alone. At first they despise the Word; then they blaspheme, rail, and curse it. And finally they do as the Jews in our text: they pick up stones and are ready to commit murder. Thus despisers of the Word become blasphemers of the word, persecutors and murderers of human beings. The devil reveals his true colors by not wanting to hear God's word, by blaspheming, reviling, and cursing it, by doing evil to, and killing, people. The one who despises and slanders and murderously assaults his neighbor is a child of the devil. This is what reveals the devil and his children; for he is a liar and a murderer, despising God and his Word.

14. When the Lord here threatens the Jews, he is admonishing followers against committing such sins, teaching them that if they want to be his disciples they must learn to be on guard against despising God's Word, gladly hearing and keeping it, ordering their lives according to it. Then they may be assured that they are of God and are God's children.

15. The rest are children of the devil. For since they do not wish to hear God's Word, they have forfeited righteousness and life, and, if I may be so bold as to say it, they are mired in the devil's cloaca, and they are in no way able to mitigate their sins through their reputation, accomplishments, and economic status. The pope with his adherents is up to his ears in such sins. For he will not tolerate God's Word and persecutes and slays Christians because of it. This is the devil in his true colors.

16. On the other hand, it is an attribute of God that he justifies and quickens. For just what kind of a God is he? He is no murderer but a creator, from whom all life flows. The devil has never created and given life to any man. To create and to grant life are exclusive works of God. Now then, just as God is a God of life whose very nature is life, so also those who are of God and hear his Word have life

in themselves, exactly as Christ here affirms with striking and beautiful words, "Verily, verily, I say unto you, If a man keep my saying, he shall never see death."

17. However, what is meant by keeping Christ's Word? Nothing else than to believe what he promises us in the gospel concerning the forgiveness of sins and eternal life, that it is true and that in faith we should hold fast to such hope. He who does this, says Christ, has eternal life and has nothing to fear with respect to sin, death, hell, and final judgment, for in Christ are found grace and mercy in fullest measure. Man, of course, will be overcome by death, but his soul will not see corruption. When man dies in God's Word, he will not die as horribly and dreadfully as those who die in the devil's name and without God's Word. These people die in sullen resentment, stomp and stumble about, roar like lions, for they do not wish to die, and yet must die since they cannot escape death. If it were possible, they would certainly try to build a mighty wall about themselves.

18. It will not be thus, Christ says, with my followers who hear and keep my Word. Even though they must lie down on their beds and die, they will not experience such fear and anxiety. In their hearts they will be at peace with God and hope for a better life. They will fall asleep in this hope and depart from this life without fear and trembling. For even though death will overpower their bodies, its power will be so weak that they will feel nothing of it, but peacefully fall asleep as though lying on a couch with their head resting on a pillow, somewhat like the unfortunate fellow who finds relief in being put to death by the hangman and gladly goes to the gallows in order to leave this wretched existence. But then there are others, like Clemens,* who became crazed with fear and acted as though he was possessed of a devil.

19. Therefore, consider, dear children, what benefits are yours when you gladly and diligently hear God's Word. First, you know that you are of God and have overcome the devil and hell, and that neither sin nor God's judgment can harm you. Whatever other kind of trouble you may encounter, you will be able to deal with it. On the

*hanged at Wittenberg

other hand, the world becomes troubled and impatient when the slightest thing goes wrong, eventually despairing completely.

20. To be sure, Christians will have to suffer a whole lot at the hands of the devil and the world who oppose them and subject them to hurts against life and limb, possessions, and honor. How is it possible for them to bear all this with patience? In no other way than by holding steadfastly to the Word and affirming: Let happen what may; I am not of the world but of God, else the world would comport itself differently toward me; but I much prefer that it hate and harass me on every hand than that it be fond of me and I be not of God. Where the heart is so minded, there all tribulation and adversity pass over, just like clouds in the skies and birds of the air; for a while we see them and then they're gone.

21. Our sole comfort in this life must be that we possess the power of the Word, particularly when our final hour approaches, so that death then becomes a sleep. It will be as though we are entering a dense fog, unaware of a murderer, and he is shot dead and murdered before he is aware of what has happened. Thus it will also be in this instance. The devil is a murderer and is determined to slay us, as we well know. But while we have the Word and hold steadfastly to it, we shall not really become aware of being involved in a death struggle. For the Word produces fine, gentle people and quiet, joyful hearts, which in times of anxiety do not despair or become fretful but pass through everything buoyantly, taking comfort alone in this, that through Christ they have a gracious heavenly Father. This is something they derive from the Word and nowhere else.

22. Now, then, tell me, because of daily trials and adversities shouldn't it be our primary goal to achieve this consolation to which the Word points us, in order that we might have an untroubled heart? Yet, this is nothing when compared to the last and greatest evil—death, from which no doctor, counselor, or advocate can rescue us, save alone our dear Lord Jesus Christ. He supplies us with the remedy that will benefit us more than anything else.

23. But what happens? When he offers us this help, straight to hearth and home, we are loathe to accept it. As a result we get our due reward: We are not of God and fall from one sin into the next, thus becoming more wicked each passing day, as we already have

pointed out above. When the final distressing hour arrives, we are left without comfort or recourse. That, as you know, is what happened in the case of the bishop of Trier, who as he was about to die became wild, like a bull in the slaughterhouse. For he had despised, blasphemed, and persecuted God's Word. Who can console a person like that? There is no help or consolation anywhere.

24. Thus the chief lesson to be learned from today's Gospel is that we diligently hold to the Word, gladly hear it, and receive it in faith. If we do this, we shall conquer sin, death, devil, and hell. Even though death consume us, we yet shall not feel its sharp fangs, for Christ's Word is our armor that supplies us with a confident life and a quiet, peaceful death and eternal life.

25. On the other hand, we could wish no greater judgment on the godless who despise God's Word than that which they already have hanging around their necks, namely, that they are not of God, nor are they God's children. No more terrible judgment than this could be pronounced upon them. As in the case of a wicked child who despises God's commandment and disobeys father and mother, what more devastating thing could be wished upon him than what already is hanging on his neck, namely, that he is a child of the devil and not a child of God? This is not something to be taken lightly. I would rather be in the hands of the executioner or the Turk than to be a child of the devil. For then I am in the hands of the arch-murderer and the liar who leads me astray and into eternal death. Beware of him, dear children, and take this to heart, I beg you. It is a priceless gospel. Amen.

JUDICA SUNDAY—FIFTH SUNDAY IN LENT

Second Sermon—1534

John 8:46–59

1. This long Gospel lesson is very rich in meaning and we can hardly do justice to it, because our time is necessarily limited; yet, with our Lord God lending us his grace, we want to treat it at least briefly.

2. First of all, Christ, our Lord, says to the Jews, You can fault me neither for my life nor for my teaching. "If I say the truth, why do ye not believe me?" He then poses the following syllogism, "He that is of God heareth God's words; ye therefore hear them not, because ye are not of God," but of the devil, from whom you will receive your due reward, namely, death and hell.

3. This is a particularly severe judgment upon all those who despise God's Word; everyone ought therefore be on guard against this sin and avoid it. But what happens? Despising the Word is such a prevalent evil everywhere in the world that no sin is more commonplace. God's Word nowadays is despised by people in high and low places, in the secular and spiritual realms; peasant and burgher do not want to listen to it, and they run amuck like wild beasts. We preach to them as best we can, but they don't want to listen. Hence they are of the devil, and he will reward them, as he did the Jews and other scornful persons.

4. But listen to how the Jews answered Christ, the Lord, over this judgment, "Say we not well that thou art a Samaritan, and hast a devil?" In other words, Underneath you're nothing but a mischievous rogue and a heathen; you are a deceiver and an apostle of the devil, because you do not teach correctly. It's the same response we get at the hands of smart alecky peasants and burghers today when we reproach them for their shameful scorning of God's Word. They begin

to mock and say, You clowns ought to preach the gospel but instead you only want to scold us; you don't teach as Christ's apostles but like the devil himself. This is what we have to listen to. Yet why should we lament? This is what Christ himself experienced at the hands of his people, as he details at length in this Gospel lesson how they slandered him when, to the glory and praise of God alone, he preached for the sake of the people's spiritual well-being. We can't expect anything different.

5. The second point is made in the Lord's statement, "Verily, verily, I say unto you, If a man keep my saying, he shall never see death." So, we have not only the glory of being God's children when we give heed to his Word, in contrast to those who because they refuse to hear God's Word are of the devil and are his children; but we also have the benefit that whoever heeds and trusts God's word will never see death, that is, he will not die nor come into hell; indeed, even physical death he will not see since he has forgiveness of his sin and beholds only grace and righteousness. Of course, we naturally have dread for the moment of death, but if we cling to Christ's Word and believe it without doubting, we shall not see death, that is, feel it and experience it eternally, but will pass from this life as in a sleep and live forever.

6. For the ungodly life's story is: I live, I know not how long; I die, I know not when; I pass away, I know not whereto; I'm filled with wonderment, yet I rejoice. These are they who will see death, feel and experience it, for they have not believed Christ's Word, and as a result will be terrified by death. They will not be able to outrun it but must forever remain in everlasting death, because they have disdained the wonderful, mighty medicine of God's Word which makes death into everlasting life, yes, even initiating it already in this life. For believing Christians, therefore, the song is: I live, I let God decide how long; I die, God wills when and what way; I pass away, I know where I am heading; I am mystified that I still am sorrowful. These are they who will not see or experience death. Though death holds some dread for them (indeed they, too, are Adam's children and must suffer death), they will nonetheless not come into eternal death nor will death's sting pierce their heart, but they will fall asleep without angst or sorrow.

7. St. Paul affirms this in Romans 1:16: "I am not ashamed of the gospel of Christ: for it is the power of God unto salvation to every one that believeth." That is precisely what Christ says here, "If a man keep my saying," that is, firmly believes, "he shall never taste of death" and shall be saved. This is the wonderful, mighty thing about Christ's Word that in whatever heart it is apprehended there salvation has surely come and death with sin, devil, and hell is overwhelmed and throttled by Christ's victorious resurrection.

8. Whoever, therefore, heeds God's Word has both its glory and benefit: glory, in that he is of God and is God's child; benefit, in that the Word which he believes saves him. And though he will still become ill, be assailed somewhat by the devil, and experience physical death, yet at the moment his soul is released he will, as it were, fall asleep and come into Christ's bosom, with the angels ministering to him and bearing him up, so that his foot is not dashed against a stone, as promised in Psalm 91:12.

9. On the other hand, whoever does not have nor heed God's Word will have both shame and hurt: shame, because he is of the devil and is called a child of the devil; harm, because he must despair in his sin and exclaim: Oh, where shall I now go? I must die! He feels and experiences death forever. That is the second point in this Gospel, urging that we should treasure God's Word in our hearts as a priceless possession that is able to eradicate death with sin, devil, and hell, no longer a reality to be seen or felt.

10. The third point is this: "Your father Abraham rejoiced to see my day: and he saw it, and was glad." And a little farther on: "Verily, verily, I say unto you, before Abraham was, I am." He does not say, before Abraham was, I was; but rather, before Abraham was, I am. For that is an attribute belonging to God alone, to be neither created nor made like Abraham or other creatures. It is God's nature to be neither created nor made, but I AM, that is, of eternal essence, without beginning or end. For God was present at the beginning and it is his nature to be eternal and without end.

11. That really vexed the Jews to the core that Christ said he was God. They take it to be blasphemy against God and say, That is the very devil that this individual, born a human being, states that he is God; and they become so violently aroused that they take up stones to stone him to death.

12. For us, however, it is consolation and verification of the highest kind to know that Christ is the true and everlasting Son of God. And that is the ground for Christ's Word being so mighty and able to save all who believe it. For because he is the very and eternal God, he is able also to give life and salvation to all those who cling to and believe his Word.

13. In this connection we should also note that the Lord says, "Abraham rejoiced to see my day: and he saw it, and was glad." That was tantamount to his saying, Abraham understood that I, the everlasting, almighty God was to become man. And by his perception and trust of my Word, he was saved and did not see death. If he had not accepted and heeded my Word, he would have remained in everlasting death. But he saw my day, and because he saw it he was glad.

14. For his saying that, the Jews become very angry and say, Ugh, you're crazy, how can that be?! You're certainly not old enough to have seen Abraham who lived two thousand years before you. They obviously saw and were aware of his being of human descent and not existing before Abraham. What they did not see or perceive, however, was that according to his divine nature he was before Abraham, before all creatures, before the whole world, and, therefore, they were unable to see the wonderful identical predication being true of him, that this man was God, a truth which human reason is incapable of harmonizing.

15. Briefly then, these are the three points contained in this Gospel lesson. The first, that we ought eagerly listen to and learn God's Word. If we do so, we become God's children; if we refuse, we remain children of the devil. The second, that by virtue of the Word's power and capacity to save, those who believe on it will not see everlasting death. Third is the fact that Christ is true, eternal God, who has such power that by his Word we come to live forever and will not die. May our dear heavenly Father give us his grace, so that by his Holy Spirit we firmly believe his Word and by it are saved eternally, for the sake of his beloved Son, Jesus Christ. Amen.

PALM SUNDAY

1534

John 12:12–19

On the next day much people that were come to the feast, when they heard that Jesus was coming to Jerusalem, Took branches of palm trees, and went forth to meet him, and cried, Hosanna: Blessed is the King of Israel that cometh in the name of the Lord. And Jesus, when he had found a young ass, sat thereon; as it is written, Fear not, daughter of Sion: behold, thy King cometh, sitting on an ass's colt. These things understood not his disciples at the first: but when Jesus was glorified, then remembered they that these things were written of him, and that they had done these things unto him. The people therefore that was with him when he called Lazarus out of his grave, and raised him from the dead, bare record. For this cause the people also met him, for that they heard that he had done this miracle. The Pharisees therefore said among themselves, Perceive ye how ye prevail nothing? behold the world is gone after him.

1. We call this day Palm Sunday—the day our dear Lord Jesus Christ rode into Jerusalem, thereby fulfilling the word of the prophets who foretold that he would thus ride into the city on a donkey. The prophet Zechariah, for example, proclaimed this, and the Evangelists Matthew and John cite this prophet. It's important that we Christians learn and treasure this story. There was a time when we acted it out in school, riding on a donkey and strewing palms; we did this for the sake of the youngsters, so that they would better grasp and remember this event. After that the pope took this child's play into the church itself, and because of that the day was called Palm Sunday.

2. It could just as fittingly be called the day of Christ's triumphal entry. From Galilee and Capernaum he had traversed the whole land up to Jerusalem, and on this day rode into the city on a donkey.

He wanted to be in Jerusalem for the Passover, and there take over his kingdom, even as kings and princes make their entries so that the whole country may pay them homage and swear allegiance.

3. Because Christ's kingdom is spiritual, however, the prediction of the prophet Zechariah had to precede, announcing to the people that their King would come riding in, not with lordly pomp as earthly kings were wont to do, but meekly and humbly, so that the Jews who rejected this King could never excuse themselves by saying, We just did not know that this was our promised King. How could we receive him when he made his entry not like an earthly king, but riding on a donkey, a poor and miserable figure indeed! That's why the prophet spoke as he did long before; Christ's entry was made exactly as had been proclaimed and pictured, so that the Jews would have no alibi. On top of that, his own disciples publicly hailed him as King. And since he had nothing of his own, they covered his path with palm branches and spread their garments before him—all to honor him as a King! And most significantly, the people themselves went out to meet him with their cry, "Hosanna, blessed is the King of Israel that cometh in the name of the Lord." That's how both his followers and the people gave honor and homage to this King!

4. All of this, I say, was announced and written about long ago by the prophet Zechariah, so that the Jews would never gawk and gape for a parade of worldly power, external pomp, and splendor—the very thing they are still expecting today, namely, that their Messiah and King will presently ride into Jerusalem in the same fashion as Babylonian kings entered Babylon, or a caesar rode into Rome. For that very reason the prophet said, "Do not be afraid, O Daughter of Zion; see, your King is coming, gentle and riding on a colt, the foal of a donkey." He wrote that way as if to say, You, Zion's daughter, listen and heed it well; even though your Messiah will make his entry on the back of a donkey, in such lowly fashion, he will nevertheless be received with royal honors. Be earnestly concerned, therefore, that you truly receive him as your King, lest you miss him entirely! He will ride into Jerusalem in this humble manner, and will then weep over a city which did not accept him. Terrible times will indeed come upon you because you despised your King, refusing to recognize the time of God's visitation.

5. It's evident, therefore, that the Jews have no justification whatever for not having accepted him. They will of course reply, How could we have known that this might be our King? After all, there was nothing royal about his entry to alert us; he rode into our city on the back of a donkey! He will answer you as follows, Look at the prophet Zechariah! Long beforehand he proclaimed exactly how your King would come riding in; but in spite of that—and even after I have now fulfilled his word—you have paid no attention either to your prophet or to me, your King. So now you have no excuse!

6. This was, of course, foretold beforehand also for us, and is preached to us year after year, so that we might learn the difference between Christ's kingdom and the kingdoms of the world, between our Christ-King and other earthly kings. This Christ-King comes to Zion's daughter humbly, riding on a donkey; he does not rule a realm where men gather wealth and property, conduct wars, become rich and powerful in this world—all the marks of worldly kings. These are obligated to maintain peace in their territory, so that their subjects may live in quiet and unity as they go about making a livelihood. Now Christ does not reject or even condemn earth. But in the realm where he is King and Lord, he's not concerned about teaching us how to farm, plow, sow, harvest, be a housekeeper, pile up money, conduct war, or rule over land and people. All such things he entrusts to earthly kings and lords.

7. Here, then, is the difference between this King and worldly rulers: They are concerned about people managing house and home, governing lands and subjects, acquiring money and property, becoming rich and powerful—all for the present time. Our Christ-King, on the other hand, wants us to know how to inherit the kingdom of heaven, how to be saved and become eternally rich, so that we may finally enter that other better life. Over there, eating, drinking, and working to sustain physical life will no longer be necessary, as it always is in this world. Yes, there these bodies of ours will be more beautiful, more lovely than the dear sun itself! There we will no longer be sad, weak, or sick, but everlastingly happy and healthy, strong and vigorous.

8. In his kingdom and by his Word Christ not only teaches us that we are poor lost sinners, condemned to death and in the devil's

clutches, but also that through his death and blood, he has redeemed us from all sins, from death and the power of the devil, so that by faith in him we are righteous and blessed forever. What wonderfully different teaching, wisdom, and insight this is compared with what is offered by human reason, legal experts, and the wise of this world—namely how to live here and now, managing house and home, acquiring goods, and protecting land and people. Even if we do live here a long, long time, finally and eventually we still have to depart and leave it all behind.

9. This is the reason why Christ entered Jerusalem as he did, without worldly pomp, meekly riding on a donkey. Thereby he not only wanted to fulfill the words of the prophet, but also to point out the manner and character of his kingdom, so that we may never be deluded into thinking that he came to earth to help us become rich and heap up treasure, when actually he came so that we might be delivered from sin, death, and the devil, and become truly rich in the life beyond. To sum up, this then was his true purpose in coming to earth, his kingdom's real nature and power and fruit, namely, that we may one day escape this wretched, mortal, decaying existence and enter that happy, glorious, eternal life beyond.

10. It was just such a King that God promised through his prophets. Had God intended him to be an earthly king, reigning in worldly fashion, there would have been no need for him to be especially promised. Because God made a very particular promise about him, there was no way he could have come as an ordinary king, ruling in the usual royal style. David and other kings reigned in that traditional manner, over territory and people, and thereby also gathered treasure. This King, however, is a very extraordinary King, especially promised by God; he set up a spiritual, eternal kingdom, over which he holds sway with unique power and might—his Word and the Holy Spirit.

11. But the Jews simply didn't want this kind of King—even though he came to them exactly as their prophet Zechariah had said: a righteous helper with eternal, heavenly blessings. Just because he made his entry in that lowly fashion—riding on a donkey—they paid little attention. And so they "missed the boat" entirely, so to speak, and to this day are still waiting for another, worldly-type king who

will ride in on a handsome Spanish charger, sitting on a golden saddle, clad in cloth of gold, to make everything appear as glittering and splendid as possible. But their waiting is vain and useless; no such king was promised and so, obviously, no such king will ever arrive!

12. The pope, likewise, has no taste for such a king; worse yet, corrupts his gospel. He boasts about being Christ's vicar on earth, and yet conducts himself like any other earthly lord and king—gathering treasure with the best of them! But in the treasures that Christ brings, which neither moth nor rust can consume, nor can thieves break in and steal—because these are heavenly treasures—he has little interest.

13. We Christians, however, should get really well acquainted with this Christ-King, and place all our hope boldly in the life which is to come, where we will be forever happy, free of all sin and infirmity. It's for that reason that Christ came, and was crucified, died, rose from the dead, and ascended into heaven to occupy his kingdom. That's how he overcame sin, death, and the devil for us, and by his blood and Holy Spirit swept us clean of all filth, so that all who believe in him are righteous and blessed, and will someday pass through temporal death into his eternal, heavenly kingdom.

14. That's why all of us should truly welcome this Christ-King, recognizing him as our righteous helper, and by the power of the Word, Sacraments, and faith, enjoy him now and forever! A Christian, you see, has not been baptized, so that he may collect treasure and get rich here on earth—all of which he can do as well without the gospel and baptism; instead he was baptized so that through Christ he may attain eternal life. To reach that life is why we should faithfully use the gospel and our baptism. I am a baptized Christian so that I may inherit and attain Christ's kingdom. And if I'm also blessed with possessions, I use these for my physical needs—certainly not to lift myself up into heaven!

15. We should, therefore, mark all the difference between Christ's kingdom and worldly powers, as he himself clearly showed by his extraordinary entry into Jerusalem, riding on a donkey, without a saddle, the animal a borrowed one at that! He sat on it without pretense, just as he was, barefoot, without boots and spurs. From the human point of view the whole incident looked ridiculous, and yet

this beggar-King, riding on a donkey, was Israel's King, promised by God and foretold by the prophets. That was evident also from the way his followers greeted him, "Hosanna!" Blessings on this King and upon his new kingdom! "Blessed is he who cometh in the name of the Lord, even the King of Israel!" All of which made it crystal clear that he was in no way like worldly rulers who have amassed a lot of treasure and property for the purpose of displaying worldly pomp and circumstance for their public appearances. Christ was no such earthly king; on the contrary, he is an eternal King, with an everlasting kingdom where one needs neither gold or silver, and yet will never suffer any want or need in all eternity.

16. The world has nothing but high disdain for this King and his kingdom with its eternal blessings; it is concerned only with temporal goods: power, honor, and riches on earth. We Christians, however, are to labor here and use the world's goods for our bodily needs, all the while not forgetting the other life. After all, we must in the end depart and leave behind the goods of this earthly life; that should help us remember where we really want to be, namely with Christ, our eternal King. For if we accept him here, that is, believe in him and heed his gospel, he will also receive us over there, saying to us, "Come, O blessed of my Father, inherit the kingdom prepared for you from the foundation of the world."

17. This, then, is what our dear Lord Jesus Christ meant to show by his entrance into Jerusalem, so that we might truly understand him and his kingdom. On the left hand, as it were, we still live here in the kingdom of this world, but always on the right hand we reach forward and upward to his kingdom everlasting in the world to come. It was for that future life that we were baptized. May God grant us his grace so that we may joyously welcome and accept this King and remain with him forever. Amen!

HOLY WEEK

OR STORY OF THE SUFFERING AND DEATH OF JESUS CHRIST, OUR SAVIOUR

*First Sermon**

THE HAPPENINGS IN GETHSEMANE

Matthew 26; Mark 14; Luke 22; John 18

1. We are approaching the season when in our sermons we give special attention to the suffering and death of our Lord Jesus Christ. So we want to arrange our customary preaching schedule in such a way that we give due consideration to the account of Christ's passion. Though it is always right and proper to have our Saviour's suffering and death in remembrance, so that we grow in appreciation of his tremendous love and blessing, it is nevertheless very good and necessary to set aside a special time during the year to devote our preaching to the story of Christ's suffering, so that our maturing young folks and people in general not forget it but always have the story refreshed in their minds.

2. Our sermons during the year regularly treat the fruit and benefit of Christ's suffering as we, through faith, believe on him, come to salvation, and are declared righteous before God; and with this article especially, we contend against false teachers, yes, the devil himself, who would gladly deter and strip us of this article of faith. For it is on this story that our salvation is grounded; on it we build and defy the gates of hell, as St. Paul says in 1 Corinthians 15:3–4: the gospel which he first of all delivered to them, which he himself first of all accepted, and which they, too, had received and appropriated to themselves, was "that Christ died for our sins according to the scrip-

*Preached at the parish church on Judica Sunday, 1534.

tures; and that he was buried, and that he rose again the third day according to the scriptures."

3. That is why this story must not be shoved into oblivion among us Christians, like the Jews forgot Moses and the mighty acts and blessings which God had shown them, to the extent that for a long time the Book of the Law was even lost among them, as in our day under the papacy preaching concerning the Lord's passion has dealt more with the beloved saints and especially about the Virgin Mary's suffering than about Christ's suffering.

4. Accordingly, we want to consider the story of Christ's passion in several segments or sermons, since the account is lengthy and rich in detail. If we divide the story of Christ's passion most accurately and succinctly there are six parts: first, the Lord's Supper; second, the story in the Garden; third, the happenings in Caiaphas' house; fourth, the events before Pilate; fifth, the account of the cross; sixth, concerning the Lord's tomb. That, in outline, constitutes the story of the Passion.

5. For the present, therefore, we will postpone the first part, the account concerning the Lord's Supper, until Maundy Thursday when it is customarily treated. Now we will treat the story of the passion in five segments. First, we will speak of the things that happened to Christ in the Garden; then of the happenings in the high priest Caiaphas' house to which Christ was led bound; third, the events before the governor Pontius Pilate; fourth, the things that occurred at Christ's crucifixion; and fifth and last, the account of Christ's burial—thus a brief summary of the whole story in five successive segments. May God graciously lend his blessing for our comfort and need.

6. Above all, however, we must carefully note the chief thing in preaching about the passion—we certainly must not neglect or omit it!—namely the ground and ultimate meaning of Christ's suffering. This is vital if we are to retain a clear-cut and correct understanding of the difference between the suffering of our Lord Jesus Christ and that of others. For where the devil does not assail the story or get people to completely forget about it, he strips away its fruit and blessing, so that even though they hear and know the story, they receive no comfort from it.

7. That is why we must be very careful to distinguish well between the Lord's suffering and that of others. For the devil and his cohorts suffer too; so also the pious and godly. The beloved saints, prophets, apostles, and martyrs suffered in their time, as do pious Christians in our day wherever they have been driven by persecution. The devil—along with his angels, apostles, disciples, and pupils—endures the fire of hell, but without becoming better thereby or holier. The beloved saints have suffered, and to some extent they still endure persecution and martyrdom at the hands of the devil and also the hostile world. But none of this suffering has the ultimate meaning and purpose of our Lord Christ's passion.

8. Accordingly, this is a necessary distinction: a Christian or saint, though he suffer much, does so only as regards the world, and by his suffering honors and praises God, as stated by Christ to Peter in the last chapter of the Gospel of John (21:18–19): "Verily, verily, I say unto thee, when thou wast young, thou girdedst thyself, and walkedst whither thou wouldest; but when thou shalt be old, thou shalt stretch forth thy hands, and another shall gird thee, and carry thee whither thou wouldest not. This spake he," states the Evangelist, "signifying by what death he should glorify God." There you have it: the suffering of the saints—like that of John the Baptist and the virgin Mary—has the sense and ultimate significance that thereby God is glorified and exalted. "Jesus should die for that nation; and not for that nation only, but that also he should gather together in one the children of God that were scattered abroad" (John 11:51–52).

9. We may indeed preach of the saints' suffering, but with due restraint we must distinguish it from the suffering of Christ. Previously, under the papacy, Christ's passion was preached only as an example for us to follow after. Then the pains and suffering of Mary were hitched to his, so that people might lament in sympathy with Christ and his mother and be moved to tears. And whoever could do this best of all was deemed to be the foremost preacher of the passion. We, however, preach the Lord's suffering in the way Holy Scripture does, emphasizing every aspect of Christ's suffering in the way the Scriptures do. That means that we show that Christ's suffering pertained to his obedience under the will of his heavenly Father, as St. Paul says (Phil. 2:8): "He humbled himself, and became obedient

unto death, even the death of the cross." He exalted and praised God by his suffering, as other saints praise and thank God through theirs. However, beyond this there was specific purpose for which Christ suffered, a purpose which distinguishes it from all suffering of the saints, namely, that through his suffering the whole world was to be redeemed, heaven opened, hell closed up, and eternal life won.

10. This underlying significance cannot be ascribed to any other suffering than to Christ's alone. Christ suffered to the praise and glory of God, rendering a well-pleasing service, but it was for you and me, all of us, for the sake of our redemption and salvation that he suffered, in order to free us from the power of sin and death, and open heaven for us. This glory I must not ascribe to any other, however holy he's presumed to be—also not to the compassionate suffering of the Virgin Mary! I do not attain to God's grace and forgiveness of my sins through the saints' suffering, not even for the least sin. True, the blood of the saints is holy, but I do not become holy thereby. And even though I pour out my blood, as the beloved saints did, I cannot thereby atone for my sins nor be saved. If I die for the sake of God, I do well and render God a God-pleasing sacrifice and service; but thereby I cannot be saved nor can anyone else.

11. The barefoot monks, therefore, were particularly reprehensible when they devilishly misled poor sinners and evildoers by comforting them with the words: My dear man, now you have to die a miserable death, but don't despair; God will view the ignominious death you now suffer as compensating for all your sins. Similarly, when they came to some dying persons on their sick bed and said, Dear fellow, for the sake of your soul you must endow many vigils and Masses, give generously to the cloisters, be on guard for your poor soul, and petition the saints to share their merits with you, in order that you may be saved. That amounted to not preaching Christ's death but our own death, as though we thereby could and would be saved, without any need at all of the suffering and death of our Lord Jesus.

12. If they had pointed the poor people in the right direction, they would have instructed sinners as follows: My dear man, you indeed deserve death, first, because before God you were conceived and born a sinful human being, like all of Adam's descendants who have

inherited sin and death (Rom. 5); second, before the world you are guilty of death by virtue of the evil done. See to it, therefore, that you patiently endure death as your due, serving God and the world faithfully. For the judgment and penalty attaching now to your body is also God's judgment and penalty; but with your death you do not wipe out your sin, for how can the sword or rack you've earned atone for sin? Your death serves, rather, as an example for others that they might learn. If, however, you want to be saved, then call upon God's Lamb who carries the world's sin. That is how they should have directed sinners, showing them that their sufferings belong here in this world where there is plenty and enough to make them guilty of death, not to mention that before God they are sinners and worthy of eternal death.

13. But when a person suffers as a Christian he should say, I will bear this to the honor and glory of our Lord God, for before God I am guilty—all of me, head to toe—not only of this suffering, but of death. Therefore, in obedience under the will of God, I accept and endure it, be it grief, anxiety, persecution, hunger, nakedness, peril, or sword, and I will suffer it in staunch faith, so that God may be praised and glorified thereby. Only Christians, however, believe this; nonbelievers and heathen do not.

14. The grounds and purposes, *causae et fines,* of suffering in the world differ, namely, that in the eyes of the world they are compensation for evil done, while in the case of the saints and Christians they are for praise and glory of God; but the ground and purpose, *causa et finis,* of Christ's suffering meant: He suffered for us! No other suffering can be accorded such glory, as before stated. Never should it have been said, as under popedom the preaching shamelessly proclaimed, O holy Virgin Mary, you have suffered more than you were guilty of; let your surplus suffering and merits help and comfort me. Nor should a person say, Oh, blessed John and, Oh, holy martyrs, let me partake of the benefits of your sufferings; and particularly you, holy Mother of God, show your breasts to your Son Jesus and obtain grace from him for me. That sort of blasphemy was initiated and endorsed by the pope; it was his treasury of the saints; merits, into which, by his shameless boast, he could enter with his key and hand out some of this treasure to other people—for a price!

15. Such were the horrible, shocking sermons we heard under the papacy. There were sermons, of course, about the sufferings of Christ but with no distinction from the saints' sufferings; that is, the sufferings of Christ were dealt with as examples to serve us and learn from. Indeed, in completely contradictory ways people were pointed towards the sufferings of the saints and how they might share in them. So, even though Christ's passion was preached, the fruit and benefit of his suffering was not only concealed but perverted.

16. Therefore we must distinguish very carefully. All other sufferings have their own ground and purpose, *causas et fines,* for which they are ordained. Christ's suffering also has its own ground and purpose, *causam et finem,* for which it was ordained. Of the Virgin Mary and the rest of the saints, I may say the following: Sancta Maria, Sancte Johannes, and so on, you have indeed suffered greatly, but your suffering does not help me that I might be saved thereby; you bore and did these things for yourself, glorifying God thereby; but my Lord Christ's suffering was special and unique. By it, when I'm in the throes of sin and death, I can and will be comforted. Accordingly, our whole trust, with all our heart, depends alone on the once-and-for-all suffering of Christ Jesus, upon whom alone our salvation rests, above and apart from the suffering of all others.

17. We must note this very carefully and preach it year after year, repeating it again and again, so that it may be firmly set in people's hearts, not only to know the story and history of how Christ suffered, but also why he suffered, the ground and ultimate purpose of his suffering and death. It matters little if I don't know why Isaiah, John the Baptist, and other prophets and saints suffered, though it is good, if I do; but if I'm ignorant of that, I still won't be damned. But what really counts is that I know what, how, and especially why, for what reason, Christ suffered; for if I do not know that, I will be damned and lost.

18. Now then what was the purpose for which Christ suffered? Of this the prophets and apostles inquired. Isaiah 53:5: "But he was wounded for our transgressions, he was bruised for our iniquities: the chastisement of our peace was upon him and with his stripes we are healed." 1 Peter 1:18–19: "Forasmuch as ye know that ye were not redeemed with corruptible things, as silver and gold, from your

vain conversation received by tradition from your fathers, but with the precious blood of Christ, as of a lamb without blemish and without spot." 1 Peter 2:21: "Christ also suffered for us." Idem, v. 24: "Who his own self bare our sins in his own body on the tree, that we, being dead to sins, should live unto righteousness: by whose stripes ye were healed." And 1 John 2:1–2: "We have an advocate with the Father, Jesus Christ the righteous: and he is the propitiation for our sins: and not for ours only, but also for the sins of the whole world." There we have the ground and ultimate purpose for the suffering and death of our dear Lord Jesus Christ clearly and eloquently expressed. Hold on to this and let nothing divert you from it.

19. Since, then, we are to preach the Lord's passion in such a way that people don't forget why Christ suffered, and correctly and precisely distinguish between Christ's suffering and that of the saints, we must now proceed herewith to take up the story of the passion beginning with the happening in the Garden, in order that our young folks may know and retain it. Matthew records the event, as do all four Evangelists.

Matthew 26:36–46

Then cometh Jesus with them unto a place called Gethsemane, and saith unto the disciples, Sit ye here, while I go and pray yonder. And he took with him Peter and the two sons of Zebedee, and began to be sorrowful and very heavy. Then saith he unto them, My soul is exceeding sorrowful, even unto death: tarry ye here, and watch with me. And he went a little farther, and fell on his face, and prayed, saying, O my Father, if it be possible, let this cup pass from me: nevertheless not as I will, but as thou wilt. And he cometh unto the disciples, and findeth them asleep, and saith unto Peter, What, could ye not watch with me one hour? Watch and pray, that ye enter not into temptation: the spirit indeed is willing, but the flesh is weak.

He went away again the second time, and prayed, saying, O my Father, if this cup may not pass away from me, except I drink it, thy will be done. And he came and found them asleep again: for their eyes were heavy. And he left them, and went away again, and prayed the third time, saying the same words. Then cometh he to his disciples, and saith unto them, Sleep on now, and take your rest: behold, the hour is at hand, and the Son of man is betrayed into the hands of sinners. Rise, let us be going; behold, he is at hand that doth betray me.

Luke 22:43–44

And there appeared an angel unto him from heaven, strengthening him. And being in agony he prayed more earnestly: and his sweat was as it were great drops of blood falling down to the ground.

Matthew 26:47–56

And while he yet spake, lo, Judas, one of the twelve, came, and with him a great multitude with swords and staves, from the chief priests and elders of the people. Now he that betrayed him gave them a sign, saying, Whomsoever I shall kiss, that same is he: hold him fast. And forthwith he came to Jesus, and said, Hail, master; and kissed him. And Jesus said unto him, Friend, wherefore art thou come? Then came they, and laid hands on Jesus, and took him.

And, behold, one of them which were with Jesus stretched out his hand, and drew his sword, and struck a servant of the high priest's, and smote off his ear. Then said Jesus unto him, Put up again thy sword into his place: for all they that take the sword shall perish with the sword. Thinkest thou that I cannot now pray to my Father, and he shall presently give me more than twelve legions of angels? But how then shall the scriptures be fulfilled, that thus it must be?

In that same hour said Jesus to the multitudes, Are ye come out as against a thief with swords and staves for to take me? I sat daily with you teaching in the temple and ye laid no hold on me. But all this was done, that the scriptures of the prophets might be fulfilled. Then all the disciples forsook him, and fled.

20. This constitutes the first phase of the passion, describing what happened to Jesus in the Garden, and from it there are two things to learn. First of all, my beloved, from Christ our Lord's words given here by the Evangelist Matthew, we learn that his suffering had a unique and singular basis, a purpose which the sufferings of the saints did not have. For, as Peter seeks to defend him with the sword to keep him from being taken captive by the Jews, the Lord stops him by saying, "Put up again thy sword into his place: for all they that take the sword shall perish with the sword. Thinkest thou that I cannot now pray to my Father, and he shall presently give me more than twelve legions of angels? But how then shall the scriptures be fulfilled, that thus it must be?" One angel would have sufficed to pro-

tect Christ from the violence of the Jews, but Christ says he could have mustered more than twelve legions of angels—that would be more than 70,000 angels! For that matter, one angel would have been sufficient to safeguard Christ against the whole world. But, as St. Luke records, Christ says, "Suffer ye thus far," or as St. Matthew gives it, "Peter, put up again thy sword into his place. How then shall the scriptures be fulfilled?" In other words, if I do not suffer, the Scriptures will not be fulfilled; but the Scripture must be fulfilled; therefore these things must take place. Here then is the ground of Christ's suffering: not because he had to, or because God could not find another way to effect his praise and glory, but in order that God might be vindicated as true to his Word which he had spoken through his prophets.

21. The Evangelist has reported this for the sake of the know-it-alls and wiseacres who question God concerning all of his works, Why are you doing so and so? There is no more pitiful pupil—if I may speak this way—in heaven and earth, and beneath the earth in hell, than our Lord God. The devil not only wants to be God's master but the whole world also thinks itself so smart that it must teach God how to run the world. Could not God, says master wiseacre, have found another way than this to redeem the human race, causing his Son to suffer an ignominious death? Why does God surrender his Son into his enemies' hands? Could he not have sent an angel to smite the whole world, not to mention this mob of Jews? Indeed, he could very well have done so, for he is almighty, also omniscient. He knows and understands very well in his benevolent nature what he wants to do without any of your savvy. But here it is not a question of power but of volition.

22. Our enthusiasts (Schwaermer) are also very smart in upstaging God. Why does Christ, they ask, take bread and wine in the Supper? Why water in baptism to wash people from their sins? Why does he not create people righteous and without sin, as he created the first man, Adam? Does he not have power and might great enough for that? The devil is at all times at work in the world, especially among the enthusiasts who want to take God to school and instruct him on what to do.

23. That is why the Evangelists state that Christ suffered in order that the Scripture might be fulfilled. God wanted things done in the

way it pleased him. He could very well have done otherwise but it was not his will to do so. Would God stoop to having some brash individual teaching and directing him first of all? Yes, says our clever reason; if I were in God's shoes then I would demonstrate my benevolence and mercifulness thus and thus in the world. This is the world's worst plague, that the children of mankind perceive our Lord God to be some kind of fool, because, while mighty, wise, and kindly above all things, he appears against all reason to be incapable of doing otherwise than to let his Son be born of a woman, be crucified, and die.

24. To be sure, the world cannot do otherwise, for everything that God says and does, it judges to be foolishness. Those who are genuine Christians, however, to whom God's Word is a serious matter, trust in God their Lord without subtle sophistry and contend that God manifests greater might in what the world perceives as weakness and foolishness than we can fully comprehend or understand. Non-Christians and unbelievers call it foolishness, just as our bishops and the worldly wise opine concerning the things God has created. They say, It is foolish and foolish to talk about, and if I were God I would do so and so. However, if you want to be a Christian, guard yourself against such sophistry and say, In the things of God it is the better part of wisdom to be silent; I will remain with the little remnant of genuine Christians who say rather: I could also engage in sophistry, but before God, who is almighty and knows how to do all things, I will refrain from debating and disobeying his Word, presuming to tell him how to do things, when he knows them better than I do.

25. Accordingly, Christ now says here, "Thus it must be, in order that the scriptures be fulfilled," as much as to say, I would have been glad if it could have been otherwise, but don't inquire further, believe the Scripture; if you don't want to believe and follow the Scripture, so be it. Therefore, we also respond to present day sophists: We don't bring you a new teaching, nor do we preach a different faith from that of the Scripture. And having done that in our preaching, there's nothing more to do but let the sophists ruminate. For ourselves, we will stand with the little remnant of the faithful, trusting the Scriptures.

26. With twelve legions of angels the Lord could have totally wiped out, not only the Jews, but the whole world, indeed a hundred

thousand worlds, one upon the other. But he needed to suffer that the Scripture might be fulfilled; so, not because he was compelled or forced, but to fulfill the Scripture, that God might be found faithful and true to his Word. Human reason says, Is God really so weak that he lets himself be crucified? Why does he humiliate himself this way? But Christ replies, Begone with your sophistries! I could well have arranged things differently; I have more than enough angels, and in fact one angel is stronger and mightier than ten Turkish potentates; but things are to be resolved peaceably, not by sword, as the Scripture says (Isa. 2:3–4). Micah 4:2–3: "The law shall go forth of Zion, and the word of the Lord from Jerusalem. And he shall judge among many people, and rebuke strong nations afar off; and they shall beat their swords into plowshares, and their spears into pruninghooks: nation shall not lift up a sword against nation, neither shall they learn war any more." So much for the first part.

27. The Evangelists, secondly, describe very carefully Christ our Lord's struggle with death in the Garden, because of its importance. After the supper Christ went out over the brook Kidron, as St. John records, into a garden on the nearby Mount of Olives where there was an area or enclosure for the Jews to keep their sheep. St. Luke tells how the Lord customarily liked to go to the Mount of Olives. We must understand this to mean that, after the Lord had preached in the city of Jerusalem carrying out his mission, he then would go his way to the Mount of Olives, where he had a resting place under the trees on the grass till morning. In the morning then he would again go into the city to accomplish his office. The betrayer Judas knew this pattern very well.

28. But now, on this occasion, as the Lord, following his custom, left and came to the Garden, something new and different occurred. He divides his disciples and takes Peter and the two sons of Zebedee with him, saying to the rest of the disciples, Sit down here; I must go on a ways to pray. And after doing this he fell down on his face praying, "O my Father, if it be possible, let this cup pass from me: nevertheless not as I will, but as thou wilt." This petition was new and unusual. Earlier, he had also many times prayed. But he had never separated his disciples in the manner he did here. Three disciples he took with him, Peter, James the elder, and John, leaving the other

disciples behind to rest. These three disciples were to be privileged to hear him speak in his anguish and need.

29. Our dear Lord Christ here presents himself for our sakes as a poor, sinful human being, his divine nature now held in abeyance and no longer sustaining him as before with consolation and security. The tempter, the devil, is thus given elbow room to draw closer with severer attack than before. Accordingly, Christ speaks here as mere man struggling in death's throes, seeking for support from his disciples whom he before had often consoled. With tremors and shuddering his heart is overwhelmed with grief, and in despair of life, sensing death, he knows that he must now die and pours out his grief before his disciples. His deep anguish and need overwhelm him utterly and cause him to take refuge in his disciples who are much weaker than he.

30. The suffering of our beloved Lord Jesus Christ in the Garden exceeds the ability of human tongue to tell, exceeding, in fact, all human understanding and thought, particularly in such an exalted and sublime person. Had any other person been attacked with such severity by the devil, he would have been strangled in the blink of an eye, especially as regards human existence when thought of in terms of soul and body conjoined. In the life to come it will be even more bitter for the damned, since in spite of everything, they will not die but remain forever in great agony. That is why we are unable to understand and comprehend it, let alone express the anguish Christ encountered in the Garden.

31. He himself exclaimed, "My soul is exceeding sorrowful, even unto death." These words are pressed from him by his agony. He states, I am in such great anguish, so terrified, afflicted, and filled with despair that my soul is at the point of being torn from me. The average man could not have survived if he had experienced such agony for even a split second but would have succumbed immediately. God the Lord has here yielded over a perfectly pure Lamb to the jaws of the devil, who with a vengeance gnashes on it with his teeth and fancies that he will wolf it down. But finally he will have to leave it undevoured. Such was the grief Christ here poured forth as he exclaimed, "My soul is exceeding sorrowful even unto death." In other words, There is nothing left of life, no way out, I must die.

32. But why are you, O Lord Christ, so overcome with grief and terrified? Did you not say that you could petition your Father to send

you more than twelve legions of angels—except that the Scripture must be fulfilled? If you are so terrified and afflicted by death, what hope is there for us poor, miserable people and sinners, if we are brought to the gallows or stake, or plague and other illness stare us in the face. We most certainly would despair, if death causes you so to tremble and shake. Of course the world makes light of it and finds it amusing that Christ, the Lord over death, should fall so low that he laments, "My soul is exceeding sorrowful, even unto death."

33. But it was for our sakes that this man, like no other person upon earth, was so afflicted; no one has ever been so terror-stricken by death as he was. When a man who has languished in jail for a long time is told, Get ready, you're going to be put to death, there's no alternative, he begins to agonize and fret, wrenching for a day, or three or four, his terror ever mounting, even more than when the hangman actually comes and executes him. That is to experience true death, when the incarcerated wretch gnaws away inwardly and the devil prompts the thought, You are mine and you must suffer. Then life takes on an entirely different aspect for the man; he speaks and acts differently. In short, his affliction is quite different from the plague or syphilis, for he experiences the anguish and throes of death, quite apart from bodily ailment or physical death.

34. It is in the nature of things for us human beings to find the struggles before death worse than death itself. When the devil has his way, despair reigns. The face of the individual involved in such struggle becomes tense, pale, and white, the eyes sunken and gloomy, the ears cold, and so on. But none of this compares with Christ our Lord's struggle in the Garden. Accordingly St. Luke states, "And being in agony he prayed more earnestly: and his sweat was as it were great drops of blood falling down to the ground." Christ went further than we; the heat and the fire he experienced pressed a bloody sweat from him.

35. Of this battle, as said, we know nothing, for in Christ's case it was greater than for all mankind together. The fact is that Christ had to become the chief martyr among all martyrs on earth. We human beings are conceived and born in sin, with unclean, calloused and leprous flesh, without real sensitivity. The fresher and sounder an individual is, with healthy skin and blood, the faster he senses when

things are not well with him; the filthier his skin and blood, the less he will sense something wrong, as with a leprous man. Now Christ's body, his flesh and blood are fresh, healthy, clean and without sin, while our bodies, our flesh and blood are leprous, unclean and full of sin, and this accounts for the fact that when we hear of death and feel its terrors, the intensity barely reaches the second rung, while for Christ is on level ten. Inasmuch as he had to be the greatest martyr and bear the deepest suffering, terror, and sharpness of death—though in his own nature he is perfectly clean—he felt and experienced death's throes more than all of us together.

36. That is why we don't read of any of the saints experiencing such anguish that bloody sweat was pressed from them, as the Evangelists report of Christ. We know very well that a terror-stricken individual, particularly when wrestling with death, cannot even cry tears; his sight and hearing fail, his tongue becomes dry like bark, his eyes dry like a stone. All fluids and blood throughout his body converge on the heart. But in Christ the terror and anguish is much greater. For we see how his heart, which by nature is so strong that it circulates again the blood which under stress has converged there, presses drops of blood from him, as St. Luke writes. It must, therefore, have been such overwhelming sorrow, anguish, and grief as no human heart could ever even imagine. We human beings experience sorrow to the point where our tongue becomes dry, ears deaf, hands numb, and yet without a drop of blood oozing from our whole body. That is the way it is for us, but in Christ's case the heart caused the blood to be pressed from his body, something which goes beyond all human comprehension.

37. Christ, our dear Lord, voluntarily bore this great agony for the glory of his heavenly Father and for our benefit, so that henceforth we might have a champion over against anguish when our appearance becomes strained, our eyes dark and gloomy, our tongue speechless, and our head cannot think; then we must hold to this man who has overcome this terror by absorbing it within himself. As a result our anguish can no longer be as great as it was in his heart, for Christ overcame the greatest agony with his innocent heart, and with his perfectly pure blood, extinguished and quenched the devil's bitter fury and poisonous, fiery darts, so that we may be comforted

by his conquest. The devil has already shot his fiery darts into him and pressed them into his heart, charging, You have fallen into God's disfavor, and so on. Such are the very darts he has extinguished in his innocent heart, in his sinless body and pure blood, driving them so deep within that they have been blunted and no longer have power against us. The suffering of the saints could never have accomplished this, for by their blood the devil's arrows are not blunted nor made powerless. Only Christ's blood could accomplish this.

38. This was the battle our dear Saviour, Jesus Christ, waged in the Garden, a struggle which, prior to his actual dying, pressed him with the necessity of dying; and the devil jibed at him, terrifying his heart with the thought, You must pay the penalty, and so on. His holy nature was horrified thereby, because the very purity of his nature made the agony all the greater, all for the purpose, as said, that we might be comforted. For such great, boundless love and goodness we must be eternally grateful from the bottom of our hearts. Amen.

HOLY WEEK

*Second Sermon**

THE RECORD OF THE EVENTS THAT TOOK PLACE IN THE HOUSE OF CAIAPHAS, THE HIGH PRIEST

Matthew 26, Mark 14, Luke 22, and John 18

1. My dearly beloved, you have already heard a portion of the passion the history of our Lord Christ's suffering which took place in the Garden of Gethsemane. For our sakes he subjected himself to the terrible fear and agony of death. His suffering was so great that he broke out in a bloody sweat which poured from his body onto the ground.

And Judas, the betrayer, brought with him a whole platoon of soldiers provided by Pontius Pilate and the high priests of the Jews. Dear friends, you have heard how all of these things happened for our sake. It was for us that our dear Lord Jesus Christ took upon himself this burden of indescribable distress of soul and mind, not for his own sake, but rather for our sake. No one forced him to do that, neither an angel nor a devil, for he said, I could have summoned twelve legions of angels. But he was determined that by his suffering he would save us, just as it was for our benefit that he did everything, including the conquest of hell and death.

2. And that is the most important part of the passion of Christ, which was a spiritual suffering far greater than any kind of physical pain! Lashing, beheading, crucifixion—all of these are a physical and temporal suffering which result in the dying of our five senses. But spiritual suffering, which is experienced by a person's heart and soul, that is a torture immeasurably greater than physical death. That is

*Preached at the parish church, March 25, 1534.

why Christ, through his agony in the Garden, took upon himself the poison and bitter hatred of the devil. At the same time he also took upon himself the full wrath and condemnation of our Lord God and drained that cup to the dregs, so that we would not have to suffer those things, or, even if we might be asked to bear suffering, being in Christ, we would be able to bear that suffering and overcome it. God wants us to seek our comfort and consolation in that fact, and then, if spiritual terrors and despair do attack us, cling to our baptism in that man who for our sake has overcome all such suffering. This we must firmly believe and not harbor any doubts about it.

Now there follows the second part of the passion that befell our Lord in the home of the high priest Caiaphas. The holy Evangelists write thus:

Matthew 26:57–61

And they that had laid hold on Jesus led him away to Caiaphas the high priest, where the scribes and the elders were assembled. But Peter followed him afar off unto the high priest's palace, and went in, and sat with the servants, to see the end. Now the chief priests, and elders, and all the council, sought false witness against Jesus, to put him to death; But found none: yea, though many false witnesses came, yet found they none. At the last came two false witnesses, And said, This fellow said, I am able to destroy the temple of God, and to build it in three days.

John 18:19–23

The high priest then asked Jesus of his disciples, and of his doctrine. Jesus answered him, I spake openly to the world; I ever taught in the synagogue, and in the temple, whither the Jews always resort; and in secret have I said nothing. Why askest thou me? ask them which heard me, what I have said unto them: behold they know what I said. And when he had thus spoken, one of the officers which stood by struck Jesus with the palm of his hand, saying, Answerest thou the high priest so? Jesus answered him, If I have spoken evil, bear witness of the evil: but if well, why smitest thou me?

Matthew 26:62–75

And the high priest arose, and said unto him, Answerest thou nothing? what is it which these witness against thee? But Jesus held his peace. And the high priest answered and said unto him, I adjure thee by the living God, that thou tell us whether thou be the Christ, the Son of God. Jesus saith unto him, Thou hast said: nevertheless I say unto you, Hereafter shall ye see the Son of man sitting on the right hand of power, and coming in the clouds of heaven. Then the high priest rent his clothes, saying, He hath spoken blasphemy; what further need have we of witnesses? behold now ye have heard his blasphemy. What think ye? They answered and said, He is guilty of death. Then did they spit in his face, and buffeted him; and others smote him with the palms of their hands, Saying, Prophesy unto us, thou Christ, Who is he that smote thee? Now Peter sat without in the palace: and a damsel came unto him, saying, Thou also wast with Jesus of Galilee. But he denied before them all, saying, I know not what thou sayest. And when he was gone out into the porch, another maid saw him, and said unto them that were there, This fellow was also with Jesus of Nazareth. And again he denied with an oath, I do not know the man. And after a while came unto him they that stood by, and said to Peter, Surely thou also art one of the them; for thy speech betrayeth thee. Then began he to curse and to swear, saying, I know not the man. And immediately the cock crew. And Peter remembered the word of Jesus, which said unto him, Before the cock crow, thou shalt deny me thrice. And he went out, and wept bitterly.

3. These events transpired in the palace of Caiaphas, the high priest. St. John writes: The Jewish soldiers took charge of Jesus, bound him, and first of all led him to Annas. The order of events was as follows: As soon as Jesus was captive in the Garden, he was led out from there to Caiaphas' house. But because the house of Annas, father-in-law of Caiaphas, was located along the road that led to the house of Caiaphas, they brought Jesus there first. By doing this the older man and father-in-law, Annas, would be honored by being the first one to see Jesus bound and captive. In Annas' house nothing further happened to our Lord, but in the house of Caiaphas false witnesses were brought forward to level charges against him.

4. So nothing really happened to Jesus in the house of Annas, except that the servants indulged the old priest by bringing Jesus bound before him and saying, Look! We are bringing Christ, the man whom you have so long been anxious to arrest, first of all to you. And Annas merely said, That's fine, very good, just lead him to the house of Caiaphas, for he is the high priest this year. You see, all the high priests, elders, and council members ruled not only over the city of Jerusalem, but also over the entire country. These were all assem-

bled here in the palace of Caiaphas, who was, so to speak, the head of the whole Jewish nation. That's the way they commanded that it be done: As soon as Jesus was apprehended, the servants were instructed to bring him to Caiaphas' house. In keeping with that order he was led directly to the house of Caiaphas, except that for the sake of the old priest, Annas, in his honor, they first took him to his house, as said. I mention this so that we properly understand and grasp the account of our Lord's suffering.

5. Now, the holy Evangelists clearly and diligently describe what took place in the palace of Caiaphas as follows: The high priests hauled Jesus before the entire council, his hands being bound, and interrogated him there. Second, the Evangelists inform us that there Peter denied the Lord three times. And in the third place, they record the fact that the Jews mocked, ridiculed, reviled, and spit upon him, all the night long, until the morning dawned. All of this transpired in the palace of the legal rulers of Jerusalem and the whole nation of the Jews.

6. First of all, St. Matthew and St. Mark write that the high priests and Bible scholars, the elders of the people and the entire council, had assembled. These were the people who controlled the entire spiritual regimen of the Jews, just like cardinals and bishops, and their doctors and scholars under the papacy. The elders and the council also controlled the secular government. That is why Jesus, with his hands bound, was hauled before the high priests and the council of Jerusalem, which meant before the spiritual and secular authorities. It was just as if today the pope, together with his cardinals and bishops, and the imperial monarch, with the princes of the empire, were to condemn someone to death. The whole regime at Jerusalem was based on both such authorities; it was something that existed from the very beginning of Judaism. Aaron was the high priest, and the tribe of Levi was the source of the entire spiritual government. The tribe of Judah, however, was the source of the reigning kings or secular government. That is why, in this trial of Christ, we see both levels of government represented by the foremost and highest officials, the most intelligent people of the land; these are the ones who scheme and plot against Christ, and finally pronounce the judgment of death against him.

7. It is both terrible to hear, and also nonetheless worth pondering, that these two levels of authority, the priestly order and the kingly order here join hands in opposing Christ. The high priestly forefathers were Moses, Aaron, and Levi. Here, however, we see the descendants of those forefathers who have sunk so low that they presume to betray Christ and condemn him to death! The council's forefathers were Abraham, Isaac, Jacob, and Judah; now such noble people have fallen so low that they betray and dispose of their God, who had been promised to them. It would not have been the least bit surprising were God to have been so filled with wrath against both ruling orders that he would no longer have provided either spiritual or secular government in the future, for if these two orders pursue after Christ, what is left on earth to protect him?

8. This is what happens: Christ is betrayed, disposed of, and condemned to die, not by evil, lowly people, but by the spiritual and secular heads! In addition to that, it is his very own people, whom he himself had chosen and whom he had provided with such stringent laws, laws to which the whole land had to conform. And everything which they resolved and adopted as law, that was then the law of the land, just like the papal council and the laws of the empire were for us. Whatever they agreed upon, that became the law of the land. This is how the spiritual and secular governments functioned—next to God they were the highest power on earth. You see, in Judaism no one was on a par with God except for the high priest and the council at Jerusalem. Whatever the high priest at Jerusalem ordained, you either obeyed or you died. Whatever the king or his advisers commanded, you dared not disregard or disobey. Consequently, no one dared to disregard or contradict the laws which Moses had recorded in the Law and earnestly commanded the people to obey.

9. Very well, they had the power to do what they did; no one can deny that. Whenever the people saw that someone had been condemned to death by both the spiritual and secular courts, they had no recourse but to silently approve that decision. In their "heart of hearts" they might very well be thinking, That man is being treated unjustly; but no one dared to interpose a protest against such a decision. And because theirs was unrestricted power, they deliberately misused and abused it. As a result of having this power, they killed

all the prophets, yes, even Christ himself, the greatest of all the prophets. For Moses had said, Whatever the high priest and the king order or command, you are to obey; they rationalized that they had the right and power to torture and slaughter, like an ox, anyone whom they disliked, for any reason whatsoever.

10. Thus Christ was not killed in a rebellion, nor in a riot, nor by people who had no legal power; no, he was killed by those who held full, legal power. It is still true to this day, that whatever happens to the detriment of Christians as a group, happens to them under authority of law, as we unfortunately must testify about our persecutors—princes, bishops, and officials who have divine sanction so far as secular power and also church authority are concerned, based on God's Word, provided they use that power properly. Sad to say, however, those who possess legal power are now persecuting the gospel!

11. The case of Christ is an exceptional one, different from any other. He is killed by those who not only possess legal power, but also by those who are his friends, cousins, and blood relatives, yes, even those whose office God had authorized and confirmed with special, miraculous signs. The Roman emperor and the princes of his realm, though ordained by God, are not mentioned by name in Holy Scripture, as were Moses, Aaron, Levi, and Judah; nor are they confirmed by being led out of Egypt, through the Red Sea, which was a miraculous sign. Those now have nothing more than the government ordained of God, regardless of who is exercising it. They remain "nameless." In contrast to that, the Old Testament rulers are named individually and are confirmed by miraculous signs.

12. Here we see how we should evaluate the spiritual and secular realm; also how we should evaluate ourselves who are preachers, princes, or government officials, for we are the ones who persecute God and crucify Christ who has given us that power! I tell you, it would not be surprising at all if God were to say, I shall no longer put up with any kind of government or power; I shall destroy every last one of them! For if the emperor and his princes had no power, they would have to cease from persecuting the gospel so bitterly.

13. Now God has raised up the Jews before all the world as an example from which we are to learn that his wrath burns hot against his enemies and against those who persecute his gospel. From the exam-

ple of the Jews, we are also to learn that in the long run he will repay in full all those who hold legal power but abuse that power by persecuting the gospel. He has taken away from the Jews every trace of both spiritual and secular power. The priesthood of Aaron has been so totally abolished that every last stone of the temple has been destroyed!

The same thing is true of the secular government of Judah; it has been so totally destroyed that not even a single strand of it remains. There they lie, and now they have neither the secular kingdom nor the priestly realm, and they are scattered all over the world, confused and in error. For God had made them kings and priests and had given them great authority, so that they might serve him with these powers. But because they misused their powers by killing the prophets and murdering God's own Son, he had to humble them by stripping them of their power, so that they could no longer go on killing the prophets or publicly crucifying Christ. That is the reason why they cringe in the dust, expecting at any moment to be driven out. They raved against God and refused to give him any peace, and because they refused to let up, they had to be destroyed.

14. God will do the same thing to the pope, his cardinals, bishops, emperor, kings, and princes, if they now persecute his gospel. They do have authority, but I am not now speaking of the power which, contrary to God's Word, the pope arrogates to himself, but rather of the power which emperors, kings, and princes have in the secular government and the power which the pope as a bishop, along with other bishops, could have in the church in keeping with God's Word, if only they would serve God with that power! Unfortunately, they accept the power gladly but serve the devil with it. And now they have decided that people should think of them as having power over everything, while they call us traitors! They are the spitting image of Annas and Caiaphas!

But when the time is ripe God will destroy them, so that they can no longer harm any Christians. They will finally be brought to realize what horrible things they have done, just as God destroyed the Jews so that they would no longer be able to crucify Christ. You see, the words of Psalm 110:1 and 1 Corinthians 15:25 must forever remain true: "The Lord said unto my Lord, Sit thou at my right hand, until I make thine enemies thy footstool," and "For he must reign, till he hath put all enemies under his feet." He does not say, I will elevate your enemies to positions of power but he says, I will put them all under your feet as a footstool. The Jews were turned into a footstool! Emperors, kings, and princes who persecute the gospel will not escape his wrath either! They do, indeed, receive their power from God, but he who gave them that power can also bring them abjectly down. The one who elevated them to power, can also jerk them off their thrones and humble them in shame!

15. Our dear Lord Jesus Christ did not suffer in secret, nor did he suffer at the hands of those who had no legal power. No, he suffered in public and at the hands of those who exercise public power. Here in Germany that happens to be the emperor and the pope. However, we should not be offended when we see that both kinds of power, spiritual and secular, such as the pope and emperor, are enemies of God. As we confess and say in the Christian Creed, "I believe in Jesus Christ who suffered under Pontius Pilate." That is what has happened in every age of the past and is also happening today, namely that Christians and true martyrs are being killed by both the legally established authorities, spiritual and secular. It is indeed the responsibility of all spiritual and secular authorities to protect and defend Christ and his adherents in the same way that King David and other godly kings have done; but the exact opposite of that is what is always taking place. Those people who should be offering help to Christians are the very ones who persecute and bedevil them.

16. Therefore, when we see that the same thing is happening today—pope, emperor, and other persons in positions of authority are persecuting the Christians—we should remember that this is nothing new, for that is the way it has always been. No prophet was murdered by an assassin, but all of the prophets were publicly murdered by those who occupied legal positions of public power and trust. That has continued till this present day. All the blood that was shed was shed by those who were kings, princes, judges, councils, and the like, all members of the secular government, along with bishops, preachers, and so on, all members of the spiritual realm. They were the very ones who murdered and betrayed our Lord Christ, as the history of his passion teaches us and as the examples of holy martyrs testify. The other murderers on the street and in the woods are assassins,

and that kind of murder is an assassination and is not a prophet's death. It is a "prophet's death" when it is carried out by legal power and the people have to remain silent and say, That was done by pope, bishop, prince, king, and emperor.

17. Note this well: Christ is condemned and killed by the highest ranking heads of both the spiritual and secular realms, which God has ordained. These men, who occupied positions of unrestricted public power, killed Christ! God had ordained the high priests, elders, and the council at Jerusalem to discharge their duties in full harmony with God's Law. But they paid no attention to that Law of God. Instead, they misused their legal power to deliberately defy God. Yet God had invested the pope, emperor, kings, and princes with power, so that they might serve God with the powers vested in them. As head bishop the pope was given the spiritual power to bind and to free people from their sins. To the emperor, kings, and princes, power was given to govern the land and the people so as to punish evildoers and preserve peace on earth as the secular government. These powers, given to them by God, were to be exercised in accordance with God's Word. But what happens? God does indeed tell them, You, O emperor, are vested with the sword; therefore go ahead, hang the thieves on the gallows, execute the murderers, and so on. You, O pope, as bishop are vested with the keys to the kingdom of heaven; therefore cast the incorrigible sinners to hell, in accordance with my Word and command. But they completely disregard God's Word. They say, What we do and decree, that will be the law, that and nothing else.

18. But what will happen someday when the tables are turned? God will do what fills them with hatred, and he will refuse to do what they want him to do, just as now they do what fills God with wrath and leave undone what they know is God's will. A person indeed ought be terrified knowing that he is a preacher, bishop, prince, or ruler in the world, and wish instead that he was a servant or a maid! For those people occupy a station in which God has been frequently blasphemed and persecuted. It is the damnable devil who has terribly distorted the two offices that are so great and noble. He is the one who misleads the people with false doctrine and who sheds innocent blood with the sword, yes, the one who crucifies Christ himself—not

to mention the unusual fact, that he is condemned to death and is crucified, not only by those who hold positions of legal power, but who are actually Christ's own blood brothers!

19. In addition to that, the Evangelists record how the high priests, elders, and the whole council, having caught Christ, hailed him before themselves, and cross-examined him. Those tyrants rejoiced in the fact that they had apprehended Christ, and they thought, There! Now we've got him in our power. What shall we do now, so that we can find cause to have him also killed? Up till this moment they had not given any thought to whether they had sufficient charges to bring against Christ, charges that would be worthy of death. Up till now they had spent all of their efforts in planning his capture. But now that they held him as a handcuffed prisoner, they couldn't think of any justifiable reasons to kill him. They racked their brains trying to find legitimate or illegitimate reasons to do away with him. They searched for false witnesses who could testify against him, but they couldn't find anything that would justify the death penalty.

20. One false charge or testimony is described by St. Matthew who reports that two false witnesses stepped forward with the accusation that he had publicly proclaimed that he had the power to destroy the temple of God and rebuild it within three days, all by his own power. That charge is immediately suspect, for in John 2:19–22, we are told what Jesus meant by that statement. He was not speaking of the temple in Jerusalem, but about the temple of his own body. Nor did he say that he would destroy his own body, but that they, the Jews, would be guilty of his (pointing to his own body) death, and that he himself would raise his own body from the dead! St. Mark writes that they (the Jews) testified falsely that he had said, "I will destroy the temple made by human hands and I will replace it within three days, with a temple not made by human hands." But their false witnesses did not agree as to what Jesus had actually said.

21. St. Matthew reminds us that prior to the testimony about the destruction of the temple, they brought false witnesses to testify against Christ, witnesses who are not listed or named by Matthew. Those testimonies also contradicted one another. Later on, as St. Luke informs us, when they were bringing their false accusations before the governor, Pontius Pilate, they again used the same self-con-

tradictory charges, saying, "We find this man guilty of misleading the people by forbidding them to pay tribute to Caesar," and so on. That was a terrible, barefaced lie. For, after the Pharisees had asked Jesus whether or not they should pay taxes to the emperor, according to Matthew 22:21, Jesus responded by saying: "Render therefore unto Caesar the things which are Caesar's; and unto God the things that are God's." We will have more to say about this same charge later on, when we deal with Pilate.

22. Right now we shall hear how the high priests, elders, and the council itself disagreed with one another in Pilate's palace. They were not agreed on what kind of a charge they should lodge against Christ in the court of the governor, Pontius Pilate. You see, the Romans had taken away from the Jews the right of capital punishment. As a result this was a sore spot for them under Roman law, that unless Pilate granted permission, they were forbidden to execute anyone. If they had still retained the power of capital punishment, they would quickly have agreed on what they would do with Jesus, namely, kill him. But because they no longer had that authority, they conspired together saying that since this Jesus has deliberately sinned against our laws, unless we can prove that he has committed murder or sedition, or some other offense against Caesar, we cannot charge him with anything. However, we must keep in mind that the crime with which we want to charge him must be the crime of lesé majesty, an offense against Caesar's crown and authority, a crime that even the emperor in Rome must punish with death! Such a charge the Jews wanted to level against Christ, but they couldn't turn anything up.

23. If they had accused him by saying that he claimed that he would destroy the temple of God, and so on, Pilate would have responded, Who is this fellow anyway? What if he did claim that he would destroy the temple of God, so what? For even if the Jews considered it a great sin to destroy the temple—the pope would consider it an even greater crime to threaten to destroy the monasteries and churches—it would be an even greater sin to rebuild the temple without authorization to do so, because even King David was not allowed to build the temple. Therefore the governor would not have considered it a crime, but would no doubt have told them, You must be off your rocker to come up with such a silly charge, for the temple

is still standing there and is not destroyed! And even if they had then charged Christ with having said that he would destroy the temple, or that he claimed to be God, those charges could not have been sustained either. For Pilate, being an intelligent, astute heathen, would have responded, Why all this fuss about what he says? Any old fool can boast that he will do so-and-so, but that doesn't mean it is going to happen! You are even greater fools to even bring up that kind of an accusation of crime. Or if he claimed that he was God, let him be God; that's his problem! In other words, the high priests and the members of the council had to acknowledge in their hearts that they really had no grounds whatsoever for their charge against Jesus.

24. This, therefore, proves that Christ is suffering innocently. Just as in the Garden he voluntarily and gladly is weak for our sake, when he might well have been strong; for he says at this point, "I could ask my Father to send me more than twelve legions of angels and he would do so." His available power is furthermore proven by the fact which St. John records, that with a single word he sends the entire Jewish guard reeling backwards and falling to the ground. Jesus, in other words, voluntarily assumes here the role of a sinner, even though he is completely innocent and without sin. He allows himself to be accused of being a blasphemer and a revolutionist, even though he is innocent of both of those charges. Consequently, he is condemned to die as a blasphemer, a revolutionary, and murderer, even though his accusers and everyone else knows in his heart that he is exactly the opposite of these trumped-up charges. They all know that he has done all things well, that he healed every kind of disease, raised up the dead, and so on, but it was God's eternal plan that he be the Lamb of God that bears the sins of the world.

25. St. John here records an unusual bit of dialogue that also occurred in the house of Caiaphas. In this dialogue the high priest questioned Jesus about his disciples and about his doctrine. Jesus answered Caiaphas as follows: "I spoke openly to the world; I ever taught in the synagogue and in the temple, whither the Jews always resort; and in secret I have said nothing. Why askest thou me? Ask them which heard me, what I have said to them." The high priest is interrogating Jesus in an attempt to catch him in a misstatement for which they could find him guilty of a crime against the Roman Em-

pire. But Jesus eludes the trap by directing him to his disciples and listeners. That sort of answer infuriates the high priest's servant, so he tries to flatter his master by delivering a smashing blow to Jesus' face, saying, Is that the proper way to answer the high priest? Why don't you say, Oh, my dear lord high priest, I'm sorry! I was in the wrong and I plead for your forgiveness. But neither the high priest nor the servant of the high priest prove anything against Jesus by such interrogations and beatings. Therefore, Jesus says to the high priest, "If I have spoken evil, bear witness of the evil; but if well, why smitest thou me?"

26. Thus all of these things have been carefully recorded, so that we can see beyond any doubt, that our dear Lord Jesus Christ died in perfect innocence, not only in regard to his person, which is without sin, but also so far as his accusers are concerned; they can find no fault in him which would allow them to make their charges stand up before the heathen, Pontius Pilate. Contrary to what the high priest's servant claimed, the testimony of the false witnesses was contradictory.

27. Finally, since they cannot prove Christ guilty of any crime against the emperor, the high priest gets up—as recorded in Matthew and Mark—and says to Jesus, Have you nothing to say in response to the charges these witnesses have brought against you, that you plan to destroy the temple of God and then rebuild it? And since Jesus maintained his silence, the high priest became even more angry and says, "I adjure you by the living God, that you tell us, whether you are Christ, the Son of God!" Here we see how the devil effectively uses God's name and talks about him. "I adjure thee by the living God, that thou tell us whether thou be the Christ, the Son of God." They sin knowingly, and such sin is inexcusable.

28. Jesus says to them, "You have said it," or as St. Luke writes, "You are telling the truth, for I am he." Because the high priest had adjured him in the name of God, his Father, Jesus now gives an answer, whereas he had previously maintained silence. Hereby he is teaching us this lesson: When we are questioned under oath or in the name of God, we are to step up boldly and confess the truth, regardless of what the consequences might be. And he goes on to say, "I say unto you, hereafter shall ye see the Son of man sitting at the right hand of power, and coming in the clouds of heaven." In

effect he is saying, You will see and experience the fact that I am the Son of God, and I am the Lord, who will judge you and the whole world in great glory!

29. When the high priests and the council members hear that, they become filled with a raging anger and they say, Such an answer is altogether too haughty and defiant; now we have the trump card; away with him, beat him to death! That is the same as if we were to say to our opponents, Today you refuse to hear the truth; but on that future day you will have to listen to it; on that day when we will pronounce judgment upon you! On that day they would cry out, Is that a proper way to reply to the pope, the bishops, emperors, and rulers? Then the high priest would tear his clothes, pretentiously in great and holy wrath. Oh yes, what great honor and love this holy man has toward God! He cannot abide being denied the honor that is due him! He cries out, "What further need have we of witnesses?" As if to say, Wouldn't we be fools to spend more time listening to more witnesses testifying against him? You've heard him freely give evidence that he is a blasphemer against God and is therefore guilty of death; for there is no greater guilt than a man's own confession. Since he has sworn an oath that he is God's Son, and has also sworn that he will be seated at the right hand of power—which would make him equal to God, sitting in the seat of judgment—therefore he has testified against himself, manifesting that he deserves to die! Therefore we have no further need for more witnesses, because we ourselves have heard his blasphemy against God. What do you think? He must surely die!

30. Nevertheless they do not fully abide by this charge. Before the governor, Pontius Pilate, they do not charge him with blasphemy against God, but accuse him of being a revolutionary rebel against the emperor, one who leads the people astray, forbids them to pay the imperial tax, and is himself intent upon becoming both king and emperor. Then in their next breath they repeat this same charge (as St. John writes), "We have a law, and by our law he ought to die, because he made himself the Son of God." However, because that is insufficient cause and because from that moment forward the governor is seeking to release Jesus, they therefore drop this charge and reinstate the first charge, sharpening its demands even more,

saying to the governor, "If thou let this man go, thou art not Caesar's friend; whosoever maketh himself a king speaketh against Caesar."

31. This now was the hearing and arraignment which took place in the home of the high priest, Caiaphas. And it all has been recorded for our instruction, that we might know that Christ humbled himself so deeply for our sakes and allowed himself to be indicted, convicted, and killed as the greatest of evildoers. However, since he is completely innocent, even his adversaries knew in their hearts and had to admit that nothing was to be found in him to warrant a death sentence. The charges, which they later advance before Pilate, are not stated here; nor was he afterwards questioned in Caiaphas' house about this; but we shall hear about this later when we deal with the third part of the passion. However, since the same two reasons are stressed, they are tied together in a single brief, discussed, and stated as follows, We wish to charge before the governor that he is an insurgent and terrorist inciting rebellion against Caesar. In Caiaphas' home they do not discuss this matter with Jesus himself; but they confer secretly among themselves, resolving to say, We wish to denounce him before Pilate and accuse him of having stirred up rebellion in the land and making himself king. For, stirring up rebellion and making oneself king were serious matters, deserving of death, matters which Pilate could not nor should tolerate.

32. But even if the case were to have been handled in this way, these two matters would have achieved nothing before the governor. For Pilate knew very well that Jesus was not an insurrectionist, nor was he insubordinate to the emperor. For when he asked him (John 18) whether he was King of the Jews, Jesus answered and acknowledged that he was a King, but not in opposition to the emperor; for his kingdom was not of this world. He was a King, but he was born to bear witness to the truth. Yet, it could not be otherwise; he would have to die for these two reasons, as his title implies, although the very title is false and deviously fabricated for the Lord. For he is not a king opposing Caesar, nor an insurrectionist alienating the people. Therefore, it is an inflammatory title, really only attributable to the Jews. For Jesus was crucified by them as an insurrectionist and murderer, and as a blasphemer of imperial majesty who dared to organize insurrection in the land and make himself king. Pilate well

knows that Jesus is not such a man; nevertheless, under pressure he yields and has the innocent one crucified. Such were the two lethal offenses the high priests and elders falsely concoct against him, and these charges prevail. After all, insurrection is more than murder and blasphemy against the imperial majesty, since the one involved opposes Caesar and is guilty of death.

33. Third, the Evangelists, Matthew, Mark, and Luke, tell how men spit upon and slandered the Lord in the high priest's home. Who can repeat all these blasphemies? This blasphemous maltreatment went on continuously through the night until morning. The Evangelists touch on this just briefly, telling how they covered up his face and struck him in the face with their fists, toying with him, saying, "Prophesy, Christ, who is it that smote thee?"

34. As I have averred above, so I repeat now: Just as Christ of his own free will gladly became weak for our sakes, and allowed himself to be taken captive and bound, so also for our sake, of his own free will and gladly, he allows himself to be accused, mocked, spit upon, sentenced, condemned, and killed as a sinner, even though he was not guilty of death. We ought to mark this well, so that we do not explain the Lord Christ's suffering as human reason and the Jews do by saying, If he was that mighty, why didn't he resist? If he was righteous and without sin, why did he allow himself to be condemned to death? But we say, He testified clearly that it was of his own choosing and willingly that he became weak and a sinner for our sakes; otherwise, he could well have exercised his might and warded off all prisons, sentences, condemnations, and death.

35. Human reason and the Jews reproach us Christians for worshiping a God who was an insurrectionist and blasphemer. On the other hand, however, we Christians exult in this, that Christ, true God and man, suffered of his own will gladly. He did not wish to exercise his might, and his adversaries were not able to prove him guilty. What he did, he did for our sakes, so that he might break the stranglehold which sin, death, and the devil had on us. On account of our sins we deserve to suffer death, terror, and hell. But Christ takes our place and innocently endures death, terror, and hell, so that through him and in him we escape all this. Through his undeserved and innocent death he saves us from the rightful death which

we deserved, that is, from the sins whereby we merited death and hell. But if we now cling to him in firm faith, we have salvation. The Jews, who because of their clever cunning and conceit, scoff at us, will one day find out where they are headed.

We shall discuss Peter's fall another time.

HOLY WEEK

*Third Sermon**

WHAT HAPPENED BEFORE PONTIUS PILATE IN THE PASSION OF CHRIST

Matthew 27; Mark 15; Luke 23; John 18–19

1. We have now heard two parts of the passion story. First, how things went with the Lord in the Garden, where for us he endured great anxiety and agony, sweating blood because of it. Thus in his own body, in his holy flesh and blood, he prevailed in that great, hellish conflict, so that we Christians need not be terrified by it, but should cling to him who in our stead triumphed in that battle and shared his victory with us.

2. Second, we have also heard that the Lord was led captive, as an object of mockery, to Annas. However, nothing was accomplished there, but within the hour he is next hustled to the high priest, Caiaphas, in whose house he was interrogated by the high priests, elders, and the entire council. There false witnesses came forward, but were unable to cite any factual evidence against him which might constitute a legitimate charge before the heathen Pilate. It was there that Peter not only forsook his Lord but denied him three times, an incident which, by itself, requires a special sermon. For it is so very rich in comfort for all poor sinners, that a great man, an apostle, suffers such a fall and yet receives grace and forgiveness. However, sermons are preached about this often during the year; now we wish to preach briefly on the passion account, to help us understand and remember it better.

3. Now follows the third part of the passion: how the Lord fared before the governor, Pilate. In the house of high priest, Caiaphas, it became obvious, also to the consciences of the witnesses themselves, that the Lord was innocent, since the witnesses could not agree, until

*Preached Palm Sunday, March 29, 1534, at the parish church.

the high priest asked him whether he was Christ, the Son of God. But here before Pilate his innocence becomes apparent before all the people, and his adversaries and accusers have the wind taken out of their sails, not only in the council, privately among themselves, but also publicly before the Roman court. For, as stated above, criminal jurisdiction was removed from the Jews by the Romans and entrusted to Pilate as governor of the entire country. Accordingly, the Lord faced both spiritual and secular authorities, and he made an exemplary confession before the high priests and before Governor Pilate; thus not only before his own people, the Jews, who were agitating for his death, but also before the whole Roman Empire. Now everyone would perceive that he suffers innocently, and his suffering would be regarded as all the more precious in all the world. Of this third part, the holy Evangelists write as follows:

Matthew 27:1–10

When the morning was come, all the chief priests and elders of the people took counsel against Jesus to put him to death: and when they had bound him, they led him away, and delivered him to Pontius Pilate the governor. Then Judas, which had betrayed him, when he saw that he was condemned, repented himself, and brought again the thirty pieces of silver to the chief priests and elders, saying, I have sinned in that I have betrayed the innocent blood. And they said, What is that to us? see thou to that. And he cast down the pieces of silver in the temple, and departed, and went and hanged himself. And the chief priests took the silver pieces, and said, It is not lawful for to put them into the treasury, because it is the price of blood. And they took counsel, and bought with them the potter's field, to bury strangers in. Wherefore that field was called, The field of blood, unto this day. Then was fulfilled that which was spoken by Jeremy the prophet, saying, And they took the thirty pieces of silver, the price of him that was valued, whom they of the children of Israel did value; and gave them for the potter's field, as the Lord appointed me.

4. The Evangelist Matthew reports two things here. The first is that the high priests and elders of the people have taken counsel concerning Jesus and delivered him to the governor, Pilate. The second point has to do with events as they developed for the betrayer, Judas.

5. First, the record tells how the high priests and elders of the people plotted together to put Jesus to death. This deliberation

among themselves was done without and apart from the testimony of witnesses. It was a secret, clandestine meeting where they connived to formulate what they would allege and present as evidence before the governor, Pilate. Because it is a secret consultation, the Evangelist does not want to announce it at this place. But later the gist of their counseling together is submitted in the accusation before the governor. They allege and accuse Christ of being a murderer and heretic. But now they debate how they want to formulate their accusation before Pilate, namely: We want to accuse him of being an insurrectionist and a murderer; if that will not do the trick, we shall then say that he is a blasphemer and seducer of the people. There they plot secretly, but later these thoughts erupt publicly.

6. Once again we see how all that happens to Christ occurs under the aegis of the two established authorities, the spiritual and the secular, as it is written: *ut eripias animam meam a judicibus,* "that you might deliver my soul from the judges." Accordingly, Christians will not suffer at the hand of murderers, but at the hand of emperors, kings, rulers, and bishops, that is, at the hand of those who possess both swords, thus evidencing before the world that the latter commit injustice while the former suffer injustice, just as Christ suffers at the hand of both authorities and yet his innocence comes to light and wickedness is exposed, for they are doing him an injustice. The high priests have already condemned him to death, and now Pilate condemns him as well; yet both, high priests and Pilate, are the constituted governing authorities.

7. After this the Evangelist describes how Judas met his end. But I will let the case of Judas rest for now; it would take too long to talk about him. When the betrayer, Judas, sees the Lord being led from one place to the next bound in chains and handed over to the governor, Pilate, by the high priests (just like the pope burns no one at the stake, nor kills Christians, in accord with his spiritual office, but commands the emperor to do this; so the high priests do not kill Jesus, but turn him over to Pilate). To repeat, when Judas now sees Jesus bound in chains and led before Pilate, he despairs and commits suicide. Before this he felt secure, but now his hour has come. However, listen to how the high priests consult him. When he comes to return the thirty pieces of silver and says, "I have sinned in that I

have betrayed the innocent blood," they say: "What is that to us? see thou to that." Miserable consolation! We must see in Judas an example that warns against betrayers and scoundrels who do not kill Christ and yet are responsible for getting him killed.

Matthew 27:11

And Jesus stood before the governor.

8. The place for the hearing must have been a building with an open courtyard located in front of the other chambers in the building; in the same open area, on a bench, sat the governor, as judge, with the defendant standing before him, so that all the people standing outside on the street were able to see what was going on; for the court of justice discharged its functions in a very conspicuous manner.

John 18:28–32

Then led they Jesus from Caiaphas unto the hall of judgment: and it was early; and they themselves went not into the judgment hall, lest they should be defiled; but that they might eat the passover. Pilate then went out unto them, and said, What accusation bring ye against this man? They answered and said unto him, If he were not a malefactor, we would not have delivered him up unto thee. Then said Pilate unto them, Take ye him, and judge him according to your law. The Jews therefore said unto him, It is not lawful for us to put any man to death: that the saying of Jesus might be fulfilled, which he spake, signifying what death he should die.

9. Once the high priests and elders have gotten Jesus before the court, it is their plan, first, to make the accusation: God's people have interrogated this man and condemned him to death; we now hand him over to you, Pilate, and want you to find him guilty of death. For this is how their thinking went: We are anticipating that Pilate will not interrogate him any further but will let the case rest as we have presented it; for after all they are head not tail, when it comes to running things in Israel. So they feel that Pilate will take immediate action and say "Yea" and "Amen" to their entire proposal.

10. What St. John reports is that all they needed to do was state their case before Pilate and he would immediately send him straight

to the cross. But when Pilate goes out to them and says, "What accusation bring ye against this man?" they reply haughtily, "If he were not a malefactor, we would not have delivered him up to you." So their initial strategy was not to make mention of their accusation but have Pilate sentence him to death without first interrogating him.

11. Events here in the passion parallel closely what Christians experience in the world. For what befell Christ, our Head, in the world, also befalls Christians in every century. The high priests and elders want Pilate to consider their sovereignty and authority in spiritual and secular matters unquestioningly; for, since by divine law they are the people of rank in Israel, they simply cannot err or be wrong. But our Lord God intended this whole matter to come to light and not be kept under wraps. For this reason he also has the criminal court at Jerusalem turned over to the Gentiles, so that it would come to light, since the Gentiles were naturally hostile to the Jews, and, vice versa, the Jews against the Gentiles.

12. For this reason Pilate says, "Take ye him, and judge him according to your law," as if to say, If I am to punish him, then I must first interrogate him; but since you know that he deserves to be punished, and that is your obvious intention, why are you coming to me? They would gladly have dealt with him in secret and shamefully put him to death. But they wanted him to be arraigned publicly. For this reason, also, God had removed jurisdiction of the criminal court from the Jews and given it to the Romans. Now it was Roman justice, and to the present day it still is Roman law that no one be put to death without being interrogated. It was similar in the case of Festus' reply to the high priests and elders of the Jews when judging Paul: "It is not the manner of the Romans to deliver any man to die, before that he which is accused have the accusers face to face, and have license to answer for himself concerning the crime laid against him" (Acts 25:16). The same obtains among us: no one is to be executed upon one man's accusation. Also, in his law God had forbidden the Jews to do this (Num. 35:30): *Ad unius testimonium nullus condemnabitur:* "One witness shall not testify against any person to cause him to die." Deliberately, however, the high priests and elders choose to ignore this. That is why the Lord's innocence had to be made public, to their sin and shame, also before the Gentiles.

Luke 23:2

And they began to accuse him, saying, We found this fellow perverting the nation, and forbidding to give tribute to Caesar, saying that he himself is Christ a King.

13. They now began to accuse him; and this is the other part of their plan. The first tactic had failed, so they try the second. For, as stated, they had resolved that if Pilate will not listen and permit him to be judged without interrogation, we shall then charge him as follows: We accuse this man of being a subversive who is seducing the people, opposing payment of taxes to Caesar, and claiming that he is a king. Really these are two charges, but St. Luke treats them as one, while St. John construes them separately. He is an insurgent and a scoundrel, they say, for he is seducing the people into refusing payment of taxes to Caesar, and trying to make himself Caesar. For this reason he is guilty of death. This was the plan they had agreed on secretly behind closed doors, not out in the open.

14. These are serious charges. An insurgent is not only a killer and murderer of some person but a destroyer of the whole country and kingdom. For one who tries by force to get and destroy a kingdom kills and murders many people. Christ now had to bear the accusation of being an insurgent and murderer.

John 18:33

Then Pilate entered into the judgment hall again, and called Jesus, and said to him, Art thou the King of the Jews?

15. Pilate has listened to the plaintiffs. Now he asks the defendant what he has to say to this, for the principle of law is: *Audiatur alters par,* that is, "the other side must be heard." Is it true, he asks, that you are seditious and wish to be king of the Jews? John is the only Evangelist to give such a lengthy account of Jesus' reply to Pilate. However, it is not at all surprising that the Evangelists do not give all details in the same or identical words; for no narrative is so fixed that it cannot be told or described differently by another person. Nonetheless it is remarkable that St. John gives such a detailed account of the Lord's reply to the question, Art thou the king of the Jews? That,

after all, was the main accusation for which Christ suffered and was crucified. The high priests and elders reason like this: If all the other accusations lose out, this one accusation, that he has incited insurrection and forbidden taxes to be paid to Caesar, will succeed. For this reason, therefore, St. John has described it in such detail.

John 18:34–35

Jesus answered him, Sayest thou this thing of thyself, or did others tell it thee of me? Pilate answered, Am I a Jew? Thine own nation and the chief priests have delivered thee unto me: what hast thou done?

16. The Lord Jesus and the governor, Pilate, address each other directly. The Lord says, Pilate, you are a wise man; you should indeed perceive who I am; as much as to say, If this is your own idea, then you are contradicting yourself, for you surely know better. If others have told you this about me, then ask them about it, and have them prove it.

17. Like an arrogant Roman, Pilate replies, Why should I inquire about your Law and your religion? Your people and the high priests have handed you over to me; if there is something behind this which we Romans do not understand, then say it. Christ then preaches him a lengthy sermon, saying:

John 18:36

Jesus answered, My kingdom is not of this world: if my kingdom were of this world, then would my servants fight, that I should not be delivered to the Jews: but now my kingdom is not from hence.

18. This is a proper response to such an accusation and question. It is true, says he, I confess it; I have even preached that I am a King and have a kingdom; but with one difference. The situation is this: The kingdom about which I have preached and in which I am King is not a worldly kingdom. I have done Caesar no harm; nor have I harmed you, the governor, as far as your office is concerned; I have taught that one should give to Caesar what is Caesar's. For this reason my kingdom is of no concern at all to the Roman emperor. This is the Lord's defense and response before the governor, Pilate.

19. He adds moreover, Understand this very clearly; I shall in very truth prove to you that my kingdom is not of this world; were my kingdom of this world, my followers would be fighting to save me from being handed over by the Jews. So, his meaning is clear: If my kingdom were a worldly kingdom, I would have come into the city with a large army and there would have been many casualties. But I cause nothing like this to happen; no one is drawing a sword here; no one is killing anyone. No king seizes power over a kingdom without force, as I am doing. Since now no one is fighting for me—what's more, my disciples and followers are fleeing from me—just don't take my word for it but judge and see for yourself that I am not a worldly king, nor is my kingdom of this world. In this way the Lord vindicates himself against the Jews' accusation, and publicly thwarts his accusers before the governor, showing what liars they are.

John 18:37

Pilate therefore said unto him, Art thou a king then?

20. Since you are not a worldly king, and your kingdom is not of this world, and yet you confess that you are a King and have a kingdom, I now ask you, What kind of a king are you, and what kind of a kingdom do you have?

John 18:37

Jesus answered, Thou sayest that I am a king. To this end was I born, and for this cause came I into the world, that I should bear witness unto the truth. Every one that is of the truth heareth my voice.

21. Do you want to know what sort of a King I am and what sort of a kingdom I have? I will tell you. My kingdom is called and is a kingdom of truth, having nothing to do with lies and falsehoods nor with ghouls; it is, however, an eternal, enduring kingdom in which are found lasting, genuine, eternal blessings. And I am a King of truth; to that end was I born. It is my office, and I have come into the world in order to bear witness to the truth, so that the world might accept the truth. This is what I preach to people everywhere—kings, emperors, townsfolk, peasants, and people of high and low estate. In

this way Christ preached a beautiful, powerful sermon before the court and the governor, clearly differentiating between his kingdom and the kingdom of the world.

22. When Pilate hears that Jesus is not a worldly king and his kingdom is not of this world, but is a King of truth, and by his teaching and preaching, rather, furthers and helps Caesar in his kingdom, he responds, saying, "What is truth?" (John 18:38).

23. As if to say, O you poor Jesus, what a poor King you are. If you are a King of truth, you are indeed a poor King. For one who wants to become rich and attain great prominence should not begin with God and lofty title, nor make a pitch for truth. If you are going around with truth, then go merrily along; you are not disturbing me at all with your kingdom. If you are not armed, nor allow your followers to fight for you, then you will do no harm to Caesar or to me, God willing. Thus he perceived Christ's kingdom to be a make-believe kingdom, like a comedy, a kind of game.

24. That word of Pilate, "What is truth?" accurately paints our age. For the way things are going, people are wondering, What is truth? What do faithfulness and faith amount to anymore in the world? What is integrity? After they take your coat, next it's your shirt. The one who has a concern for truth is already lost. The one, however, who wants to climb the ladder of success needs to lie, deceive, dissemble, and betray.

25. So, also, the second tactic, designed to get Jesus, fails and squelches the high priests and elders. Just as they were unable to get Pilate to put Jesus to death without an interrogation, so the charge of being a seditionist also fails. Once again these "pious" people are publicly thwarted.

John 18:38

And when he had said this, he went out again unto the Jews, and saith unto them, I find in him no fault at all.

26. Thus Pilate is saying, You high priests and elders have accused this Jesus of being a seditionist and murderer; but from what I hear, he is no worldly king but a King of truth and is letting Caesar be. Also, you see that he is by himself and did not come with a crowd of followers, but proceeds more like a beggar and a poor preacher.

27. The high priests and elders become irritated when they hear this. For it must have knocked the wind out of them, these important personages and religious leaders, to be publicly called liars by a heathen judge. They say, This man is an insurrectionist and murderer. Pilate says, "I find in him no fault at all." What else is this but saying, You lie like scoundrels and rogues?

Luke 23:5–7

And they were the more fierce, saying, He stirreth up the people, teaching throughout all Jewry, beginning from Galilee to this place. When Pilate heard of Galilee, he asked whether the man were a Galilean. And as soon as he knew that he belonged unto Herod's jurisdiction, he sent him to Herod, who himself also was at Jerusalem at that time.

28. Pilate would be happy to be rid of the Jews and the prisoner Jesus. So when he now hears the word "Galilee," he logically thinks, Herod is ruler and king in Galilee; I shall send the high priests and Jews, along with the prisoner, to him. The Romans were not happy if a judge governed poorly; and if they were to hear about it, he (Pilate) would suffer for it. Accordingly Pilate would be happy to be rid of this matter. And since he now hears Jesus accused of being a King and an insurrectionist, he sends him to Herod. Reluctantly the Jews go to Herod, but they had no choice.

Luke 23:8–12

And when Herod saw Jesus, he was exceeding glad: for he was desirous to see him of a long season, because he had heard many things of him; and he hoped to have seen some miracle done by him. Then he questioned with him in many words; but he answered him nothing. And the chief priests and scribes stood and vehemently accused him. And Herod with his men of war set him at nought, and mocked him, and arrayed him in a gorgeous robe, and sent him again to Pilate. And the same day Pilate and Herod were made friends together: for before they were at enmity between themselves.

29. Now Herod is happy that Jesus is brought to him, for he thinks that Jesus would have to be fearful of him and play the hypocrite. The Jews raise a hue and cry, accuse him and say, This one is an in-

surrectionist and murderer; he wants to be king in the land where you yourself, Herod, are king; therefore, have him punished. However, Herod knew very well that there was not a grain of truth to this; for he had sharp eyes for this sort of thing and was on guard when it came to insurrectionists. Pilate and the other governors before him had also put many insurrectionists to death. If Jesus now were one, Herod and Pilate would not have allowed him to wander around the country for very long.

30. Once again Jesus is found innocent, this time before King Herod. However, Herod vilifies him, out of deference to the Jews and the governor, Pilate. The servants at court mockingly say, Is this the prophet who has performed so many signs and wonders among the people? And Herod is very displeased when Jesus does not perform a miracle in his presence. Who does this man think he is? How come he doesn't try to please and ingratiate himself with me? If he thinks me a fool, I will show him who's a fool, and he sends him back to Pilate again.

31. Once again the Jews have lost, this time before King Herod. The two regents, King Herod and Governor Pilate, both testify that Christ is innocent and the Jews are liars. For Christ should then have died even though he could honestly not be condemned while sun, moon, and stars attest to his innocence.

32. When they return to Pilate, he wonders, How can I rid myself of these people? Herod refuses to render a verdict. What am I going to do with him now? The Evangelist, accordingly, states:

Luke 23:13–17

And Pilate, when he had called together the chief priests and the rulers and the people, said unto them, Ye have brought this man unto me, as one that perverteth the people: and, behold, I, having examined him before you, have found no fault in this man touching those things whereof ye accuse him: no, nor yet Herod: for I sent you to him; and, lo, nothing worthy of death is done unto him. I will therefore chastise him, and release him. (For of necessity he must release one unto them at the feast.)

33. Herod and Pilate both acknowledge the Lord's innocence. Similarly today, yet, God calls upon those who have the authority to

acknowledge that Christians are being dealt with unjustly. But Pilate, like Herod, after getting nowhere, tries a two-pronged tactic to secure Jesus' release. First, he says to the people, You have a custom that at this festival I release a prisoner of your choosing. I have a prisoner by the name of Barabbas, who is a notorious insurrectionist and murderer (for in a rebellion he had committed a murder, and was, as Matthew states, especially well-known); I shall release either him or Jesus, who is called Christ. Pilate was cagey and so he reasoned, They will not ask for Barabbas but for Jesus, whom King Herod and I, and also they in their conscience, pronounce innocent. Therefore, he says, I would like to give you someone other than Barabbas who is the worst scoundrel among all the prisoners I have. This heathen is not worth further debate; I could well propose a lesser scoundrel to you; however, I shall not do so. Take either Barabbas or Jesus. Pilate could well have sworn an oath on this and thought that heaven would cave in before they asked for Barabbas.

Luke 23:24–25

And Pilate gave sentence that it should be as they required. And he released unto them that for sedition and murder was cast into prison, whom they desired.

34. Even though not happy about it, Pilate felt compelled, for he had made a promise to the Jews; but he never thought the Jews would ask for Barabbas. Since he is their choice, Jesus is repudiated, and Pilate must keep his promise to release to them the arch-scoundrel who was deserving of death. This is in the nature of Christian crossbearing, as it happened to Christ and his gospel—in spite of the fact that the very stones and wooden planks witness in behalf of the Lord Christ's innocence and his gospel.

John 19:1

Then Pilate therefore took Jesus, and scourged him.

35. Since Herod is of no help, nor even Barabbas, Pilate opines, What am I going to do now? Should I have him crucified? No, I will try one more thing; I'll give him a public flogging, have him scourged

so that their venomous anger is stilled, and then I can release him. Pilate thinks, Even though the high priests and Jews are still very spiteful and evil, nevertheless, when they see that I have had him publicly scourged, they will be satisfied; and so he hands Jesus over to the soldiers in the hall. There they removed his clothes and scourged him horribly. Just give such brutes an inch, and they will take a mile.

John 19:2–3

And the soldiers platted a crown of thorns, and put it on his head, and they put on him a purple robe, and said, Hail, King of the Jews! and they smote him with their hands.

36. The soldiers acted here on their own, without the governor's command. They put a purple robe on Jesus, placed a crown of thorns on his head, put a reed in his hand, bowed the knee, mocked and jeered, saying, "Hail, King of the Jews!" You have a crown for your head, a scepter in your hand, and you are robed in royal purple; so now where are your people?

John 19:4–5

Pilate therefore went forth again, and saith unto them, Behold, I bring him forth to you, that ye may know that I find no fault in him. Then came Jesus forth, wearing the crown of thorns, and the purple robe. And Pilate saith unto them, Behold the man!

37. Pilate thinks that since he has had Jesus flogged the Jews will want him released. For he personally is aghast and horrified at what he sees, so badly had he been maltreated. The Evangelist John carefully describes Jesus' exit from the hall where he had been scourged, stating how terribly torn and pitiable he looked. We can well believe that the Lord appeared dreadfully hurt since even the heathen Pilate feels sorry for him. It caused him to say, "Behold the man!" In other words, In my opinion you ought to be satisfied now because he has been so horribly brutalized.

John 19:6

When the chief priests therefore and officers saw him, they cried out, saying, Crucify him, crucify him. Pilate saith unto them, Take ye him, and crucify him: for I find no fault in him.

38. The high priests and Jews show no concern whatsoever, even though Jesus has been so horribly beaten, and even Pilate is filled with great pity. Instead they cry, Crucify him!

39. Pilate shouts back, You crucify him; I cannot crucify him because I can find no fault in him—as much as to say, You are ghouls and scoundrels.

John 19:7

The Jews answered him, We have a law, and by our law he ought to die, because he made himself the Son of God.

40. They then hurl the final accusation at him, that he is a blasphemer. The first accusation had been murderer. With this second charge they argue, How long do we have to accuse and denounce him? He is a heretic and blasphemer. He has blasphemed God in his preaching and said, I am God, and has seduced the people.

41. These are the devil's two specialties—lies and murder—and Christ must bear these innocently, as innocent Christians must also bear them. The real blasphemers, seducers, and murderers have the reputation of being holy, of being upright and pious people who honor and serve God, righteous, faithful teachers and leaders who show people the way to heaven. On the other hand, those who truly honor and serve God, and are upright teachers and leaders, are the ones who are upbraided as blasphemers of God and seducers of the people. Under that pretext the world is seduced.

John 19:8–11

When Pilate therefore heard that saying, he was the more afraid; and went again into the judgment hall, and saith unto Jesus, Whence art thou? but Jesus gave him no answer. Then saith Pilate unto him, Speakest thou not unto me? knowest thou not that I have power to crucify thee, and have power to release thee? Jesus answered, Thou couldest have no power at all against me, except it were given thee from above: therefore he that delivered me unto thee hath the greater sin.

42. Pilate becomes more fearful; for he thinks that Jesus is one of the old heathen gods. But when he boasts of his power, Jesus preach-

es him a good, pointed sermon. And since Pilate hears that this charge of the Jews is also untrue and worthless, he tries to conceive a way of setting Jesus free.

John 19:12

And from thenceforth Pilate sought to release him: but the Jews cried out saying, If thou let this man go, thou art not Caesar's friend: whosoever maketh himself a king speaketh against Caesar.

43. Now they come back to the first charge; they repeat it, hone it, and say, You, Pilate, refuse to listen and grant that this man is an insurrectionist; however, consider this: If you free this man, we will press charges against you before Caesar charging you with vindicating a man who is openly against Caesar.

John 19:13–16

When Pilate therefore heard this saying, he brought Jesus forth, and sat down in the judgment seat in a place that is called the Pavement, but in the Hebrew, Gabbatha. And it was the preparation of the passover, and about the sixth hour: and he saith unto the Jews, Behold your King! But they cried out, away with him, Away with him, crucify him. Pilate saith unto them, Shall I crucify your King? The chief priests answered, We have no king but Caesar. Then delivered he him therefore unto them to be crucified.

44. When Pilate hears that the Jews want to press charges against him before Caesar, and that Caesar might become provoked for his not having loyally discharged his official duties, he gives orders to hand Jesus over to be crucified. In letting himself be importuned by the Jews, he had no chance of winning. So when he hears that the people are threatening to write the emperor and accuse him, he renounces the testimony he previously bore towards Jesus and incriminates himself with Jesus' innocent blood.

45. But to cap it all, he, in the end, renders a judgment that shows his disagreement with the Jews, has water brought, as Matthew writes, washes his hands in front of the people, and says, "I am innocent of the blood of this just man; see to it yourselves." In other words, If something comes of this, either before the emperor or otherwise, I

want to bring this to an end and assign all the blame on you. And the Jews defiantly reply, "His blood be upon us and our children."

46. Then Pilate pronounces the sentence, I, Pilate, on behalf of the Roman emperor, condemn this Jesus to death on the cross because he wanted to be king of the Jews. The Jews pressed this sentence from Pilate, the judge, through their incessant, insistent screaming.

47. This is the story of what happened before the governor, Pilate. First, the high priests and rulers of the people try to get Pilate, as judge, to pass sentence on the prisoner, Jesus, without an interrogation. Second, they accuse him of being an insurrectionist and murderer and yet cannot sustain the charge. Third, Jesus is sent to King Herod. Fourth, the insurrectionist Barabbas is set free, and the innocent Jesus is handed over to be crucified. Fifth, Jesus is scourged and horribly beaten, and still the malicious Jews are not satisfied. Sixth, he is accused of being a blasphemer but then the Jews drop the accusation and go back once more to their first attack, sharpening their case by using the emperor's name and rank.

48. Accordingly, Jesus must die a heretic and blasphemer, a murderer and evildoer, in tune with what the people sing about him as he hangs on the cross, "If he be the King of Israel, let him now come down from the cross, and we will believe him. He trusted in God: let him deliver him now, if he will have him: for he said, I am the Son of God." However, the main reason why Christ had to die is that he was pronounced guilty of being an insurrectionist and enemy of the emperor.

49. It is that way also today. When the pope, bishops, and the malicious papists can come up with nothing against us, they say that we are insurrectionists. First, they reproach us with being heretics. When that does not stick, they say, We are disobeying the emperor; and the disobedient must be punished. Accordingly, we also must endure two of the devil's tactics—lies and murder—just as Christ, our Head, bore them. Thus it has been, and thus it will be to the end of time: the devil with his followers, seducers, liars, and murderers bears the title and reputation of being a faithful leader, faithful teacher, and source of life; but Christ, who is truthful and the true source of life, must with his disciples die a murderer, insurrectionist, and heretic. Amen.

Holy Week

About Christ's Suffering and Mission on the Cross, and the Malefactor on his Right Hand.

*Fourth Sermon**

We have heard Scripture's account of Christ's passion or suffering up to where he is hung on the cross. However, in order to complete the picture of Christ's suffering we would like to read to you what St. Luke says about the Lord on the cross.

Luke 23:32–43

And there were also two other, malefactors, led with him to be put to death. And when they were come to the place, which is called Calvary, there they crucified him, and the malefactors, one on the right hand, and the other on the left. Then said Jesus, Father, forgive them; for they know not what they do. And they parted his raiment, and cast lots. And the people stood beholding. And the rulers also with them derided him, saying, He saved others; let him save himself, if he be Christ, the chosen of God. And the soldiers also mocked him, coming to him, and offering him vinegar, and saying, If thou be the king of the Jews, save thyself. And a superscription also was written over him in letters of Greek, and Latin, and Hebrew, THIS IS THE KING OF THE JEWS. And one of the malefactors which were hanged railed on him, saying, If thou be Christ, save thyself and us. But the other answering rebuked him, saying, Dost thou not fear God, seeing thou art in the same condemnation? And we indeed justly; for we receive the due reward of our deeds: but this man hath done nothing amiss. And he said unto Jesus, Lord, remember me when thou comest into thy kingdom. And Jesus said unto him, Verily I say unto thee, Today shalt thou be with me in paradise.

1. In this fourth part of Christ's passion or suffering on the cross, I intend to deal particularly with the words which the Lord spoke on

*Preached at the parish church on Good Friday, April 2, 1534.

the cross. For we ought to look not only at this man's passion and suffering but also at what he says; for what he says explains what he is doing and accomplishing by his suffering.

2. Above all else, however, as we heard in the first sermon on the passion, we must distinguish our Lord Christ's suffering from that of the saints, in general, not just on account of his person, since Jesus Christ is eternal God, by whom heaven and earth were created and all things made, but also on account of the reason for his suffering, and the benefit and fruit resulting from this suffering. For no man's, no angel's, no other creature's suffering has accomplished and is able to accomplish what this man's suffering has. For he suffers not for his own person but for us, that in this way we might be free and rid of sin and death.

3. By virtue of the person, this suffering is extremely, indescribably great. For one drop of Christ's blood is incomparably greater than heaven and earth. There is a great difference between the killing of a king and the killing of a peasant. The greatness of the person makes the wrong committed against him all the greater. But we shall skip this now, and only state that his suffering must be highly esteemed because of its fruit and benefit, namely, that through this suffering all creation is radically altered and all things made new, heaven too. This is what the words spoken on the cross make plain, words which every Christian should know by heart.

4. The first word Jesus spoke on the cross was his prayer for his crucifiers, "Father, forgive them; for they know not what they do." These words are indeed brief but very comforting. The Lord may have spoken other words, but only these are recorded, and they are written for our consolation.

5. Now as our dear Lord Jesus Christ is lifted into the air to hang on the cross, suspended between heaven and earth, with nothing any longer on earth to call his own, he is exercising his true, real, priestly office, accomplishing the work he came on earth to do, not only with his suffering, by offering up himself, but also by his intercessions. For both constitute a priest's work, to sacrifice and to intercede.

6. The purpose of his suffering and priestly offering is, as he himself states in the Gospel (John 17:19): "For their sakes I sanctify myself, that they also may be sanctified through the truth." And John

10:15: "I lay down my life for the sheep." There it is stated that his suffering is a suffering for us, not for himself personally. Plainly he affirms in those words that he is a faithful shepherd, priest, and bishop of our souls, who accomplishes his priestly work so that the entire world may become new.

7. But when he offers himself thus for us, what garment or priestly garb does this priest, Jesus Christ, wear and what is his altar? His adornment is not a gold or silk cloak, decked with pearls or jewels, like the pope's bishops adorn themselves, nor like the Old Testament high priest who had his special priestly resplendent robes. Instead he hangs on the cross bare and naked, covered with wounds, and has, so to speak, not a thread on his body. Instead of a purple robe he is red with blood, his body covered with wounds and welts, badly swollen. Instead of a priestly headdress he wears a bloodied crown of thorns.

8. That's the adornment of this High Priest. For he is "a priest for ever after the order of Melchizedek," as Psalm 110:4 states. This High Priest is both priest and offering; for he offers up his body and life on the cross. It appears to be totally out of priestly character for him to hang on the cross, naked and bare, bloody and swollen, wearing a crown of thorns. Yet, he is the true Priest and Bishop, who in great love offers up himself and lets his own body be consumed for the redemption of the whole world. The old priesthood possessed great splendor. When Aaron and his descendants sacrificed rams, oxen, cows, and calves, it was quite a spectacle to behold, accompanied as it was by singing and clashing cymbals. But in the case of this High Priest, there is no extravagance like that.

9. The altar of this High Priest is the cross and gallows. For similar to how we now view the bar of criminal justice and capital punishment, so we must view the cross on which Christ hangs. Today we call it the holy cross, for Christ has made it so glorious; but at that time it was nothing but the gallows on which the Jews hung and executed him. This was the altar on which this High Priest performs his sacrifice.

10. It was a shameful, horrible, uncommon altar. In those days the Jews opined that the person placed on such an altar was utterly despicable and accursed. In fact it was Moses who said, "He that is hanged is accursed of God" (Deut. 21:23). When oxen, cows, and

calves were sacrificed in the temple they were brought with pomp, incense, and great ceremony to the holy, consecrated altar. But Christ, the true High Priest and preeminent sacrifice, who consecrates and sanctifies everything, is led before a public tribunal to an inglorious, unconsecrated, yes, to an altar of abomination, to be executed as a criminal. We human beings count no place so repugnant as the place where a cross or gallows stands. With a curse the man of the street says, Be hanged, and may the crows devour you! But now the cross, the most shameful piece of wood on earth, an abominable, repugnant place, becomes the altar for our high priest and bishop. There he is offered up as the most accursed man who has ever lived on earth.

11. In addition, this High Priest is slain not as the other malefactors lifted up alongside him. Sheer venom and the devil move his crucifiers. They have compassion for the two malefactors. But this man, crucified between them, is treated as the worst of malefactors. No one shows him compassion, but things are made as spiteful as they possibly can be. Everything he says is grossly distorted. The wine, customarily given to criminals in order to pluck them up, they pollute for him with vinegar, gall, and myrrh so that the suffering of poor Jesus will not be mitigated. Then he prays and cries out, "Eli, Eli, lama sabachthani," which they twist mockingly into, "He calleth Elias; let us see whether Elias will come to help him." They do not treat the other two malefactors this way. But this man has to endure it.

12. The venom poured out over this Priest and his sacrifice is so great that it cannot possibly be described. No thief or murderer dies so shamefully and disgracefully as does Jesus here on the place of the skull where scoundrels, rogues, and murderers were buried. Not only does a crown of thorns pierce his head, but he is also spit upon, vilified, and taunted. Nowhere in history does one read that a human being was ever so unmercifully punished, as was this man. People usually don't scoff at an evildoer who has been condemned or mock the person about to be executed. It's not something to sport about. Rather they offer them wine as a sedative, speak kindly, and befriend the victim as much as possible. But this High Priest is treated differently, for he must be the most shameful thief and scoundrel that ever lived.

13. That is also why he still is a sorry, contemptible High Priest to the world now, on a disgraceful, inglorious altar, himself an offering abhorred by the people. The prophet Isaiah who foretold this, says (53:2–3): "When we shall see him, there is no beauty that we should desire him. He is despised and rejected of men; a man of sorrows, and acquainted with grief: and we hid as it were our faces from him; he was despised, and we esteemed him not." When he was taken captive, he was dealt with viciously, both before the high priest, Caiaphas, and the governor, Pilate. As he was lifted up on the cross, they poured out all their venom and malice upon him; yet no amount of spitting, scoffing, and blasphemy could satisfy them. No criminal was ever so terribly inundated and maltreated, nor has there ever been a more unglorious place of sacrifice.

14. So this is now our High Priest, Jesus Christ, with his altar and offering, so terribly mistreated by the Jews and soldiers. Nevertheless, all our sins lie on his shoulders, as the prophet Isaiah clearly attests in that same passage (vv. 4–5): "Surely he hath borne our griefs, and carried out sorrows: yet we did esteem him stricken, smitten of God, and afflicted. But he was wounded for our transgressions, he was bruised for our iniquities: the chastisement of our peace was upon him; and with his stripes we are healed." And Isaiah 9:6: "The government shall be upon his shoulders." There we all are, you and I and all men, from the first man, Adam, to the last man to be born into the world. For our sakes he was taken to that despicable place and there died so shameful a death that all creation and the stones of the pavement cry out in protest at people's refusal to show him compassion.

15. Along with his priestly office and work of offering up his body on the cross, came also his intercessory prayer. Priests not only performed the sacrifices, but also interceded with God. Christ's intercession was spoken in the words, "Father, forgive them; for they know not what they do." Thus he both prays and offers himself to his heavenly Father. The Epistle to the Hebrews states (5:7), that in the days of his earthly life Christ offered up prayers and petitions, with loud cries and tears, to him who was able to deliver him from death, and that his prayer was heard, for which reason he also gave glory to God.

16. It is our comfort (and we are therefore exhorted to take comfort in this) that this High Priest has prayed for you and me and for

us all, that is, for his crucifiers. For just as he suffers for us all, so he also prays for us all. Thus his crucifiers are not only the Jews and Gentiles, who at that time laid hands on him and nailed him to the cross, but also we ourselves and the whole world. For it was our sins which crucified him, wounded, and crowned him with thorns. Those crucifiers were simply our sins' servants and lackeys. Had your sins and mine not nailed Christ to the cross, those crucifiers would have had to let him alone. Christ is there as the true Priest and Lamb of God paying for the sins and death of the whole world with his offering; that is why the Jews and Gentiles seize him. For that reason his prayer covers the entire world. When Christ prays for those who crucify him, he is praying for all men, also for us who by our sins were the cause of his cross and death; and he does not pray for our condemnation but for our salvation.

17. For this reason we should look on the gallows, the judicial proceedings, and the cross on which Christ suffered in no other way than as the altar on which Christ sacrificed his body and life for our sins, and in the midst of which he prayed, thereby manifesting his priestly office to bring us to grace, so that we would be rid of sin and be freed from eternal death. For the one who takes away sin also takes away death. The fact is, "The wages of sin is death," as St. Paul teaches (Rom. 6:23). Consequently, where sin has been removed, there death has no more power. And where there is no death, there likewise is no hell or devil, but lasting righteousness, life, and salvation instead. Since by his sacrifice and prayer on the cross Christ has rooted out sin, neither death, nor devil, nor hell have any claim on us.

18. All of this Christ accomplished on the cross, not by reason of our works and merit, but by reason of his body and blood, by his becoming a curse for us and dying on the cross for our sins, and not least, by praying for sinners. This is to be our joy and consolation, and for this we ought to thank Christ with all our hearts and diligently preach about it.

19. Under the papacy this also was preached about. Disregarded, however, were the words and story which are so clear and true that Christ sacrificed himself on the cross for our sakes and prayed for us. Instead they went about teaching another way to salvation, urgently exhorting people to be priests themselves, bring their own sacrifices,

and with their own works repay God and earn eternal life. And today still, the pope and his adherents condemn our doctrine because we teach that we are saved alone by Christ's body and blood, which he sacrificed on the cross. Indeed, is this not a terrible vehemence, blindness, and judgment that has fallen upon these people, that year after year they preach everywhere of Christ's passion and his death on the cross for us and yet rant against us, curse our doctrine as heresy, and condemn us for promoting this teaching and pointing people to this sure, everlasting comfort? That is (as Isaiah threatens the despisers of God's Word) to see with the eyes and yet be blind, to hear with the ears and yet be deaf, to have an obdurate, insolent heart. For what else can one say when they are so blind? They even teach and confess that Christ offered himself for us; yet they persecute and shed the blood of those who proclaim and believe this. They extol the High Priest, Christ, as the brilliant sun because he offered himself on the cross for our sins; and yet they rush to put a monk's hood over a dying man, place a paternoster chaplet in his hand, and say that he must trust in his works, in indulgences, in a miserable hood, in Masses, and so on; and thereby they pitiably deceive people. The light shines into their eyes; they see well; but they still do not understand.

20. Clear and manifest it is that Christ, our one and only High Priest, proffers us his wounds and tears and says, Father, here am I, a mediator between you and mankind. I am a man and have brothers who are mired in sins and in peril of death and hell; but I am dying for them, I am offering myself for them, I am gracious to them, and so on. This our opponents hear and see, yes, confess and preach, but at the same time they clamor and rant so against it and condemn us as heretics. So be it, it is God's avenging wrath; and may God graciously protect us against it. Were God ever to let us fall, may it be into such sins that we feel and confess, not into that which opposes itself against his grace, vaunts itself in so doing, extolling it as righteousness and holiness.

21. Therefore, let us open our hearts and view our High Priest Christ in his true glory. If you let your reason guide your ears and eyes, and perceive only how disgracefully, miserably, and wretchedly he hangs on the cross, you will find no more adornment on him than Aaron had. However, if you are guided by God's Word and look into Christ's heart, you will

find his beauty and dress embellished with every virtue, and a treasure of such worth that we shall never be able to thank him enough.

22. That is so because, in the first place, he is adorned with truly perfect and absolute obedience toward the Father, so that in accord with his will and to his glory, he allows himself to be spit upon, scourged, tormented, and shamefully put to death. How glorious this adornment is we will never comprehend in this life. Nevertheless, this much we are able to discern from God's Word, that all rubies, precious stones, pearls, the finest velvet and pure gold, are as nothing compared to it.

23. The second aspect of his adornment is his great love for us, his whole heart being aimed at helping us. His suffering does not deter him; indeed he hardly gives it a thought, so greatly is he concerned about us and our distress. First, he prays for us, "Father, forgive them; for they know not what they do," and only then prays for himself, "My God, my God, why has thou forsaken me?" and, "Father, into thy hand I commend my spirit." Who can tell all that deserves to be said about such love and adornment? His heart overflows with more ardor than the entire world could ever understand or muster. In his greatest suffering, torment, and disgrace, he appears not to see or feel anything; his only concern, all that he sees and cares for, is your and my misery, our anguish, and great distress.

24. Could there be greater, more fervent love than that? If someone were to take a look at his enemies in such a way as to intend to help them in their distress, shame, scorn, and mockery, and while himself suffering did nothing else but help his enemies, every reasonable person would have to grant this to be greater love than if father and mother were to walk through fire or be slashed with a knife in order to rescue their children from danger. Paternal and maternal love is very strong. It's part of its nature not to feel adversity and pain. But this man has the interest of his enemies so at heart that he does not think about his own misery; his only concern is how they might be helped. The heart of our loving Lord Christ burns as if he were being dragged through fire, suffering, blood, spear, crushing load, and wounds, and yet he embraces us with great love and mercy, prays for us, and says to his Father, I am here for their sake, Father, forgive them; for it is for their sake that I am enduring all this.

25. This, then, is the glory with which our great and everlasting Priest is adorned. It is a raiment we must view and discern with spiritual eyes. Outwardly one does not see it. Instead, Christ appears to be a malefactor, rogue, and scoundrel above all scoundrels. But inwardly we discern—and his words attest it—that his heart is adorned much more beautifully than the sun and earth's greatest glory. For there is, first of all, sincere and willing obedience toward his Father; then, on our behalf, love, mercy, patience, gentleness, and all virtues heaped together. It is a beautiful cloak and priestly splendor far different from that of Aaron, the high priest. And it's been my purpose to apprise you of this, in order to make it clear why Christ suffered.

26. Accordingly, in all the segments of his suffering we should have our eyes fixed especially on this point and never lose hold of it, nor let it be taken from us. The chief point simply is this, that Jesus Christ, God's Son, offered himself on the cross for us, and there was nothing else that moved his heart but our distress and misery. For you and I, all of us, are implicated in the wounds, thorns, and spittle, because by those very wounds, thorns, and spittle, he snatches and grabs at us in order to deliver us.

27. We need to know this article not simply for the sake of comfort, but also to gird us against the devil's poison that is poured into people through the pope and others directing them to heaven through their own righteousness, merit, and works. But had this been possible to achieve by our works, why would it have been necessary for Christ, God's Son, to suffer and endure such great pain? But now he stands there and intercedes with his Father, saying, I, the High Priest, am bringing my offering, my body and blood, in all obedience and patience, praying that you will be gracious to poor sinners and forgive them their sins, also that you will be their Father and have regard for my person and offering. His prayer was not only spoken with his mouth but also substantiated by what he did; it truly accomplished what was required, expunged our sins, and reconciled us with God, whether we believe it or not.

28. This is evidence enough to show that by our works we are unable to accomplish the likes of this; for to obtain forgiveness of sins is not as easily achieved as the papists and teachers of works think. The works the pope has commanded are indeed difficult, but they

are not for that reason impossible. Not much is required to put on a hood, keep the vigil, fast, and sing, all of which may be good to do. However, by doing these things nothing is really accomplished. If one is to obtain forgiveness of sins, something other and greater than your or my works must be there; God will be slow to hear me because of my fasting, vigils, and praying; for the truth is, as Isaiah says, that he was wounded for our transgressions and was bruised for our iniquities; he bore all our griefs.

29. Now, the papists have to admit that the suffering and death of the Lord Christ are far and above my praying, my good works, my suffering, my almsgiving, and my fasting. The one who wants to employ these things against sin, death, and the devil will assuredly accomplish nothing. In order to atone for sins and bear the wrath of God another man is needed, other works and merits required, if sins are to be atoned for and God's wrath borne. The one who wants to bring his own merits and works to bear in this situation and employ them against sin, blasphemes Christ's vicarious death and intercession, since he thinks as much of his offering and prayer as he does of Christ's sacrifice and prayer. We must diligently guard against such abomination.

30. But now the Lord does not merely petition in a general sort of way but singles out those for whom he prays, saying, "Father, forgive them; for they know not what they do." Many are disturbed over why the Lord spoke this way; however, the simple explanation is that he wants to underscore two kinds of sins. Some sins are those which a person acknowledges to be sins; other sins, those which a person does not recognize. Some people know that they are doing wrong and continue doing so unabashedly, out of hatred and loathing for known divine truth. It is called sinning against the Holy Spirit when one continues to insist that it is right. Such people sin knowingly and out of malice, persist in these deliberate sins, do not desist from them, do not pray to be forgiven for them, like our prelates, the papists. They well know that our doctrine is right, that Christ has commanded the Sacrament to be received in its entirety, has not forbidden marriage, has in no way mandated the sacrifice of the Mass, also, that Christ has died for our sins, and so on; and yet they condemn us as heretics for such things, and rebuke their followers

when they learn that they are devoted to our teaching and the Sacrament as Christ instituted it. These leaders sin not in ignorance, but against the Holy Spirit. Now, whether in accord with his will our Lord God could turn one or the other of these people away from such sins, is beside the point; for it is in the nature of such sins that they cannot be forgiven, since they run headlong against grace and the forgiveness of sins, inasmuch as forgiveness of sins requires both that one must confess the wrong and be absolved of it, and also pray for forgiveness.

31. There are also those sinners who sin in ignorance. This you have to understand in this way: David knows well that he is doing wrong and is sinning against God when he takes Uriah's wife and has Uriah killed. However, in that instance evil, lust, and the devil drive him so fiercely that he falls into these sins before he can ever give thought to what he is doing. Later, however, he confesses his sin, regrets having done it, wishes that he had never done it, and asks for mercy. All of us have such sins hanging around our necks, where all too easily and unawares, we become ensnared and fall, at times coerced by the devil and by our flesh, at times by fear (as Peter), at times by carelessness and folly because we do not understand, at times by being secure and arrogant. These sins Christ bore on the cross and petitioned in their behalf. For they are sins which do not militate against grace. This kind of sinner does not say, I have done right; but stands naked and stripped, admits and confesses his sins, and prays for forgiveness. That is why we see many a poor thief, many a murderer, many a harlot, and other wicked people coming to grace; for they do not offer excuses for their sins but confess them, acknowledging that they have done wrong, petitioning for forgiveness.

32. This, therefore, is a necessary distinction we must make: that Christ's vicarious sacrifice and intercession stand between all sin and God. God will not impute them as long as they are confessed and the penitent holds fast to this High Priest with his offering and intercession on the cross. However, sins which stand opposed to grace and are not acknowledged to be sins, like the blasphemies of the malefactor on the left and the high priests, these are not included here under Christ's prayer. A great difference obtains between the sins which a person acknowledges as sins and the sins which he does not

acknowledge to be sinful. The sins which a person acknowledges as sins, be it unbelief or weakness in faith or other failings, are all careless sins. God does not want to reject me on account of such sins but is ready to forgive me as long as I confess them to be sins, pray for grace, and lay hold on Christ. However, the sins, which a person does not acknowledge as sins but offers excuses for them, are not trivial; for they do not want to be considered sins but contend against grace.

33. Our papists and their adherents knowingly and willingly do not want things to be otherwise; nor do they want to acknowledge their sinfulness or have a desire for Christ's offering for sins. They sin against the Holy Spirit and repudiate God's grace. Christ does not pray here for them but for those who do not know what they are doing; these are to take comfort in his sacrifice and intercession and know that their sins are forgiven.

34. So much in brief about Christ's prayer on the cross. With it he is telling the reason for his suffering there, so that these sinners who sin unknowingly and are contrite might know that because of his offering they have a gracious God, who does not want to impute their sins to them, but graciously forgives them.

35. The other thing which Jesus says on the cross is to the malefactor on his right, "Verily I say unto thee, Today shalt thou be with me in paradise." The malefactor on the left blasphemes Jesus and says, "If thou be Christ, save thyself and us." But the malefactor on the right rebukes him and says, "Dost thou not fear God, seeing thou art in the same condemnation?" and so forth. He then turns to Jesus and says, "Lord, remember me when thou comest into thy kingdom." Then Christ directs him to the kingdom of heaven and says, "Today shalt thou be with me in paradise." This is a beautiful heart-stirring story, the likes of which you can find nowhere else.

36. For, in the first place, it is a great miracle and very comforting that this malefactor on the right, who is justly condemned to death—temporal and eternal, just like the malefactor on the left, and possesses no good works, but on account of his sins has reason to be fearful of God, nevertheless courageously and confidently trusts that Christ will receive him into his kingdom.

37. Second, it is also a great miracle that this malefactor and murderer pays no heed to the deep offense when he sees how Jesus is con-

demned, blasphemed, and shamed by both the spiritual and temporal authorities. For the Jewish leaders mock him and say, "He saved others; let him save himself, if he be Christ, the chosen of God." The soldiers mock him also, give him vinegar to drink, and say, "If thou be the king of the Jews, save thyself." And posted above his head is the superscription: "Jesus of Nazareth, the King of the Jews." The malefactor on the left, likewise, blasphemes him and says, "If thou be Christ, save thyself and us." In short, everyone is offended at him, in fact counts him as done for, including the disciples, who, though they stood around the cross for a while, no longer had any hope. It is only the malefactor on the right who takes no offense because of him, to the point that he even rebukes the malefactor on the left. Indeed, it is a great, powerful vexation, shocking the whole world, that Christ dies such an ignoble death. Nevertheless, this malefactor struggles right on through all this with such great faith that he dares to call Christ, who hangs next to him on the cross, a Lord and King. Who has ever heard of anything like this? He reproves the entire world of lies and takes no note of what other people think or say about him, but addresses him as an everlasting King. Others look upon Jesus as a wicked person and a fool, but he calls him a Lord, declares that he has a kingdom and earnestly begs that, when he enters his kingdom, he would remember him. By now it was apparent that none of them would live the night through. But he believes that Christ is a Lord of another, of an eternal, life. Indeed his was a strong and glorious faith, a wonderful confession, in view of how the whole world despairs of Christ and holds him in lowest esteem.

38. This is how we ought to esteem Christendom, as the handiwork of God, while all the world crumbles, the Jews and Gentiles blaspheme and crucify Christ, the disciples forsake him, and meanwhile God enlists this malefactor. Thus today he still wants to uphold his Christian church. Should all fall away from Christ—emperors, kings, pope, bishops, the high and mighty and wisest on earth—God still will retain a few who possess his Spirit and confess him before the world. It is, therefore, a comforting picture and example for all Christendom that God does not want faith in Christ and confession to become extinct. If the disciples, along with others who are kindred to the Lord Christ, do not confess or believe, but out of fear deny,

are offended in him, and go away, then a malefactor or murderer must come forward to confess this Christ, preach about him, and teach others what we are to think about him and what comfort we should find in him. For our Lord God does not want Christ to be without people to confess him, even though it be only a thief on the gallows or a murderer on the torture wheel.

39. Accordingly, this is a comforting story from which we learn what kind of people Christ has in his kingdom, who find their way to him and to whom he wants to show the fullness of grace, namely, they are sinners who confess their sins and with all their heart plead for grace; they indeed shall find grace and forgiveness. For in keeping with his intercession he now confirms it in very fact that the reason for which he came is that he wants to forgive the sins of those who confess their sins, yearn for forgiveness, and believe; for as soon as this malefactor pleads guilty and appeals to Christ, in that very moment he is heard and becomes the firstfruits of the Lord's intercession on the cross.

40. Why doesn't Christ first take care of Peter or some of the other saints? Why does he allow the firstfruits of his prayer to be a scoundrel and murderer whom he redeems and saves from sin and eternal death through his blood and wounds? Answer: By this he wanted to show that his kingdom is meant not for saints but for sinners; that it is for the comfort of all poor sinners that they firmly believe and do not doubt that Christ did not die for the righteous but for the unrighteous and sinners, as he himself says, (Matt. 9:13): "I am not come to call the righteous, but sinners to repentance." For this reason the one who thinks he would like to die holy and without sin will enter that "heaven" where flames leap up to the window and devils dance. For the one who is unwilling to acknowledge his sin never stands in need of the Lord Christ and his suffering. But he did not die for himself but for sinners!

41. For this reason we should regard this story as an example in which Christ substantiates, in deed, what he sought to do and did accomplish by his suffering, inasmuch as he makes a saint out of a murderer on the cross, who does not remain in sin but becomes a saint in eternity. Of course, Christ did not die in order for sinners to remain and continue in sin. He died in order to redeem them from sins

and to change them so that they become upright and holy, just as we see happening here with the malefactor. Out of this person Christ makes a saint for eternity (for he does not remain a scoundrel and murderer but is converted), and out of the gallows and death, which the malefactor, as he himself confesses, has deserved, Christ makes a divine altar of worship, so that he no longer suffers as a murderer but as a Christian and a true saint. For he dies confessing and believing in Christ, repents of his sins with all his heart, and intends, should God permit him to live longer on earth, to sin no more. By such faith he receives the happy verdict that he not only is rid of his sins, but is saved and possesses the promise that he will be an heir of paradise.

42. Thus we have now shown the fruit of Christ's suffering: first, in the words of his intercession; and then, also by the word of his work and deed as he promises paradise to the malefactor on his right who calls upon him for help. This example we should emulate and not be influenced by coarse, godless people who carry on and say, I shall go on sinning so that Christ might redeem me and demonstrate his grace on me. No, never. Heretofore our flesh was filled not merely with sickness and filth, but also with sins. But while before we were caught up in sins and in death, that is no reason for us to continue in sins. Now it must be our concern how to crawl out of this, how to become reconciled with God, and ever more and more, by God's grace, sweep sin out. So much, then, for the two words of Christ on the cross. May God grant us his grace to keep and remember this. Amen.

HOLY WEEK

*Fifth Sermon**

About the Events of Christ's Burial

We have considered the passion and the events of Christ's suffering up to the last episode when he was placed in the tomb and the tomb secured. The Evangelists John and Matthew write of this event as follows:

John 19:31–42

The Jews therefore, because it was the preparation, that the bodies should not remain upon the cross on the sabbath day, (for that sabbath day was a high day,) besought Pilate that their legs might be broken, and that they might be taken away . . . But when they came to Jesus, and saw that he was dead already, they brake not his legs: But one of the soldiers with a spear pierced his side, and forthwith came there out blood and water. And he that saw it bare record, and his record is true, and he knoweth that he saith true, that ye might believe. For these things were done, that the scripture should be fulfilled, a bone of him shall not be broken. And again another scripture saith, they shall look on him whom they pierced. And after this Joseph of Arimathea, being a disciple of Jesus, but secretly for fear of the Jews, besought Pilate that he might take away the body of Jesus; and Pilate gave him leave. He came therefore, and took the body of Jesus. And there came also Nicodemus, which at the first came to Jesus by night, and brought a mixture of myrrh and aloes, about an hundred pound weight. Then took they the body of Jesus, and wound it in linen clothes with the spices, as the manner of the Jews is to bury. Now in the place where he was crucified there was a garden, and in the garden a new sepulchre, wherein was never man yet laid. There laid they Jesus therefore because of the Jews' preparation day; for the sepulchre was nigh at hand.

*Preached publicly in the afternoon of the Saturday before Easter, 1531.

Matthew 27:62–66

Now the next day, that followed the day of preparation, the chief priests and Pharisees came together unto Pilate, Saying, Sir, we remember that that deceiver said, while he was yet alive, After three days I will rise again. Command therefore that the sepulchre be made sure until the third day, lest his disciples come by night, and steal him away, and say unto the people, He is risen from the dead: so the last error shall be worse than the first. Pilate said unto them, Ye have a watch: go your way, make it as sure as ye can. So they went, and made the sepulchre sure, sealing the stone and setting a watch.

1. There are two incidents here: first, the Jews begged Pilate to remove the bodies of Christ and the thieves from the cross; second, the grave was to be made secure until the third day.

2. The reason why the Jews wanted the body of Christ taken down were twofold. The first is given by the Evangelist John who stated that, because it was the Sabbath it was a special day; the second referenced Moses' precept that a victim's body should not remain on the cross overnight, but should be buried that same day before sundown. If a corpse remained overnight on the cross, the countryside would be designated unclean and sinful because such a person was an abomination before God. The Jews, having previously maneuvered Christ to judgment by an accursed death on the cross, now begged that he and the murderers, as individuals cursed by God, be removed from the cross so that the countryside not be designated unclean. In this way, the Jews figured that they were protecting and defending themselves against any criticism of not having obeyed God's Law to the letter. That's why they had persisted in crying out for his crucifixion, yelling without letup, "Crucify, crucify!" For they reasoned that once he was on the cross, God's Law which states that a crucified individual was cursed by God would protect them from criticism by the people. They didn't anticipate that God would put a hole through their plan and foil their scheming, nor that God would move the robber on the cross to openly testify of Christ that he was innocent, the Lord of life, and the Saviour of the world. Much less did they anticipate that God would resurrect his Son.

3. Also, there was the binding requirement of the Sabbath, the highest and most revered of all the festivals. Nothing was holier than

the Sabbath, as Moses stated (Lev. 23:3): "But the seventh day is the sabbath of rest, an holy convocation; ye shall do no work therein: it is the sabbath of the Lord in all your dwellings." The other three festivals, the Feast of Unleavened Bread (or Passover), the Festival of Weeks (or Pentecost), and the Festival of Booths (Tabernacles), were all great and glorious festivals, but the Sabbath was the greatest and most sacred. The Sabbath was ordered in the Ten Commandments which Moses calls the Ten Words (Precepts). That is why it is called the highest; the other festivals were designated but not ordered in the Ten Commandments.

4. Whether that was the intent of the Jews or whether they had some other reason for their haste, I do not know. Maybe they thought that since he was not yet dead, his legs should be broken to add to his misery. Or if that wasn't their intent, perhaps they just couldn't wait until he died. So they hurried to demand that Pilate remove the body from the cross without delay. They weren't satisfied that he was condemned to death and raised on the cross, but begged that his legs be broken or that he be stabbed to hasten his death or increase his agony. It seems nothing satisfied their grim hatred—not even that he was condemned to death, and that judgment was meted out to nail him to the cross. Eagerly they awaited the moment he would die. But how his body would be cared for and how it would be buried was of no concern. Their only concern was that he be dead. His body could be devoured by birds and wolves as far as they were concerned. If only he might be dead and be removed from the cross as one accursed by God, then by their calculations they would have won. His burial was the least of their concerns.

5. As a matter of fact, they are not worthy to take his body from the cross to bury it or see to it that others bury it. They did not deserve such honor and privilege, like beloved children of God, that they should bury Christ's body. The Holy Spirit had called other people for this, namely, Joseph and Nicodemus. They were inspired with courage and bravery: Joseph, petitioning Pilate for the body of Christ; Nicodemus, arranging for the burial. They were disciples empowered by Christ's suffering. Before they had been anxious and frightened; now they are confident and courageous. Christ's sacrifice and prayers on the cross penetrate and bear fruit. The thief at

Christ's right was the first fruit of Christ's death; Joseph and Nicodemus, the second. They, like the thief, became courageous. Joseph went to Pilate to ask for the body of Christ; Nicodemus brought an hundred pound weight of myrrh and aloes. Once they were secret disciples of Christ for fear of the Jews; now, they are his disciples and confessors openly.

6. These were men of power and influence. Joseph hailed from Arimathaea and was a wealthy man, an esteemed official in Jerusalem. Nicodemus was a Pharisee and a member of the Sanhedrin. Thus in that very hostile crowd of high priests, scribes, Pharisees, elders, and people in general, Christ at his death finds two gallant men to claim his body that hangs disgracefully on the cross, and to give it burial most honorably, discounting all risk to life and limb, to earthly possessions and reputation. Now they have greater faith, confidence, and courage than when the Lord was alive, so great is the fruit and power of the suffering and death of Christ.

7. The second incident is that the Jews ask Pilate to place a guard for three days at the tomb where Christ's body lies buried. Will wonders ever cease? What a series of events because of their godless plans! How they maneuver, how they fuss, how they scurry around! The high priests, the Pharisees, and the elders have now accomplished what they wanted. Christ has been crucified, he is dead, his body has been taken down from the cross like they wanted—their purposes have been accomplished, but they still are not satisfied. They are nervous and fearful because of the crucified man who is dead and has been buried. Before Pilate they use the excuse that his disciples might steal the body and say that he is risen. However, in their hearts they have not forgotten the Lord Jesus' words which he had spoken while still alive, namely, that in three days he would arise. This was a sharp stinging thorn in their minds. What if it were true? What will happen to us if he arises from the dead?

8. There is a warning here: Let us not be confused about the man who is crucified, Jesus Christ. See what happened to the Jews! Let their example be a warning for us. They wanted to tangle with him; now, however, he leaves them no peace or rest.

9. The Jews became so uneasy that their deed would lead to shame that they offered the guards at the tomb a generous

amount of money to say, "His disciples came during the night and stole the body while we were asleep." Pilate, however, had the grave guarded and placed his seal on it, and the guards, placed by the Jews themselves, gave strong testimony that the disciples had not stolen the body. But what difference does that make with such wicked people? Even though they have been assured by their own guards, yes, and know in their minds that the tomb was secure, nevertheless they remain implacable and hard like an anvil. This brief is a summary of the fifth incident of the passion, the burial of the Lord.

10. However, what is the most important, the vital part of the passion is that we not only know the details of his suffering, but that we understand the reason for it and the fruits of his suffering. That is why we must remember the details of the suffering and engrave them on our hearts, never to be forgotten. For in the details of the passion are many points, bits and pieces, that testify and remind pious hearts how Christ suffered for us and for our sins. Through these examples and attestations, our forebears (without doubt many of whom were saved) were sustained when they, too, heard and learned from the details of the Passion how Christ died for our sins. So beside the details of the passion, we must also point out the purpose of Christ's suffering. Now that purpose we confess in our Creed when we say, "I believe in Jesus Christ who suffered, was crucified, died, and was buried," and so on. Why was he crucified and why did he die? In order that you might have the forgiveness of sins and be saved, as we confess in the third article of the Creed: I believe in the forgiveness of sins, resurrection of the body, and life everlasting. All this has been made possible through Christ's suffering and death. By the working of the Holy Spirit, we confess Christ, and through faith in him receive forgiveness of sins, life, and salvation. Therefore, the most important aspect of the passion is that we preach and learn why Christ suffered and died, namely, for our sins and that he has saved us from sin, death, and hell.

11. Now then, in order that we might gain deeper appreciation for the power and the benefit of Christ's passion and be strengthened thereby, let us hear the text of the 53rd chapter of the prophet Isaiah which deals with Christ's suffering and resurrection.

Isaiah 52:13–53:12

Behold, my servant shall deal prudently, he shall be exalted and extolled, and be very high. As many were astonished at thee; his visage was so marred more than any man, and his form more than the sons of men: So shall he sprinkle many nations; the kings shall shut their mouths at him: for that which had not been told them shall they see; and that which they had not heard shall they consider. Who hath believed our report? and to whom is the arm of the Lord revealed? For he shall grow up before him as a tender plant, and as a root out of a dry ground: he hath no form nor comeliness; and when we shall see him, there is no beauty that we should desire him. He is despised and rejected of men; a man of sorrows, and acquainted with grief: and we hid as it were our faces from him; he was despised, and we esteemed him not. Surely he hath borne our griefs, and carried our sorrows: yet we did esteem him stricken, smitten of God, and afflicted. But he was wounded for our transgressions, he was bruised for our iniquities: the chastisement of our peace was upon him; and with his stripes we are healed. All we, like sheep, have gone astray; we have turned everyone to his own way; and the Lord *hath laid on him the iniquity of us all. He was oppressed, and he was afflicted, yet he opened not his mouth: he is brought as a lamb to the slaughter, and as a sheep before her shearers is dumb, so he openeth not his mouth. He was taken from prison and from judgment: and who shall declare his generation? For he was cut off out of the land of the living: for the transgression of my people was he stricken. And he made his grave with the wicked, and with the rich in his death; because he had done no violence, neither was any deceit in his mouth. Yet it pleased the Lord to bruise him; he hath put him to grief: when thou shalt make his soul an offering for sin, he shall see his seed, he shall prolong his days, and the pleasure of the Lord shall prosper in his hand. He shall see of the travail of his soul, and shall be satisfied: by his knowledge shall my righteous servant justify many; for he shall bear their iniquities. Therefore will I divide him a portion with the great, and he shall divide the spoil with the strong; because he hath poured out his soul unto death: and he was numbered with the transgressors; and he bare the sin of many, and made intercession for the transgressors.*

12. In these verses we hear how the prophet Isaiah prophesied concerning the Lord Christ's suffering long ago. He points out very definitely that such suffering was foreordained and indicates that it was to be a sacrifice to pay for our sins and secure redemption for the human race. The prophet describes the suffering of the Lord almost

more clearly than the Evangelists in the New Testament. In the entire Scripture of the Old Testament there is no place where the purpose of Christ's suffering is so precisely and clearly delineated as in this text. Truly, we can say that this chapter of the Old Testament is an exemplary summary of that purpose, just as St. Paul's Epistles are in the New Testament. That is why every father should read it often to his children, so that they might learn it by heart and that our youth might become familiar with it and be strengthened in their faith.

Behold my servant shall deal prudently, he shall be exalted and extolled, and be very high. As many were astonished at thee; his visage was so marred more than any man, and his form more than the sons of men.

13. Christ was to be a great glorious and exalted King, but at the same time also the kind of person who would jolt and offend many. He would be a glorious, but also a controversial King because his appearance would utterly lack in comeliness. The prophet sets forth both: a great King, but repulsive to look at, so that no one would turn his eyes toward him. With that, the prophet wishes to warn the Jews and everyone else about the offensive visage of Christ. He will hang wretchedly on the cross, die a miserable death, and project an offensive image. Be careful, therefore, and be forewarned.

So shall he sprinkle many nations; the kings shall shut their mouths at him; for that which had not been told them shall they see; and that which they had not heard shall they consider.

14. "To sprinkle" here means to preach, as Moses used the word in Deuteronomy 32:2: "My doctrine shall drop as the rain, my speech shall distil as the dew, as the small rain upon the tender herb, and as the showers upon the grass." Just as the drops of rain and dew sprinkle grass and herbs, so also the drops of God's Word descend upon people. What the prophet wished to say was this: Even though this King, Christ, would be so disfigured and marred, yet will he sprinkle the nations, that is, his battered appearance would be proclaimed around the world. The Gentiles would come to hear of his awful, tortured appearance, how he was piteously nailed to the cross and how his own people were shamefully angered and offended by him. Kings

will hush before him and prostrate their wisdom under this King's feet. This King who was crucified shall be so exalted that the kings of the world will be pleased to hearken to his wisdom.

For that which had not been told them shall they see; and that which they had not heard shall they consider.

15. Though the Jews were offended by this King, the Gentiles who were called accepted him.

Who hath believed our report? And to whom is the arm of the Lord revealed?

16. How wonderful will the preaching of this sermon be! But who will believe it? The Jewish people will not; instead they will be offended. They expected the promised Messiah to be an earthly king. Because this King had no earthly domain, they would not believe that he was the promised Messiah. Yet this King will be exalted and his kingdom will sprinkle the Gentiles. He will reign through his Word, and in no other way. Then will be revealed to the Gentiles that he is the arm of the Lord. They will understand how mighty he is, namely, that he has conquered death, overcome the devil, and taken him into captivity. The Jews will say, He is dead, how can he help others? However, the Gentiles will recognize and believe that he is the only Saviour and helper against sin, death, and the devil.

For he shall grow up before him as a tender plant and as a root out of a dry ground.

17. So, in that way he grows; first his kingdom becomes a delicate shoot but soon it grows into a great tree by God's grace. The shoot had no fertile soil and no moisture, yet it thrives. The gospel and the kingdom of Christ thrive in the midst of trouble and turmoil. Like dry arid land on which nothing can grow, that is how the Christian people are despised and ignored by the world. Nevertheless, by God's grace the tender plant thrives. On both counts, his person and his kingdom, Christ receives no recognition from the world. The gospel is maligned, so that it has no esteem, but is considered foolish and suffers

persecution; yet it prospers. All the world figured that after three days we would be as nothing; nevertheless, we are still here and growing.

He hath no form or comeliness; and when we shall see him, there is no beauty that we should desire him. He is despised and rejected of men; a man of sorrows, and acquainted with grief: and we hid as it were our faces from him; he was despised and we esteemed him not.

18. People don't desire this King, but flee from him, as from the devil, because he is so lowly and so persecuted. The Jews look for a way out and say, In Holy Scriptures it is written that there will be two Messiahs, one who will suffer, another who will not suffer, but will be glorious. They interpret this text of the prophet to mean that two Messiahs will come, the one who came long ago as a beggar, the other, a glorious King, for whom they are still waiting. But words are very plain and clear, and definitely refute this interpretation of the Jews. For it is precisely indicated here that he will be of miserable appearance and yet glorious in the selfsame person.

19. The Jews were unable to reconcile these two aspects, the miserable form and the glorious majesty. That's why they gave up on a suffering Messiah and beggar, and focused instead on one who would be a mighty, glorious King. But they are overruled. The words are clear, that both the despised and the glorious Messiah and King are one and the same person. The prophet clearly states that the Messiah and King would be grossly despised and rejected, yet also most glorious. What is said does not portend two Messiahs, two persons, two Kings, but one Messiah and King, one and the same person. The Messiah will be so despised that people will scowl and say, I don't like that King. That's how the gospel is received today yet. People don't want to hear it; don't want to see; can't tolerate it. Yet he will be glorified, according to the prophet, even though he is despised. The devil, the world, and death force themselves on him, yet they cannot thwart his kingdom.

Surely he hath borne our griefs and carried our sorrows.

20. The prophet describes this King as a sorrowing person. But now why does he sorrow? Why the suffering? The reason is because

"he hath borne our griefs." The text is so wonderfully plain. This King's suffering is our grief and sorrow. What we should have borne eternally, that he assumes. The pain we deserved—to die eternally, hunger, thirst, suffer, and so on—has been placed upon him. His suffering has been for me, for you, for us all—for our benefit.

Yet we did esteem him stricken, smitten of God and afflicted. But he was wounded for our transgression, he was bruised for our iniquities.

21. That is true. As we have heard, Moses himself said, "Cursed is everyone that hangeth on a tree." For that reason he was railed upon as a condemned and accursed man. He couldn't help himself; how was he to help others? But they failed to look at him rightly. The fact is, he is carrying our sorrows. From outward tokens it appears that he is damned; but from a spiritual perspective we understand that he is bearing all our sorrows, yours and mine. The prophet repeats the reason why Christ suffered when he says that he was wounded and bruised as one rejected by God, and that this happened to him on account of our sins. This we must earnestly bear in mind, all the more so because under the papistry the suffering of Christ has been so obscured, that what the prophet Isaiah and the apostle Paul have written was largely lost sight of by us, who were led away from Christ's suffering to our own works. For this reason we should engrave the words of the prophet on our hearts as he says, "He was wounded for our transgressions, he was bruised for our iniquities."

The chastisement of our peace was upon him; and with his stripes we are healed.

22. He is punished; we have peace. I, you, all of us have angered God; for that he needed to atone, so that we might be redeemed from sin and obtain peace. He suffers; we go free. The indulgence hawkers assured us that our desperate beads of sweat and gross carousings would, by the pope's indulgences, be freed from pain and punishment. They directed us to believe that our souls must suffer in purgatory, when in reality (even as they spoke) they already had departed in grace and love. Does not the prophet say, "The chastise-

ment of our peace was upon him," in order that it might be well with us and we might enjoy good days? This great love and grace no person should ever so shamefully forget. The great harm the devil caused us in paradise has been healed by Christ's wounds.

All we like sheep have gone astray; we have turned every one to his own way; and the Lord hath laid on him the iniquity of us all.

23. None of us kept on the right path. We all went astray like sheep. There was no redemption from sin, no salvation, we all went astray. The only way to salvation is through Christ's suffering and death, because our sins are placed on him and he is punished for them. Whoever strays from this way and does not look for peace in Christ is on the wrong road. We must set these words against the pope and all the works-righteous. It is incredible that one could be so blind and not regard this text, especially when it is sung every day in the *responsoriis.* Indeed the pope's followers sing it to this day, and yet do not understand it rightly. The prophet states it very clearly, The Lord placed on him not only the sin of one individual, but the sins of all people. You cannot rescue yourself from even the smallest of sins. So, if you want to be helped, you need to have this man's wounds before you. It is most deplorable that in the abominable darkness of the papacy people were not aware of this. But now it is even much worse, that in the bright light of the gospel people refuse to see.

He was oppressed and he was afflicted yet he opened not his mouth: he is brought as a lamb to the slaughter, and as a sheep before her shearers is dumb, so he opened not his mouth.

24. The prophet here points out how Christ suffered, that is, how patiently, never even uttering a word of complaint. St. Peter points this out, (1 Peter 2:23): "Who, when he was reviled, reviled not again; when he suffered, he threatened not; but committed himself to him that judgeth righteously." Here the apostle points out the meaning of the words, "he opened not his mouth." Not that Christ did not speak during his suffering, for the passion account tells how

on the cross he prayed to his heavenly Father and also spoke with his mother, Mary, and his disciple John. But he did not scold, did not curse, did not threaten, nor say, Watch out, you doubting Jews, you are going to be paid back. He did not seek revenge, nor did he say, Father, punish those who crucified, ridiculed, and despised me. But he suffered like a sheep which does not cry out against its shearer. Swine and other animals squeal and bellow, but a sheep does not cry out or curse its butcher or shearer. Christ's suffering was excruciatingly great and severe, so that he had every reason to complain and threaten, but he neither complained nor threatened, reasonable though it might have been for him to do so. But here there are only words of patience, compassion, benevolence, love, and gentleness; there is no evidence of anger, impatience, or revenge. With heartfelt willingness he suffered for our sake, wishing no retribution, harboring no feelings of revenge. It is as the prophet said, "So he opened not his mouth."

He was taken from prison and from judgment; and who shall declare his generation?

25. He will die, and yet at the same time live. He will be transported out of this life where people taunted, judged, damned, and mocked him, and be placed into another life. Even though he died and was buried, nevertheless, he did not remain in the grave in terror, judgment, death, and mockery. None of this could any longer affect him. All that is past and, praise God, all judgments as well. He is no longer in anguish, no longer subject to the shameful, mocking verdict, judgment and death. For now he has been transported to the place where he lives in highest glory. Through the words of the gospel the Holy Spirit will reveal and proclaim him in all the world. This has happened in richest measure, so that he has also now come to us in these latter times.

And who shall declare his generation?

26. The prophet has now declared that Christ died and that he yet lives. One might ask how long shall he live? The prophet says that no

one will be able to tell the length of his life; in other words, his is eternal life. He says both things of Christ, that he will die and yet that he has life eternally. In the same way the apostles teach that Holy Scripture testifies that Christ would die and be resurrected from death, as St. Paul states (1 Cor. 15:3–4): "For I delivered unto you first of all that which I also received, how that Christ died for our sins according to the scriptures; And that he was buried, and that he rose again the third day according to the scriptures." Thus, also, the prophet here states that Messiah will die and yet will attain to a life that cannot be spanned, in other words, eternal life.

For he was cut off out of the land of the living: for the transgressions of my people was he stricken.

27. This is said in the manner of the Hebrew tongue. "Life" in Hebrew means to be of pulsing vitality. That is why the prophet says he was torn from the land of the living, meaning that he is no longer among people who live and breathe day by day, but rather in another place and life. This happened at the time when he was punished "for the transgressions of my people." If he is punished "for the transgressions of my people," it follows that he will be torn from the land of the living. The prophet Isaiah wishes to lock the reason for Christ's suffering into our hearts; that is why he repeats so frequently. At the time when he is punished for the transgressions of my people, he would depart from this life.

And he made his grave with the wicked, and with the rich in his death; because he had done no violence, neither was any deceit in his mouth.

28. That is as much as to say that he was judged and killed as a godless man. The Hebrew speech designates a rich man as a godless man. The rich man's epitaph will be as Christ says (Matt. 19:23): "A rich man shall hardly enter into the kingdom of heaven." The rich place their confidence and trust in their riches and are generally godless people. David, though he was king of Judah, nevertheless is not rich, as Psalm 132:1 testifies: "Lord, remember David and all his afflictions." People who have much sorrow and grief are not rich. Our

sovereign Duke John, even though he is a prince in the realm, nevertheless is not a rich man. But H.G., M.J., and B.B.M. are rich.*

29. That is why Scripture equates a rich man with an ungodly man who relies on his riches. The prophet wishes to say that Christ died as one worthy of death and the devil, although he was not an ungodly man. In his entire life not the slightest evil deed is to be found, nor in his teachings one tiny false word. Rather, in his teaching there is nothing but truth, and in his life nothing but innocence and holiness. In other words, he did not die for his own sake, for he did not deserve death; rather he is innocent and just in all his preaching and works.

Yet it pleased the Lord to bruise him; he hath put him to grief.

30. That he was crushed is God the Father's gracious and good will. Christ was not guilty—he did not deserve this. But thus it graciously pleased God that by the innocent death and cross of his Son our sins would be wiped out and we be saved. Thus, also, Christ said in the Garden, "Not as I will, but as thou wilt." Neither the Law of God nor the ruler Pontius Pilate had any claim against him personally but it was in accord with the Lord's gracious and good will.

When thou shalt make his soul an offering for sin, he shall see his seed, he shall prolong his days, and the pleasure of the Lord shall prosper in his hand.

31. The prophet has indicated up to this point the reason for Christ's suffering, namely, that he suffered for us and for our sins. Now he also addresses the power and fruit of this suffering, in that across the world many will embrace and benefit from this suffering, rejoice that Christ suffered for them and thank him from the bottom of their hearts. "Guilt offering" means a sacrifice to pay a debt. "Seed" refers to beneficiaries and offspring. So the prophet wishes to say that Christ, by his suffering and death, would pay our debt and therewith gain many offspring. Even though he has neither a wife nor household, nevertheless, he will have a multitude of children. The prophet speaks of the Messiah (Isa. 9:6), as "Everlasting Fa-

*The references apparently are to Duke George of Leipzig, Margrave Joachim of Brandenburg, and the Bishop of Mainz, Joachim's brother, Albert.

ther." If he is to be an everlasting Father, he must have children and heirs in abundance.

32. In order, therefore, that the Jews can't say, The Messiah has no wife, so how can he have offspring? the prophet adds that the Messiah will have many children because he has yielded his life as a guilt offering. The fact that he has children is because he gave himself as a guilt offering. He lives, and his children will also live with him. He draws children to himself by baptism and the gospel. We and all believers are his seed, his children, born through Word and Sacrament. We have not earned being his seed, the children of God, but Christ has acquired and earned this for us because he took and carried our guilt himself.

And the pleasure of the Lord shall prosper in his hand.

33. What Almighty God had in mind was to be accomplished through this King. That which God purposed through him, to redeem the world from sin, death, and hell, would certainly be accomplished. Even though emperor, king, Turks, pope, world, devil, death, and hell stand opposed, yet they will not be able to hinder God's plan. God will entrust his plan into Christ's hand and through his hand carry it out, not by the emperor's might and sword, nor through the pope's work and holiness. Christ, God's Son, will do it. For he alone died for us; he alone carried all our sins.

He shall see the travail of his soul and be satisfied.

34. I will reward him well, says God, because he permitted himself to be in such travail. Because he suffered, he shall, after his death, experience joy. I will resurrect him from the dead and fill him with rapturous joy in abundance forever.

By his knowledge shall my righteous servant justify many; for he shall bear their iniquities.

35. This text is the main point of this chapter and, therefore, we must heed it diligently over against the pope and those who teach

works-righteousness. The prophet points out very clearly how we ought to grasp the salvation earned by Christ. We human beings are all sinners and eternally lost. If we are to be made righteous and be saved, it must happen through Christ. Because we can only be justified and saved through him, it was necessary that he be more than a perfect man. Human power and might can justify and save no one. God alone can do this. Now since the prophet testifies of Christ, that he will justify all who believe on him, he is testifying that Christ is not only true man, but also true God.

36. The prophet declares that Christ will justify many "by his knowledge," not by man's works, strength, wisdom, or holiness, but only because they have come to know him. The bottom line is that our justification is solely dependent on our confessing Christ, that is, believing that he died for our sin and God placed our punishment on him. This we must firmly believe and not despair of because of our sins. When we find comfort in his suffering and death and believe that he, the righteous and innocent Saviour, has paid for our sins, then we perceive him correctly. That is a powerful thunderbolt against works–righteousness; it topples all monastic ritual, monastic life, and human holiness. Here one must resort to a bit of ancient wisdom, which states *bene definire et dividere,* "to delimit and divide correctly." To accept Christ is not a matter of a cowl, clerical collar, a Mass, pilgrimage, good work, or merit, and the like; but rather we must hear what the prophet says of Christ in Holy Scripture, accept, and find comfort in him alone. The pope and the devil also hear this message, but they do not accept it. When I, however, confess and receive this message, it enables me to overcome sin and death.

37. The prophet says that Christ will give us his Word, understanding, and his Holy Spirit, who will write it into our hearts convincing us of its truth. The thief at Christ's right had such understanding as we learn from the passion history. He could do nothing other than confess in his heart that Christ is the Lord of death and life, even as he stated, "Lord, remember me when thou comest into thy kingdom." You and I, and everyone else, must do likewise, convinced of the worth of Christ's suffering.

For he shall bear their iniquities.

38. How does he justify mankind? By taking their sins upon himself, as John the Baptist says of him, "Behold the Lamb of God that taketh away the sins of the world." Those who confess him to be that, and believe that he carries their sin, know him rightly. Justification, in the Christian sense, is not my work, my merit, my obedience of the Law, but rather that I firmly believe that Christ has borne my sins.

Therefore will I divide him a portion with the great, and he shall divide the spoils with the strong:

39. I will give him a multitude of the heathen, God promises. Because of Christ the devil will be robbed of many of the high and mighty of this world, the wise and the powerful, and the devil will not be able to thwart him.

Because he has poured out his soul unto death: and he was numbered with the transgressors; and he bore the sin of many, and made intercession for the transgressors.

40. From the history of the passion we learned how Christ was crucified between two murderers and how from the cross he prayed in behalf of poor sinners. Therefore, two truths are juxtaposed: that Christ died, and that he is Lord over all. If he died, he must be a true natural man. If he is to bring people to receive him in faith and win many as his reward, snatching away the strong for his booty, then he must be true God. The prophet cannot emphasize this enough and for that reason repeats it so often: Christ died for us, bore our sins, and was shamefully killed as the vilest malefactor. Because he did that, God says, I will exalt him.

We have covered this chapter in cursory fashion. Christians should read it often and meditate upon its meaning.

HOLY WEEK

*Maundy Thursday**

On the Lord's Supper

As you know, today we are celebrating the institution of the blessed Sacrament of the Body and Blood of our Lord Jesus Christ. For although we constantly preach sermons on this blessed Sacrament, it, nevertheless, has been common practice to set aside special days for the consideration of its origin and beginning. So we want to speak about it now on the basis of our text and under God's gracious guidance. The Evangelist Luke writes as follows:

Luke 22:7–20:

Then came the day of unleavened bread, when the passover must be killed. And he sent Peter and John, saying, Go and prepare us the passover, that we may eat. And they said unto him, Where wilt thou that we prepare? And he said unto them, Behold, when ye are entered into the city, there shall a man meet you, bearing a pitcher of water; follow him into the house where he entereth in. And ye shall say unto the goodman of the house, The master saith unto thee, Where is the guestchamber, where I shall eat the passover with my disciples? And he shall shew you a large upper room furnished: there make ready. And they went, and found as he had said unto them: and they made ready the passover. And when the hour was come, he sat down, and the twelve apostles with him. And he said unto them, With desire I have desired to eat this passover with you before I suffer: For I say unto you, I will not any more eat thereof, until it be fulfilled in the kingdom of God. And he took the cup, and gave thanks, and said, Take this, and divide it among yourselves. For I say unto you, I will not drink of the fruit of the vine, until the kingdom of God shall come. And he took bread, and gave thanks, and brake it, and gave unto them, saying, This is my body which is given for you: this do in remembrance of me. Likewise also the cup after supper, saying, This cup is the New Testament in my blood, which is shed for you.

*Preached at the parish church on Maundy Thursday, April 2, 1534.

1. So far, the account of what took place at the Lord's last supper. What is described here must be distinguished from the Sacrament of his Body and Blood. For in this scene it is not the Sacrament of Christ's Body and Blood that is treated, but the eating of the paschal lamb, concerning which Moses had issued instructions in the Old Testament. The Law prescribed (Exod. 12) that in the afternoon of the fourteenth day of the first month, around five or six o'clock, the Jews were to begin the observance of the Festival of Unleavened Bread, or the Passover, which was to be celebrated for seven days. They were to rid their houses of all leaven and leavened bread, and for seven days eat unleavened bread only; also, on the first day of this Passover observance they were to eat the paschal lamb.

2. This same Jewish Passover, according to our reckoning, is being celebrated on the evening of this particular day by Christ and his disciples. He states, "With desire I have desired to eat this passover with you before I suffer: for I say unto you, I will not any more eat thereof, until it be fulfilled in the kingdom of God." His meaning is, I have had the earnest desire and heartfelt longing to eat this Passover with you; for it is the last Passover I shall celebrate with you. For with this Passover, the Mosaic and Jewish Passover, priesthood, kingdom, and worship are being brought to a close, and I am beginning a new Passover in my kingdom of the New Testament. So now I wish to eat the last Passover with you, namely, in order to bring its observance to a close.

3. The Jews were required to eat the old Mosaic paschal lamb in the following manner: They had to have their loin cloth girdled about them, sandals on their feet and staffs in their hands, eat in urgent haste, fully prepared for departure. It was the Lord's Passover; therefore, one and all were to have their sandals and girdles on, equipped as pilgrims who were ready to leave quickly. Just as a bearer of a message stands at the table, and eats and drinks in haste, in order to refresh himself before taking his leave, so the Jews had to eat their paschal lamb. In like manner Christ and his disciples stood ready—or, as the Evangelist says, reclined there—with sandals on their feet and staff in hand, eating in haste, as though ready to depart.

4. This eating of the ancient paschal lamb the Lord celebrated with his disciples as though it were his last, not merely as one who is eating

and drinking with another before departing this life, but also as regards further observance of the Mosaic Law. The Jews were required to celebrate the Passover in order to extol and praise the grace and mercy of God, for their deliverance and establishing his rule and priesthood among them, and choosing them as his people. The Passover was to call to their remembrance this blessing and stir them to give thanks to God for it. All this Christ now terminates. It would no longer be necessary every year to observe the deliverance from Egypt, nor would there be need for the Jewish kingdom and priesthood any longer. All this should now come to an end and become obsolete, even though it had been ordained by God through Moses.

And he took the cup, and gave thanks, and said, Take this, and divide it among yourselves: for I say unto you, I will not drink of the fruit of the vine, until the kingdom of God shall come.

5. This, likewise, has nothing to do with the Sacrament of Christ's Body and Blood but is the final drinking of the cup associated with the Passover. As though the Lord were saying, We are sharing a farewell drink of remembrance. I am drinking it with you as it was ordained through Moses, but henceforth it will be no more. With this cup and drink I shall dismiss the ancient paschal lamb, and there shall henceforth be a new Passover and a new paschal lamb, of the New Testament.

6. In this manner Christ celebrated the old Passover with his disciples. And we should bear in mind that we are properly to distinguish this from the Sacrament of Christ's Body and Blood. True it is that a person eats and drinks here just as he does in the Sacrament. But here it is simple bread and wine only with which Christ for the last time celebrated the old Jewish paschal lamb, kingdom, priesthood, proclamation, and thanksgiving for the deliverance from Egypt. Thereupon he immediately institutes a new paschal lamb, a new kingdom and priesthood, a new proclamation and thanksgiving, as follows:

And he took bread, and gave thanks, and brake it, and gave unto them, saying, This is my body which is given for you: this do in remembrance of me. Likewise also the cup after supper, saying, This cup is the New Testament in my blood, which is shed for you.

7. Here now the Lord institutes the Sacrament of his Body and Blood. And this text ought to be committed to memory, for it is not long, and at the same time it is very plain and clear. Our Lord Jesus Christ did not wish to burden us with a lot of ordinances, as the Jews were in the Old Testament. He does nothing more than take bread and wine and say, "Take, eat, this is my body; drink, this is my blood"; or, "This is the cup, the New Testament, in my blood"; also, "This do in remembrance of me." Let us then open our eyes and prick up our ears and firmly apprehend these words.

8. Above, when the Lord gives his disciples the cup, stating, "Take this, and divide it among yourselves," he does not say, "This is my blood," but, "This is the fruit of the vine whereof I shall not henceforth drink." But here, when he takes the bread, he says, "This is my body"; and when he takes the cup, "This is my blood," or, "The New Testament in my blood." So, we do not here have mere bread and wine, but the bread is his Body, which he gives to eat, and the wine is his Blood or the New Testament in His Blood, which he gives to drink. For this is what the words state, "He took bread," "he took the cup," and he adds the words, "This is my body," "This is my blood," or, "This cup is the New Testament in my blood." These words cause the bread to be his Body and the wine his Blood. Whosoever then eats this bread eats Christ's true Body; and whosoever drinks this cup drinks Christ's true Blood, be he worthy or unworthy.

9. This we are steadfastly to believe. For Christians are to give glory to God and to confess that what God says, he is also able to do. St. Paul writes (Rom. 4:21) that this was true of Abraham. Whoever wishes to be a Christian should not be like the fanatical spirits who question how it is possible for bread to be Christ's Body and wine to be Christ's Blood. They have their own ideas of God and want to comprehend him with their reason; therefore, if something does not rhyme with reason, God also is unable to do it. But just why is it that man has puzzled about this for so long? The more man struggles over it, the less he is able to comprehend our Lord God with human reason. For our Lord God is not a God who allows himself to be mea-

sured and comprehended by human reason, nor are his works and words to be subject to the canons of human reason. St. Paul says (Eph. 3:20): "[God] is able to do exceeding abundantly above all that we ask or think." Why is it then that we torment ourselves by presuming to resolve and establish that God's Word and work must conform to our reason? If God says it must be so, then because it is God's Word and he is all-powerful and truthful, he is able, also, to effect what he says.

10. Therefore, we should hold steadfastly to these clear words of our Lord, The bread he proffers is his Body, and the cup or wine is his Blood, or the New Testament in his Blood. In childlike faith we should partake, without doubting, and believe it to be so. We should give thanks to Christ for such grace, rejoice over it, and strengthen our hearts by it, considering why Christ has done what he did, not disputing whether he is able to do it. Impertinent are the hearts which question why Christ did it this way and doubt that he is able to do it.

11. None of us is able to comprehend what our eyes behold here. Nor are we really able with our reason to explain how it comes about that we fall asleep and then awaken. When I open my eyes, my view extends for several miles. Also, the voice of one preacher reaches many hearts and ears. Such are the things I see and hear, and yet I cannot comprehend how they happen, even though I should break my neck over it. Now, since we do not understand things with which we are in daily contact and experience, why do we want to be master and judge of God's great works which are hidden from us? Our tongues make rattling noises in our mouths, rouses itself to action, and emits understandable words. No one is able to understand how this comes about. Nor is anyone able to tell us how hair grows on our heads. Now since you cannot comprehend how things you daily experience come about, dear friend, give glory to Christ for the truth he speaks when he says, "This is my body," "This is my blood," even though you do not understand how it is possible.

12. It is very troubling when people try to make God's works conform to their reason. We cannot even measure or grasp things with which we are in daily contact. How then can we measure or grasp what God declares only in his Word and wherein we have no compe-

tence and experience whatever? For this reason we should give God the glory and let him be all-powerful and truthful, and believe that he is able to do what he says. That a cow eats hay and grass is something which you are able to judge and reason about. The same is true for things like gold, silver, stone, wood, corn, and so on. What a man is to make out of all this is something to cogitate about; there you can be as proficient as your ability allows. But human reason will never be able to explain the things God effects, how the eyes come to see, the ears to hear, and man's tongue to speak. Let the learned, wise, and clever smart alecks go on with all their sharp reasoning to dispute, question, and investigate; they will never be able to basically state how the simplest thing God does comes about.

13. Therefore, we should leave God's Word and work undisputed and ask only who has spoken the Word and who has done the work, whether God or man has spoken it, whether it is God's or man's work. If it is God's Word and work, close your eyes, do not dispute and inquire as to how it comes about, but believe that God is all-omnipotent and truthful in his words and work. I should allow myself to be baptized in the name of the Father, and of the Son, and of the Holy Spirit, and believe that through the washing of regeneration, I am cleansed of all my sins and not dispute about how it all comes about. For there stands God's Word, command, and promise, "Go ye therefore, and teach all nations, baptizing them in the name of the Father, and of the Son, and of the Holy Ghost. Whosoever believeth and is baptized shall be saved."

14. So, in clear words, Christ also says here, "Take, eat, this is my body; drink, this is my blood; this do in remembrance of me." Therefore, in the Sacrament, under the bread and wine his Body and Blood are truly and essentially proffered and received. For it is his Word, command, and ordinance. This is not something which man has spoken, but Christ himself has ordained, instituted, and commanded it. For just as baptism is not man's word and work but Christ's, in like manner this Sacrament also is not man's word and work but Christ's alone. How it comes about we shall not be able to ascertain with our reason. For that matter I cannot fully understand how I am able to see, hear, read, even though I sense it all. Much less should I expect to be able to know how it happens that in the Sacrament Christ dispenses his Body and Blood.

15. If you don't want to be misled, give up listening to the disputing of the fractious spirits with their subtle, critical questions; rather look to the benefit and joy you are to receive from this Sacrament. Of his own will Christ ordained and instituted it most freely and lovingly. It is of no consequence whether Christ was standing or reclining with his disciples when this took place; but what is of consequence is that we hold to his Word, institution, command, and ordinance.

16. It is not a difficult task. For eating and drinking come naturally, things we would much rather do than anything else. Yes, eating and drinking are the happiest things in the world for us to do. As the adage has it, Eating comes before the dance; also, Where the belly is full, you'll find a happy man. In a word, eating and drinking are a pleasant, necessary task which a human being learns quickly. It is this pleasant, necessary routine which our dear Lord utilizes and says, I have prepared a joyful, delightful, and delicious meal; I don't wish to lay on you some hard, difficult task, like donning a monk's hood, going on a crusade to Jerusalem, being circumcised, slaughtering and sacrificing animals, washing garments, as commanded in the Law of Moses. But I am instituting a supper: When you come together in my name and wish to preach and teach about me, then take bread and wine and speak these words over the elements, and know that my Body and Blood will be there, truly and essentially.

17. Since our dear Lord now undertakes such a loving and necessary task, and prepares such a delicious, comforting meal, it is astonishing that people find it so hard to partake of the Sacrament, and shun it. To them, preaching about the Sacrament is a nuisance. Exhort them to commune, and they will regard it as a greater nuisance. Indeed, for they have anxieties; they must first become righteous and let off sinning. Under the papacy it was not surprising to see that people, when burdened with such thinking, were hesitant and fearful of it. In that context this comforting Sacrament was corrupted with gall, vinegar, and wormwood, and the joy which should have been in the Sacrament was taken from us. For this is what was taught: We are to be so pure that not the least particle of daily sinning remains in us, so holy that our Lord God would barely be able to bear with our great holiness. I was not able to find that in myself, and so I became terri-

fied at the Sacrament. And this terror, which I acquired under the papacy and to which I became accustomed, still clings to me, when I ought to be approaching the Sacrament gladly.

18. It is true, we ought to be righteous and forsake sin. For if you love sin more than God's grace, then you ought to stay away from the Sacrament rather than to partake of it. But people should certainly not be scared away from the Sacrament, for it is a lovely, comforting repast. Christ did not institute a Sacrament where he dispenses poison and death to us. For since we previously were drowning in sin and death, there was no need to add poison to poison. Pay attention to his words and you will hear him saying, I gave my life and shed my blood for you. He does not say that he gave his life and shed his blood in order to harm you; but he did this for you, for your benefit, to your comfort and strengthening, for the redemption of your soul, so that you might show more and more revulsion for sin, and more and more become a stronger Christian. So Christ does not give you the Sacrament of his Body and Blood to act as poison and death for you. It is like when he baptizes you and puts you in the water, not to drown you, but that through the same blessed washing from sin you will be redeemed and born again, in order that by grace you will become a new man; so he gives you his Body and Blood to eat and drink in this Sacrament, not to hurt or destroy you, but to quicken you and give you new life.

19. For this reason we should diligently learn what the benefits and purpose of this Sacrament are, and why indeed Christ has instituted it for you, for me, and for us all. When I become conscious of my sin, that I have been a knave and a disobedient child, that the devil has taken me captive, that I have not done what I ought to have done, then it is that I should go to this table and receive the Sacrament, in order to get rid of my sins and be refreshed. People who are conscious of their sins and sincerely desire to be rid of them should be urged to receive the Sacrament and not regard it as a judgmental occasion to be feared, but as welcome and comforting food for distressed souls. Undoubtedly it occurred under the papacy that people came to fear this Sacrament. But Christians should be instructed to approach it with joy, confident and comforted, saying, I am a poor sinner, I need help and comfort, I wish to attend the Lord's Supper,

and take nourishment from the Body and Blood of my dear Lord Jesus Christ. For he instituted this Sacrament so that all hungry and thirsty souls might be nourished and refreshed. He will not reproach me, much less hold me back, if I but come in his name to receive his help and comfort.

20. And even though this treasure and rich comfort, which clearly are to make this Sacrament a happy, joyous repast for us, were not there, we should still partake of it, in order to honor our Lord God, who has commanded us to do so. Many ancient fathers called it "Eucharist," a thanksgiving. Under the papacy it came to be called a sacrifice, that is, to define it accurately, a divine service. When I preach God's Word, I offer a sacrifice; when with all your heart you give ear to God's Word, you offer a sacrifice; when we pray for or give help to a needy neighbor, we are bringing sacrifice. So also when I receive the Sacrament, I am offering a sacrifice, that is, I am doing God's will, I am confessing and giving thanks to God, who has given us this Sacrament along with all the blessings of the kingdom of heaven, as he has commanded me.

21. It may well be called a sacrifice, not that the Sacrament itself is a sacrifice, but that the receiving or use of the Sacrament is to be called a sacrifice, not a sacrifice for sin but an offering of thanks and praise, where I confess that Christ died for my sin. The pope has made the Sacrament into a sacrifice, and a sacrificial action whereby the entire world is reconciled with God. Yet neither the Sacrament nor its use is a work offering whereby God's grace and help can be merited and won. But the use of the sacrament or the remembrance of Christ, as the Lord himself calls it, is a thank offering wherein we acknowledge and give thanks to God for our redemption, justification, and salvation solely by grace through Christ's suffering, death, and shedding of blood. Just as the preaching of the gospel is *sacrificium laudis,* that is, a thank offering in which we praise and thank God for having given us the treasure of his Word, so also the reception of the Sacrament is a thank offering. Hence, whosoever receives the Sacrament thereby shows that he is expressing gratitude to Christ for his suffering and grace.

22. Therefore, if its rich comfort does not move us to receive the Sacrament, we should at least reflect on the honor of our Lord Jesus

Christ and partake of the Sacrament often, so that he will be praised and honored by such remembrance and receive our gratitude. In a similar way, Moses kept the remembrance of the exodus and deliverance from Egypt alive among the Jews, so that when they ate the paschal lamb, they were required to praise and give thanks to God for delivering them from Egypt, leading them through the Red Sea, and giving them the kingdom and priesthood. It was a joyous repast for them. And today still the Jews celebrate it as a glorious event and eat the paschal lamb, happily, as though dancing merrily. Thus Christ wanted to keep alive a remembrance of his suffering and death among his people of the New Testament. Therefore, when we partake of the Sacrament, we should give thanks to him for his deliverance, not from Egypt and the Red Sea, but from sin, death, devil, hell, God's wrath, and every affliction. This should not be a frightening experience for us but one of pure joy and laughter, particularly in the spirit, so that we serve, praise, and give thanks to God for the grace and blessing shown us in Christ. For this reason we should willingly and happily go to the Sacrament, in all confidence saying, I, too, shall attend upon the true paschal lamb, and eat and drink of the Body and Blood of my dear Lord Jesus Christ, hold him in remembrance, and thank him for his redemption, so that I may not be found among the despisers and the ungrateful, who throw this precious redemption to the winds and disdain it.

23. Christ says, "This do in remembrance of me," With the words "of me" he annuls the remembrance of the Old Testament paschal lamb, which called to mind the deliverance from Egypt and the promise of the kingdom and priesthood. In a word, it was a remembrance of a salient happening and was ordained to proclaim the deliverance from Egypt, for which blessing the Jews gave thanks to God. Now he says, Just as the Jews in the Old Testament sacrificed the paschal lamb and ate unleavened bread, and by this eating and drinking remembered how with these great signs and wonders God had delivered them out of Egypt and slavery and given them the land of Canaan, a land which they had not developed, along with houses fully furnished that they had not built, and vineyards and olive groves which they had not planted, so, when you partake of my Sacrament in the New Testament, you should call to remembrance that I died

for you, that I gave my life into death and hell and shed my blood for you, thereby bringing an end to death, sin, hell, and God's wrath.

24. This is a different deliverance. It is a spiritual, eternal deliverance, whereby we are set free not from an earthly king but from the devil, who is a king of sin and death. He is that pharaoh from whom Christ has delivered us, and by this rescue he has brought us not into a material but into an everlasting kingdom and priesthood, where we shall be kings and priests forever. These are his deeds and blessings which have become ours, not by our wisdom, righteousness, strength, and power, but by his having procured them for us by his Body and Blood, given and shed for us. This is what he gives us in the sacrament, and for this we ought to praise and thank him.

25. That is the service we render God in the New Testament—like the service of the Jews in the Old Testament—that when we receive the Sacrament, we proclaim with heart and mouth that Christ has shouldered our guilt and expunged our sin through the sacrifice of his Body and Blood. We ought to celebrate our Passover by extolling and praising the man who bears the name of Jesus Christ for his great, boundless redemption and for the everlasting kingdom and priesthood which he has won and granted us through his Body and Blood. He alone has conquered sin and death, in himself, in his Body and Blood. And this is what he grants to us, and as a sure sign, pledge, and seal, he gives us his Body to eat and his Blood to drink in the sacrament.

26. Ah, dear Lord God, how frightful and dreadful it has been under the papacy, where this Sacrament has been so shamefully distorted; and yet what a frightful and dreadful situation, on the other hand, will be created in the world if we do not make proper use of this Sacrament and thank God for his unspeakable blessing. In the papacy very little worthwhile has been preached either about the Sacrament or about its use. Relative to the passion we have hardly had the bare text explained. What has been taught about the Sacrament is this: You must comply with what the mother church, that is the Christian church, requires of you and be obedient to its teaching; also, you must show sorrow and remorse, worthily prepare yourself, and perform this work of obedience. Nothing was said about the joyous, comforting, and precious repast which we ought to have in the Sacrament or about faith. The Sacrament thus became simply a human work.

27. Now you see that Sacramentarians and Anabaptists have sprung up everywhere. They are particularly overbearing and impertinent spirits because they do not thank our Lord God for his grace and blessing. Yes, our Lord God must even be in the wrong and endure rebuke from them for lying; they turn his Word around, refuse to partake of the Sacrament, do not praise and extol God, but seek their own esteem, honor, and praise. We must, therefore, pray God to grant us his grace and preserve in us a true understanding of his Word and Sacrament; especially, however, a true understanding of his Holy Supper so that we may receive it with joy and give thanks to Christ for his goodness and love.

28. But someone might say, Are we to proclaim nothing but that Christ died for us? Isn't it enough to preach about this one time only? I have heard it so often and know it so well. Answer: The Jews were required to hold the deliverance from Egypt in remembrance not only once, but always, year after year. But should we Christians trouble ourselves continually to repeat the remembrance of the deliverance Christ wrought for us from sin, death, devil, and hell? Are you among those who say, I have heard it all before; why must I hear it again? If so, your heart has become dull, satiated, and shameless, and this food does not taste good to you. This is the same thing that happened to the Jews in the wilderness when they grew tired of eating manna. But if you are a Christian, you will never grow weary, but will long to hear this message often and to speak about it forever.

29. Allow me a personal comment: I am a doctor of the Holy Scriptures; yet the more I consider the Children's Creed, the Lord's Prayer, baptism, and the Sacrament, the better it all tastes to me. I also could easily say with the bored, satiated spirits, I know the Creed, the Lord's Prayer, the words of baptism and the Sacrament, the Psalms, and so on; but daily I experience and must confess that, even though I have already confessed my faith in the words of the Creed, spoken the Lord's Prayer, reviewed the words of baptism and the Sacrament, yet, if tomorrow I do not review these things item by item, my heart will become cold and lazy. And if I don't repeat it on the day following, I will become even colder and more indolent, ultimately arriving at the point of disdain. For seven years I had no desire to partake of the Sacrament, because I was then so very perfect.

That is what I got out of the papacy. But when I became aware that it was the devil who was impeding me and leading me away from the Sacrament, I said, Devil, perfect or not, I am in the need of the Sacrament and cannot do without its comfort; therefore, I shall attend and no longer offer excuses; and so I went, sometimes even without confessing my sins. Not that I had rejected confession, despised or neglected absolution; but that I sometimes went without confessing my sins only to spite the devil who wanted to keep me away, for I didn't need to go to the Sacrament since I was already so perfect.

30. So, it is not true when you say, I know it well, and there is nothing to be gained from hearing it again or repeating it. If I were to stop praying for one day, I would lose a great deal of my desire and faith. For as the prophet Isaiah testifies (55:10–11): The Word will not return fruitless; just as rain waters the earth and makes it bear fruit, in the same way God's Word waters and ameliorates man's soul. If you abandon God's Word and prayer, and yet feel that you will continue to pray, your soul will lose power and ardor. For this reason we should not look at God's Word in this light, that, once we have heard it, we don't need it anymore. Even apart from that, it can easily happen that one gets himself involved in some other activity that causes him to forget all about the Word. Therefore, we should daily take recourse to the word. If you do not do this, the danger is there that you will become so cold and laid back that ultimately you feel nothing anymore and you do not partake of the Sacrament for several years.

31. Now then we have heard about two things that ought to rouse and prompt us to partake of the Sacrament. First, there's what we have to gain and what our need is, for Christ ordained and instituted the Sacrament for our benefit, comfort, and joy. Second, God's honor and glory ought to motivate us. If we have no desire for our own sake, to pray the Lord's Prayer, confess our faith, and so on, and to receive the Sacrament to our salvation, then we should pray for God's sake and partake of the sacrament in order to glorify and serve him. I exhort you in this way so that we make use of the glorious gifts and great blessings while we have them and so that they will not be taken from us, as it happened a while back to the papists and is now happening to today's fanatical spirits. Once the treasure has been

taken away, we will yearn to have it again, but then there will no longer be pastors available to instruct us.

32. These are the two things that occurred on this particular evening. First, Christ ate the paschal lamb with his disciples in observance of the Jew's Passover, kingdom, and priesthood. Second, he instituted the Sacrament of his Body and Blood. We ought to partake of it often and in remembrance of him. May the merciful God grant us his grace so to do. Amen.

HOLY WEEK

*Good Friday—1533**

The Suffering and Death of our Dear Lord Jesus Christ

John 19:13–30

When Pilate therefore heard that saying, he brought Jesus forth, and sat down in the judgment seat in a place that is called the Pavement, but in Hebrew, Gabbatha. And it was the preparation of the passover, and about the sixth hour: and he saith unto the Jews, Behold your King! But they cried out, Away with him, away with him, crucify him! Pilate saith unto them, Shall I crucify your King? The chief priests answered, We have no king but Caesar! Then delivered he him therefore unto them to be crucified. And they took Jesus and led him away. And he, bearing his cross, went forth into a place called the place of a skull, which is called in Hebrew, Golgotha: Where they crucified him, and two others with him, on either side one, and Jesus in the midst. And Pilate wrote a title, and put it on the cross. And the writing was, JESUS OF NAZARETH THE KING OF THE JEWS. *This title then, read many of the Jews: for the place where Jesus was crucified was nigh to the city: and it was written in Hebrew, and Greek, and Latin. Then said the chief priests of the Jews to Pilate, "Write not, The King of the Jews; but that he said, I am King of the Jews. Pilate answered, What I have written I have written. Then the soldiers, when they had crucified Jesus, took his garments and made four parts, to every soldier a part; and also his coat: now the coat was without seam, woven from the top throughout. They said therefore among themselves, Let us not rend it, but cast lots for it, whose it shall be: that the scripture might be fulfilled, which saith, They parted my raiment among them, and for my vesture they did cast lots. These things therefore the soldiers did. Now there stood by the cross of Jesus his mother, and his mother's sister, Mary the wife of Cleophas, and Mary Magdalene. When Jesus therefore saw his mother, and the disciple standing by whom he loved, he saith unto his mother, Woman, behold thy son! Then saith he to the disciple, Behold thy mother! And from that hour that disciple took her unto his own*

*Preached at home in the Lutherhalle.

home. After this, Jesus knowing that all things were now accomplished, that the scripture might be fulfilled, saith, I thirst. Now there was set a vessel full of vinegar: and they filled a spunge with vinegar, and put it upon hyssop, and put it to his mouth. When Jesus therefore had received the vinegar, he said, It is finished: and he bowed his head, and gave up the ghost.

1. Today we are considering the events of the suffering and death of our Lord Jesus Christ, as we confess in the Creed, "I believe in Jesus Christ, his only Son our Lord who . . . suffered under Pontius Pilate, was crucified, died, and was buried." Christians really should have the suffering and death of Christ always in mind and on their lips every day. But since the events are given at some length, it's impossible to consider them all at one time. We, therefore, customarily assign them to additional times of observance. However, this day is especially devoted to considering and preaching about Christ's suffering, in order that we realize all that happened to Christ on this day, namely, in the Garden, at the house of the high priest, Caiaphas, in the judgment hall before Pontius Pilate, and on the cross. Under God's gracious guidance we shall speak of these events at some length.

2. The Jews dealt with Christ for an entire day and night, it being the time of the Passover. God had ordered them, through Moses, to commence observing the Passover the evening of the fourteenth day of the first month; this they observed zealously. The question is, Was he crucified on the first day of the Passover? According to our reckoning, it was on Good Friday. We must start with the evening of Maundy Thursday and proceed to the following night. Christ's Passion thus extended from about eleven o'clock in the evening until the next afternoon at three o'clock. Christ had left Jerusalem for the Garden at approximately seven o'clock; there he agonized with death so that his sweat was as great drops of blood falling to the ground. Soon after, about nine o'clock, he was apprehended in the Garden, bound, and led before the high priest, the elders of the people and the Sanhedrin who were assembled in the house of Caiaphas, the high priest. At about eleven o'clock he was examined and accused by false witnesses. Approximately at twelve o'clock the mocking began, and he was spit upon, slandered, and ridiculed. This continued through

the night till morning. In the morning he was led before the tribunal where Pilate, the governor, witnessed three times that he was innocent and that he found no cause worthy of death in him.

3. The first accusation of the Jews was that he roused the people, had forbidden them to pay taxes to Caesar, and incited insurrection, declaring himself to be a king and ruler. After Pilate had listened to the charge against Christ, and had heard his answer and confession that his kingdom was not of this world, and that he contemplated no harm to Caesar in his realm, he responded to the high priest and the people as follows, "I find no fault with this man," and then sent Jesus to Herod. That was the first time Pilate exonerated Jesus.

4. After Jesus was again returned to Pilate from Herod, Pilate called together the high priest and elders of the people and said to them as regards his examination of Christ, "Ye have brought this man unto me, as one that perverteth the people and behold: I have examined him before you, have found no fault in this man touching those things whereof you accuse him: No, nor yet Herod: for I sent you to him; and lo, nothing worthy of death is done unto him" (Luke 23:14). Pilate then offered the people the choice between the seditionist and murderer, Barabbas, and Jesus, saying, "Whom do you wish that I release, Barabbas or Jesus who is called Christ?" The high priest and elders persuaded the people to petition for Barabbas and call for crucifixion. This was the second time Pilate sought to exculpate Jesus.

5. Then as regards the third, since the former strategy failed, Pilate had Jesus scourged and then wished to release him. St. John writes that Pilate permitted Christ to be miserably lashed, smitten, beaten, and lacerated. He thought that this would move the Jews and satisfy them as sufficient punishment. That is why he led him out clothed in a purple robe, crowned with thorns, scourged and torn, and said to the Jews, "Behold the man!" As though he wished to say, Look at the man! Haven't I allowed him to be scourged enough? That was his third excuse or apology concerning Christ's innocence.

6. But this did not help. Jesus had to be disposed of. The Jews pressed Pilate harder and harder, saying, "If you release him, you are no longer Caesar's friend." The procedure at the court was long drawn out, lasting from seven o'clock in the morning until ten o'clock. After that Jesus was crucified around noon, between eleven

and twelve o'clock. At that time the sun's light was extinguished and there was darkness until three in the afternoon. Before the darkness came to an end, Christ died, having hung on the cross for three hours. After that he was taken from the cross and buried at about five o'clock in the evening. All these things, from the previous night till the evening of this day.

7. This is the record of events as described by the Evangelists, especially St. John, who indicates the time and the hours, from which one can figure that Christ's suffering spanned the entire night and the following day. He specifically states that Christ suffered on the day of the Passover: "And it was the preparation of the passover, about the sixth hour" (John 19:14). That is a suffering of eighteen hours, and even longer. For three hours he hung on the cross; three hours he was before the court; for seven hours, that is the entire night he was falsely tried, mocked, and spit upon in the house of Caiaphas. For two hours he agonized with death in the Garden; two hours elapsed during which he was seized, bound, and led from the Garden, first to Annas, then to the home of the high priest, Caiaphas; and this does not take into account the agony of spirit at the Passover meal, indicated by St. John in chapter 13.

8. So, our dear Lord Jesus Christ really and truly celebrated the Jewish Passover, dutifully, quietly hearing God's Word, and in obedience to his heavenly Father enduring the suffering. Holy Scripture foretold that he would suffer and die, as we read in 1 Peter 1:11: "Searching what, or what manner of time the Spirit of Christ which was in them did signify, when it testified beforehand the sufferings of Christ, and the glory that should follow." The Holy Spirit indicated beforehand the suffering that Christ would endure. Christ heard these same words and this same preaching on that Passover day. In those eighteen hours, or more likely twenty-four hours, he not only had to hear with his own ears the counsel of the high priests and the judgment of the Jews with the murderous mob crying, "Crucify him, away with him, crucify him"; but in his heart he also heard the witness of Holy Scripture that he must suffer and die. Over this he pondered the entire night and day, how the prophets' witness was being fulfilled in him. It seems to me the suffering of the night was much greater than that of the day.

9. In recording the events of the suffering of Christ, the Evangelists always repeat these words, "These things happened so that the Scriptures of the prophets might be fulfilled," for everything that Christ suffered happened in accord with Holy Scripture. For that reason the Evangelists not only record the events of Christ's suffering, but also repeat, "This happened that the scriptures might be fulfilled." As though they wished to say, Ask the prophets about it; they will tell you why Christ suffered. Great and severe is his suffering, his martyrdom, and the cross; but great also is his love, compassion, ardor, and all-encompassing grace toward us, in that the devout Lord and Saviour with his suffering and death fulfilled the Scriptures for our sake.

10. We read in Genesis 3:15: "And I will put enmity between thee and the woman, and between thy seed and her seed; it shall bruise thy head, and thou shalt bruise his heel." Christ must have been hearing this verse from time to time during his suffering, the words ringing in his heart and preaching to him. For he had now arrived at the time where he was to crush the head of the serpent—not the species that crawls in the grass and eats the vegetation, but the devil. This he was to do not with oxen hooves, not with sword and gun, but with his body and life as he permits the devil to run over him, pouring out all his fury and anger upon him. He crushes and squashes the devil that we might have rest and peace from him.

11. When the head of the serpent is crushed and smashed, that is the end—good riddance once and for all! Because Christ crushed the head of the serpent, the devil, his might and power were now at an end. The devil still remains a devil for us, and the world remains the world. But the head of the devil has been crushed, and Christ has taken away his power and destroyed his realm of death, sin, and hell.

12. It was this verse, undoubtedly, that Christ had in mind as he suffered and said, This is the hour that I crush the head of the devil and he bruises my heel. This I must needs suffer. Today is my Passover and true celebration. The pain, the suffering, the fear, and the misery are indescribable. Throughout that night and day this sermon out of Scripture's testimony dinned in his ears. This is what he endured on the Passover of the Jews, and thereby he celebrated the Passover to the letter, and through his suffering destroyed the reign

of the devil, so that now he has overcome the devil's dominion. When he utters one word the devil with his reign of death, sin, and hell is undone. And whoever believes in him may be certain that sin, death, and the devil will not harm him.

13. There are also other passages in the prophets, like in Psalm 16:2–3: "O my soul, thou hast said unto the LORD, Thou art my Lord; my goodness extendeth not to thee; But to the saints that are in the earth, and to the excellent, in whom is all my delight." Here David is speaking in the person of Christ and says that Christ had to suffer for the Lord's sake, and, nevertheless, endured such suffering for the saints on earth, for the blessed, that is, for the elect and chosen ones whom he has called and in whom he delights. This passage was preached and sung to Christ on that Passover and it reminded him that he must suffer.

14. Psalm 22:1: "My God, my God, why hast thou forsaken me? Why art thou so far from helping me, and from the words of my roaring?" Verse 6: "I am a worm, and no man; a reproach of men, and despised of the people." Again, verse 8: "He trusted on the LORD that he would deliver him . . . seeing he delighted in him." Also, verse 16: "For dogs have compassed me: the assembly of the wicked have inclosed me; they pierced my hands and feet." Verse 18: "They part my garments among them, and cast lots upon my vesture." That is a prophecy of Christ's suffering, and points clearly to his martyrdom on the cross, how his hands and feet were pierced through, and how his body would be stretched out so that one could count the bones; likewise, how his garments would be parted among them. That is why the Evangelists Matthew and John introduce this psalm when they describe how the soldiers parted his garments among them. And finally the Lord himself used the words of this psalm when he cried out, "My God, my God, why hast thou forsaken me?"

15. Psalm 69:21: "They gave me also gall for my meat; and in my thirst they gave me vinegar to drink." Here, too, David speaks in the person of Christ as he laments about those who crucified him and those who mock him giving him gall and vinegar to drink. That is also why St. John refers to this psalm as he writes, "After this, Jesus knowing that all things were now accomplished, that the scripture might be fulfilled, saith, I thirst." With this he wished to indicate that Christ had in his heart the prophets' prophecies concerning his suffering.

16. The entire 53rd chapter of the prophet Isaiah is a glorious prophecy concerning Christ, of his passion and resurrection. In this same chapter the Holy Spirit witnessed so clearly and distinctly of Christ's suffering as later described in the New Testament by an apostle. And this prophecy is wonderfully fulfilled in Christ. The Evangelist Mark drives this home in his Gospel when he says, "And with him they crucify two thieves; the one on his right hand, the other on his left," in fulfillment of Scripture, that "he was numbered among the transgressors." The Lord himself points to these prophecies about himself when he says to his disciples (Luke 22:37): "For I say unto you, that this that is written must yet be accomplished in me. And he was reckoned among the transgressors: for the things concerning me have an end."

17. Thus our dear Lord Jesus celebrated the Passover, hearing God's Word about his suffering and fulfilling the same in every detail. For he was the kind of preacher who had God's Word not only in his mouth, but verified it with his deeds, as St. Luke says of him in Acts 1:1: "Jesus began both to do and teach." The prophets witnessed concerning these things, through the Holy Spirit, long before so that we might know Christ died not for his own sake, but in obedience to his heavenly Father, in love and service to us.

18. And that is the paramount significance of the passion, that we realize and consider how Christ suffered in obedience to his heavenly Father and in our behalf to benefit us, that the Scripture might be fulfilled. It is well that we consider the true price of the redemption with which Christ redeemed us. It was not the exodus from Egypt. The redemption is nothing temporal, but rather, eternal, from sin, death, and hell. It is also well to consider the price paid for our sins, namely, that Christ did not pay gold or material goods, but rather his body and life, himself the offering for our sins, as St. Paul exults (Gal. 1:4; Eph. 5:2; Titus 2:14). At the same time one should bear in mind what great agony he suffered for us and how excruciating it was for him; how his sweat was as great drops of blood; how he was mocked, crowned with thorns, spit upon, scourged, nailed to the cross, and pierced for our sake. But this is the greatest and noblest consideration, that Christ had to suffer in order that he might fulfill the Scriptures.

19. We should diligently ponder all this, in order that we might not only recognize the greatness of the redemption, the price and the martyrdom, but also discern the love and good will toward us; how deeply concerned he is about us, and how his great heart, love, and compassion motivated him to give himself for us. That is why we should lovingly esteem both him who suffered such martyrdom for us and also the heavenly Father who ordained this and placed this martyrdom upon him. Such love should generate within us the realization of his goodwill toward us which prompted his voluntary martyrdom and suffering in our behalf. A human heart would need to be harder than stone, yes, harder than iron or steel not to be softened by this.

20. Nevertheless, the dear, pleasure-loving world goes merrily along, takes none of this to heart, is lazy, cold, unthankful, and despises this great treasure. As a result God finally rejects these godless people, and they distance themselves farther away all the time. Is not our Lord God right when he says to the unthankful world, Do you not have regard for the great love with which, as a Father, I so cordially embraced you that I subjected my dearest to this great martyrdom? Very well, then I have nothing to do with you. If you are not concerned about what I have done for you, then I will no longer be concerned about you. If you do not want my Son, Jesus Christ, then take Barabbas, yes, take the devil himself. I give you over to the factious spirits, to false teachers, to the Turks, to avarice, to arrogance, and the like.

21. We need not be surprised. Who can blame our Lord God for this? For while he gives his Son at the cost of his body and blood, to rescue you from death and hell, you spurn this as being nothing, and for his grace and love smash him in the mouth. So then he is doing right by you when he says to you, If that's the way you want it, you fine gentlemen, then coast along and go to the hangman. When one realizes how unthankful people are and how they seem to find no joy in Christ, is it any wonder that God becomes angry and lets the world go heedlessly along? For whoever rejects and refuses love and friendship from Christ should go to the devil and become a devil himself. Who can turn the world around?

22. We do not preach about the passion in order for people to become ingrates; but rather that they recognize our heavenly Father's

great love for mankind and his Son, our Lord Jesus Christ, through whom we again gain the Father's and the Son's favor. For he who believes with his whole heart that Christ suffered for him will not be a thankless rogue, but will with his whole being be grateful to Christ. If someone came to my rescue in an emergency, when death threatened by fire or water, I would have to be a wretch not to feel grateful toward him. We hold that person dear who gives or loans us ten gulden. What should our response be when God's Son is given for our sakes and endures sin, death, and hell? Should we not respond, My Lord Jesus Christ suffered for me; therefore, in return, I will love him, gladly preach, hear, and believe his Word, be obedient to, and follow him. If we do not do this, we are a thousand times more malicious than the people of the world. They know nothing of this grace, but we know, and yet we are ungrateful, thoughtless, and forgetful of the fact that we, through Christ, are redeemed from sin and death. He says to us, Neither sin nor death shall harm you for I have obtained eternal salvation for you through my death. It is terrible for anyone to despise such a love!

23. We need to study the passion of Christ, in order that we might remember that it happened for our good and for our eternal benefit. I must have regard for his bloody sweat, his agony, and his crucifixion, and say, That is my help, my strength, my life, my joy. All this happened for our sakes and for our benefit. We must believe this and thank him from the bottom of our hearts. Whoever does that and views the suffering of Christ in this way is a Christian.

24. He has shown us great kindness and we should never forget it, but always thank him and find comfort for ourselves, confessing, His pain is my comfort; his wounds, my healing; his punishment, my redemption; his death, my life. No one can preach it sufficiently; no one can be sufficiently amazed that so great a person came from heaven, stepped into our place, and suffered death for us. We have been visited graciously and redeemed with a great price. When in this life we experience harsh mistreatment and evil, we can usually trace it to our unthankful living. It serves H.G. and M.J.* and all the

*The reference is to Duke George of ducal Saxony and Margrave Joachim of Brandenburg, both opponents of the Reformation.

other papists right when God abandons them. For when people despise God's wonderful and eternal comfort, love, and help, as they indulge their wantonness, they get what they deserve as they go headlong on their way. Therefore, we should hold firmly to our Saviour and sacred Head, Jesus Christ, who for our sins was crucified and died. To this end may the gracious God help us. Amen.

EASTER EVE

*1532**

About the Article of our Christian Faith: I believe in Jesus Christ, who . . . descended into hell; the third day rose again from the dead.

1. On Easter we celebrate the great, comforting article of our Christian faith: the descent into hell and the joyful resurrection of our Lord Jesus Christ. This festival was instituted in order that this article might be preached, inculcated, be truly comprehended, and retained by the people. For this reason we now want to devote our attention to this article and discuss it. We owe it to our God to praise and honor him, and to preach his Word as long as we live.

2. We confess it in the Creed, the holy Gospels teach and testify to it, and it is customary to preach about it during this season, that our Lord Jesus Christ died and was buried, descended into hell, and on the third day rose again from the dead. I would like now to speak on that theme. I have not been well** and do not know how long I shall live; fanatical spirits are everywhere; and because that is so, I want to leave my teaching and confession behind for pious hearts that they might know my thoughts on this article.

3. There have been, and there still are, many who have wanted to sound the depths of this article with their reason and their five senses, particularly that before Christ rose from the dead and ascended into heaven, while still in the grave, he descended into hell. The best and safest is simply to stick with the words, just as they read, with childlike understanding.

4. You know how some are wont to paint the Lord's descent into hell, namely, that Christ wore a choir robe or mantle, with the angels preceding him, and he has a battle standard in his hand. With it he is

*Preached publicly on March 31, 1532.

** Concerning the nature of Luther's illness, see preface, pp. 13–14.

beating against hell, while the devils try to defend themselves; but finally he batters hell open and drives out the devils, just as an earthly castle or house is taken by force. Chancel dramas have also portrayed this on Easter Eve for children, and the people sing: Christ has burst the gates of hell and vanquished the foe. However simple these portrayals are for the children in dramatic form and song, I am generally pleased with such graphic depictions for they help the average folks and children to understand a little better, and that's all that is necessary.

5. It is true, you may talk about the Lord's descent into hell in two ways. First, plainly and simply, by means of childish words and pictures, which may also be the best and safest, as stated. Second, it may be discussed point for point, just as the account gives it, that Christ descended into hell, while his body lay there in the grave until the third day.

6. Some teachers, indeed, have been very concerned about it and argued skillfully and sharply as to just how it was possible for Christ's body to lie in the grave and for his soul to descend into hell. A few have stated that personally and actually he did not descend according to the soul, but simply in a spiritual manner, according to his work, power, and effect. But why is it that they have been concerned and sharply argued about it for so long? They will not comprehend or fathom it with their thoughts, even as learned teachers themselves have not understood it, though they have troubled themselves greatly and disputed sharply about it for so long already. I readily grant that in things that lie far beyond my mind and reason to comprehend, I should refrain from speaking and hold my tongue. The same holds true here, that I should presume to speak with my tongue and penetrate with my heart how the Lord's spirit was troubled in the Garden as drops of blood were pressed from him and fell to the ground—it would be impudent for me even to try. Similarly I would never be able to put into words or generate the thoughts that would explain the heart, love, and ardor out of which Christ's prayer and supplication on the cross welled forth with loud cry and tears. I must let that rest with the Word and faith; never would I be able to achieve it with my words and thoughts.

7. Now, then, just as I cannot fathom or grasp this, as well as other things, so I also cannot fathom or grasp how Christ descended into

hell. Christian faith confesses that he descended into hell, and Holy Scripture established this article as true in very explicit words, "Thou wilt not leave my soul in hell; neither wilt thou suffer thine Holy One to see corruption" (Ps. 16:10). And Ephesians 4:9: "Now that he ascended, what is it but that he also descended first into the lower parts of the earth?" But how it all took place, that you will not fathom; and even though you were ten times wiser than Solomon, you still would not get it. Therefore, my sincere advice is, stick to the simple words and childish pictures and do not let the astute spirits, who want to cogitate deeply, without sketches and apprehend it with their keen intellects, trouble you. But just as this article is expounded in the Word, and is illustrated in pictures with a procession of angels and Christ going down to the gates of hell with battle banner and smashing them, so let us grasp it unquestioningly. For even though it is stated with simple straightforwardness, and the pictures seem childish, these words and pictures still illustrate nicely the power and significance of this article, as we shall hear.

8. If quibbling mattered, I would want to be as cunning as they who scoff at us and disdainfully ask, Just how did it happen? Was the banner made of paper or cloth? How did it happen that it was not burned up in hell? What kind of gates, locks, or bolts did hell have? Were they iron or wood? Thus they indulge in subtle argumentation, in order to scoff at and mock us Christians and our Christian faith. I, too, could create allegories and spin fanciful explanations about the significance of the banner, staff, cloth and the gates of hell. But if I wanted to speak about this article in precise, dialectical terms, without pictures, you would not understand me, and I myself wouldn't know what I was saying.

9. Therefore, I shy clear of quibbling and high-brow questioning and allegories, and speak simply and in childlike manner about this article, even as the words, paintings, and graphic portrayals present it. Some picture the child Jesus as stepping on a snake. That is but a simple, elementary sort of illustration, but it clearly portends the first promise of Christ, when God promises Adam and Eve and the human race that Christ, the woman's seed, was to crush the serpent's head. In the wilderness Moses erects a bronze serpent and whoever looks at it will recover from the venomous bite of the serpent. This

likewise is an imperfect picture and image but see how lovely and excellently it portrays Christ lifted up on the cross, as Christ himself explains it (John 3:14). For just as the Jews, who looked up at the bronze serpent in the wilderness, recovered from the venomous bite of the serpent, so whoever looks at Christ lifted up on the cross, that is, believes in him, will recover from the devil's bite and venom, and have eternal life. But if I try to comprehend, fathom, and explain these promises dialectically, without pictures, as a thing itself is, I would really be unable to discuss it at all, and you would be unable to understand it.

10. For this reason the pictures, allegories, and figures of speech are good and beneficial, in order to depict something, and to apprehend and retain it. Yes, they also serve to check the poisonous darts of the devil, who wants to divert us from the Word by means of profound thoughts and subtle questions; and through such wonderfully lucid pictures, which every ordinary person can comprehend, we will be able to retain the proper understanding of the Word. So, in this article of Christ's descent into hell, when a child or an average person sees a painting on the wall of Christ storming hell with a banner in his hand and driving out the devil; or when he hears the hymns at Easter telling how Christ crushed hell and overcame the accursed devil, thereby delivering Christendom, and so on, he from that moment on thinks, If that is true, then Christ has overcome and bound the devil. That is rightly stated, in truly Christian fashion, for it also is the truth. Although it is not precisely stated how it came about, nonetheless, it is the absolute truth.

11. It sounds ludicrous that Christ should descend with the banner and the banner yet remain intact—when in hell's roaring fire brass would disintegrate, yet the banner not. So how should one treat it? Since we must inculcate this on the minds of people who are unable precisely to comprehend it, we need to picture it in some way and just simply say, Since you are unable to understand and comprehend the Lord's descent into hell, then envision it for yourself. It is as if a mighty conquering champion were to approach a fortified castle with his army, banner, and battle ordnance, occupy it, tie up and take captive the enemies therein; that is the way I understand also Christ's descent into hell. Whoever now hears this should clearly un-

derstand that Christ, who descended into hell and bound the devil, is the conquering Lord over the devil and hell.

12. When I, therefore, say, Christ is Lord over the devil and hell, and the devil has no power over him and over them who are his, that is stated without picture and embellishment. When I apprehend that and believe it, well and good. But if I would paint it with flourishes and graphic colors, sketch in a banner with which Christ batters hell open, so that a child and the common man who are unable to understand without a picture, might also comprehend and believe, that is well and good also. Whether we comprehend it with or without pictures, is an indifferent matter, as long as we don't become heretics and this article remains intact, that our Lord Jesus Christ did descend into hell, battered hell open, overcame the devil, and delivered those who were held captive by the devil.

13. I say this because I am seeing and learning that the world now wants to discern things in tune with the devil, govern the articles of faith, and explain everything in harmony with its own reason. Thus, in reference to this article the world comes and asks many useless, futile questions, whether Christ's soul only descended into hell or whether the Godhead went with it; also, what he did there, what kind of resistance the devils offered, and how he overcame them. Then after they have raised a lot of questions, they conclude, Christ died on the cross, his body was laid in the grave, his soul is in heaven with the Father to whom he commended it, so how then can it be possible that he descended into hell? and thus finally this article is thrown into complete doubt.

14. Therefore, continue in your childlike faith, which goes like this, I believe in Jesus Christ, God's only Son, our Lord, conceived by the Holy Spirit, born of the Virgin Mary; that is: I believe in the entire man, who as true God and true man, with body and soul, undivided, descended into hell and overturned hell. The whole person, that is, Jesus Christ, true Son of God and true man, born of Mary, has done this. The same God and man, in one person, descended into hell but did not remain there. He did not leave his soul in hell, as Psalm 16 states about him. But where the soul is, there also belongs the body according to the Scripture passage which calls the entire man soul.

15. But how it happened that the man lay there in the grave, and yet descended into hell, there say, That I do not know, I am unable to conceive or engage in dialectic about it. But I can roughly paint it for you and comprehend it in a picture: As a conquering hero Christ took up the banner and with it stormed the gate of hell, smashed it open and drove the devils into turmoil, causing one to fall through a window, another into a hole. Along then comes an immature smart aleck who scoffingly says, Ah, what are you alleging? Do you think that hell has a wooden door? Whereupon you reply, Dear master wiseacre, I know as much as you do; I could engage in sharp dialectic about it as well as you, if it were apropos and helpful; I know very well that no carpenter made hell's door, for hell existed before there ever was a carpenter. It has no wood, iron, bolts, nails, and the like, as have castles and houses on earth. The door is not of wood nor of iron, and the banner with which Christ knocked open the door is not of cloth.

16. I could also explain and allegorize about all such pictures and figures of speech—banner, door, bolts, staff, and so on—as to what they signify, and without the help of any wiseacre. But I shall not do it, but simply stick to the clear words and the simple pictures which accurately portray this article. For by intricate reasoning and barbed questions the devil would like to lead me off the right path, from the clear Word and simple meaning to reliance on human reason. It is better, therefore, that here I remain a child, who understands this picture and believes that Christ entered hell just like a person goes through a door. Such a picture cannot hurt or mislead me, but serves and helps me to comprehend and retain this article at all points; and, of course, the knowledge that Christ has overcome the devil and hell remains pure and unadulterated, whether the gates, door, banner, and staff be of wood or iron or nonexistent. If in other respects we employ pictures to explain things hard to understand—even though they may not exactly be equivalent or actually exist as the pictures paint them—why then are we unwilling to apprehend, by means of pictures, this article which we cannot fathom or elucidate, since the picture does indeed help to achieve the proper, plain meaning, namely, that Christ himself personally destroyed hell and bound the devil? If Christ did this with his back, head, banner, or staff, then

nothing else matters; but what does matter is that I know and believe the door was broken open, the devil bound and taken captive, and hell shattered, so that neither hell nor the devil can take me captive or harm me, and all who believe in Christ.

17. Christ touches on this somewhat when he states (Matt. 16:18): "Upon this rock I will build my church; and the gates of hell shall not prevail against it." And 2 Peter 2:4: "God spared not the angels that sinned, but cast them down to hell, and delivered them into chains of darkness, to be reserved unto judgment." And St. Jude, v.6: "The angels which kept not their first estate, but left their own habitation, he hath reserved in everlasting chains under darkness unto the judgment of the great day." But what gates, everlasting bonds, and chains of darkness these are, remains hidden to reason. And even though I would venture to speak more exactly about it, I still would not comprehend it.

18. Therefore, I am pleased that this article is painted in pictures and childish activity so that ordinary people can understand it. Turks, Gentiles, and Jews hold us to be big fools, as those who believe that hell is a wood or iron building and has doors, locks, bolts, and windows made by carpenters or smiths. But that simple we are not; we merely say that one should depict this article in paintings and pictures, so that it may be understood, and we stick with the words and unsullied Christian understanding.

19. That is the first part of this sermon, concerning the article that Christ descended into hell, that is, that he has overcome the devil and smashed hell, so that no Christian need henceforth fear and be terrified of the devil. This he did with the banner, that is, with the heel whereby he crushed the serpent's head. The very same banner and heel we shall, of course, see on that day, though as yet in this life we do not understand nor can say precisely what it is. It is not a banner like we make banners, out of cloth or paper; but we let it be a banner, in order that we hold on to the main point: Christ has crushed hell, opened up heaven, bound and taken captive the devil, and delivered the prisoners.

20. The world with all its powers was unable to deliver anyone from the devil's bonds or take away the agony and power of hell for a single sin, even though all the saints were to go to hell for one man's

sins. Indeed all of them together, as many as have ever lived on earth, would have to stay in hell eternally, if the Son of God had not gone there personally and overthrown it and gained the victory by his divine power. For no Carthusian hood, no sash of a barefooted monk, nor the holiness of all monks, nor all the world's power and might are able to extinguish one spark of the hellish fire. But it is accomplished when this man himself goes down with his banner, before which all devils must run and flee, like from death and venom, and extinguishes all the fires of hell in front of him, so that no Christian need be afraid any longer; and if he were already experiencing hell, he still would not suffer its pangs, just as through Christ he also will not taste of death eternally but made his way through death and hell into eternal life.

21. The second part of our sermon deals with the fact that our Lord Jesus Christ rose from the dead on the third day. For this a strong, firm faith is required, making this article strong, firm, and salutary. The words, Christ is risen from the dead, we should blazon and inscribe with letters so large that just one letter would be as large as a steeple, yes, as heaven and earth, so that we would see and hear, know and think of, nothing but this article. For we speak and confess this article in prayer, not just as an incident that has occurred, as we routinely tell some idle tale, or story or happening, but as something firmly set in our hearts, real and alive. And we call this faith, when we are so grounded on it and as firmly caught up in it as if nothing else were ever written, for Christ is risen.

22. This is where Paul is a true master as he treats this article. Romans 4:25: Christ "was delivered for our offences, and was raised again for our justification." Ephesians 2:5–6: "Even when we were dead in sins, [God] hath quickened us together with Christ, (by grace ye are saved;) And hath raised us up together, and made us sit together in heavenly places through Christ Jesus." 1 Thessalonians 4:14: "For if we believe that Jesus died and rose again, even so them also which sleep in Jesus will God bring with him."

23. If now we believe this, we can live and die in peace; for Christ did not overcome death and rise from the dead only for his own person; but we must perceive that it ties us mutually together with Christ, so that we also are included in the resurrection, and on account of and

through it we also must rise and live with him eternally; also that our resurrection and life in Christ have already begun and are as sure as if they had already happened, save that they still lie hidden and are not manifest. So intently should we look upon this article that by comparison, all other considerations are as nothing, as if there was nothing else for us anywhere, in heaven or earth. When you see a Christian dying and being buried, and nothing but a dead corpse lying there, and nothing else to see and hear but grave, funeral chants, words of death, yes, utter death itself, you should still put the picture of death out of sight and beneath the surface, by faith, a grave and a dead corpse, but pure life and a beautiful, cheerful garden and paradise, in which there are no dead people but new, living, happy human beings.

24. For because it is true that Christ rose from the dead, we already possess the best part of the resurrection, so that the bodily resurrection of the flesh from the grave (which is still in the future) is really secondary by comparison. For what are we and the whole world compared to Christ, our Head? Hardly a drop of water compared to the ocean, or a particle of dust compared to a great mountain. Since Christ, the Head of Christendom, through whom it lives and possesses all things and who is so great that he fills heaven and earth—compared to him, sun, moon, and all creatures are as nothing—has now risen from the grave, and thereby has become a mighty Lord over all things, also of death and hell, so must we also, as his members, be affected by his resurrection and actually become partakers of what he has thereby accomplished for our sake. For as by his resurrection he has taken everything with himself, so that heaven and earth, sun and moon, and all creatures must both rise and become new, so he will also take us along. The same God, who awakened Christ from the dead, will also quicken our mortal bodies and with us also all creatures, now subject to vanity and anxiously longing for our glorification, will be freed from the perishable existence and be glorified. Therefore, because we already possess better than half of our resurrection, since head and heart are already in heaven, only the least still needs to be done, that our body be buried in the ground so that it also may be renewed. For where the head is, there also the body must be presented, as we see in the case of all animals as they are born into this life.

25. Moreover, a second half has also occurred, yes, far more than half; namely, that already through baptism we have in faith spiritually risen from the dead, that is, according to the best part in us; and so not only bodily has the best part of it occurred, that from the grave our Head ascended into heaven but also spiritually our soul possesses its portion and is with Christ in heaven, and only the husks and shells or fragments remain here below; but for the sake of the main part, they must also journey there. For the husk and shell must still rise, but the chief part and the kernel has already risen.

26. This now we must firmly believe so that when we see a Christian who is ill, in throes of death, and then laid in the grave, or if we ourselves must die, we must put everything out of sight, and affirm and confess the resurrection, and say, The principal part of the resurrection has already taken place; Christ, the Head of all Christendom, has passed through death and risen from the dead. Moreover, the foremost thing has taken place in me: my soul also has passed through death and is with Christ in the heavenly existence. What harm can then death and grave do me? As St. Paul says (2 Cor. 5:1), this body is merely a tabernacle of the soul, as made of earth or clay, and an out-of-date garment, or an old, shabby, miserable pelt. However, since by faith the soul is already in the new, eternal, heavenly life, and cannot die or be buried, we thus have nothing more to await but for this poor tabernacle and old pelt to follow along and become new and no longer be perishable since the best part is above and cannot be left behind. As Christ, who is called the resurrection, has left death and the grave, so also must everyone who says, I believe, and clings to him. For the reason he preceded us is to get us to follow after him; and he has even now begun this in us, that through Word and baptism we daily rise in him.

27. In that way, you see, we ought to accustom ourselves to such thoughts of faith, against the outward, bodily view of the flesh, which sets before our eyes absolute death and with such a picture wants to frighten us and cast doubt on and eradicate the article of the resurrection. For it is an affront to the Head when one allows reason with its thoughts to give way to the eyes, and does not rather embrace the word in the heart. For in that case one can have only thoughts of death, because he sees the body lying there in pitiable and horrible

decay and stench; for the fact is, no carcass smells worse than the body of a dead human being, and no one on earth can stand it. Moreover, there's nothing that helps, no medicine of any kind, nothing other than burning and burying of the ashes in the ground as deep as one can. That leads St. Paul to say (1 Cor. 15:42–43): "It is sown in corruption; it is raised in incorruption: it is sown in dishonour; it is raised in glory: it is sown in weakness; it is raised in power." It is especially exasperating, as the Saxons say, Do you suppose one fellow is embedded in another? I see this one dead and buried, six or nine feet deep, and he stinks so badly that no one can stand being near him. What do you suppose will become of that fellow?

28. No one can deny that a dead human corpse is a miserable thing. But if it were a matter for human reason to adjudicate, then I could speak just as derisively as you do. People regard reason's judgment as very keen. But if I wished to judge according to what I see, I would be willing to bet that in any contest of intellects, I could make it much worse and more miserable than you could. You see a lifeless corpse decaying; I see it also. You see a dead man's corpse being torn to pieces and devoured by worms, fish, wolves, or other animals; I see it also. But if I am to judge according to reason how and what I see, then I am lost.

29. But I have a greater insight than what the eyes behold and senses feel, something which faith teaches me. For there stands the text, which reads: He is risen; he did not remain lying in the grave and in the ground but rose from the dead; and not for his own sake but for our sake, so that his resurrection is ours, and we also shall rise in him and not remain in the grave and death, but in our body celebrate with him an eternal Easter.

30. Look what the farmer does when he sows seed in the field and tosses it into the ground so that it must decay and rot; it appears as if it is lost altogether. Yet he shows no concern, as if it had all been in vain. Yes, he forgets where the seed is. What is happening to it does not worry him in the least, whether the worms will devour it or otherwise destruct. He just leaves the scene with only thoughts like this, that around the time of Easter or Pentecost, beautiful stalks will come forth, bearing many more ears and kernels than the seeds he has sown. If a young farmer, who had never before observed seeds

grow, were to see that, he would surely say, O father, what are you doing? How did you hit upon the folly of sowing seed into the ground? There it is lost, it will decay, there it can benefit no one. Let it remain on the floor, so that we can bake bread from it.

31. When our Lord God therefore sows our body and has it buried in the grave, our reason says, Is it really true that God gives life to his Christians? Just see how he allows them to be beheaded, crucified, burned to death, become dust and ashes, die and decay in the ground. But what does God say? Much the same as a father to his young, noodle-headed son. The son thinks he is intelligent and says, Dear father, how did you hit upon such folly as to plant seed helter-skelter in the ground? But the father says, Dear boy, just shut your eyes and let me do the sowing; I'm not intending it to be lost. God speaks the same way: My dear fellow, let me deal with my Christians and don't be bothered about whether they will be beheaded, burned to death, and killed; let me take care of this.

32. Yes, says reason, I see it there. When I go to the field in summer, the grain is nice and beautiful. But here the sights are terrible to behold: in one instance you see a person being strangled to death; in another a person being buried in the ground and decomposing. Response: Were the grain to become visible immediately upon being planted in the ground, you would need no practical experience, nor have to wait every year for God to do his work. Likewise, if the body were raised from the dead as soon as it is buried, you then would not need any faith, and God would not need any interval for demonstrating his wisdom and might over our wisdom and understanding. But now faith confesses and says, I believe in Jesus Christ risen from the dead; I believe in the resurrection of the flesh. And Holy Scripture testifies (Ps. 34:19–20): "Many are the afflictions of the righteous: but the Lord delivereth him out of them all. He keepeth all his bones: not one of them is broken."

33. If you look at the body degenerating, decaying, and being devoured by snakes and worms, you are lost. But if you look to God's Word and continue in faith, you are buoyed up. For as God's work year for year, and experience also, attest, the seed which the farmer casts into the ground, letting it decay and in the summer come out of the ground, in another form and with much fruit, so our faith and

Holy Scripture attest that our bodies, which God has buried during the winter and lets decay, at his time, on Judgment Day, will again rise much more beautifully than the sun.

34. It is a sore trial when we die so wretchedly. Man howls, cries, and moans; he sees before him not life but the form of death. When faced with such trial, we must cling to God's Word in faith and conceive comforting and joy-filled thoughts of life to counteract the face of death; and bear in mind that the grave is not really a grave but a beautiful, fragrant garden in which are planted beautiful and fragrant cloves and roses, which during the summer are to thrive and bloom on and on. For just as the Lord Christ's grave had to become vacant and not stink but become lovely, glorious, and beautiful, so also must the graves of the Christians become vacant and not stink. These are the Christians' thoughts, art, and wisdom.

35. Consider the story about St. Agatha: As she was led away to prison and to death, she said, I am going to dance; and when she was martyred, she said, Behold, how deep is my hurt; they are piping me music that I might dance. Indeed, this pious virgin was more firmly convinced of the article of the resurrection from the dead than any farmer is sure that the grain, sowed over the winter months, will sprout and thrive during the summer. Would to God, I could muster such hope of the resurrection from the dead as a farmer musters hope from a grain of wheat. And about St. Vincent and others, we read that they went to their death with joy and laughter, scoffing the meanwhile at their judges and hangmen. When they threatened St. Vincent with sword, fire, and death, he said, O you fools, do you think I am afraid of that? This buoys me up. To him it was ludicrous and preposterous that people taunted him; for that reason he defied them and said, The martyrdom with which you are threatening me is to me pure joy in Christ. He was so firmly convinced within himself of the resurrection and believed it so firmly that he could but scoff at the hangman.

36. Let us also learn to imbed this article into our hearts and take comfort in it; then we can ward off the devil when he sharpens his spear to use against us and threatens us with death and hell; we can respond to him and say, Devil, don't you know any better than to threaten with death? Hold on, I am not afraid of your threats; you are

singing me a beautiful little song and persuading me to dance; my grave is a pretty garden. For since Christ, my Head, on whom everything depends, has risen, lives, and is seated in heaven, and I am baptized in him, I thus am more than halfway there already, and but little remains for me to do but completely to remove the old skin, so that it too might again be renewed. For since the inheritance is already wholly mine, the husks and shells must then surely follow as well.

37. Thus we should put out of sight the wretched spectacle of death, before which human reason becomes terrified, and not look at the outward specter but at Scripture and to faith, where we learn that, since Christ rose from the dead and is exalted above all the heavens, and our soul has also risen with him, our body must in the same way again come forth from death and the grave and shine beautifully as the sun. To that end may God grant us his grace, that we may apprehend it and with it comfort ourselves and others. Amen.